The People's Army in the Spanish Civil War

The People's Army in the Spanish Civil War

A Military History of the Republic and International Brigades 1936–1939

Alexander Clifford

Pen & Sword
MILITARY

First published in Great Britain in 2020 by
Pen & Sword Military
An imprint of
Pen & Sword Books Ltd
Yorkshire – Philadelphia

ISBN 978 1 52676 092 0

A CIP catalogue record for this book is
available from the British Library.

Printed and bound in the UK by TJ International Ltd,
Padstow, Cornwall.

Pen & Sword Books Limited incorporates the imprints of Atlas,
Archaeology, Aviation, Discovery, Family History, Fiction, History,
Maritime, Military, Military Classics, Politics, Select, Transport,
True Crime, Air World, Frontline Publishing, Leo Cooper, Remember
When, Seaforth Publishing, The Praetorian Press, Wharncliffe
Local History, Wharncliffe Transport, Wharncliffe True Crime
and White Owl.

For a complete list of Pen & Sword titles please contact

PEN & SWORD BOOKS LIMITED
47 Church Street, Barnsley, South Yorkshire, S70 2AS, England
E-mail: enquiries@pen-and-sword.co.uk
Website: www.pen-and-sword.co.uk

Or

PEN AND SWORD BOOKS
1950 Lawrence Rd, Havertown, PA 19083, USA
E-mail: Uspen-and-sword@casematepublishers.com
Website: www.penandswordbooks.com

Contents

For Róisín, with love and admiration

Acknowledgements

First and foremost, this book would simply not have been written were it not for the passion and expertise of Dr Peter Anderson of Leeds University, who introduced me to the fascinating field of the Spanish Civil War as a wide-eyed first year. During the writing of the book, he was kind enough to provide vital advice, reassurance and encouragement at a time when I needed it most. The other person without whom the book could not have been written is my flatmate and friend José Del Pino, a talented linguist and teacher who has enabled me to access a huge range of texts in Spanish and spent countless hours translating old soldiers' memoirs with me completely voluntarily (although sometimes bribed with takeaway pizza). I wish to thank my mother, my primary proofreader and cheerleader as always, and my father for his healthy scepticism and grounded thinking. My brother Freddy helped me with research in his field of expertise, firearms, and has written an excellent appendix on the topic for this volume. Ian Aird assisted me greatly in sourcing the images that illustrate the book and I wish to thank him for his kindness and readiness to help. My commissioning editor Rupert Harding and publisher Pen and Sword placed their trust in me and this project, and have shaped it into the engaging book it has become. In particular, Rupert has been a constant source of guidance and encouragement from the start as I entered the unfamiliar world of publishing and I wish to thank him for his efforts. My editor Linne Matthews has made this book distinctly more readable and has done a huge amount of work to help it reach publication, for which I am extremely thankful. Finally, my partner Róisín has tolerated our room becoming a research office, my mind being in Spain and our flat being overrun with books; my sincere apologies.

The author and publisher gratefully acknowledge the permission granted to reproduce the copyright material in this book. I would like to thank the following for granting permission for quotations used: Edwin Mellen Press, United Writers Publications, University of Illinois Press, Hachette/Orion, Penguin-Random House Group, and Simon & Schuster. Every effort has been made to trace copyright holders and to obtain their permission for the use of copyright material, be they images or quotations. The publisher apologises for any errors or omissions in the above list and later credits, and would be grateful if notified of any corrections that should be incorporated in future reprints or editions of this book.

Note for the reader on Spanish naming customs

Most Spaniards have a given name and then two surnames, first the surname of their father, followed by the surname of their mother. It is common practice to refer to someone on most occasions using only their given name and first surname, as is the case in this book; for instance, Francisco Franco Bahamonde is referred to simply as Francisco Franco. The exception tends to be those who have exceedingly common paternal surnames, who then often have their maternal surnames given also. To provide an example from this work, the Republican General Juan Hernández Saravia is always referred to with his full name, Juan Hernández being a very common name in Spain.

List of Illustrations

Plate 1

From militia to People's Army – the transformation of Republican forces from the badly organised militia bands of 1936 (1) to something approaching a regular army by summer 1937 (2).

Plate 2

3. Troops of the People's Army's 46th Division reviewed by (from left to right) Republican Prime Minister Juan Negrín, President Manuel Azaña, General José Miaja, Major Valentín González (El Campesino), and Major Enrique Líster.

4. Chief of the General Staff of the People's Army Colonel (later General) Vicente Rojo, visiting the front.

Plate 3

5. Major Attlee Company, British Battalion. Named after the Labour Party leader, commander Sam Wild is in black crouched by the Maxim machine gun.

6. Tough Slavic volunteers of the Dimitrov Battalion.

7. Men of the Machine Gun Company of the Abraham Lincoln Battalion.

Plate 4

International Brigaders: Fred Copeman (8), Royal Navy mutineer and commander of the British Battalion at Brunete; Bill Alexander (9), industrial chemist and British Battalion commander at Teruel; Robert Merriman (10), Economics doctoral student and Chief of Staff of 15th International Brigade at Belchite; and Milton Wolff (11), machine gunner then Lincoln-Washington Battalion commander in 1938.

Plate 5

12. Ernest Hemingway (centre) conversing with officers of the German-Austrian 11th Thälmann International Brigade.

13. General José Miaja, 'Saviour of Madrid'.

Plate 6
Nationalist commanders; the Caudillo and Generalíssimo Francisco Franco (14) and General José Enrique Varela (seated) with staff (15).

Plate 7
16. & 17. Propaganda shots of the Nationalist army's advance on Madrid, autumn 1936.

Plate 8
The Rebel elite: General Miguel Cabanellas salutes Moroccan Regulares (18); 'Bridegrooms of Death' Foreign Legionnaires resting at Navalcarnero (19).

Plate 9
The Nazi Condor Legion in Spain; Messerschmitt Bf 109 (20), Junkers Ju 87 Stukas (21), Heinkel He 111 being armed (22), and Flak 36 88mm cannon (23).

Plate 10
24. Major Enrique Líster with men from his famous 11th Division during the Brunete campaign.
25. & 26. Lieutenant Colonel Juan Modesto, commander of V Corps, overseeing operations at Brunete.
27. Major Valentín González, El Campesino, directing Republican troops on horseback during the advance on Quijorna.

Plate 11
The Battle of Brunete: a Soviet-built T-26 passing through Villanueva de la Cañada (28); British machine-gun crews in action (29); the ruins of Villanueva de la Cañada, the church steeple housed an AT gun (30); and Republican transports under bombardment on the road to Brunete (31).

Plate 12
32. The Belchite siege; the fortified Purburrel Hill outside Quinto.
33. The old town of Belchite today; the San Martín parish church is visible the background.

34. & 35. Exterior and interior of the San Agustín, stormed by the Lincolns on 4 September 1937.

Plate 13

36. Republican troops advance confidently into Teruel, December 1937.

37. The diversion: Republicans pose with a captured Nationalist placard celebrating the anticipated fall of Madrid to Franco's shelved winter offensive.

Plate 14

38. People's Army machine-gunner killed in the hills around Teruel.

39. A T-26 abandoned in the snow.

Plate 15

40. Republican troops fighting house to house in the city itself.

41. A Carlist Requeté of the Navarrese Corps in a snowbound Teruel trench, February 1938.

42. A lone soldier advances on the Teruel bullring.

Plate 16

43. 'Liberation': Nationalist troops enter the ruined outskirts of Madrid, March 1939, as the populace look on.

List of Maps

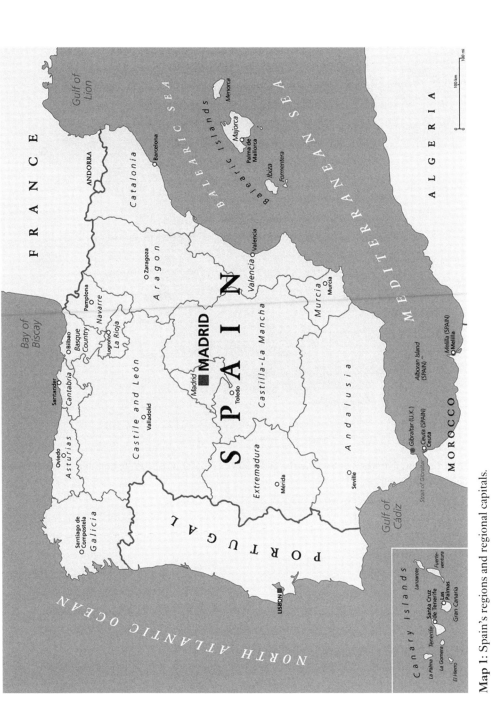

Map 1: Spain's regions and regional capitals.

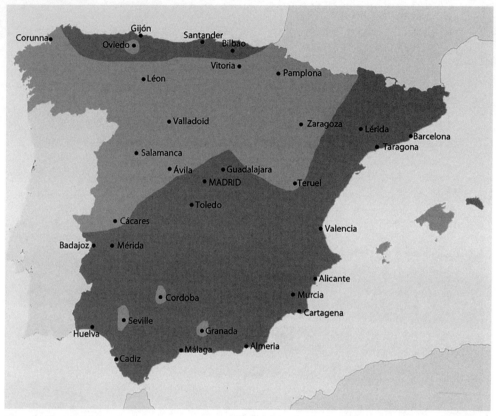

Map 2: Territorial division of Spain at the outbreak of civil war in July 1936. Republican-held territory is dark, Nationalist light.

Map 3: Territorial division of Spain by spring 1937, after the Madrid battles. Republican-held territory is dark, Nationalist light. Note the substantial gains Franco was able to make against the militias in just a few months.

Introduction

In November 1936, just four months after its outbreak, the world awaited the end of the Spanish Civil War. Since the late summer, General Franco's Nationalist Rebels, amply aided by Hitler and Mussolini, had put their Republican adversaries to flight and stolen a march on Madrid. The advent of a fascist victory seemed so certain that several overeager foreign journalists filed reports describing the Generalissimo's triumphant entry into Spain's capital on a white horse. The beleaguered Republican government had fled to Valencia. Nationalist prisoners were murdered by communists, desperate not to allow them to be liberated. *Daily Telegraph* correspondent Henry Buckley was informed by his editor in London that Franco's forces were in the centre of Madrid, quite contrary to Buckley's own report from the scene.[1] They had all jumped the gun.

The Nationalist steamroller was halted on the outskirts of the city; halted by a combination of loyal army officers, workers' militias, the timely arrival of Soviet weapons, advisors and international volunteers, and, perhaps most of all, by the exhaustion and depletion of the colonial troops that Franco relied so heavily upon. Once it became clear that the city was not about to fall, the Nationalists attempted to cut Madrid off, first from the north in December, then from the south and east in the February and March of 1937. All these efforts were frustrated, with huge losses on both sides. After these failures, what had started as a military coup was to become a protracted civil war. Franco, under pressure from his generals and fascist allies, moved his focus to the Northern Front, where the Basque Country, Asturias and Santander represented a Republican enclave that was a thorn in the Nationalists' side and a drain on troops and resources. This allowed the Republicans to take the initiative on the main battlefront, and this they did during 1937. The workers' militias, formed on the outbreak of war to defend the Republic against military insurrection, were transformed into a People's Army (Ejército Popular, sometimes translated as Popular Army, although People's is more accurate), supplemented by thousands of idealistic foreign volunteers in the International Brigades and advanced

Russian tanks and aircraft. It was no easy task to transform disparate bands of revolutionaries and countless conscripts into a coherent fighting force, but against the odds, the Republicans created their People's Army. In less than a year, the Republic went from being defended by peasants armed with swords and shotguns to having a regular fighting force capable of launching bold combined-arms offensives using modern military hardware and infiltration tactics. The aim of this book is to give an account of this new army at the peak of its powers, telling its story through the three great offensives it launched over the course of six months in 1937, the battles of Brunete, Belchite and Teruel. Quite deliberately, the narrative focuses on two unique aspects of the People's Army: the International Brigades and the Republican officer corps. The International Brigades were a unique physical and martial manifestation of global class solidarity during the rise of fascism. They were to be the shock troops of the People's Army, often better led and more motivated than most Republican formations, and units such as the largely anglophone 15th Brigade of volunteers from Britain, America, Canada and Ireland would be called upon time and again to serve as the tip of the spear. Meanwhile, the People's Army was commanded by a motley blend of amateur militiamen, brave but uneducated, and Loyalist professional officers, who had not joined Franco's coup but often found themselves promoted by necessity far beyond their experience and abilities. The struggles of these underqualified commanders, leading a citizen's army into its baptism of fire against a superior foe, is a fascinating aspect of the conflict and tells us much about the People's Army and its performance as a whole.

The Spanish Civil War lasted from July 1936 until April 1939 and was fought between General Franco's Nationalists (at various times also referred to as the Rebels, Insurgents, Francoists and, by their enemies, fascists) and the Republicans (also referred to as the Loyalists, and, again, by their enemies, reds). It was a war of great intensity and passions, where feelings ran high and as many as 238,000 civilians from both sides were murdered behind the lines.[2] The war was triggered by a *pronunciamiento* (military uprising) of a large section of the Spanish army against the Republican government. However, the coup d'état failed and the country was split in two between supporters of the coup and sympathisers of the government, resulting in a long and bitter civil war. The brutal battles that will be described below could hardly be further removed from the dreary stalemate on quiet sectors of the front portrayed in George Orwell's *Homage to Catalonia*.

While its proximity to the Second World War has led to Spain's civil war being labelled as a 'curtain-raiser', or prelude to that conflict, it would be wrong to imagine Spain's war as similar to the Second World War. Certainly, modern weapons, such as the German Messerschmitt Bf 109 or Stuka dive-bomber, were used for the first time. And the Spanish war, like the Second World War, was also a conflict between democracy and communism on the one hand, and fascism and militarism on the other. However, this is where the similarities begin to dry up. In terms of tactics, theory and even military hardware, Spain's civil war owed much more to the First World War, and to the bitter colonial conflict in the Moroccan Rif, which the Spanish were embroiled in from 1909 to 1927. This is hardly surprising given that, at this time, most of the world's militaries (with the notable exception of Germany) primarily based their conception of warfare on the supposed lessons and certainties of 1914–1918.[3] Despite the fact that Blitzkrieg was only just around the corner, it remained, in 1936, simply a theory; such ideas played a very limited part in the Spanish war. Stanley Payne has convincingly argued that the Spanish Civil War was 'typical neither of World War One nor of World War Two, but rather represented a kind of transition war halfway between the two and exhibited certain characteristics of each.'[4]

The period from July 1937 to February 1938, encompassing the battles of Brunete, Belchite and Teruel, represents a unique period within the Spanish Civil War. The early months of the conflict saw something of a mismatch as Franco's professional colonial troops took on disorganised, untrained Loyalist militias. By contrast, from mid-1937, the Republicans had managed to create a proper, conventional army, almost from scratch, albeit with serious deficiencies. All three battles would start with Loyalist offensives aimed at seizing the initiative on the war's main front. On the other hand, the Nationalist military went from strength to strength during 1937, with an ever-increasing supply of Axis arms. Brunete, Belchite and Teruel were therefore perhaps the greatest battles of the war because they saw the Republican and Nationalist armies go toe to toe, both sides confident of success. From the spring of 1938, the Republic was crippled and for the superior army of Francisco Franco it was a question of when, not if, final victory would come. For a few months in the second half of 1937, the war stood at a crossroads, and though the two sides were never equal, this period was the closest the civil war came to a fair fight. The grinding down that the People's Army suffered in the second half of 1937 led directly to the collapse of the Aragon Front in the spring of 1938, and the subsequent fatal division of the Republic into two zones by Franco's advance to the sea. At this point, Republican victory became inconceivable, even to contemporaries, and the war's remaining twelve months were a slow, dying agony. The later Ebro offensive of July 1938, although spectacular initially, was too little too late; the Republic had already been mortally wounded, the war was already lost. Effectively, therefore, the three big offensives of 1937 marked the People's Army's best shot at success – the short window of the conflict where there was a real prospect of Republican military triumph, albeit with little prospect of ultimate victory. Equally, it was to prove the greatest test for Franco's Nationalists, whose army had never faced so strong and disciplined an enemy before Brunete, nor would ever face such setbacks as they did at Teruel during the whole war.

Throughout the book, the Republic's People's Army is the primary protagonist. Given the speed of its conception and the unique pressures it was under, and despite its ultimate defeat, the People's Army was a fighting force that probably achieved more than could have been expected of it. While at the time, the formation of the People's Army was politically controversial (many revolutionaries opposed the creation of a regular army), there can be no doubt that it was the only reason the Republic was able to resist for so long against Franco's armies. In his recent military history of the war, Charles Esdaile said as much when he explained the factors that delayed the Nationalist victory: 'the Republic, in the very nick of time, turned its back on the militias and organised a regular army … the mere existence of the People's Army was enough to ensure that the war was long and drawn out.'[5] Ultimately, like other total wars of mass mobilisation, the American Civil War or the First and Second world wars, the Spanish Civil War was a 'wearing-down' war, decided by which side could amass the most men and material and use them most effectively to grind down and finally crush the opposition. Defeating the Nationalists in detail, fighting a guerrilla war or adopting a defensive footing was simply not an option for the Republic in this sort of conflict, given the superiority in resources enjoyed by Franco. In these circumstances, with an inferiority in planes, artillery, and arms of almost all kinds (often qualitative rather than quantitative), the Republic could never win a war of attrition. Yet the People's Army did the best it could to deprive the enemy of the initiative and prolong the conflict through diversionary attacks. Historians have not been especially kind to the Republican army, nor its leaders, and indeed rarely are to defeated militaries. However, when compared to other armies built in wartime, for instance the American

Expeditionary Force of 1918, it can be seen that the People's Army actually performed rather admirably and the issues it did have are in fact common to other similar attempts to build an army.

Unfortunately, there is no account in English of the Army and its battles. Michael Alpert's definitive study of the Republic's military is an institutional work, which mentions the battles it fought only in passing. More than anything else, this volume seeks to synthesise eyewitness testimony with the grand overview to provide the reader with a clear, comprehensive account of the strategy, tactics and combat experience of the Republican People's Army during its three greatest battles: Brunete, Belchite and Teruel. The reader will soon become familiar with the scorching heat of the arid plains around Brunete, with the shattered streets of Belchite, still ruined to this day, and with the frozen hills of Teruel. Through the words of the combatants on both sides, battlefield reporters and the recollections of commanders, the reader will experience what it was like to be at the sharp end in some of the civil war's most intense hotspots.

The book begins with a brief overview of the events that plunged Spain into civil war, followed by a description of the course of the conflict up to the spring of 1937, when the People's Army had finally begun to take shape. Then, the narrative pauses as we take an in-depth look at how and why the People's Army was created and what challenges it faced, before closely examining their Nationalist adversaries. Next, the People's Army's three great offensives of 1937 are described in detail, with the context for each campaign set out, followed by a blow-by-blow account of the battle and a final assessment. Lastly, the concluding chapters summarise the slow demise of the Spanish Republic and take stock of the Republicans' combat performance, and weigh up their successes and failings.

Chapter 1

Peace Was Not Possible:
Spain from 1898 to the Civil War

In July 1936, a cabal of Spanish generals carried out an uprising against their elected government. The failure of their coup to swiftly seize power led to a civil war that would last more than thirty-two months and claim hundreds of thousands of lives. 'Peace was not possible,' wrote José María Gil-Robles, the charismatic leader of the Spanish Right before the war, in his autobiography published thirty years after the conflict. Despite the whitewashing of his own responsibility implicit in his words, Gil-Robles' analysis of Spain's situation in 1936 was not far from the mark. How had Spain come to find itself in a position where its people were at war with themselves?

On 13 April 1931, Spaniards went to bed living in a monarchy and woke up in a Republic. Spain had been in steady decline for centuries from its sixteenth-century Golden Age, and by the time the twentieth century dawned, it was a backward nation. This was cruelly highlighted by a humiliating defeat in the Spanish-American War of 1898, which resulted in the loss of the last remnants of Spain's once great empire. The political system was moribund, unrepresentative and corrupt. In the so-called *Turno Pacífico* system, political power was passed between two monarchist parties at regular intervals thanks to large-scale gerrymandering and electoral fraud. This system proved unable to cope with the pressures brought about by a combination of the First World War, the Russian Revolution, army discontent, colonial conflict and regional particularism. The first signs of breakdown came in 1917 when the army crushed an attempted general strike, having been bought off with offers of better pay and conditions. Following the end of the First World War, and the general European downturn that it brought about, worker unrest became steadily greater. In particular, Barcelona, Spain's main industrial centre, was the scene of a bitter social war between unions and employers, both of whom engaged in assassination and dirty tricks. Into this maelstrom was thrown an unpopular colonial war in Spain's Moroccan protectorate. The divisive issues of conscription and military profiteering corroded the popularity of the army and the monarchy, which was seen as intimately tied to both the generals and the war in Morocco. This criticism reached fever pitch thanks the Annual disaster of 1921. In a devastating display of incompetence, the Spanish suffered another humiliating defeat at the hands of the Riffian rebels. Over 13,000 Spaniards were killed, many mutilated, and tens of thousands of weapons fell into the hands of the triumphant insurgents.

Even Spain's stagnant political class could not ignore such a catastrophe and demanded answers. A detailed enquiry was undertaken, which heavily implicated the army command and King Alfonso with responsibility for the disaster. Partly to suppress the publication of the report, partly to bring an end to worker unrest in Catalonia, General Primo de Rivera staged a coup in September 1923. His paternalistic dictatorship, condoned by the king, lasted until shortly before his death in 1930. Against a backdrop of world depression and a discredited monarchy, a landslide victory for liberal Republicans and Socialists occurred in the municipal elections of April 1931. Despite the fact that these elections necessitated neither the abdication of the king, nor his new military regime, the tide of public opinion was clear. The royal family quietly fled and the Spanish Second Republic was proclaimed. The new government, made up of centrist Republicans of several parties and the Spanish Socialist Party (PSOE), faced an unenviable task. Spain was in dire need of modernisation; vast swathes of the population were illiterate, the Catholic Church still had exclusive control over education and the rural South was dominated by wealthy, semi-feudal landowners. All these and more problems had to be addressed alongside the intimidating challenges of building Spain's first true democracy amid a global economic crash. Worker and peasant hopes were raised beyond all reasonable expectations by the advent of the Republic, while the traditional bases of power within Spain – the military, Church and landowners – were intransigent in their attitude to reform. They were embittered by the fall of the monarchy and the Republic's attacks on their privileged positions, through cuts to the army, the separation of Church from state and tentative steps towards land redistribution. A class war was beginning to escalate in the south, typified by longstanding hatreds between landowners and landless peasants. The situation is described well by one such peasant in Toledo province, Timoteo Ruiz:

> Five large landowners practically owned the village. Apart from some
> 500 smallholders like my father, the rest of the 4,000 inhabitants
> were landless day-labourers who every morning waited in the village

square to be chosen to work by the foremen of the big estates. There was work for all only at harvest and olive-picking times. The only way the landless labourers could keep themselves and their families alive was by cutting firewood on the communal land in the mountains. But this was forbidden, and the Civil Guard [the paramilitary police force] confiscated the wood if they caught the men.[1]

Faced with these huge structural problems and a failed military coup in August 1932, the Republican-Socialist coalition ran out of steam. The PSOE in particular was frustrated by the lack of progress and so left the government. In the subsequent elections of 1933, the right gained a majority in the Cortes. A minority administration was formed by the centre-right Radical party of Alejandro Lerroux. Spain's urban middle class was small and weak. As a result, so was the political centre ground and the parties of the centre-left and centre-right could never hope to govern alone. Instead, they relied on the support of elements to the left and right of them respectively. For the Republican parties, their allies were the Socialists of the PSOE. On the other hand, Lerroux's Radicals relied on the votes of a new Catholic-Conservative party, the CEDA, under the leadership of Gil-Robles. CEDA was a broad church but at its core, it opposed the Republic and everything it stood for. The new rightist government immediately began a vicious campaign of reversing the reforms that the previous administration had introduced. Landowners felt empowered and took violent retribution on peasant labourers for what they saw as insubordination. Union agitation increased and the political spectrum became ever more polarised as it became clear that the goals of left and right were diametrically opposed. The centre ground was too small, the areas of agreement almost non-existent. Furthermore, CEDA used the language and visual styles of fascism; their cadres hailed Gil-Robles as the Jefe, roughly equivalent to Duce or Führer, while the CEDA youth, the JAP (Juventudes de Acción Popular), was unashamedly fascist.

It is in this context, and the context of the advance of fascism all over Europe, that the left's violent reaction to CEDA's entry into government in October 1934 can be understood. An ill-prepared revolutionary general strike was called by the PSOE and its unions, which was swiftly crushed across Spain, with the exception of in the mountainous northern region of Asturias, where miners' militias held out for weeks. Under the direction of Spain's youngest general, Francisco Franco, the elite colonial Army of

Africa was transported from Morocco to Asturias and led a brutal campaign of pacification. In total, around 4,000 people were killed and a further 30,000 arrested, including all the left's major leaders who had not escaped the country. The Asturias rising was crucial in the build-up to civil war, for both left and right began to see one another as existential threats. The left could point to the repression of workers' organisations and newspapers, as well as the security forces' brutality, as evidence of the impending return of authoritarianism, perhaps even the advent of fascism, in Spain. For their part, the right viewed Asturias as evidence of an imminent Bolshevik revolution, and of the threat that the left posed to law and order. The catastrophism of both sides was to have dire consequences.

The Radicals were brought down by a comical financial scandal in late 1935 and so elections were called for February 1936. For some time, Manuel Azaña, leader of the centre-left Izquierda Republicana, had been trying to rebuild the alliance of Republicans and Socialists. For the February elections, an electoral pact known as the Popular Front was created, encompassing not just the Republicans and Socialists but also parties to their left including the Spanish Communist party (PCE) and the anti-Stalinist Marxists of POUM. The Popular Front also enjoyed the support, if not participation, of Spain's large anarcho-syndicalist movement (CNT-FAI), which abstained from parliamentary politics but was won over by assurances of an amnesty for political prisoners. Meanwhile, the support of the Basque Country and Catalonia for the Republican project was ensured by promises of regional autonomy. The Popular Front won a narrow but decisive victory in the vote; but the old Republican-Socialist coalition was not resurrected. Instead, the Socialist leadership, dominated by leftist Largo Caballero, insisted on the PSOE remaining outside of government, in the hope that the Republicans would eventually collapse and a Socialist-only cabinet could be formed. In effect, Largo viewed Azaña's administration as like that of Kerensky in the Russian Revolution: a liberal regime that was bound to be short-lived, after which the left could inherit the state. Unfortunately, this was how the right viewed the new government as well.

The right had not taken defeat well. When the results came in, both General Franco (now Chief of the General Staff) and Gil-Robles had tried to persuade the caretaker prime minister to remain in office and declare a state of emergency, in effect to ignore the democratic process. Frustrated by the failure of this scheme, Gil-Robles almost immediately put CEDA's election fund at the disposal of a group of military conspirators. A clique of fiercely nationalist and anti-Republican army officers began to put together plans for a coup attempt, to be justified as restoring law and order and preventing a Communist takeover. During the spring and early summer of 1936, Spain was consumed by political violence. Over 300 political murders took place, triumphant peasants seized untilled land and strikes swept the country, with workers demanding better wages and the reinstitution of those sacked and blacklisted after the Asturias rising. However, just as much, if not more, responsibility for the disorder lay with the right. The Spanish fascist party, the Falange, carried out a deliberate policy of provoking unrest by murdering left-wing politicians and union leaders. The most famous of such cases took place on 12–13 July. A known leftist in the urban armed police, the Assault Guard, was murdered outside his home by Falangists on the evening of 12 July. In angry reprisal, his colleagues roamed Madrid looking for prominent right-wingers. They called on Gil-Robles but he was away on holiday. Eventually, they found the monarchist José Calvo Sotelo and proceeded to kidnap and murder him. While the government had no part in the killing, it was used by the right to highlight the Republicans' total lack of control over law and order. Now even the police were carrying out revenge attacks. Sotelo's murder provided a clear justification for the military plotters, but as we have seen, their coup had been in the works for months. In June, a representative of the ultra-conservative Carlist party had bought 6,000 rifles, 450 machine guns, 10,000 grenades and 5 million rounds of ammunition in Germany.[2] Shortly before Sotelo's death, a right-wing newspaper correspondent had hired a commercial plane and pilot in England, and was on his way to the Canary Islands in order to ferry General Franco from his distant posting to Morocco, ready for the uprising.

That revolt came on the evening of 17 July, starting in Spanish Morocco, where the colonial army seized control of the protectorate. On the morning of 18 July, military garrisons across Spain attempted to seize power. The army and security forces were themselves badly split; the Civil and Assault Guards generally supported whichever side seemed most likely to triumph in each locality, and their arms and training were vital in a number of key cities that the Republic held. In the army, more than 2,000 officers and thousands of conscripts also chose to remain loyal rather than join the uprising.[3] The Republican government vacillated, paralysed by the crisis, delaying in arming the workers who supported them and attempting conciliation with the rebellious generals. Unsurprisingly, this failed and with great reluctance, the government armed the workers' militias that had been rapidly formed by left-wing parties and unions. Within a few days, the map of Spain broadly resembled the electoral map of the previous February. In the areas where the left was strong (the industrial cities, rural south), the workers, police and Loyalist soldiers succeeded in defeating the rebellion. Meanwhile, in rightist regions (the rural north, several cities), with the help of civilian elements, the Insurgents quickly crushed forces loyal to the government. The primary reason that the coup had failed was that there very swiftly came into being two armed camps in Spain; the military Rebels were not just opposed by workers but by a significant number of army officers, the rankers of the navy, the majority of the progressive Spanish air force, as well as tens of thousands of armed paramilitary police from the Assault Guard, Civil Guard and Carabineers.[4] Longstanding divisions in the Spanish army between those who had fought in Morocco and those who had largely remained in the Iberian Peninsula played a significant part. The role played by the workers who spontaneously defended the Republic in its hour of need is probably overstated. Although armed mobs of workers did succeed in overwhelming rebellious garrisons in Madrid, Barcelona, Valencia and elsewhere, they did so with the assistance of loyal police paramilitaries and army officers and the all-important armouries that they controlled. Meanwhile, in areas secured by the Nationalist Rebels in the war's first few days, the barricades and militias were quickly overcome in large part because the security forces sided with the military uprising. One factor that is hard to quantify is the extent to which visible mass support for the Republic effected the decisions of soldiers and policemen as to whether to back the rebellion or remain loyal.

Although the coup had failed and Spain was split roughly in half, the Rebels were still confident of a quick victory. However, they faced one huge problem. General Franco and his elite Army of Africa were trapped in Morocco. Unexpectedly, the navy and air force had not joined the uprising, and so the finest units in the Spanish army were stuck on the wrong side of the Straits of Gibraltar. Therefore, on 21 July, Franco dispatched representatives to Hitler and Mussolini asking for aircraft to transport his forces. Before the month was out, the world's first military airlift would begin and in total, Nazi Ju 52s would carry over 17,000 of Franco's elite African troops across the Straits. German and, in particular, Italian aid would increase dramatically as the war progressed. As Mussolini's foreign minister (and son-in-law), Galeazzo Ciano, would later remark, 'Franco had declared that if he received 12 transport planes or bombers, he would have the war won in a few days. These 12 airplanes became more than 1,000 airplanes,

6,000 dead and 14 billion lire.'[5] With the advantages of experienced soldiers and Axis arms, Franco's columns swept through southern Spain in August and September 1936, putting often numerically superior Republican militias to flight. Throughout their rapid conquest, the Nationalists, as the military Rebels soon labelled themselves, carried out a policy of 'cleansing', a tactic developed during the long war in Morocco, specifically designed to liquidate resistance in the rear areas. Widespread looting, rape and mass murder were practised by the Army of Africa during their occupation of southern towns and villages. The most infamous example was the provincial capital Badajoz, where over 4,000 Republicans were herded into the city's bullring and machine-gunned. An American journalist who arrived on the scene several days later asked Colonel Yagüe, one of the Nationalists' most talented field commanders, for the justification of the massacre. The veteran of Morocco replied simply: 'Of course we shot them. What do you expect? Will I take 4,000 red prisoners with my column, having to advance against the clock? Or will I leave them in my rearguard so that Badajoz will be red another time?[6]

Then, Franco made the first of a number of military errors he was responsible for during the conflict. With his forces closing on Madrid, he diverted to the city of Toledo. There, in the fortress and military academy of the Alcázar, a small number of Nationalist cadets and Civil Guards had been holding out stubbornly against a rather incompetent militia siege since the beginning of the war. The relief of the heroic defenders of the Alcázar was a huge propaganda coup for Franco and probably helped ensure his appointment as Nationalist commander-in-chief. What the general could not have known was that the delay in reaching Madrid was to prove crucial. In the meantime, Republican resistance had stiffened significantly. The Republic's ragtag defenders were beginning to be organised more efficiently by the new Under-Secretary for War, José Asensio Torrado, while the populace of the capital had found new resolve and worked hard to fortify the city, motivated by the popular slogan '*¡No Pasarán!*' (They shall not pass!). Perhaps even more crucial was that Franco's delay coincided with the arrival of the first shipments of Soviet military aid to the beleaguered Republic. Russian T-26 tanks and I-15 and I-16 fighter aircraft gave the Loyalist forces a temporary technological advantage. Furthermore, the first International Brigades, composed mostly of French, German and Eastern European volunteers, were thrown into the battle, although they probably had more impact on the morale of the defenders than the actual military situation. In addition, as many as 25 per cent of the forces defending the capital were loyal paramilitary police from the Civil and Assault Guards, the former renowned for their sharpshooting.[7] Lastly, Soviet military advisors helped coordinate the defence of the city, overseen by General José Miaja and masterminded by his chief of staff, Colonel Vicente Rojo. In Rojo, the Republic had certainly their most able planner, an officer almost singularly praised by contemporaries and subsequent historians, even described by some as a 'military genius'.[8]

It had been expected by many, not least the leaderships of both factions, that the capital would fall swiftly. However, while the Nationalists' colonial troops had held the advantage in the rural south, the streets of Madrid were home turf for the Republican militias. The Army of Africa troops were exhausted and depleted after months of fighting and the Rebels were operating at a clear numerical inferiority. Franco's assault took place in November, driving into the city from the west, through the Casa de Campo park and the newly built University City. Amongst text books and laboratories, bitter hand-to-hand fighting characterised the brutal struggle for the campus. Later, the emphasis of the attack was shifted to the working-class suburb of Carabanchel, but despite moments of danger, the Republican troops held firm. Heavy air and artillery bombardment took its toll of civilian casualties but the populace remained steadfast. Much of the Nationalist momentum was drained by repeated flank attacks carried out by Miaja's forces on the thin wedge the Insurgents had punched to the city's outskirts. Within three weeks, it was clear that the direct assault on Madrid was not going to succeed. The Rebel forces then attempted to isolate the capital and broaden their foothold, first by trying to cut the Corunna road in December–January and then the Valencia road in February 1937 at the Battle of Jarama. Both attempts were frustrated by heroic, if costly, efforts on the part of the Republicans. In particular, the International Brigades suffered huge casualties, often thrown into these desperate defensive battles with inadequate training. Hugh Thomas gives figures of 15,000 losses on both sides at Corunna Road and 25,000 Republican and 20,000 Nationalist casualties at Jarama.[9]

Also in February, Málaga, on Spain's south coast, was the scene of Mussolini's first triumph of the war. The newly formed Corpo Truppe Volontarie (CTV) of Italian regulars and fascist Blackshirt volunteers took the city in a lightning attack, which would result in Asensio Torrado's dismissal. Flushed by their quick victory, the semi-motorised CTV were transferred to the Madrid front and prepared a fresh attempt to cut off the capital. The subsequent battle of Guadalajara of March 1937 was a humiliation for the Italians. Amidst an unseasonable snowstorm, the CTV (who had not been issued with winter clothing) became bogged down. As with the Italian army of the Second World War, the CTV suffered from poor morale and leadership, and, with the enemy in control of the skies, they were taken by surprise by a rapid Republican counter-attack.[10] The Italian retreat became a rout, which infuriated Il Duce, who vowed not to allow a single soldier to return home until they had atoned for their defeat. Although Guadalajara's significance was overstated, it did have three important consequences. Firstly, it was a huge propaganda boost for the Republic; it was the first time their embryonic People's Army, at that point still being forged from the myriad militias, had won a clear victory in the field. Secondly, as we have seen, it actually deepened Mussolini's commitment to the war, if only due to a fit of pique. It was evident both to the Nationalists and their Axis backers that substantially more foreign aid would be required to overcome the Republicans, leading to huge increases in arms shipments during 1937. And finally, it made it clear to Franco that Madrid was not going to fall any time soon. He was therefore persuaded by his generals and allies to shift the Nationalist focus northwards, to the Basque Country, Asturias and Santander. These industrial regions formed a narrow Republican strip on Spain's Cantabrian coast; isolated from the rest of the Republic, they would surely provide easier pickings. Furthermore, victory here would free up a vast number of Nationalist troops.

From April, with Franco distracted with his northern campaign, the initiative on the war's main front fell into the hands of the Republic. Their new Ejército Popular was to be put to the test in the offensive for the first time. By mid-1937, the Spanish Civil War appeared finely poised. Nationalist victory, seemingly so close the previous autumn, now appeared to be a distant, if still likely, prospect. For their part, the Republicans had averted the existential danger, for the time being, and were going through a thorough reorganisation on both the home and military fronts. The People's Army, created on paper months before, was about to become a reality.

Chapter 2

The Last Great Cause?
The Spanish Republic in 1937

I t is one of the great ironies of the Spanish Civil War that an uprising of reactionary generals, framed as an attempt to forestall revolution, would in fact be the trigger for one of history's most profound grass-roots social revolutions. As we have seen, the rebellion of the majority of the army, joined by around half the security forces, forced the Republican government to arm the workers as their only defence against insurrection. However, once the Rebels had been defeated in the areas of Spain that remained loyal, a revolutionary situation predominated. With the government largely deprived of its main instruments of law and order (the armed police and army), it was powerless to stop the activities of the very militias they had been forced to arm. The situation was neatly summed up by the liberal president of Catalonia, Lluís Companys, who found himself at the mercy of the anarchist militias who had helped subdue the military rising in Barcelona. He told CNT-FAI leaders:

> Today you are master of the city. If you do not need me or do not wish me to remain … tell me now, and I shall become one soldier more in the struggle against fascism. If, on the other hand, you believe that … I, my party, my name, my prestige, can be of use, then you can count on me and my loyalty as a man.[1]

Across Republican Spain there was a similar story. The liberal government found itself powerless to control the forces that the war had unleashed. The state disappeared from view for a period, a huge range of its functions simply ceasing to exist, not least, control over law and order. In this context, a 'red terror' came to Spain. The reasons for the killing of 38,000 to 50,000 political enemies in Republican territory were myriad and complex. Almost 7,000 of the victims were members of the clergy, and although contemporary horror stories about the atrocities committed against priests and nuns were exaggerated, it is clear that many workers and peasants took revenge on their local clergymen for what they saw as decades of lies and coercion. For instance, in the elections of February, some priests had told their flocks that a vote for the Popular Front was a vote for the Antichrist. Far more common was the killing of known rightists, landowners, employers and army officers, largely as retaliation for both the military coup and years of hatred, resentment and social conflict. Most important of all, however, was the absence of state control. The vast majority of the killings occurred in the first six months of the war, a period in which the dislocated Republican government could do little to prevent them. As early as 8 August, the moderate Socialist Indalecio Prieto had appealed to the Republic's supporters not to engage in violence and Finance (later Prime) Minister Juan Negrín was so deeply disgusted by the atrocities that he felt ashamed to be Spanish.[2] The red terror was not directed or controlled by the government, rather being a largely spontaneous, indirect consequence of the generals' coup.

The revolution brought about genuine radical change across the Republic. In the villages, peasants collectivised the land of their own accord, while in the cities, worker control of everything from factories, to transport, to the Ritz became a previously undreamed-of reality. However, stories of atrocities and property seizures had a detrimental effect on the Republicans' reputation abroad, dramatically reducing the likelihood of international support from the Western capitalist democracies. By no means were all of the Republic's supporters enamoured with the new revolutionary order. While the anarchist movement (CNT-FAI), radical Socialists and the anti-Stalinist Marxists of the POUM, which George Orwell was to join, thought social revolution essential to the war effort, others argued the exact opposite. The revolutionaries were opposed by the liberal Republican parties, the moderate Socialists and the Spanish Communists (PCE), who all sought to reign in revolution and restore democratic, capitalist order. It may be surprising to readers new to the Spanish Civil War to learn that the Communists, and their Soviet backers, were perhaps the most vocal advocates of counter-revolution within the Republic, but there were a number of reasons for this.

Why had Soviet Russia become involved in Spain? The two countries had not even exchanged ambassadors before the war started, and at first the USSR expressed nothing more than moral support for the Republican cause. They had signed the Anglo-French Non-Intervention Agreement in August 1936, which had sought to contain the conflict and prevent foreign involvement. However, by mid-September, two facts had become markedly clear. First, that the Non-Intervention Agreement had had absolutely no impact on the willingness of Italy and Germany to provide Franco with support, despite the signatures of these two fascist nations and their rather farcical sitting on the Non-Intervention committee. Second, that as a result, the Republic appeared to be on the brink of defeat. Stalin's foreign policy had changed markedly in the preceding years. The abstract goal of world revolution had been abandoned in favour of 'socialism in one country', i.e. preserving the communist experiment in Russia from outside threats. To this end, the Comintern (Communist International) had ordered communist parties the world over to seek alliances with democratic parties of all colours in order to avoid fascist advance. The fall of Germany, which had been the home of the largest communist party outside of the Soviet Union, to Nazism had come as an almighty shock. In order to guarantee Russian security from fascist aggression, Stalin sought friendship with the Western powers, Britain and France. In 1935, he had concluded a collective security deal for mutual protection with the French and he hoped to extend this to full military pacts with Russia's First World War allies. As a Nationalist victory emerged as the likely outcome of the Spanish conflict, the Soviets worried that France, their new partner, would soon be surrounded on three sides by hostile fascist states, namely Italy, Germany and Spain. The British ambassador to Moscow reported as much to his superiors as early as August, saying that as far as the Russians were concerned, 'the world revolution can wait; meanwhile any danger to France is a danger to the Soviet Union.'[3] Therefore, sometime in September 1936, Stalin took the decision to send aid and advisors to help the Republic, the only major power to do so.

The policy of suppressing social revolution and reinstating central government control was not merely that of the Communists and Stalin, keen on fostering friendship with Britain and France. In this goal, they were aided and abetted by the centre-left Republican parties and the moderate wing of the Socialists. Figures as powerful as President Manuel Azaña, prime ministers Largo Caballero and Juan Negrín, President of Catalonia Lluís Companys and Defence Minister Indalecio Prieto were just as crucial to the Republic's counter-revolution as Stalin and the PCE. All these factions pursued the same goal: of reigning in revolution and re-establishing order, albeit for different reasons – the Republicans and moderate Socialists because they believed in liberal democracy and were frightened by revolution, the PCE and USSR because they believed a bourgeois Republic would be more likely to receive French and British assistance, and ultimately could bring closer Russia's dream of a collective security alliance with the Western powers. It is therefore in this light that we should view Soviet intervention in Spain. Stalin was a politician prepared to subordinate ideology to all other considerations, as shown by his final, startling step to try to protect the USSR from German aggression, the Nazi-Soviet pact of August 1939. It must have come as a surprise to such a man that Britain and France seemed to ignore their imperial and strategic interests as far as Spain was concerned, with fatal consequences for both the Republic and Stalin's hopes of an anti-fascist alliance. Indeed, by 1938, British politicians such as Eden and Churchill started to realise their error, brought about by instinctive anti-communism, and perceive that a Spain under Franco, indebted as he was to Germany and Italy, would not be in Britain's best interests.[4] By then, it was too late. The Republic was as good as lost and Stalin had abandoned his plans for collective European security.

Through the prestige brought by Soviet aid, their unflinching moderation in the face of social revolution and their brilliant organisation and discipline, the PCE grew rapidly in the early stages of the war. They were transformed from a minor force on the left of Spanish politics to perhaps the single most powerful party in the broad Republican coalition; indeed, the new composition of the PCE came close to embodying the inter-class alliance that the Republican cause represented. From numbering just a few thousand in early 1936, by March 1937 the Communists had over 300,000 members and a quarter of a million in their youth wing, the JSU. Their discipline and calls for a regular army to replace the militias attracted officers that had remained loyal to the Republic, who also benefited from carrying a membership card that placed them above suspicion of Nationalist sympathies. Meanwhile, the lower middle classes, both urban and rural, were won over with the party's vigorous protection of property and opposition to collectivisation. To the well-to-do, frightened by the revolution unfolding around them, the PCE's calls for order and respect for property seemed appealing. The counter-revolution in Republican Spain involved a series of measures, including militarisation of the militias, the reinstitution of state security forces and courts, as well as normalisation of the economy, all of which took time to implement. However, the counter-revolution reached its zenith in May 1937. In Barcelona, the Catalan government of Republicans and Communists, headed by Companys, had been slowly wresting back control from the powerful anarchist movement. On 3 May, police, under the orders of the Catalan minister for public order, attempted to seize the central telephone exchange from worker control. This provocative act led to six days of revolutionary disturbances in the city, where anarchists and the POUM clashed with Communists and the forces of order. This 'civil war within a civil war' was fairly small in scale and not especially ferocious (as Orwell's account in *Homage to Catalonia* testifies to); however, it marked the decisive victory of the counter-revolution as the anarchists were forced to climb down. Further, the May Days were used as justification for a brutal suppression of the anti-Stalinist POUM by the Communists, culminating in the murder of their leader, Trotsky's former secretary Andrés Nin, by the Soviet secret police, the NKVD. After this, the Republic was for a time under the thumb of the SIM, a Communist-dominated military intelligence bureau, who would bring a miniature version of the Stalinist purges to the Spanish Civil War.

The government of left-wing Socialist Largo Caballero fell as a result of the May Days crisis, and the counter-revolutionary coalition of liberal Republicans, moderate Socialists and Communists took a firm grip on power. The new prime minister, Juan Negrín, was a social democrat of the PSOE. A highly intelligent member of the provincial middle class (he held two doctorates before he was 30), Negrín came to rely heavily on the PCE's mass mobilisation and political power to pursue his state-building project. The leading figure of the moderate wing of the PSOE, Indalecio Prieto, became defence minister, with overall control of the war effort. The priorities of the new administration were to complete the state's reassertion of power, to win foreign support for the cause, and to redouble the Republic's war effort through greater central direction of the home front and a more vigorous military policy. It was under this regime that the long, painful process of militarisation was finally completed.

Many historians in the past, and most recently Radosh et al,[5] have argued that, after this point, Soviet/PCE dominance was so great during the civil war that, in effect, the Spanish Republic represented an early example of the 'people's republics' that Stalin was to impose on Eastern Europe after the Second World War. This view overlooks the 'Spanishness' of the Republic's internal power struggle.[6] The Spanish left had been bitterly divided for years by union and party rivalries, and the disunity of the Republican zone surely owed more to these long-running animosities than Soviet takeover plots. Further, the Spanish Republic bore crucial differences to later Soviet satellite states.[7] For one, Soviet attempts at creating a united Socialist-Communist party were frustrated, and Stalin's suggestion of holding elections in 1937 was roundly rejected by the various parties of the Popular Front. This shows that the Republic continued to enjoy an autonomy and pluralism that Stalin's later puppets did not. Spain was thousands of kilometres from Russia and the Soviet Union was not yet a super power, and unlike in Eastern Europe in 1945, Russian military presence was negligible, never more than 800 advisors and technicians.

The People's Army

The Republic had faced a seemingly insurmountable task at the start of the war. Due to the nature of the war's outbreak, many military units that did remain loyal were swiftly dissolved and the inexperienced conscripts dismissed. The Republicans therefore had to fight a military rebellion without an army. This problem had initially, as we have seen, been overcome by the arming of the workers' militias. While the militias, alongside loyal police units, had performed admirably in putting down the revolt across much of Spain, by August, a more conventional war was being waged, and their deficiencies became clear.

The problems that the militia faced were obvious. They had little to no training or experience. Their equipment and supply was haphazard and they possessed virtually no heavy weapons, nor the expertise to use them. They armed themselves however they could. The same Toledo peasant from whom we heard about pre-war rural conditions, Timoteo Ruiz, recalled that on the outbreak of war, the villagers went to the house of a landowner who had a collection of old weapons: 'I remember with what pride I received the lance with which I set out to defend the Republic. Others went with old swords, bucklers, breastplates.'[8] The militias lacked military discipline or organisation; many appear to have gone on leave when they wished. Many columns operated like committees, with commanders elected and orders discussed and debated before being obeyed or discarded. Others preferred to police the rear areas (and often perpetrate atrocities) rather than go to the front. Political rivalries between the militias of different unions and parties played their part in militia ineffectiveness, as did a naivety about modern war, betrayed for instance by a deep reluctance to dig trenches. In the words of one, evidently dismayed, Republican staff officer, 'Our militia had nothing but their enthusiasm; they were deficient in everything else.' The same officer spent the first chaotic weeks of the war trying in vain to meet demands for supplies and weapons from an endless stream of *milicianos*, including an unlikely request from a group of anarchist militia-women for

400 bras.[9] Yet it was from this raw material that an army was to be forged. The process was greatly hindered by enormous distrust between the militias and the loyal professional officers who would be largely responsible for the militarisation process. Quite understandably, there existed a deep suspicion of army officers among many Republican elements, as well as objections to military power and authority. The officers, for their part, rather resented the militias as inefficient and ill-disciplined, and those that found themselves in command of militia columns found the experience deeply dislocating, with all the certainties of military life gone. This antipathy had a corrosive effect on attempts to form a regular army. As a result both of politicians' desire to ensure proper control and the officers' need for order amidst the chaos, the People's Army was to be a deeply bureaucratic one. Helen Graham has described a 'fetishistic' drive for a rigidly centralised military bureaucracy, which did not make best use of the popular enthusiasm the Republic enjoyed, nor provide for battlefield flexibility.[10]

Militarisation began in September 1936, with a decree that formally incorporated the militias into a new People's Army. However, it took months to turn these aspirations into reality. The model on which the new army was to be based was the Communist Fifth Regiment. The Fifth Regiment had been formed out of the communist paramilitary organisation, the MAOC, at the beginning of the war. The MAOC, then the Fifth Regiment, enjoyed a number of advantages over the organisations of other parties and unions. For one, it was the only militia that had had any pre-war military style training, and its development was overseen by a Comintern delegate in Spain, Vittorio Vidali, who became its first political commissar. More importantly, however, it was perhaps the only militia that had a realistic view of war. The Fifth Regiment was in fact a training school that churned out fifty militia battalions in an incredibly short time. Estimates of the strength of the regiment's output vary from 25,000 to 70,000, and these men held clear advantages over the other militias. Recruits had to be in good physical condition and only about half were actually communists; many others joined the Fifth as it seemed to be the best organised, best trained force with which a supporter of the Republic could enrol. For example, Joaquín Masjuán, a Catalan metallurgist who had fought with the anarchist Durruti militia column in the defence of Madrid, applied for an NCO training course with the Fifth Regiment in December 1936 and graduated into the Communist-led 1st Mixed Brigade.[11] The units produced by the regiment had received usually a month's military training, a brief but crucial period considering the complete absence of training in most militias. They were subject to strict discipline and organisation, again in stark contrast to the enthusiastic but chaotic nature of most of the militia bands. On the other hand, the Fifth Regiment was quite evidently a propaganda tool for the PCE and provided the platform for Communist domination of the Republican war effort. The training was rather rudimentary, amounting to little more than parade drill and the instilling of a military ethos. Antonio Candela was an illiterate Extremaduran peasant who, after fleeing the Nationalist advance through his native province, had arrived in Madrid and signed up for the Fifth in September 1936, despite holding no previous political convictions:

> None of the recruits had any military training so, on the following day, early in the morning, the sergeants divided us into groups of five and took us to some open ground where we received our first military training. We learned how to march in step, up and down and they also taught us how to handle Spanish Mausser [*sic*] rifles. We did this for two or three days, then one afternoon they told us to climb onto a lorry.[12]

Candela and thousands of others were rushed off to the front in new 'Steel Companies', each an independent military unit, with integral signals, ambulance and logistics sections. This once again was a completely different approach to most militias and mirrored the composition of the so-called 'mixed brigades' of the later People's Army.

In October 1936, the organisation of the People's Army began in earnest. The basic building block of the army was to be the mixed brigade, intended to have four infantry battalions, heavy, field and anti-tank artillery, engineers, a cavalry or armoured car squadron, and medical and communications services. The inspiration was both the Fifth Regiment and the Spanish army's own traditional use of 'columns', the basic formation used in the Moroccan war. Additionally, Franco's forces had used such combined-arms columns in their advance on Madrid with much success. Due to the speed of their conception and the material pressures the Republic was under, the brigades were rarely over 3,000 strong, with a maximum of 650 per infantry battalion, and few brigades had their full complement of supporting arms and services. Nevertheless, the pace at which this project was undertaken was eye-watering: after the initial creation of six brigades in October, by December there were fifteen mixed brigades in the field; by early 1937, forty active brigades with a further fifteen in training; and by May of that year, there was a total 153 along the main battlefront. Divisions in the People's Army were generally made up of three brigades and therefore had a total paper strength of close to 10,000, although two brigades per division was not uncommon and given that units were almost always undermanned, this figure was rarely achieved. Some of the best mixed brigades, made up of Fifth Regiment veterans of the defence of Madrid, were concentrated into the crack 11th and 46th divisions, which had already shown their proficiency at the battles of Jarama and Guadalajara. The 11th Division in particular, known as the Listers after their inspirational commander, would become arguably the finest unit in the People's Army. The Republican command would come to rely on these formations, and the International Brigades, time and again in offensive operations. However, while superior to the initial militia columns, the mixed brigades had some severe flaws, with military historian Charles Esdaile labelling the decision to opt for this structure one of the worst decisions of the entire war.[13] For one, having so many constituent parts, the mixed brigade required a plethora of staff officers, which the Republic was short of anyhow, with Esdaile estimating that the new structure required triple the number of staff officers than a more traditional approach would have done. Even worse, this structure meant the dilution of the army's artillery strength, with the limited guns and ammunition available (see below) split equally between brigades; in effect, a colossal waste of firepower as artillery is most effective when concentrated where it is required. Colonel Segismundo Casado was a Loyalist professional officer, who later wrote of the problems inherent in the People's Army's structure:

In the organisation of the People's Army, the greatest error was committed when the Spanish High Command accepted the advice of the Russian advisors with respect to the organisation of the tactical units.

As a principle in the formation of the mixed brigades, an exotic organism was introduced which might be called the 'little great unit'. This type of tactical and administrative Unit does not exist in any regular army, for the simple reason that its composition is absurd. ... It comprised 3,700 men; its armaments consisted of 1,960 rifles, 32 machine-gun rifles and 24 machine guns. Naturally, at the end of the war, the Central Army, for example, had 250,000 men, and only 95,000 rifles, 3,000 Automatics and 65 Batteries. More over, as I have said, the mixed brigades had 4 Battalions and the Spanish tactical regulations as laid down for the Republican Army were made on the basis of Regiments of three Battalions. I remember as an effect that when the People's Army had approximately 1,000,000 men, it had only 350,000 rifles and 8,000 machine guns. These figures show only too plainly that the organisation of the unfortunately celebrated mixed brigades absorbed an enormous number of men who had no means of fighting, robbing them of their tactical mobility without increasing their firing power. This waste of men meant mobilising a great number of reinforcements which meant in turn an alarming reduction of hands in all work behind the lines. It was not possible to practise the fundamental principle of the economy of forces.[14]

Effectively, the mixed brigade wasted too much manpower in supporting arms and was short on actual fighting power. Casado claims that had a later proposal to transform the 200 mixed brigades into more typical regiments been accepted, up to 150,000 men would have been saved and could have been used to form new units. While shortages of arms surely contributed to the problems the colonel alludes to, the mixed brigade was alien to the regular officers who served the Republic and necessitated yet more 'starting from scratch' in the militarisation process.

The new army faced an uphill struggle to reintroduce military discipline and to wrest away control of militias from political parties and unions. For one, the colourful titles of the militia units were replaced with a bland, non-political numbering system. However, in the task of installing order and discipline, the People's Army's commissars were vital. The propensity of commissars in the Republican army is often viewed in negative light, as the instruments of communist infiltration and control of the army. But in the context of 1936, they were entirely necessary. There was a commissar attached to each unit from company size upwards, and their role was extremely varied. It is true that in previous revolutions, the role of the commissar had been to watch over the professional officers to ensure their loyalty to the cause, and although this was important in Spain, with such suspicion of the regulars who fought for the Republic, it was not their primary function in the Spanish Civil War. Commissars had to justify orders to the troops (who until recently had been voting on whether to obey them), to motivate the rank and file, to educate conscripts on the importance of the struggle. They were also responsible for the men's welfare and morale, acting as 'shock absorbers' in the tensions between the Republic's soldiers and officers.[15]

The slogan of the Commissariat, 'The first to advance, the last to retreat', was put into practice by the majority, who often filled the absent role of NCOs and battlefield adjutants to unit commanders. Unsurprisingly, their casualties were high. As the war wore on, and, as we shall see, the People's Army's material inferiority became clear, the role of the commissar became ever more important, in counteracting the negative impact of successive defeats on morale and fortifying the will to resist in the men. The reason that so many commissars were drawn from the ranks of the PCE was because the Fifth Regiment had produced many able men ready for the role, and also because no other party grasped their importance or allocated quality and experienced personnel for Commissariat appointments. This would, however, lead to resentments and tensions with other Republican elements, with Defence Minister Prieto increasingly fighting against Communist control of the Commissariat, while Esdaile simply points out the commissars added another layer of bureaucracy to the People's Army.[16] Although a biased observer (he would go on to take up arms against the Communists in the war's final stages), Colonel Casado provided a fair assessment of the role of the Republic's commissars in his 1939 memoir:

> There were plenty of Commissars of good faith who gave their lives in the holocaust of patriotism and liberty, dying at the head of their Units, and there were others who worked honourably for the highest motives. For these, my greatest respect. But, undoubtedly, the mistaken activities of the Commissariat contributed notably to the adverse course of the war.
> Such things naturally aroused hatred and suspicion among men who were fighting for the same cause. Political differences were increased, and passions rose high.[17]

It is presumed, quite incorrectly, by many that the Spanish Civil War was in large part a guerrilla conflict. In fact, it was remarkably conventional, as was the People's Army. Perhaps Ernest Hemingway's depiction of mountain guerrillas in *For Whom the Bell Tolls* or the association between guerrilla warfare and the Hispanic world, or even the 2006 Oscar-winning civil war fantasy *Pan's Labyrinth* are responsible for this misconception. In reality, the Republic made surprisingly little use of behind-the-lines resistance fighters, although one partisan unit was formed with Soviet help. Part of the reason must be the systematic brutality of the Nationalists in their cleansing of the rear areas (to be discussed in the next chapter). Also, the Republic fought a conventional war because it believed it could win – it represented the legitimate government, while Franco's forces were the Insurgents. Furthermore, the Republicans always held out hope that Britain and France would eventually come to their aid and swing the war in their favour. Therefore, while in hindsight an extensive guerrilla war seems a logical approach, at the time the idea received little attention.

The Republic had built an army, with Loyalist officers, volunteers, militiamen and, for the most part, conscripts (twenty-seven reserve classes were mobilised by the war's end).[18] As we have seen, this was no easy task. An even bigger issue was equipping the army. At the outbreak of war, the Republicans found themselves at an immediate disadvantage. The government managed to retain control over 200,000 of the 500,000 rifles in Spain (the rest being seized by the military Rebels), but around 70,000 of these were lost in the retreats of August–September 1936. Of 1,007 Spanish army artillery pieces, the government forces found themselves with only 387. This initial inferiority in arms was only worsened by the international situation. The aforementioned Non-Intervention Agreement had banned the sale of arms to Spain. This meant quite simply that the Republican government could not buy weapons. While Hitler and Mussolini supplied the Nationalists with all the equipment they could want, the Republic was banned from purchasing military hardware on the open market. Had such an agreement not been in place, possession of Spain's gold reserves would have allowed the government to purchase all the arms they required. Gerald Howson gives one stark example: in the summer of 1936, the British Soley Arms Company had 800,000 rifles, 50,000 machine guns, a considerable number of artillery pieces and enormous quantities of the appropriate ammunition, equipment and spare parts to go with them. Had Non-Intervention not been in place, the Republic could have bought the lot, at market prices, and had them shipped immediately. This would have amounted to a greater quantity of munitions than the Republicans were to acquire for the entire war.[19] Had they been able to make such a purchase, or other similar purchases, the war would likely have turned out very differently.

Without a large domestic armaments industry, the Republic had to rely on two more malevolent sources: the Soviet Union and the black market. Following the previously discussed decision to intervene in Spain, Russian shipments of arms began arriving in mid-October 1936 and played a crucial role in the defence of Madrid. The Republic's gold reserves were for the most part transported to Moscow, where they formed a sort of current account for arms purchases. The Soviets took advantage of the desperation of their new ally in offloading large quantities of outdated equipment from the Tsarist era, all at inflated prices. Stalin did however also provide some modern hardware that was of great use: Russia supplied T-26 and BT-5 tanks (281 and 50 respectively), which were by far the best in Spain. The T-26's 45mm gun was capable of knocking out with ease any of the tanks received by the Nationalists, but they suffered heavy losses due to their thin armour and mechanical failure brought on by overuse. In addition, the Soviet DP-28 light and Maxim M1910 heavy machine guns were just as, if not more, effective than the equivalent weapons in the Nationalist ranks. Furthermore, as we shall see, the Soviets also supplied hundreds of modern aircraft. In total, they charged the Republic $171.4 million, more than $3 billion today, for this aid, paid up front in gold. The Mexican and Czech governments were also sympathetic and provided what little they could, but on the black market, the Republic was to an even greater extent vulnerable to manipulation and deceit. Huge amounts were spent on bribes or 'storage fees', while some shipments simply never arrived, with no opportunity for recompense. It was in this way that the Polish government, although in no way sympathetic to their cause, sold a large quantity of unwanted weaponry to the Republic. This included a wide assortment of First World War rifles and artillery, often with ammunition that had been in storage for decades. There were a few weapons within the Polish shipments that were useful, such as hundreds of copies of the American BAR light machine gun, widely used in the Second World War. However, these were exceptions. The Poles overcharged to such an extent that although official figures show $24 million worth of sales to Spain, military officials estimated they had in fact made in excess of $200 million, far more than the Russians, despite shipping far less.[20] A good example of this was the sale of sixteen First World War FT-17 tanks, which the Polish military had designated 'useless', for $35,000 each, when the Republic was only being charged $21,500 by the Soviets for each T-26! The FT-17 had a top speed of 4mph and a two-man crew; it was not suitable for warfare in 1936. When a Polish officer challenged his superior as to the outrageous dishonesty, he simply laughed and said, 'Why should we worry, it's only the Spanish Republicans!'[21]

British, American, Canadian, Japanese, Austrian, Russian, Mexican, French, Czech, German and, of course, Spanish-made rifles therefore found their way into the hands of the Republic's armed forces, and that is by no means a comprehensive list. By mid-1937, although the People's Army never achieved total uniformity, most units wore a baggy brown uniform with Sam Brown belt. Helmets were not ubiquitous but the French Adrian style was common, as were Czech and Spanish designs, the latter resembling an enlarged German Stahlhelm. Wherever possible, battalions were fitted out with a single rifle, and while the lucky ones might get brand new Mosin Nagants or Mausers, most had to make do with old rifles in poor condition, such as thousands of Mexicanskis, American Remington rifles ordered by the Tsar during the First World War that had been offloaded on neighbouring Mexico after the Russian Revolution. Even worse, some Republicans found themselves equipped with outdated single-shot rifles, such as the Italian Vetterli dating from 1870, or else unwanted First World War weapons such as the utterly dreadful French Chauchat machine rifle.

One issue rarely mentioned by historians is artillery. Artillery was the by far the most important weapon of the First World War, accounting for the majority of battlefield casualties. From 1914–18, it was the key offensive and defensive weapon; without artillery support, infantry could never penetrate fixed defences, while the best way to counter an enemy attack was to catch them in the open with a timely barrage. What had transformed the First World War in its final year back into a war of movement was not the invention of tanks, but a massive increase in the size and complexity of both sides' artillery arms, which were capable of obliterating even the best-prepared defences. Equally, artillery and mortars almost certainly accounted for the majority of battle casualties in the Second World War. This was a weapon of which the Republic were desperately short, both in terms of quality and quantity. They received just 302 field guns and 191 howitzers from the Russians, as well as 393 anti-tank and 64 anti-aircraft guns. Other than modern anti-tank guns, the majority of the artillery pieces that the Republic received were in hopelessly poor condition. This was a serious issue, because, as shall be seen in the coming chapters, Republican offensives often became bogged down in attacks on fortified towns or hills. Without adequate artillery support, it is always a slow and costly affair for infantry to capture well-defended positions. Even more critical was the shortage of shells. While the Soviet Union dispatched 659 million rounds of small arms ammunition, and the modern 37 and 45mm AT guns and tank cannons were also well supplied, they sent just 1.2 million shells for conventional artillery, the equivalent of 2,700 per gun.[22] To put this figure in some context, for their initial assault on Verdun in 1916, the Germans gathered 850 artillery pieces and 2.5 million shells.[23] For six days' combat, the German force of 140,000 men enjoyed the support of more guns and twice as many shells as the Republican army of perhaps 800,000 received from the Russians for the entire duration of the war. Meanwhile, the British army had at its peak 6,800 guns on the Western Front and fired almost a million shells in twenty-four hours during their attack on the intimidating Hindenburg Line in September 1918.[24] The deficiencies, therefore, are clear. The Republic lacked the artillery firepower to fight a modern war effectively. The sum of all this was that the People's Army found itself with a vast array of different weapons of various ages and calibres, a deeply impractical situation. Most armies use one standard rifle, several machine guns (sub, light, heavy), and perhaps ten different artillery pieces (field guns, howitzers, anti-tank, anti-air etc.). A report of the victorious Nationalist army, upon inspecting the myriad arms they had captured by the war's end, concluded that the Republic used at least 49 rifle types, 41 different automatic weapons and 60 different artillery pieces.[25] The difficulties this caused cannot be overstated. Each weapon was different, having its own quirks and features, was maintained in a different way, and crucially, used a different sort of ammunition. In these conditions, if a soldier found himself mixed up with another unit, he might not be able to reload his weapon. Rifles often came without cleaning kits, artillery without sights, equipment without instructions. It was in this position of acute material inferiority that the Republican forces were forced to operate from the spring of 1937 onwards.

It was no small mercy, therefore, that there were a small number of talented senior officers who either remained loyal to the Republic or else emerged from the militias. General José Miaja was the first to rise to prominence, having been given command of the dramatic defence of Madrid. Miaja was an ageing, unspectacular professional officer of conservative leanings but found himself in the Republican zone when war broke out. He collaborated closely with the PCE in organising the defence of the capital and it was largely thanks to their propaganda that he gained an almost mythical reputation as the 'saviour of Madrid'. He may have been seen as 'in with the communists', but as American journalist Louis Fischer joked, 'he probably knew as much about Communism as Francisco Franco.'[26] Although Miaja was an inspirational figure, touring the front and whipping up the enthusiasm of the city's beleaguered defenders, his military talents were limited (he had only previously commanded a regiment in combat), and as the war progressed, he would abuse his new-found prestige to get his own way. Hemingway described him rather scathingly as the 'old bald, spectacled, conceited, stupid-as-an-owl, unintelligent-in-conversation, brave-and-as-dumb-as-a-bull, propaganda-built-up defender of Madrid'.[27] The real mastermind of the Republican victory that winter was Miaja's chief of staff, Colonel Vicente Rojo. Praise for Rojo is virtually unanimous across all accounts and he was even allowed to return to Francoist Spain in the 1950s, such was the esteem in which he was held. He was an unlikely Republican hero, being a devout Catholic from a military family. Although no friend of revolution, the 41-year-old Rojo was equally repulsed by his own rebellious colleagues, with whom he felt no affiliation. President Azaña described him as 'hardworking, competent, silent, disciplined. He should have been the true general, but he lacks leadership skills.'[28] For a decade, Rojo had taught at the military academy, and it appears he was a keen student of military theory. Before the war, he published a book a month on the subject, at a loss, mostly translated works such as those of British military theorist J.F.C. Fuller, in the hope that his fellow officers in the resolutely backward Spanish army might 'read and study a little more'.[29] The new defence minister, Indalecio Prieto, made him chief of the general staff, in effect, the head of the People's Army, in June 1937. In this post, Rojo was to plan all of the Republic's major offensives and direct their overall strategy. Both Miaja and Rojo were probably typical of the roughly 2,000 active professional officers who served in the People's Army in the sense that their service to the Republic was a marriage of convenience. Only a minority of those officers that did remain loyal were ideologically committed to the Republican project. Most were merely what Michael Alpert terms 'geographically loyal', in the sense that on the war's outbreak, they found that they and their families were in the Republican zone and it was therefore prudent to serve the Loyalists rather than join the rebellion.[30] A number of genuine Republicans who had taken retirement in previous years under a misguided scheme of then War Minister Manuel Azaña did return to the fold, although these men were naturally older than most active officers. On the whole, most of the regular officers who served in the People's Army were aged Peninsula soldiers, who had seen little of the war in Morocco, with many belonging to the artillery and engineers rather than the infantry. This was due to the fact that the vast majority of those that had fought in the Rif in the infantry and cavalry, as well as most of the younger generation of junior officers, sided with the Rebels. As a result, not only did the Republic enjoy the services of considerably fewer professionals than their adversaries, those that did serve were often of limited quality.

With a shortage of professionals, many of the field commands were taken by men drawn from the militia. A number of anarchists became famous leaders, such as Durruti and Cipriano Mera, but it was from the communist ranks of the Fifth Regiment that the most prominent militia officers would rise. The most talented was undoubtedly Juan Modesto (real name Juan Guilloto León). According to Louis Fischer, 'He was a handsome, jovial little fellow in his thirties, a woodworker who had been a corporal in Spain's pre-war Foreign Legion of toughs.'[31]After his military service, Modesto had joined the PCE, and became commander of the MAOC militia. He was sent to the Soviet Union to attend a military training course at the Moscow Frunze Academy, which he reportedly passed with distinction. In the war's early months, he quickly won plaudits for his leadership and bravery in combat. The stocky Andalusian was not always popular with his communist colleagues, having a reputation for being sarcastic, ruthless and often short-tempered (President Azaña reports that he berated a group of Soviet advisors during a battle for resembling a mother's meeting).[32] Despite this, Modesto commanded respect and was highly rated by Rojo, who said that he inspired great confidence, and modern historians have labelled him an outstanding figure.[33] By mid-1937, he was a lieutenant colonel in command of a corps at the tender age of 30. More famous was Enrique Líster, commander of the elite 11th Division. Like Modesto, Líster was young, from working-class stock and made his name with the Fifth Regiment. However, he was a very different character – a charismatic, personable man, cunning but something of a maverick. Idolised by his men, he was a strict disciplinarian and a committed communist. He had also attended the Frunze course but had been thrown off it for poor behaviour, and ended up working on the construction of the Moscow metro.[34] It is interesting comparing the memoirs of the two worker-soldiers. While Modesto's prose is terse and matter of fact, Líster's is petulant and emotional, full of anecdotes of arguments and lavish praise for his division. This surely reflects their respective characters. Another famous communist was El Campesino, 'the peasant', real name Valentín González. El Campesino was a former army deserter, who was, it seems, promoted far beyond his abilities on the back of Communist prestige and shameless self-aggrandisement. Unquestionably he was a tenacious fighter, suited to battalion command perhaps, but he was basically illiterate and could not read a map. Hemingway, while expressing some distaste at the fact these supposed spontaneous people's heroes had been picked and groomed by the Communists, described Modesto as 'much more intelligent than Líster or El Campesino', and concluded that the 'truth' of these men 'was much better than the lies and legends' produced by PCE propaganda.[35]

Despite this crop of talented militia leaders, a major problem the People's Army faced was the lack of junior officers and NCOs. The Republicans were desperately short of leaders of all levels; at the outbreak of war, 90 per cent of the Spanish army's officers and NCOs within Republican territory disappeared, either joining the rebellion, deserting or being imprisoned (or worse) for treachery, real or imagined.[36] Those lieutenants, captains and majors that did remain loyal were, due to necessity, rapidly promoted, and found themselves commanding brigades, divisions and corps. The most striking example was Vicente Rojo, a mere major in July 1936, who, in less than a year, was elevated to chief of the general staff! Such shortages were incredibly difficult to make up, and in a war of movement, lower leaders are crucial in maintaining momentum, especially in the face of tough resistance. Without skilled squad and section commanders, attacking élan can quickly be lost and low-quality information makes it up the chain of command. There was both a shortage of officer candidates *and* instructors due to the pressures of civil war, and courses were often only a month or less and purely theoretical. The situation called for rapid battlefield promotion, as problematic as that can be, but the Republican army list of 1938 reveals a total of only 9,458 war-temporary officers, less than half the figure in Nationalist forces.[37] To make things worse, the dearth of experienced NCOs, the backbone of any army, was exacerbated by misguided efforts to address the junior officer issue by simply promoting many of those NCOs that did remain. The overall picture, seen again and again in military reports, was that the People's Army simply did not have enough quality in its junior leadership roles.

One of the unique features of the People's Army was the famous International Brigades. In total, around 35,000 people from over fifty nations would come to fight for the Republicans over the course of the war, with the largest contingents coming from France (9,000), and Germany and Austria (5,000). Perhaps 2,800 Americans and 2,000 British and Irish also joined. A remarkable 20 per cent of volunteers were Jewish, for whom the fight against fascism was all the more pertinent.[38] They went on to form up to forty different battalions, usually in national groups, spread across seven mixed brigades, including the renowned 11th-15th 'International' Brigades. Volunteers flocked to the Republic, especially from the autumn of 1936 to the spring of 1937, for a variety of reasons. Some because they believed the

Republic's cause just, others because they felt sympathy with the suffering of the Spanish people, or they were appalled by the flagrant intervention of Hitler and Mussolini and the lack of an international reaction. For some it was also the belief that fascism must be combatted, that democracy must be protected, and that if fascist aggression could be beaten in Spain, a world war could be prevented. The idea that the volunteers were largely composed of adventurers, misfits and mercenaries, perhaps seeking to escape 1930s mass unemployment, was put about at the time by the right-wing press in Britain and elsewhere, and has subsequently been repeated by some historians, as has the idea that men were 'duped' into going with promises of high-paid jobs.[39] There is scant evidence for this accusation and it has been roundly dismissed by the extensive studies of Richard Baxell, who nevertheless concedes that the thousands of volunteers had an extraordinarily diverse range of reasons for going to Spain.[40] The motives of many can be typified by Tommy Nicholson, a Brigade volunteer from Glasgow, who was initially prevented from joining up due to his political differences with the Communist party:

> I worked in the Govan wireworks in 1937. In Glasgow then you couldn't but be active in the class struggle. Poverty was rife. Glasgow had a strong workers' movement then as now and we all fervently believed in the emancipation of the working class across the world. I was anxious to get to Spain. Like many another I believed that the whole future of humanity was being fought out there. Either socialism or fascism would win through. That's why we felt we had to go. Spain became your lifeblood.[41]

Between half and three-quarters of the total volunteers for the brigades were communists, the rest were a broad range of socialists, liberals, democrats, trade unionists and a surprising number of no political affiliation. Around 80 per cent of the British volunteers were working class, and it can be presumed that figures were similar for other nationalities, dispelling the myth that the Brigaders were largely poets and intellectuals.[42] A remarkably common conviction amongst the Brigaders was the idea that fascism had to be confronted, that it could not be allowed to grow unchecked, and that Spain offered a battleground on which that could happen. It appears that many of them fervently believed that if Nazi Germany and fascist Italy could be stopped on Spanish soil, a world war could be avoided. To many of the idealistic volunteers, the Republic truly was 'the last great cause'.

There remains a lively historical debate about the nature of the International Brigades. In his 1982 book *Comintern Army*, Dan Richardson sets out a strong case that the brigades were a political and propaganda tool for the USSR and Comintern. The brigades were organised and administered by the Comintern, taking orders from Moscow, and were subject to a harsh disciplinary regime. There have been accusations that volunteers' passports were taken by Soviet secret services for use by their agents, and that those who did not conform politically ended up in prison.[43] On the other hand, Baxell has challenged many of these points directly in his works on the British volunteers. For one, the flow of volunteers to Spain predated Comintern involvement in Spain, with Communist funding and organisation merely providing the means for a greater number of working–class volunteers, who often lacked passports, to make the journey. Baxell also points out that much of the evidence for political intolerance comes from derogatory reports on individual volunteers from the Moscow archives. However, these files were confidential reports on the political quality of the volunteers with a view for future work for the party, rather than some sort of blacklist.[44] Undoubtedly there were many who regretted going, or who were undisciplined once in Spain, yearning for leave or respite. This was more the result of severe combat stress and the astonishing casualty rates the International Brigades suffered as the Republic's main shock troops, (perhaps only 7 per cent of volunteers survived the war completely unscathed, i.e. never suffering a wound or being killed), rather than political dissatisfaction.[45] Even Richardson sympathises with the Comintern's position of denying home leave; no army could allow its soldiers to leave whenever they wished, and the practicalities of returning to a blockaded Republic were problematic.[46] Thousands of Brigaders were imprisoned, or dispatched to camps or labour battalions for weeks or months for offences such as drunkenness, desertion, insubordination, cowardice and defeatism. Additionally, several hundred, although there are no exact figures, were executed, mostly for repeated desertion, looting, mutiny or rape of civilians. There seems to have been a spate of executions in the spring of 1938 during and after the great retreats that saw Franco advance to the sea amidst disintegration in much of the People's Army and a wave of desertion. From this time onwards, military intelligence informants spied on their comrades, reporting back on morale and troublemakers. While official reports are full of references to Trotskyism and accusations of political weakness (which has led to some historians seeing the brigades and their disciplinary regime as an extension of the Soviet purges), it appears that in fact this was a term thrown around by communist officials to explain many ills, not least the poor discipline and disrespect for authority exhibited by some volunteers. Confidential reports on Brigaders tend to use phrases such as 'Trotskyist elements; drunks and immoral characters' to describe the unreliable minority, suggesting that Trotskyism was simply a catch-all term for brigade leadership for those they disliked or distrusted, the dedicated Communist's go-to explanation for any and all ills ('That one word covers everything', wrote one volunteer later).[47] Certainly there is no evidence of Brigaders being executed for divergent political views, although repeatedly questioning the wisdom of the party or brigade leadership did in some cases lead to demotion if not a spell in the labour company. Of the 2,000 or so British and Irish volunteers in Spain, there is evidence two were executed, one for attempting to take information to the enemy, the other for shooting at his comrades with a machine gun while drunk.[48] Of 1,700 Canadians, 150 recurved a punishment of some form or another during the war, mostly for desertion – a primarily military rather than political crime, brought about by high casualties.[49] One only has to think of the disciplinary regimes of European militaries in the first half of the twentieth century and the ways they dealt with cowardice and desertion, whether it be the British or French in the First World War or the Germans and Soviets in the Second, to see the ridiculousness of the claims that the International Brigades represented some form of exported Stalinist terror. Whether in democracies or dictatorships, military crimes such as desertion or disrespect of officers tended to be met with severe punishment in this era. While not a lenient military to serve in, the volunteers were by no means operating under totalitarian conditions either. In fact, most deserters and political nonconformists actually found themselves back in the front lines after a period of incarceration due to the heavy losses suffered at the front.

The International Brigades have also been criticised as no better than the militias, thrown into combat without any real training, their lives frittered away at an alarming rate.[50] However, there are several nuances that this argument ignores and which go some way to proving that the brigades really were an elite within the People's Army. Firstly, it is true that when the first International Brigades were formed in the winter of 1936–37, they were thrown into action with only rudimentary training, often against some of the Nationalists' finest troops. The British Battalion was founded less than two weeks before facing the full fury of the Army of Africa at Jarama in February 1937, and subsequently only 80 of its original strength of 630 men did not become casualties in just three days of combat.[51] The Abraham

Lincoln Battalion received live ammunition for the first time just a few hours before going into combat. During the battle of Corunna Road, the Thälmann Battalion of German volunteers was ordered to 'not retreat a single centimetre', and in fulfilling this suicidal order lost all but thirty-five of their men.[52] However, as the threat of imminent Republican defeat receded in the spring of 1937, more time could be taken to train new arrivals and equipment was not quite so scarce in the rear areas. The diary of Sid Hamm, a Cardiff volunteer, who arrived in Spain in April 1937, reveals that he was in training, both behind the lines and at the front, for almost ten weeks before seeing combat and his instruction involved practice with various weapons, field manoeuvres and lectures from experienced Brigade officers.[53] The Mackenzie-Papineau battalion of Canadian and American volunteers received extensive training, overseen by Robert Merriman, who had himself seen combat at Jarama with the Abraham Lincolns. The Mac-Paps were not used haphazardly, having to wait until October 1937 to taste battle for the first time, months after their formation in the summer. Not only were new arrivals given more training after the Republic had been brought back from the brink, but the remnants of the International Brigades that had been thrown into the battles around Madrid were left with grizzled cores of veterans who had learnt the lessons of modern war the hard way. The British Battalion was in the front line from February to June 1937, 125 days in which to learn their craft, the 11th International Brigade were now heroes of the defence of Madrid, and the Garibaldi Battalion had won plaudits for their successful counter-attack against Mussolini's CTV at Guadalajara. Therefore, by the time of the Brunete offensive in July 1937, the Internationals had experienced more real combat than most troops in the People's Army and had been given a chance to rest and reorganise after the trying battles of the winter. In addition, their ranks were boosted by the inclusion of Spanish volunteers who wished to fight alongside the Internationals, motivated by a desire to be in the thick of the fighting. Due to heavy losses, by 1938 the majority of personnel in the International Brigades were in fact Spanish.

The battalions were commanded by volunteers who had a modicum of military experience, often more than commanders in People's Army units, and discipline and motivation were generally higher than in all-Spanish formations due to the lack of conscripts.[54] At Jarama, the Americans were led by Robert Merriman, who had been in the US Officer Training Corps while at college, while the CO of the British Battalion at Brunete was a former sailor in the Royal Navy, Fred Copeman. Higher command, of the brigades and the 'International' divisions, was conferred on a number of Red Army officers of non-Russian origin who were dispatched to Spain. The Soviets clearly had a 'type' that they picked out for this role. Many of them were former soldiers of the Austro-Hungarian army, who had been captured by the Russians in the First World War. The Russian Revolution had seen them freed, and they had joined the Red Army in the subsequent civil war. These men had then pursued military careers in the Soviet Union. The reason that such individuals were chosen was that they professed to simply be international volunteers from their home nations, therefore masking Red Army involvement in Spain. As such, many took on *noms de guerre.* The most famous was General Kléber (real name Manfred Stern), a Romanian of German-Jewish stock, who took his alias from a French revolutionary general. Kléber commanded the first International Brigade (the 11th) in the defence of Madrid and subsequent battles, winning a heroic reputation both for himself and the volunteers through their steadfastness and self-sacrifice during the Republic's darkest hour. While Beevor criticises Kléber as never exceeding 'the level of a tough First World War commander', what more could be expected in the circumstances?[55] The First World War was the only model to follow in 1936, and the Republic could certainly have done with more officers with his resolve and leadership. Though Hemingway accuses Kléber of being 'limited', he concedes that he was 'a good soldier' who had done 'a fine job'.[56] His career was, however, stunted by accusations of 'Kléberism'; of taking all the glory for himself and the Internationals. The Pole Karol Świerczewski (*nom de guerre* General Walter) led first an International Brigade and then a division in Spain, and was, in the words of Modesto, 'an expert in offensive operations'.[57] On returning to the Soviet Union after the war, he would command an army and be appointed minister for war in post-war communist Poland. The commander of the anglophone 15th International Brigade was yet another Austro-Hungarian-cum-Red Army veteran, Vladimir Ćopić. The Yugoslav seems to have divided opinion; Brigade veteran Walter Gregory wrote decades later that he was popular, admired, 'an intelligent man with a great appreciation of the tactics and strategy of warfare', whom he could not recall ever being the subject of criticism.[58] On the other hand, Marion Merriman's account of her late husband's role in the civil war, in which the American was Ćopić's chief of staff, paints a picture of an arrogant, stubborn commander who was easily piqued.[59] Despite mixed opinions on individuals, it cannot be argued that the International Brigades actually enjoyed the leadership of far more experienced and qualified senior officers than other Republican units, further adding to their status as elite formations. With more experience, training and motivation than the vast majority of Republican units, as well as the pick of Soviet arms, the International Brigades can undoubtedly be regarded as the elite shock troops of the People's Army, as they were perceived at the time.

As already alluded to, the Republic received hundreds of modern aircraft from the Soviet Union to equip their squadrons. This was just as well, because though the Spanish air force had, on the whole, not joined the military rebellion of July 1936, it was equipped with desperately obsolete planes. The main fighter, the Nieuport 52, was a biplane dating from 1924, which, with a top speed of 140mph, could be outpaced by most commercial airliners of the day. The main bomber meanwhile was the equally antiquated two-seater CASA Breguet 19, a model based on a successful First World War design. Hence, the advantages implicit in retaining control of the majority of the air force were in fact not so great, especially given the fact that within a fortnight of the war's outbreak, modern Italian and German aircraft were arriving to support Franco. There was also a shortage of skilled pilots, with 300 of the Republic's airmen vanishing in the first weeks of war, most joining the Nationalists, others simply deserting.[60] Fortunately, the first few shipments of Russian fighters came with pilots to fly them, but by mid-1937, the majority of the Republic's aircraft were flown by Spaniards, many of them hastily trained in the Soviet Union. There was also a small squadron of international mercenaries in the early stages of the war who effectively ripped off the Republic with extortionate pay demands and limited combat effectiveness. Other than a handful of unarmed, outdated French aircraft, the Republic was totally reliant on Russian-supplied planes, 623 of which were shipped over the course of the war.[61] They received 151 Polikarpov I-15 'Chato' fighters (and manufactured 237 themselves under licence), an effective biplane, soon to be outdated but better than what the Republicans had. The best aircraft supplied by the Soviets was undoubtedly the Polikarpov I-16 'Mosca', a modern monoplane fighter, capable of 282mph and with a ceiling of 9,280m. A total of 276 reached the Republic. When it arrived in Spain, the Mosca was by far the most advanced fighter on either side; fast, agile and well-armed, and it proved decisive in winning air superiority for the Republicans in the battles in the Madrid region. From mid-November 1936, so total was the I-16's dominance that only two were shot down in the subsequent three and a half months.[62] Unfortunately for the Republicans, the arrival of the Luftwaffe's latest fighter in the spring of 1937 was to alter the situation in the air dramatically. In terms of bombers, like artillery, the Republic was desperately short on numbers. The Soviets supplied 124 R-5 and R-Z reconnaissance biplanes, collectively referred to as Natachas, which could operate as light bombers, and 92 SB Tupolev 'Katiuskas'. The Katiuska was sleek and speedy but had several flaws; it was able to carry a payload of just 500kg, was difficult to maintain and, lacking in defensive features, it was highly vulnerable. The numbers and quality of the bombers supplied to the Republican air force compare unfavourably with those supplied to the Nationalists, which were both far more numerous and included several models that went on to see extensive service in the Second World War. The lack of an effective bombing arm, combined with the aforementioned lack of artillery, left the Republican military severely outgunned.

The Spanish navy had mostly remained loyal to the Republic in rather unlikely circumstances. Most naval officers had supported the Rebels; however, across much of the fleet, the working-class crews had mutinied and either arrested or murdered their traitorous commanders. While this left most of the decrepit navy in Republican hands, without the expertise or leadership of the officer class, their effectiveness was severely hampered. Other than a few ill-fated voyages, the Republican navy was to prove totally impotent during the course of the war.

Finally, Republican land, sea and air efforts were aided by hundreds of Soviet advisors who arrived from the autumn of 1936 onwards. While numerous figures have been given over the years, it is probable that a total of approximately 2,000 Russians served in Spain, with no more than 800 present at any one time.[63] These included tank drivers, pilots, engineers, artillerymen, interpreters, signals and communications experts, as well as army, navy and air force advisors. It is difficult to ascertain the extent of their influence on the Republican military as Spanish commanders naturally played down the importance of foreign advice in their memoirs. They certainly exercised influence over the use of Russian-supplied tanks and aircraft, at least at first while they remained Russian-operated. For instance, the advisors refused to allow Soviet planes and pilots to be deployed to a proposed offensive in Extremadura in spring 1937 because they opposed the plan. As a result of this, and the opposition of Miaja, the operation was shelved. Worse, General Walter reported to Moscow in 1938 that many Russian advisors overestimated their abilities, treated their Spanish colleagues like amateurs and were just as culpable for tactical errors as the People's Army's leaders.[64] These criticisms must be balanced against the fact that the Soviet presence did provide the Republicans with invaluable expertise and training, especially in technical matters, which simply would not have been available otherwise.

Conclusions

It should by now be clear to the reader that the Republican People's Army was beset by huge problems. Political divisions, issues with supply and equipment, poor organisation and a shortage of experienced officers of all ranks – all these and more were insurmountable challenges. Yet despite this, the People's Army was a huge step forward from the militias, and its creation, however troubled, ensured that the Republic would not be defeated quickly. As far as advantages go, the Republicans had a limited selection of quality hardware, especially in terms of tanks and fighter aircraft, thousands of dedicated foreign volunteers and a handful of talented commanders. By the spring of 1937, the Republican army had 360,000 men under arms, formed into the new, self-sustaining, if inflexible, mixed brigades.[65] This new army would be put to the test in three large-scale offensives that would pose Franco his greatest challenges of the war.

The People's Army has been labelled as the key instrument of Communist dominance of the Republic, and it is true that not only was the PCE instrumental in its formation but also that Communists held many of the field commands and commissar postings. However, the rank and file of the Republican army was composed of members of all parties and none, indeed for the most part conscripts. Furthermore, for professional officers and the bourgeoisie, membership of the PCE represented merely a marriage of convenience. It seems highly unlikely that they, or many in the ranks of the Republic's military, would have fought and died to ensure the creation of a Soviet satellite at some unspecified point during or after the war. Most important of all, in the last days of the war, a group of anti-communist officers and politicians were able to seize control of the Republic and oust both the PCE and their ally Prime Minister Negrín. Further, during this coup, regular officers such as Miaja, who had seemingly been in the PCE's orbit, proved more than capable of leaving it. If the Communists really had achieved total dominance over military and political affairs in Republican Spain, it seems unlikely that, even on the brink of defeat, their enemies would have been powerful enough to topple them.

The Spanish Second Republic was therefore a historically unique case. Globally, it was seen as democracy fighting against authoritarianism; however, the wartime realities were murkier. Communists were in office, in command of much of the army, but not in supreme power. Certainly, the international solidarity for the Republican cause is without parallel, with the most potent example being the thousands of foreign volunteers who made the journey to Spain. Finally, the Republicans, with the help of Soviet arms, had done their best to forge an army from disparate militias in the direst of circumstances – civil war. We shall discover how this historical anomaly performed in the merciless furnace of modern war. But first, to fully understand the Republic's army and its performance in the field, we must examine the army it was opposed by and the Spain it was fighting against, the Spain of General Franco.

Chapter 3

One Fatherland: Spain. One Leader: Franco. Nationalist Spain in 1937

Politics in the Nationalist zone

The shape of politics in Nationalist Spain was naturally very different from that of the Republic. Franco's Spain was not a democracy, and although there was a limited plurality of political factions, there was no room for the debates, controversies and internal dissent that racked the Republican zone. In this way, Rebel Spain was to a far greater extent an authoritarian regime than the nominally democratic Republic. However, Nationalist Spain was never supposed to have existed. A cabal of military plotters had hoped that their coup of July 1936 would allow them to swiftly seize political power, which they would use to restore order, crush what they perceived to be the Marxist threat to Spain and bring about some form of corporative, right-wing state, perhaps similar to the Primo regime of the 1920s. The new system would likely have been built on top of, rather than destroying, the existing Republic, although some generals certainly harboured hopes of restoring the monarchy. But as we know, the military uprising failed in half of the country and Spain was plunged into civil war.

Why had thousands of Spanish army officers rebelled against their government? The initial justifications included the murder of monarchist Calvo Sotelo and the assertion that a Communist takeover was imminent, but as we have seen, the former occurred when the plot was already in motion and the latter was a fabricated lie. The Spanish military had a long tradition of involvement in politics; in the nineteenth century, so-called *pronunciamientos* had been commonplace and just over a decade previously, in 1923, the army had seized power when they perceived politicians to have lost control of the domestic situation. The Spanish army saw its mission as not just defending the nation, but also as being the ultimate guardian of internal order and supposed 'Spanish values'. The Republic did have a serious law and order problem in the spring and summer of 1936, but the generals' coup was by no means an innocent attempt to protect the rule of law. As we have seen, the conspiracy began in the immediate aftermath of the Popular Front's victory in the elections of February 1936, proving an ideological basis for the military revolt. What was the ideology of the conspirators? Many in the Spanish Officer corps held violently nationalist, authoritarian beliefs and were opposed to the Republic's democratic, secular project, which included limiting the size and power of the army. Some coalesced in the UME (Unión Militar Española), a secret society of right-wing officers who conspired against the Republican government. The majority of their members were young, patriotic and even pro-fascist junior officers, and in early 1936 they made contact with the high-ranking Africanistas, who were to lead the coming rebellion and put themselves at the conspirators' disposal.

Africanistas, literally Africanists, was the term used to denote a sizeable minority within the Spanish army who were defined by their service in the long, bitter colonial war in Spanish Morocco from 1909–26. These men would be the key figures in Nationalist Spain and it is hard to overstate their importance in the Insurgent war effort; Africanistas were the core of the initial conspiracy, dominated the military commands during the civil war and shaped the coming regime. The Moroccan war had been a long and traumatic experience – it was an irregular conflict against a determined and cruel guerrilla enemy that had seen countless atrocities committed by both sides. This savage struggle cultivated a brutalised, proto-fascist military culture within the Army of Africa, the starkest example being the Spanish Foreign Legion. Founded in 1920 by Colonel Millán Astray and later commanded by Franco, it had been intended to replicate the more famous French unit, but was in fact composed mainly of Spaniards, men who had failed to settle in civilian life; criminals, veterans, even anarchist terrorists. Encouraged by their officers, they massacred civilians, burnt down villages, raped natives and mutilated their enemies, wearing severed noses and ears on their uniforms.[1] Furthermore, La Legión was built around a cult of death promoted by Astray; the soldiers called themselves the 'Bridegrooms of Death' and once presented volunteer nurses with a basket of roses complete with two severed heads as thanks for their services.[2] This brutal, dehumanising culture was not confined to the Foreign Legion; many of these ideas were widespread in the Army of Africa, and after the 1921 Annul disaster, use of inhumane tactics pervaded the Moroccan war. Undoubtedly the Moroccan experience deeply affected the men who would go on to lead the military rebellion of 1936. To give just one example,

General Emilio Mola was utterly brutalised in Morocco; his memoirs of the conflict are full of morbid scenes of crushed skulls and billowing intestines.[3] General Sanjurjo demonstrated how the Moroccan war had infiltrated the minds of the Africanistas in 1931; after four Civil Guards had been killed in a rural village by anarchists, he told the press: 'In a corner of the province of Badajoz, Rif tribesmen have a headquarters.'[4] This was part of a trend that saw officers increasingly looking inwards and applying the lessons of Morocco to perceived problems in Spain.

The war in Morocco had been against a religiously defined, foreign, dehumanised 'other', against whom any and all tactics, including the use of chemical weapons, were acceptable.[5] Increasingly, a hatred of an internal 'other' developed; Africanistas described workers, peasants and labourers in the same racist terms as the Moroccan natives. These views were exemplified by one of Franco's propaganda officers in the civil war, Captain Aguilerra. A landowner and retired soldier, he shot six of the peasants who worked his estate (whom he described as 'slave stock') when the war broke out, simply to discourage the others from picking the wrong side.[6] He outlined his views to foreign journalists, explaining that Spain's problems were caused by sewers; by giving the masses sanitation, uncivilised people had multiplied and become rebellious. Furthermore, the extreme views that Aguilerra expressed were said to be 'completely representative' of the mentality of Africanista officers that US journalist John Whitaker came across during the civil war.[7] Marxist and liberal ideas were perceived as being fundamentally foreign, their adherents 'Anti-Spain', a phrase that in Spanish is far more pejorative, literally denying the subject Spanish nationality. The ultra-nationalist UME and Africanista officers were infected with similar conspiracy theories as those seen across the European Right in the interwar period, as well as some peculiar to Spain. It was believed that the activities of Spanish Socialists and anarchists were part of a global Jewish-Bolshevik conspiracy aimed at nothing less than the destruction of Spain, its traditions and the Catholic way of life. Additionally, there was a long-running suspicion of Freemasonry, dating back to the nineteenth century, and it was common to assume Republicans and liberals were Freemasons and therefore part of a secret, foreign conspiracy. Often, these prejudices were combined and the Francoist press would frequently refer to mortal Jewish-Masonic threats to Spain. General Franco expressed many of these ideas in an interview with a *Daily Mail* journalist during the war's early months:

In Spain we are fighting, not a Spanish internal foe, but the Russian Communist International, which had its affiliations in every country.

We are determined to free our Spain from the deadly influences of those Marxist principles, which are not only false and anti-Christian, but are also entirely foreign to all our traditions and culture.[8]

The Africanistas passed on their culture and ideals to the next generation of officers through the General Military Academy at Saragossa, established in 1927 under Franco's directorship. The academy was dominated by Africanistas teaching the lessons of the Moroccan war rather than the First World War, and passing on the values of La Legión.[9] A remarkably high percentage of the young officers who went through Franco's academy would join him a few years later in rebelling against the Republican government. These men, and their superiors, sought to rechannel Spanish colonialism inwards, to almost colonialise their own country and rid it of internal enemies, and, as we shall see, apply the brutal methods of the Rif War in Spain. They believed their Republican adversaries were adherents to a foreign, anti-Spanish ideology, or even that they were puppets of the Soviet Union, International Freemasonry or Jewish-Bolshevism, or all three. This helps explain the motivation of the soldiers who prosecuted a war against their own government and a sizeable portion of their own countrymen.

However, Rebel Spain was composed not just of military men, but also enjoyed significant civilian support. As we have seen, the CEDA was the most powerful right-wing party in the pre-war years, but their attempts to protect conservative interests through legal means had been discredited by defeat at the ballot box. After the outbreak of war, and to some extent in the months before the military rising, CEDA members moved en masse to the most prominent civil war rightist parties: the Falange and the Carlists. The Falange was the Spanish fascist party, founded by the son of General Primo de Rivera, José Antonio, in 1933. Much like the Communists on the left, before the war the Falange (Phalanx) had been a small but militant organisation on the far right, with little parliamentary representation but boisterous paramilitaries. In a further parallel with the PCE, the ranks of the Falange had swelled considerably on the war's outbreak, with many right-wingers flocking to the party as a way of expressing support of and aiding the Nationalist uprising. Fascism, both in terms of its styles and imagery, and its ideology, were in vogue in Rebel Spain. Similar to the Communist Party in the Republican zone, membership of the Falange placed one above political suspicion, and there were accusations that leftists who found themselves in Insurgent territory flocked to the party. Undoubtedly, tens of thousands from the JAP, CEDA's youth organisation, joined the blue-shirted fascists, and *japistas* alone probably outnumbered the pre-war membership, known as the 'Old Shirts'.[10] However, unlike the Communists, the Falange was unable to use its newfound popularity for political gain. José Antonio had been arrested several months before the war's outbreak for provoking disorder, and remained in a Republican gaol until his execution in November 1936. Rumours, but crucially not confirmation, of his death reached the Nationalist zone and triggered an acrimonious power struggle within the party, leaving it rudderless for some time. Manuel Hedilla, an unsophisticated, unapologetic 'Old Shirt' thug, led the more radical reforming wing of the party and was officially elected leader. In spite of this, José Antonio's cousin, Sancho Dávila, and other so-called *legitimistas* insisted on the 'absent one' remaining as the party's head and resisted Hedilla's authority. This internal division was to prove the undoing of the party's leadership.

The Carlist movement dominated the rural northern region of Navarre but, especially after July 1936, had members and militias across Nationalist Spain. Carlism was a radically traditionalist, vehemently Catholic ideology, and in the nineteenth century Carlists had fought several wars attempting to place the conservative Infante Carlos and his descendants on the Spanish throne. Their fierce opposition to modernity, liberalism and secularism had seen them enjoy a revival during the Republican era; since 1931, the Carlist rank and file had been fed propaganda that insisted the Republic and its supporters were the embodiment of the Antichrist.[11] After the war's outbreak, the Traditionalist Communion (as the Carlist party was known) hoovered up monarchist, nationalist and lay Catholic support, and even gained traction among Basque Nationalists who did not join the Republicans. While they shared a common enemy with the military Rebels, the Carlist aim of restoring the Carlos line of the Bourbon dynasty and creating a confessional, traditionalist state was at odds with the vision of many in the Nationalist coalition. Further, clashes with Franco over the independence of their Requeté militia led to the leading figure in the movement, Manuel Fal Conde, leaving Spain for exile in Lisbon in December 1936.

Initially, the territory controlled by the Nationalist Rebels was administered in a rather haphazard manner. Officially, the central authority was a military Junta, based in the northern city of Burgos and headed by the most senior of the Insurgent generals, the 64-year-old Miguel Cabanellas.

However, General Emilio Mola effectively ran much of the Rebel-held north and General Quiepo de Llano controlled Andalusia almost as a personal fiefdom, much to the annoyance of his colleagues. Meanwhile, Francisco Franco had been labelling himself head of the rebellion almost from the outset. A short, quiet man with a piercing gaze, Franco was from a lower-middle-class naval family from provincial Galicia, in Spain's far north-west. Aged 16, having been rejected by the navy, the young Franco had enlisted at the Infantry Officers' academy at Toledo and graduated ranked 251 from a cohort of 312.[12] Diminutive, thin, and with a high, squeaky voice, Franco made up for his physical deficiencies through his bravery, cunning and cold determination. The Galician gained fame fighting in Morocco, eventually leading the notorious Foreign Legion, married well, and became Europe's youngest general aged 35. While no expert on military theory, he had long been considered the leading figure among the Spanish officer corps, politically dangerous by Republicans, and enjoyed the complete confidence of the Army of Africa. Franco had directed the brutal suppression of the 1934 Asturias rising using colonial troops and had been made chief of the general staff by the then-rightist government in 1935, before being dismissed after the Popular Front's electoral triumph. Personally, he held conservative, monarchist views, but was equally influenced by the Africanista ideas of Millán Astray and others, writing: 'My years in Africa live within me with indescribable force. … Without Africa, I can scarcely explain myself to myself, nor can I explain myself to my comrades.'[13]

Additionally, Franco had long been a believer in the vague Jewish-Bolshevik-Masonic conspiracy to destroy Spain that many of his comrades adhered to and would continue to include such fears in his public speeches into the 1970s.

As it became clear that the war would not be over in a matter of weeks, the issue of leadership became more pressing for the Rebel generals. There was no unified command and Cabanellas was not trusted, having previously held Republican sympathies. General Mola had been the self-appointed 'director' of the military coup, organising the plot from his base in Pamplona and winning the support of the Carlist movement for the rebellion. As well as being a capable military figure, it appeared that Mola aspired to a political future. The confusion had arisen when, just three days into the conflict, General José Sanjurjo, the official leader of the military rebellion, the most senior and respected of the Africanistas, died. A small biplane had been dispatched to Portugal, where Sanjurjo was in exile having led a failed coup against the Republic in 1932, to bring him to Nationalist territory. However, it crashed on take-off, having been overloaded with the general's luggage, and the 'Lion of the Rif' was killed instantly.

This left Nationalist Spain with an obvious leadership problem, one that Franco quickly sought to solve. At the outbreak of the war, even before the official military Junta, he set up a propaganda office to promote his own image (not that of the Nationalists). The press office in his headquarters under Luis Bolín got to work swiftly and soon had officers like Millán Astray extolling his virtues in the press and the wider country.[14] From his earliest contact with foreign powers, he presented himself as leader of the rebellion; on 29 July, when Franco had not yet even been appointed to the Burgos Junta, a telegram to Göring from the German Consul in Tetuán (presumably at Franco's request) informed the Reichsminister of the organisation of a military government presided over by Franco.[15] This body did not exist but clearly Franco had ambitions in that direction. Given that the press within Franco's zone were already hailing him as Caudillo (supreme leader) and 'Chief of the Movement', it is hardly surprising that a German agent in Spain reporting to his superiors on 15 August stated that 'the commander-in-chief is definitely Franco' long before he had actually been appointed.[16]

A key stepping stone in securing the supreme command was the fact that Franco was instrumental in securing Axis aid for the Nationalist cause. Approaches by the official Rebel leadership to both fascist Italy and Nazi Germany had been met with little enthusiasm in the war's first days, with German Foreign Office officials too conservative to risk embroilment in a foreign civil war, Mussolini hesitant also. Upon arriving in Spanish Morocco, as already explained, General Franco was faced with the problem of getting his elite Army of Africa across the Straits of Gibraltar. He turned to the Axis powers for help, but met with more success than his colleagues. On 21 July, Johannes Bernhardt, a German trade representative in Morocco, offered his services to Franco, and within a few days, Bernhardt, the head of the local overseas Nazi Party and a Spanish military representative were in Berlin, meeting with the Nazi Auslandsorganisation rather than the Foreign Office.[17] After a series of discussions, the party took Franco's request for aircraft to the Führer himself, who was in Bayreuth for the annual Wagner festival. On the evening of 25 July, after a short audience with Franco's emissaries, Hitler made a spontaneous, ideologically motivated decision to involve himself in Spain. The following morning, Operation Magic Fire, clearly inspired by Wagner's *The Valkyrie*, began and German transport planes were dispatched to Morocco. However, while initially enthused by ideological similarities with the Nationalist cause, by late 1936, Hitler's Spanish strategy was far more malevolent; he hoped that the civil war would last as long as possible thereby diverting the attention of Europe's major powers from his own rearmament and increasingly aggressive foreign policy.[18] Hermann Göring was tasked with overseeing Nazi involvement in Spain, using the opportunity to test his *Luftwaffe's* latest aircraft; but as head of the Four Year Plan, Göring also sought economic gain from the civil war. With German rearmament in full swing, Spain's vast reserves of pyrite, mercury, iron ore and other raw materials were coveted by the Nazis and their military support was in part paid for in kind with these natural resources. The German government gained a monopoly over all exports between the two countries and, to some irritation on the part of Franco, obliged the Nationalists to accept German economic dominance over Spain's mineral industries.[19]

At the same time as Hitler was making his fateful, spur-of-the-moment decision, Mussolini was also warming to the idea of intervention in Spain. Franco had dispatched Luis Bolín to Rome and he met Foreign Minister Ciano on 22 July, but the Italians were concerned about destabilising the international situation.[20] Mussolini waited until it was clear that London and Paris were not involving themselves in the conflict before risking intervention. By late July, the opportunity of hugely expanding their influence in the Mediterranean with little effort seemed greatly appealing to Mussolini and Ciano, and Franco's request for transports was met, albeit with one of the Savoia 81s crashing in French Morocco after running out of fuel.[21] Therefore, at least at first, the fascist regime saw the Spanish conflict in selfish, strategic terms as offering a chance to strengthen Italy's position in the Mediterranean at the expense of France and Britain by creating a potentially indebted ally. When it became clear that the war would not be over quickly, Il Duce increasingly sought to win glory for Italian arms and spread fascism, and his snowballing involvement in what was presented as an anti-communist crusade gained a more ideological flavour. Within five months, Italy had gone from sending nine bombers to transport troops to effectively being in a state of war with the Spanish Republic, sending tens of thousands of soldiers and pilots and billions of lire worth of military equipment to Spain. Italian aid was granted to Franco on extremely generous terms of credit, and all hardware sent was simply left on the war's conclusion, all of which actually served to hamper the Italian war effort in the Second World War.[22]

As well as securing the support and confidence of Germany and Italy, Franco gained great prestige from the advance of his African columns across southern Spain in August and September 1936, in sharp contrast to the stuttering progress of Mola's Army of the North. To secure the position of Generalissimo, Franco created a political campaign staff of his most senior military backers: Kindelán, Orgaz, Yagüe, Millán Astray and his brother Nicolas. None of his potential rivals had made comparable preparations. At a meeting convened by Franco on 21 September, the other leading generals reluctantly, but unanimously, appointed Franco as overall commander, thanks in part to the tireless efforts of his cheerleaders.[23] What followed was something of a fait accompli as Franco's supporters called another meeting to discuss their proposal that the office of Generalissimo carry with it the position of chief of state. In the intervening period, Franco's southern army relieved the besieged Alcázar in Toledo and the press and newsreels carried images of cheering crowds acclaiming the general as head of state.[24] Once again the Junta reluctantly accepted the proposal, with Kindelán and Yagüe working frantically behind the scenes (and threatening the insubordination of the Army of Africa if compliance was not forthcoming). As a compromise, it was agreed Franco would become chief of government of the Spanish state, but in the announcement of the decision this was changed to simply chief of state, and Franco used this term from then on, making himself formally head of state, head of government and commander-in-chief of the armed forces. Crozier hails Franco's smooth accession as the 'subtlest coup d'état of contemporary history'[25] and it certainly is remarkable how easily he was able to reach the position of Caudillo. However, his job was made easier by the lack of credible opponents. The head of the Junta, Cabanellas, who provided the only real opposition, had no reputation as a combat commander and had Republican connections. Queipo had previously betrayed King Alfonso XIII, making him unacceptable to the monarchists, and had links to a former Republican president. Mola, despite having been director of the July coup, had been somewhat outshone in the intervening months by Franco's victories in the south. Mola himself admitted as much when he explained to his adjutant why he had voted for Franco: 'He is younger than me, has higher rank, is immensely well-liked and is famous abroad.'[26] In June 1937, Mola was to die in a plane crash. The Caudillo was apparently unmoved at the news of the death of his closest military rival.

As both the military and civilian leader of the Nationalists, Franco was also keen to control the political forces within the Rebel zone. He had displayed an acute desire for unity even before becoming commander-in-chief, having told a German representative in early September that the main party of the Right, CEDA, would have to 'disappear'[27] and he made sure that their leader, Gil-Robles, was no longer welcome in Nationalist Spain. Even more ruthless was Franco's treatment of the charismatic Falange leader José Antonio Prima de Rivera. As we have already seen, José Antonio was residing in a Republican gaol in the war's early months and Falangists and German agents were keen on attempting an elaborate plan to free him.[28] However, Franco placed a number of conditions on the operation that effectively made it unworkable, and, in the unlikely event of success, he ordered that total secrecy be maintained and José Antonio only be returned with his permission. Not until two years after the Falange leader's execution did Franco publicly accept he was dead, stoking the fires of the leadership crisis that were engulfing the party. If this indeed was Franco's intention, he succeeded in his aims, as the growing conflict between Hedilla and the *legitimistas* attested to. At this juncture, Franco gained the assistance of his most important political collaborator of the early years of his regime, his brother-in-law, Ramón Serrano Suñer. Escaping a Republican prison, he arrived in the new Nationalist capital of Salamanca in February 1937. Serrano Suñer was a convinced fascist who would be the Caudillo's key backroom operator, the chief architect of Franco's new state and provide the cunning and instinctive general with political training.[29] Given the ongoing power struggle within the party, Falange leader Manuel Hedilla was more than happy to deal with Franco and his political collaborators; however, the naivety of the uneducated Hedilla allowed Serrano Suñer to manipulate him with ease. There were rumours that the Generalissimo intended to unify all political parties in the Nationalist coalition and Hedilla was persuaded into accepting the co-option of the Falange in exchange for what he thought would be his own political pre-eminence; Franco was to be the official party leader, but as his second in command, the 'Old Shirt' believed that he would be de facto political head of the Nationalist regime.[30] Serrano Suñer's task was now to manage the civil war within the fascist party so that Franco would emerge all-powerful. In April 1937, manipulated by the Caudillo's political staff, the war between Hedilla and the *legitimistas* broke out into open conflict. The *legitimistas*, with armed militia in tow, seized the Falange headquarters in Salamanca at 11.00 am on 16 April, informing Hedilla that they were taking power to prevent the sell-out of the party to Franco. Both sides then sought out the Generalissimo, professing their loyalty and begging for his backing. There were now two rival mobs of armed Falangists in the Nationalist capital, spoiling for a fight, and at 1.30 am the following night, the party headquarters was taken back by Hedilla's supporters. Several people were killed in the ensuing violence and leading Falangists were arrested for causing disorder. The Carlists had already been neutered over the winter with the departure of Fal Conde and so Franco and Serrano Suñer seized the opportunity presented to them and decreed on 19 April the unification of the Falange and Carlist movements into a single party, the FET y de las JONS (Falange Española Tradicionalista y de las Juntas de Ofensiva Nacional Sindicalista).[31] The fascist Falange had been combined with the traditionalist Carlists; the new party's uniform was the blue shirt of the Falange with the famous Carlist red beret. Although its ideology was hazy, it was made quite clear that the Movimiento Nacional, as it was often referred to, was to be under Franco's exclusive control, with the Caudillo filling its ruling political Junta with the most pliable Falangists and Carlists.

The promise of the secretary generalship that had been made to Manuel Hedilla was reneged upon, and he was publicly offered a seat on the political Junta, but only as another ordinary member. Realising too late that he had been played all along, Hedilla and the 'Old Shirts' made desperate moves to save their party from being swallowed up, first refusing Franco's offer, then informing the provincial party branches to only obey his orders. For these acts of defiance, Hedilla was arrested on 25 April and sentenced to death, although on Serrano Suñer's advice the sentence was commuted to life imprisonment.[32] Franco had now gained total control over the political factions within the Nationalist zone and created the central instrument of a one-party state that was to last for four decades.

During the civil war, the new FET had responsibility for mobilising the population as well as running Nationalist press and propaganda. The party enjoyed much success in these roles, with around one million active members by 1939, including 580,000 women engaged in various social and war work, most notably nursing.[33] Its immense propaganda machine began to manufacture the Franco myth, with the first biography of the Caudillo, in which Franco himself had considerable input, being published in 1937.[34] Already in January that year, a pamphlet was produced rewriting Franco's peripheral role in the coup of just six months previous and it was even claimed that Moscow had tried to have him killed to prevent him assuming power. Through the massive dissemination of misinformation, Franco became a crusading warrior-king, officially answerable only to 'God and history'.[35]

While the Generalissimo lacked the charisma or force of personality of other fascist dictators, his leadership cult was built on his military prowess and his pre-ordained role in saving Spain and 'Spanishness' from the Godless Marxist hordes.

The new state that Serrano Suñer constructed gave Franco total legislative power as head of both state and government, and the ability to appoint his successor; the idea that Franco's rule was a temporary wartime measure was soon dispelled. However, it was in his ability to hold together the various factions within the Nationalist zone that the Caudillo displayed his real political nous. In his first civilian cabinet (formed in January 1938), with himself as prime minister, Franco appointed three Falangists, three generals, two monarchists, two technocrats and a Carlist, cleverly balancing the different 'families' within the Nationalist coalition and pitching them against one another.[36] A German liaison officer commented that in internal politics, Franco had 'manoeuvred skilfully and had been able to hold together and balance off the divergent tendencies'.[37] Some senior Nationalist officers grated at the fact their former colleague, and in some cases equal, was now the supreme leader to whose will they had to assent. However, aside from the occasional grumbling about the conduct of the war, there was remarkably little dissent among the military. Among civilian leaders on the right, there was rather more bitterness about the hijacking of their movements by an upstart general, but those who disagreed with the Caudillo, such as CEDA Jefe Gil-Robles or the Carlist leader Fal Conde, opted for life in exile rather than meeting the same fate as Manuel Hedilla.

By the time Franco had suppressed all possible opposition from rightists in Nationalist Spain, he was already well on the way to dealing with left-wingers and Republicans in his territory. As mentioned above, the Rebel officers were quick to use tactics from colonial warfare in the civil war, particularly the policy of 'cleansing'. In the Moroccan Rif, against a guerrilla enemy, the Spanish had sought to secure their rearguard by pacifying the territory they occupied in a brutal manner. The same lessons were applied by the Africanistas to their home country. When the Army of Africa advanced across southern Spain in 1936, they left a trail of destruction in their wake. The examples of extreme brutality and cruelty are too numerous to recount. They murdered leftists, raped women, burnt villages and looted mercilessly.[38] But far from being the excesses of dehumanised soldiers, these brutal acts were sanctioned and often directed from above. Upon seizing Pamplona in the far north on 19 July 1936, General Mola called a meeting of all the provincial mayors. He told them: 'It is necessary to spread terror. We have to create the impression of mastery, eliminating without scruples or hesitation all those who do not think as we do.'[39]

It is clear that, unlike in the Republic, where for the most part the authorities tried to clamp down on violence and extrajudicial killing, in Rebel Spain, 'cleansing' was official policy. Why did the Nationalists employ such tactics? Perhaps because of their twisted attitudes towards brutality and death but also because colonial war was the only sort of war they knew. The use of terror and exemplary violence was written into Franco's orders; 'reds' were to be rounded up and disposed of in order to secure the captured ground and prevent future resistance.[40] Additionally, these tactics were useful in destroying the internal 'other' against whom the civil war was seen as being waged, fulfilling the ideological purpose of the conflict. This can be most clearly seen once the African troops had moved on. Arthur Koestler, a journalist in a Francoist prison in early 1937, described how every evening a telephone call would come through from military command with a list of those to be killed that night. He asserts that General Queipo de Llano personally chose the names.[41] In Collier's study of the Andalusian village of Los Olivos, he records the testimony of locals who said arbitrary orders from above dictated the killings. For instance, an order came through that twenty leftists must be killed; the local mayor eventually drew up a list of just seven.[42] The military carried out its own massacres and ordered local authorities to do likewise. It is therefore hardly surprising that when an Italian general in Spain telegrammed his foreign minister to complain about the Rebel conduct of the war, he accused his allies of 'behaving as if they were fighting a colonial war'.[43]

However, a brutal military culture can by no means explain all of the violence perpetrated by the Rebels. One crucial reason for this is that so many of the perpetrators were not members of the military. In fact, it was Falangists, *cedistas*, Carlists, and the Civil Guard who carried out much of the killing behind the lines.[44] Various different civilian groups were willing executioners for the military Rebels. In some cases, as shown in Ian Gibson's investigation into the killing of poet and playwright García Lorca, the perpetrators were little more than a collection of individuals who enjoyed killing.[45] These thugs, known as the 'Black Squad', came from backgrounds as diverse as former anarchist to civil servant, and worked in close collaboration with the civil governor and Falange to kill between 2,000 and 5,000 people in Granada over the course of the civil war. The account of A.R. Vilaplana, a magistrate in Burgos in 1936, further illustrates this point. The initial perpetrators of violence in the city were a right-wing militia of farm labourers organised by a local doctor who terrorised leftists in the area, killing one bricklayer for simply refusing to say *'Viva España'*.[46] In Andalusia, the civil governor set loose the various groups carrying out executions behind the lines, saying that 'victory must not stop the task of purification that the country needs'.[47] One witness described a corroborated incident in which a group of Falangists shot a heavily pregnant woman of left-wing views. Upon examining the corpse, they found that the baby had come out alive. They killed the baby with their rifle butts.[48] In Los Olivos, thirty-eight socialists (12 per cent of the village's adult males) were killed by occupying Falangists and local right-wing collaborators.[49] In the north, Carlist militia and civilians devoted themselves to the cleansing of their provinces of leftists, with perhaps more than 2,000 being murdered in Navarre, raising concern among Communion leaders as to how to stem the violence.[50] In Navarre over the course of the war, as many as one in ten people who voted for the Popular Front in February 1936 were murdered, almost exclusively by civilians and militia.[51]

A huge number of killings were therefore not carried out by brutalised soldiers but willing civilians, militiamen and police. What motivated these men to commit such terrible acts? As has already been suggested, some may simply have enjoyed killing, but this is an insufficient explanation for violence on such a scale. It is certainly true that some took the opportunity to settle old scores with neighbours or rivals while others coveted the property of those they denounced.[52] Vilaplana asserts that once the thugs realised that their violence came with no threat of reprisals, but in fact tacit approval from the authorities, they simply let themselves go and a terrible phase of bloodshed began.[53] Violent ideologies that existed within Spain before the outbreak of the war certainly played a part. CEDA's youth movement, the JAP, with 225,000 members, had long talked the 'Spain' and 'Anti-Spain' language of the Africanistas, arguing anti-Spaniards needed to be 'smashed', 'crushed' and 'annihilated'.[54] As has already been mentioned, *japistas* flooded into the ranks of the Falange militias on the war's outbreak, and so it is a fair assumption that thousands of them put their brutal ideology into practice. Elements within the Church openly advocated the extermination of 'reds', while others rationalised the struggle as a case of 'kill or be killed', particularly since stories of Republican atrocities against the clergy, real and imagined, were rife at this time.[55] Perhaps one final explanation could be that a vicious circle of violence existed. The executioners were dehumanised by their own actions and in the climate of war were even able to brag about what they had done. Whatever the root causes of the bloodshed, what is clear is that the Nationalists were able to crush internal dissent in a manner not seen in the Republic. Certainly, more than 100,000 opponents of the regime were murdered and many hundreds of thousands imprisoned in the war and its immediate aftermath. Combined with his ruthless takeover of right-wing political forces, and the outmanoeuvring of his military rivals, Franco now found himself in total control of Nationalist Spain.

The Nationalist military

Before the civil war, the Spanish army had been divided into two distinct components: the Peninsula or Metropolitan Army, based in Spain itself, and the colonial Army of Africa garrisoning Spanish Morocco. The Peninsula Army had around 8,500 officers and 112,000 enlisted men, almost all poorly trained conscripts, 40,000 of whom were on leave at the outbreak of war. Of the remainder, 4,660 officers and 19,000 of their men joined the Nationalist rising in July 1936, with 2,000 officers remaining loyal to the government, the rest disappearing, many executed and imprisoned by the Republicans.[56] The majority of the Spanish officer corps had therefore gone over to the Rebels, and, as we have seen, the Republic dismissed the conscripts who found themselves in their territory. The Insurgents managed to gain control of the majority of small arms and artillery pieces in the country during the war's early months and so mostly used the various versions of the Spanish straight-pull Mauser rifle and Spain's licensed 7mm model of the Hotchkiss machine gun in their army, in contrast to the Republic's haphazard supply situation. In Rebel Spain, the units that had successfully rebelled would form the ready-made basis for the new Nationalist army, and conscription was introduced by the Insurgents just a month into the conflict, which, according to one right-wing journalist, provided the Rebels with 200,000 recruits in the early stages of the war.[57] With incredible speed, the Nationalist army swelled from just tens of thousands at the conflict's outbreak to over a million men by 1939.

Key to the success or otherwise of the rebellion however was the Army of Africa. The colonial veterans of La Legion and the Moroccan Regulares were the only experienced, well-equipped and well-trained troops within the otherwise backwards Spanish military. Unsurprisingly, these Africanistas were unquestionably loyal to the Nationalist cause and on 19 July 1936, General Franco arrived in Spanish Morocco to assume command of the elite force. The African army consisted of 34,000 men, already more than the Rebels had in mainland Spain, and was divided between the fairly small Foreign Legion, the considerably larger body of 16,000 Moroccan mercenaries known as the Regulares and a number of conscript units on tours of duty in the Protectorate. The brutal military culture within the Spanish Foreign Legion has already been discussed at some length and shaped many of the Rebel officers, not least Francisco Franco. The Legion had often been referred to as simply the Tercio (the Regiment) as it was always a small but elite unit; however, during the civil war it was expanded rapidly to a strength of 14,000. Volunteers were attracted by the promise of 50 per cent more pay than the regular army, the sense of being part of a crack formation and the Legion's well-known ultra-nationalistic ideology. A British military observer in Spain wrote of the Legionnaires:

[They] are fit, alert and confident, conscious of being masters of their trade, certain of victory; and knowing that cheerful and gay … In battle, the Legionnaires advance in those short baffling rushes which only the finest infantry, once down, will rise to, when under fire.[58]

Peter Kemp, one of a handful of British volunteers with the Rebels, requested to be transferred from his Carlist unit to La Legion to be part of this renowned outfit. Kemp was a recent graduate from Cambridge and on the far-right of university politics who had gone to Spain more out of a sense of restless adventure and reluctance to begin his career than for any ideological commitment. He describes in his memoirs how the Legion was able to maintain their esprit de corps and elite status despite losses meaning that many of the veterans of the Rif War were replaced with swathes of new recruits. As well as retaining whipping as the punishment for cowardice or insubordination, La Legion:

impressed on the recruit that he belonged to a corps apart – the finest fighting force, he was taught to believe, in the world; it was up to him to prove himself worthy of the privilege. Battle was to be the purpose of his life; death in action his greatest honour; cowardice the ultimate disgrace. The motto of the Legion was *'viva la muerte!'* [Long live death!] It is easy for more phlegmatic nations to deride the 'cult of death'; but it produced the best soldiers of the Civil War – men virtually impervious to cold and hunger, danger and fatigue. As an Englishman I can only say that the thrill of serving with and commanding such troops was one of the greatest experiences of my life.[59]

There were only sixty-seven foreigners in the three Banderas (battalions) of La Legion at the beginning of the war, but although the Legion remained an overwhelmingly Spanish unit, many more would follow over the course of the conflict. In total, around 2,000 foreign volunteers would join either the Foreign Legion or Carlist militias, including 700 Irish, 500 Frenchmen, a number of White Russians and perhaps half a dozen Britons.[60] More significant would be the contribution of 12,000 Portuguese 'volunteers' who served in the Nationalist ranks, dispatched by the right-wing Salazar regime that feared direct involvement in the conflict. As the shock troops of Franco's army, the green tunics of the Foreign Legion were undoubtedly feared and respected, but paid a heavy price. Despite never numbering more than 15,000 at any one time, over the course of the war, La Legion lost 7,645 killed and 29,000 wounded.[61]

The Regulares had been founded in 1911 and consisted of Moroccan troops serving under Spanish officers. Franco had served as a lieutenant in this feared outfit for a number of years before joining the Foreign Legion. The Regulares were organised into Tabors (half-battalions), small but flexible tactical units that had performed well in the Rif War. They fought with great skill and courage, but their psychological impact on the battlefield was magnified by stories of atrocities committed by the 'Moorish' enemy during the Moroccan conflict. Republican troops hated and feared the Regulares more than any other Nationalist units and in the early months, militias had panicked and fled at the mere sight of their turbans or a rumour of flanking 'Moors'. However, their fearsome reputation was not without justification. The Moroccan mercenaries tended to avoid frontal attacks and split up in order to encircle their foe, confronting the enemy from several unexpected angles in order to create confusion and give the impression of overwhelming numbers.[62] The same observer who praised the combat qualities of the Foreign Legion wrote of the *Regulares*:

The Moors are solemn and patient.... They are shanky, hollow-cheeked, sinewy. They are polite. They seldom smile. They walk softly, and with the forward thrust of animals that live dangerously.... The

Moors in battle work upon their stomachs and wriggle forward at a reptilian speed.[63]

More frequently than any other troops, it was to the Moroccans that Nationalist commanders turned to lead their assaults, and understandably the Regulares had been badly worn down by the time the battles for Madrid drew to a close in the spring of 1937. Many of the veteran officers and NCOs had been lost and recruitment was stepped up in the Protectorate to an unprecedented extent. One in seven males in Spanish Morocco would either join up or be conscripted, with unscrupulous methods used to comb ever more recruits from the territory, including bribery, coercion and offers of bonuses that could transform the lives of the impoverished Moroccans.[64] However, as with La Legion, the Moroccan units were able to maintain their high fighting qualities through a variety of methods; experienced Moors were used as instructors at training camps in Spain where new recruits were familiarised with the environment, weapons and tactics of modern war. Additionally, the hardy nature and longstanding military traditions of the Moroccans stood them in good stead: 78,500 Moroccans served in the Nationalist ranks during the conflict, of whom 67,000 would become casualties, including 11,500 killed, highlighting the extent to which Rebel officers threw the Regulares into any and every danger zone.[65] Thanks to the rapid expansion of both the Foreign Legion and the Moroccan mercenary Regulares, by the end of 1937, 117 of the 640 battalions in the Nationalist army were made up of these feared colonial troops.[66]

Just as in the Republican zone, at the beginning of the civil war, the leading political parties in Nationalist Spain, the Falange and the Carlist Communion, created armed militias. As we have seen, they were often used for securing the rearguard and were responsible for many of the atrocities behind the lines, but militia units also fought at the front for Franco, with varying degrees of success. Their organisation was necessarily haphazard, with local parties recruiting Tercios or Banderas, which varied in strength from just a few hundred to several thousand. In total, around 150 Nationalist militia units were formed with up to 100,000 volunteers. However, conscription likely formed a role in building up these formations, especially after they were integrated into the Rebel military.[67] The blue–shirted Falange militia had a mixed combat record and many Falangists faced accusations of preferring to police the rear areas than fight on the battlefield. Manuel Hedilla actually used his links to the Nazi Party to request, and in fact be granted, German military instructors to create a Falange officer training school. However, these efforts were soon co-opted by the Spanish army.

By far the most formidable of the Nationalist militias were the Carlist Requetés, famous for their red berets and, in the case particularly of the Navarrese recruits, passionately devoted to their cause. Furthermore, they had received a degree of military training before the war from sympathetic army officers, most notably José Enrique Varela, who wrote a book of catechisms for the Requetés militiamen:

> *Thou of the scarlet beret wilt be: A soldier of the Faith and of the Holy*
> *   Cause of our Tradition.*
> *Thou shalt faithfully fulfil thy duties, exalt thy principles and hold thyself*
> *   in readiness for the call.*
> *Thy watchword shall ever be: 'God, Country and King.'*[68]

The Carlist red berets became known for their extreme acts of bravery, sacrifice and fanatical devotion to Catholicism, and aside from the colonial troops, were the most frequently used shock troops of the Nationalist army. They were, however, like their ideology, rather out of place in modern times; their uniform of bright red berets, shorts and white socks betrayed their naivety regarding twentieth-century warfare. English volunteer Peter Kemp eventually left the Requetés for the Foreign Legion, citing the Carlists' lack of technical training and discipline. His description of a Requeté attack early in the war is characteristic of both the superb bravery and the military limitations of the Catholic peasantry that made up the militias:

> a company in the attack was led by a captain and the chaplain, the one grasping his pistol, the other his missal; all in their scarlet berets presenting a superb target. So perished … the finest flower of Spain.[69]

In total, Carlist forces peaked at around 70,000 men before integration into the Nationalist army, 42,000 of whom would be used to form the Navarrese Corps, one of the most reliable units in Franco's army.[70] However, their repeated deployment to the toughest sectors meant that the corps had been reduced to just 23,000 by the war's end, despite constant recruitment.

After the forced unification of the Carlists and Falange in April 1937, the militias were incorporated into the Francoist army, although Carlist units in particular maintained their own identity. It was common for former militiamen to continue to wear aspects of their old uniform – a dash of blue for Falangists, red for the *Requetés*, amongst whom the famous beret remained ubiquitous, sometimes even worn under steel helmets. As already mentioned, the pick of the Carlists formed the Navarrese Corps: six brigades of red berets, which in 1938 were transformed into divisions. Throughout 1936 and into early 1937, the Nationalist army had operated with 'columns', rather loose formations to which various units were attached or detached for particular operations. This system had worked well in the irregular war in Morocco but as the civil war settled down into a more conventional conflict, the Rebel forces underwent some reorganisation. The flexibility remained and divisions were often strengthened with additional regiments or battalions if they were being used for offensives, or a Tabor of Regulares or Bandera of Legionnaires might be added to an otherwise inexperienced conscript unit to give it some backbone. Additionally, many former Army of Africa units were concentrated in certain elite divisions, such as the 13th Black Hand Division, which would be relied upon time and again to get the Nationalists out of tough spots.

The Nationalist military enjoyed a level of assistance from Europe's fascist powers that the Republic could only dream of. Italy committed itself fully to the Spanish struggle and in late 1936 established their CTV (Corpo Truppe Volontarie), made up of 50,000 ground troops at its height, 48 per cent of whom were Italian army regulars.[71] The Italian Corps was composed of the Littorio Division of the Italian Royal Army, at various times two or three divisions of fascist Blackshirt volunteers and several brigades of Italian professional officers commanding Spanish troops, which were expanded into full divisions in the latter half of the war. The CTV was a partially motorised formation, rare for the civil war, and enjoyed the support of powerful artillery units and two companies of obsolete CV 3/35 tankettes, a quite ridiculous open-topped, two-man vehicle that was no match for the Russian T-26. After being routed at Guadalajara in March 1937, the CTV's combat record did improve and it played a key role in several major Nationalist offensives. Various Italian units also served within the Nationalist ranks, for example the Moroccan Corps, created in late 1937, was granted additional firepower by an Italian artillery group. Even more integral to the Rebel war effort was Italian air support. The Aviazione Legionaria (Legionary Air Force), in which most pilots and air crews of the Italian Royal Air Force would serve at some point, provided the largest share of planes and pilots of the Nationalist air force for the duration of the conflict. The backbone of the Rebel fighter wing was the Fiat CR.32 biplane fighter, 414 of which were sent to Spain, flown initially exclusively by Italians, but as the war progressed, increasingly by Spanish pilots.[72] One Nationalist fighter pilot, the aristocrat the Duke of Lerma, received his Fiat in December 1937 and described the experience of upgrading from his old Heinkel: 'I liked the Fiat very much. It flew well – was heavier than the Heinkel 51 and needed firmer handling on takeoff and landing, but it was more solid and faster.'[73]

The CR.32 was the workhorse of the Nationalist air force; it performed well throughout the war, even though a skilfully piloted Chato was more manoeuvrable and it was clearly inferior to the I-16 Mosca. On the other hand, it was certainly superior to the Heinkel 51 fighter-bomber, which was the primary fighter of the German squadrons in 1936 and Spanish Nationalists in 1937. Two hundred and thirteen Italian bombers were also used in the civil war, including 100 of the excellent Savoia 79, almost certainly the best bomber of the conflict. As well as being resilient and carrying a large payload, it was faster than any German model, being capable of up to 267mph.[74] Overall, 5,700 air force and almost 73,000 Italian army personnel served in Spain, far and away the largest foreign contingent of the war.[75]

Italian aid alone outstripped what the Soviet Union provided the Republic. However, Franco also enjoyed the support of Nazi Germany. At the same time as Mussolini had created the CTV, Hitler merged the various German personnel in Spain into the infamous Condor Legion, without question the most technologically advanced fighting unit of the civil war. Estimates vary between 16,500 and 19,000 German military personnel serving in Spain, although the Condor Legion was never more than perhaps 6,000 strong at any one time, and the unit was undoubtedly best known for its Luftwaffe component.[76] Nazi intervention in Spain had started with the arrival of Ju 52 transport planes, which after the airlift of the Army of Africa were transferred to bombing duties. Over the course of 1937, the bomber group was re-equipped with ninety-seven brand-new Heinkel He 111s, a medium bomber that was to see extensive service in the Second World War and was superior to anything the Republic had. Additionally, a Stuka group of dive-bombers, furnished with first the Henschel Hs 123, then a small number of the famous Ju 87s, provided further bombing capability, as did the Reconnaissance squadron's thirty-two Dornier Do 17s.[77] In terms of fighters, the Condor Legion had three to four squadrons, each of twelve aircraft, which were initially equipped with the Heinkel He 51 biplane fighter-bomber. While it performed well in ground attack missions, once

Soviet I-15s and I-16s began arriving in autumn 1936, German pilots found themselves at a distinct disadvantage. From March 1937, the fighter Staffel were refitted with the state-of-the-art Messerschmitt Bf 109, one of the twentieth century's most famous aircraft and far and away the best fighter of the war.[78] Even the most advanced Russian fighters were no match for the 109's speed and firepower, giving Nationalist forces a decisive edge in the battle for air superiority. One hundred and thirty-nine Messerschmitts would operate in Spain, and as they were integrated into the Condor Legion, the older He 51s were handed over to Spanish pilots, in addition to nearly 100 Heinkels that the Francoists purchased from Germany. By mid-1937, the Condor Legion had around 100 aircraft in operation, the Aviazione Legionaria 150 and the Spanish Nationalists also around 150, highlighting the heavy reliance of Franco on foreign air power.[79] Over the course of the war, the Legion lost just 72 planes shot down while achieving at least 314 'confirmed kills', with a further 70 'probable'.[80] The Condor Legion also included substantial ground units. An anti-aircraft group was notable for the first combat usage of the notorious Flak 88, the worst nightmare of Allied tankers in the Second World War. While being a highly effective AA weapon (they brought down sixty-one Republican aircraft during the war), the '88' was found in Spain to be deadly against armour, picking off the Soviet T-26s with ease, and was also useful for destroying fortified positions.[81] With so many uses, the motorised Flak batteries were often in the vanguard of Nationalist offensives. Panzergruppe Drohne was a training unit that educated Nationalist crews in the use of the 122 lightly armed and armoured Panzer I's that were sent to Spain. These machines proved no match for the Soviet tanks supplied to the Republic; however, the unit trained 6,200 Spanish personnel and recovered and repaired scores of damaged T-26s, which were then used by Nationalist forces.[82] Given the Republic's superiority in tanks for much of the conflict, the 300 Pak 36 anti-tank guns sold to Franco and the instructors to go with them proved invaluable in breaking the back of Republican offensives. In addition, hundreds more German artillery pieces were sent to Spain and an artillery school was eventually set up. One final, oft-overlooked element of the Condor Legion was Imker-Horch, a special signals intelligence company with posts on every front that supplied information from intercepted Republican transmissions direct to Franco's headquarters. Although few in number, the Condor Legion provided the Nationalists with vital technical expertise and some of the finest military hardware used in the civil war.

As well as sending combat personnel, the Axis powers dispatched huge quantities of armaments to Spain in open defiance of the international Non-Intervention Agreement. This materiel equipped their own units in Spain and was also sold to the Nationalist forces on credit, worth a total of $1.3 billion in today's money.[83] In particular, Insurgent troops used large numbers of the reliable Gewehr 98, the rifle of the kaiser's armies in the First World War, and the MP28 and EMP sub-machine guns, updated versions of the revolutionary MP18 used by German stormtroopers in the latter stages of the same conflict. Italy sent to Spain between 689 and 759 planes, around 150 armoured vehicles, 6,751 motor vehicles, 3,227 pieces of artillery and mortars with 7.7 million shells, 3,436 machine guns, 223,784 rifles and up to 320 million cartridges of small arms ammunition. Germany shipped between 610 and 732 aircraft, 122 tanks, 838 artillery pieces with 1.1 million shells, 5,000 machine guns, 157,306 rifles and 257 million rounds of ammunition.[84] In total, Hitler and Mussolini sent up to 1,500 aircraft to support the Nationalist war effort, compared to just 623 received by the Loyalists from Russia. Although the Republicans did manage to source a small number of aircraft from other nations and also retained the majority of the decrepit pre-war Spanish air force's fleet, it is clear they were operating at both a numerical and technological disadvantage. The difference in artillery is even starker. While the Republicans received a shade under 1,000 artillery pieces of all types from the Soviets, along with 6.6 million shells, the Axis provided 4,065 with 8.8 million shells. Again, although Republican Spain received numerous cannons from other sources, their black market dealings did not come close to making good the deficit, especially as the vast majority of the shells they received from Stalin were actually for their tanks and anti-tank guns, not the howitzers or field guns. Unquestionably, the Axis sent more equipment than the Soviets, it was of a generally higher quality, in better condition, complete with spare parts and ammunition, and it was secured on credit (rather than with gold) for a lower price. This gave Franco's Rebels a decisive material advantage from the spring of 1937 onwards and was to have an immeasurable impact on the course of the war.

Given that the majority of the Spanish navy's seamen had sided with the government, the Nationalists found themselves at an initial disadvantage at sea, and indeed the Nationalist navy was to pursue a fairly conservative approach for most of the war. Once again, Axis aid proved crucial in Rebel dominance of Spanish seaways. Not only did Italian and German warships escort shipments of arms and other supplies to Nationalist ports safely, they also interdicted merchant shipping of all kinds destined for the Republic. Three German pocket battleships, six cruisers, twelve torpedo boats and fourteen U-boats served in Spanish waters, but Italian naval intervention was even greater.[85] In particular, during the summer of 1937, Italian submarines and aircraft carried out a campaign of piracy that all but closed the Mediterranean to the Soviets, severely restricting the quantities of Russian supplies that reached the Republic henceforth. At the height of the campaign, August 1937, the Italians sunk or damaged as many as fourteen merchantman and tankers that were believed to be bound for Republican Spain in just thirty days, including two Russian cargo ships.[86] With this level of support, it is hardly surprising that the Nationalists were able to dominate the sea channels around the entire Iberian Peninsula and hinder considerably the Republic's supply of arms, goods and foodstuffs.

All Nationalist forces, even the Italian and German contingents, operated under the overall command of the Generalissimo from September 1936 onwards. Franco was a cautious general, despite showing himself to be recklessly brave as a subaltern in Morocco, and was a remarkably young supreme commander, aged just 43 at the war's outbreak. His operations rarely showed verve or flair, his manoeuvres in the field were never daring, and there were no great battles of encirclement or flanks rolled up. In this way, Franco's command style was not dissimilar to the more conservative First World War commanders; his offensives relied on sheer weight of numbers and firepower to drive the enemy back, and were often both highly expensive in terms of causalities and slow in reaching their objectives. The only revealing exception was his lightning advance from Seville to Madrid in the late summer of 1936, but at that time he was facing disorganised militias with the elite Army of Africa at his disposal. It is likely he was more comfortable handling a column of tens of thousands than an army of hundreds of thousands. Indeed, writing in frustration, Italian Foreign Minister Galeazzo Ciano confided in his diary that:

> Franco lacks the synthetic view of war. He can lead the operations of a magnificent battalion commander. His objective is always land. Never the enemy. And he doesn't realise that war is won by destroying the enemy. Afterwards, territorial occupation becomes a very simple matter.[87]

This would be borne out in the battles to come, where Franco repeatedly shelved his own plans in favour of regaining lost ground, to which he seemed to attach an almost emotional importance. Clearly, he was capable of meeting the huge challenge of wielding an entire military, with all the pressures that brings, and he was not an incompetent commander as some of his biographers have implied.[88] At the same time, the comparisons to Napoleon or El Cid, the impression that the Generalissimo was some sort of military genius that hagiographers and regime propaganda propagated is evidently a gross exaggeration. A fair analysis would probably be that Franco was a mediocre general: excessively cautious yet profligate with human life, an unimaginative but certainly not incompetent commander-in-chief, perhaps the only Spanish officer ruthless enough to succeed in the role.

However, Franco also had a huge reserve of experienced and competent senior officers on which to call to command his armies, corps and divisions. While in the Republic, lowly officers such as Major Vicente Rojo found themselves catapulted into high commands by circumstance; all of the Insurgents' senior field commanders had been at least colonels before the coup. Additionally, in the People's Army, due to the fact only around 2,000 professional officers served, men from various branches, such as the artillery or engineers, might find themselves in charge of an infantry division or army corps, a role in which they had little expertise. In contrast, all formations of division or larger in the Francoist Army were headed by infantry officers who, like Franco, had trained at the Toledo Infantry Academy. There were a number of talented subordinates on whom the Caudillo could rely, the most notable of whom was General José Enrique Varela. Franco had made Varela a general during his short tenure as chief of staff before the war, for he was an Africanista par excellence. He had served for many years in Morocco, first as an enlisted man, then as an officer of the Regulares, and won Spain's highest award for bravery twice in the process. As we have seen, he was a committed Carlist and fervent Catholic, and Franco would frequently place Varela in command of his most important operations. Another rising star in the Nationalist ranks was Colonel, later General, Juan Yagüe, a brutal colonial officer responsible for many of the atrocities of the African columns in 1936. He was a fiery character, who fell out with Franco several times, most notably being dismissed after violently disagreeing with his superior's decision to divert his forces to Toledo rather than rapidly take Madrid in September 1936. Too talented to lose, Yagüe was soon restored and would eventually be entrusted with the command of the elite Moroccan Army Corps formed in late 1937, which was Franco's main assault force in many offensives. These commanders used their African experiences to great effect in the civil war, for instance employing 'active defence' tactics such as raids and ambushes, even on static fronts, to ensure that the enemy was in a constant state of insecurity.[89] While both Varela and Yagüe were of Franco's generation, General Fidel Davíla was one of the more senior of the Generalissimo's trusted officers, reaching 60 during the civil war. He took over the Northern Front after Mola's accidental death, showing more dynamism in command than his rather conservative predecessor. Juan Vigón meanwhile was to prove Franco's most able staff officer, eventually becoming chief of staff at the Caudillo's headquarters. His abilities certainly rivalled those of Vicente Rojo on the Republican side and 'Papa' Vigón was to plan many of the Nationalists' finest operations. Not only that, but he seemed to understand how to work with Franco better than most, telling a colleague in 1938:

> There are times when I think that what is about to be done should not be done and, since all you have to do with Franco is to present an objection in order for him to insist on his own way, I have decided to adopt the tactic of saying the opposite of what I think, in order for him to do what I really think.[90]

While the Republican army was desperately short of qualified officers, especially in the junior ranks, the Nationalists had at their disposal thousands of officers from both the Peninsula and African armies, many of whom had combat experience, all of whom had more training and expertise than the militia leaders who became the basis of the Republic's new officer corps. In addition to this, Franco's Axis allies were to be of great assistance in creating many tens of thousands of new junior leaders to serve the rapidly expanding Nationalist army. In March 1937, Italian officers set up a training school in Spain through which 25,000 officer cadets, artillerymen, tankers and engineers passed.[91] Even more important was the German Imker-Ausbilder. One hundred and fifty Wehrmacht instructors, assisted by retired or wounded Spanish officers, oversaw the training of 18,000 new lieutenants and 19,000 sergeants, providing the Nationalist army with the squad and platoon commanders that their Republican adversaries so evidently lacked.[92] This is a clear example of the qualitative superiority of Axis aid to Franco compared to Soviet support for the Republic; while hundreds of Soviet officers were attached to Loyalist units as advisors, there was no comparable effort to help the Republic train up its own experts.

With trained officers, many capable, even fanatical, troops, more than adequate resources and a ruthless commander-in-chief, the Nationalist military clearly enjoyed a host of advantages over its Republican counterpart. However, over the course of 1937 it would be put to the test to a greater extent than any of its generals anticipated.

Conclusions

The regime that Francisco Franco built over the first eighteen months of the civil war was to last for nearly forty years and ensure the Caudillo's supreme rule until his death in 1975. Was the Nationalist Spain of 1937 a fascist state? Certainly that is how it was perceived, not just by its enemies in the People's Army, but also broad swathes of international opinion. It is easy to see why many came to that conclusion, given the close associations Franco had with Europe's leading fascist dictators and the singularly authoritarian, anti-democratic nature of his government. Political opponents were dealt with even more mercilessly than in Mussolini's Italy and holding divergent views, even privately, was highly dangerous. The *New York Times's* Herbert Matthews, visiting Spain almost twenty years after the war had ended, wrote that 'a British Tory would be considered the most dangerous sort of radical in Franco's Spain.'[93] The Africanistas who led the military rebellion shared many characteristics with fascist movements, for example in their fetishisation of war and sacrifice, their belief that war had a positive, purifying effect on both the individual and the nation, and their certainty that brute force was a legitimate tool in the political sphere. However, not all participants in the regime were fascists, nor by any means were all of its soldiers or supporters. Fascism had played a relatively small part in Spain's political landscape before July 1936, despite the fact that several rightist parties had flirted with fascist trappings and corporative policies. It seems unlikely that millions of Spaniards were converted to such a radical set of beliefs overnight. Conservative, religious families across the country associated themselves with the Francoist cause and were the backbone of Nationalist Spain.

Therefore, it appears that the glue that held the disparate elements of the Nationalist faction together was not ideological fascism but devout, highly-political Catholicism. It was the belief that they were partaking in a religious crusade against foreign, atheistic Marxism and liberalism that bound Carlists, Falangists, Monarchists, Conservatives and the Africanistas together in a common cause. Their Catholic faith, and their abhorrence of the Republic's aggressive, nay violent secularism, was what united them and formed an integral part of Nationalist identity and propaganda. Just two months into the conflict, the Insurgents received the official backing of Spanish churchmen, with the Bishop of Salamanca declaring the rebellion a 'sacred crusade'.[94] In July 1937, this was followed up with a collective letter from the Spanish Episcopate (forty-eight of Spain's fifty bishops were signatories), which granted the Insurgents religious sanction and legitimation for their war. While the ideas and visual styles of fascism may have appealed to many within the Rebel coalition, an almost mystical, traditionalist Catholicism swept through Insurgent ranks to a far greater extent. Nationalist troops took part in huge 'field masses' before attacks, weapons of war were blessed, panzers served as mobile altars and priests charged into battle with the Requetés. The wearing of Catholic symbols or charms, especially the Sacred Heart, was ubiquitous among the soldiery. Franco would, with some success over the decades, attempt to roll back the clock and restore an idealised vision of a traditionalist, confessional Spain of years gone by. Payne argues convincingly that this resurgence of a fiercely reactionary, anti-modernity, fundamentalist Catholicism seen in Rebel-held territory during the civil war has no parallel in modern history save the wave of neo-traditionalist Islam that has swept the Middle East in recent times.[95] Like the Republic, Franco's regime was a uniquely Spanish blend of ideologies and values, fascism, Catholicism and military dictatorship, without a meaningful comparison in European history.

The Nationalist army was neither tactically nor technologically advanced – hardly surprising given it was built out of the backwards Spanish military. Cavalry remained the main weapon of exploitation; tanks were not numerous enough, nor were they used especially innovatively. Infantry still charged into combat led by caped officers and standard bearers carrying the red and gold Nationalist flag. Franco's offensives were unimaginative, and in the main plodding, attritional affairs. However, the Insurgent forces possessed several key advantages over their Republican adversaries. The Army of Africa was unquestionably the most experienced, best equipped and well-drilled military formation in pre-war Spain and was rapidly expanded, its traditions, doctrine and combat experience passed on by officers and NCOs. The Nationalists enjoyed the benefits of having a multitude of junior and senior officers, who were either veterans of Morocco or German-trained. Further, they did not face the difficulties of creating a new army from scratch; they were merely building on and recruiting into an existing one. Finally, Franco had outside support in unmatched quantity from the Italians and quality from Nazi Germany, providing him with the backbone of his air, artillery and armoured forces for the duration of the war. Thanks to Axis assistance, Nationalist forces developed effective ground-air cooperation for their offensive operations, probably the one truly modern aspect of the war. Undoubtedly, due to the advantages implicit in the last two chapters, the Spanish Nationalist army was superior to its Republican adversary, but it would be given the sternest challenge it would ever face in the second half of 1937 by an under-resourced but determined foe.

Chapter 4

The Republic's Somme: Brunete, July 1937

Background to the campaign

After the Italian rout at Guadalajara in early March 1937, it became clear to Nationalist high command that the capture of Madrid was, for the time being, an unattainable objective. The Rebels had hoped, and indeed expected, that the civil war would be short, but by the spring of 1937 this was evidently not going to be the case. Victory was no longer around the corner, as it had appeared the previous autumn. Francisco Franco therefore set his sights on an area known as the Northern zone. The Republic's Northern zone was a thin, isolated strip of territory along Spain's northern coast, cut off from the rump of Loyalist Spain and blockaded by the Nationalist navy. It was made up of the majority of the Basque Country (granted autonomy by the Republican government) and the regions of Cantabria and Asturias. Few Soviet supplies had reached the beleaguered north or international volunteers. Furthermore, this area was arguably even more politically divided than the rest of the Republic, with the conservative, Catholic Basques operating largely independently from the left-wing elements that made up the Republican Army of the North. The Northern zone was a valuable prize for Franco; not only would its destruction free up vast reserves of troops, but these largely mountainous provinces were of huge economic significance. Asturias was known for its coal and steel, while the Basque capital Bilbao was the centre of Spanish heavy industry. What little armaments production Spain had was also based here, as well as several important ports such as Santander and Gijón. By switching his focus to the north, the Generalissimo could win a quicker, easier victory than on the war's main battlefront, which wound its way down the length of Spain from the Pyrenees to the south coast, and in so doing, would strengthen his military and economic position immeasurably.

The offensive against the Basque Country began on 31 March 1937. The assault was carried out by the Carlist red beret Navarrese brigades and units of the Italian CTV, supported by the Condor Legion and Aviazione

Legionaria, against whom the Republicans could muster just a handful of mostly outdated aircraft. The operation was largely planned by Colonel Juan Vigón, one of Franco's leading staff officers and a key advocate of the northern strategy, while in command was the director of the military uprising, General Emilio Mola, who on the eve of the campaign issued a public threat to the Basques:

> If submission is not immediate, I will raise all of Vizcaya [Biscay] to the ground, beginning with the industries of war. I have the means to do so.[1]

Mola's threat was not a hollow one. The fighting was slow and bloody for much of April and May, with the Nationalists slowly pushing Basque forces back from a series of mountains on which their defence system relied. The Condor Legion proved decisive in these battles; with little opposition in the air, they bombed Loyalist positions with impunity and provided close support for the Rebel infantry. The right-wing journalist Harold Cardozo was with the Nationalists as they advanced, and describes the unmatched firepower they enjoyed:

> We went to an artillery observation post and we saw one of the greatest air and artillery bombardments that had taken place during the whole war. Scores of batteries of every calibre from field-pieces to giant 10-inch howitzers sent their thousands of shells against the rocky heights. A hundred aeroplanes came and went almost without interruption, dropping their heavy bombs.[2]

Additionally, terror raids on first Durango, and then infamously the ancient Basque capital of Guernica, shattered the defenders' morale. The firebombing of Guernica, immortalised by Picasso, was to prove one of the most controversial incidents of the whole war, and did severe damage to the Nationalists' reputation abroad. Despite this, progress remained disappointing from a Rebel perspective as the advance proceeded at a grinding crawl. Franco took a rather hands-off approach to this campaign, being largely diverted by Rebel political machinations that came to a head in April with the unification of political parties.

Driven back from the mountains, the Basques relied on the so-called 'Iron Ring', an 80km belt of fortifications constructed around Bilbao. Despite contemporary comparisons to the Maginot Line, the Ring was fatally flawed, lacking any depth and being unfinished in parts. Furthermore, it had not been sited by military experts and many of the positions were badly exposed to air and artillery bombardment, a situation exacerbated by the fact a deserter had handed the Rebels the complete plans of the defence line. On 22 May, Carlist troops reached the east side of the Iron Ring, but the assault on the defences was delayed for some time by overly cautious preparations and the death of General Mola in a plane crash on 3 June. His replacement, General Davíla, began the attack on the Iron Ring on 11 June, supported by 150 artillery pieces and three major Axis bombing raids, at 9.00 am, 12 noon and 7.00 pm, in which the entire strength of the Condor Legion was deployed.[3] German Flak 88s, without any enemy aircraft to shoot down, were employed to pick off the exposed bunkers. The following day, the defences were breached and Loyalist forces began a fighting retreat towards Bilbao. On 16 June, the Basque government fled their capital, leaving the city, and its heavy industry, intact for Franco. The Republican Army of the North retreated along the coast towards Santander, the Basque units in particular demoralised by the loss of their homeland. They had fought hard, inflicting on the Rebels 30,000 casualties, albeit at a higher cost to themselves due to superior Insurgent firepower.[4] At this point, the Rebels paused once again, allowing the Loyalist forces to escape largely intact. General Alfredo Kindelán, commander of the Insurgent air force and one of the Generalissimo's closest allies, was nevertheless critical of the campaign's conduct:

> the enemy was defeated but not pursued; the success was not exploited, the withdrawal was not turned into a disaster. This was due to the fact that while the tactical conception of the operation was masterly, as was its execution, the strategic conception on the other hand was much more modest.[5]

The Nationalist northern forces were rested, reinforced and readied for a continuation of the offensive, which was due to commence on 9 July and aimed at taking the port of Santander.

At the same time, the Republic was undergoing substantial political change. Following the 'May Days' disturbances, the aged Largo Caballero had been ousted as prime minister by a coalition of Republicans, moderate Socialists and Communists. His replacement was Juan Negrín, a social democrat of the

PSOE, who worked closely with the PCE and Soviets in an attempt to build a more efficient war effort. While accelerating the centralising militarisation project, Negrín and his new minister of defence, Indalecio Prieto, were keen to enact a more 'active' war policy. Prieto was arguably the most formidable politician on the Republican side, an industrious man who preferred to work in the shadows and therefore shunned the limelight of the premiership, allowing his protégé Negrín to take a job he had long been touted for. Bilbao fell just two weeks into Prieto's tenure in the Defence Ministry, and, as a native of the city, he was devastated at its loss, telling a Socialist colleague:

> I have been so embittered and I have judged myself so severely for my own responsibility that, not only did I send the prime minister a letter of resignation, but I also contemplated suicide. I became obsessed with the idea and I had my pistol at the ready.[6]

Republican Prime Minister Juan Negrín rejected Prieto's letter but it was clear to the government in Valencia that something had to be done to aid the north; the Northern zone could not be abandoned to its fate, and the initiative on the main battlefront had to be seized while Franco was distracted. Reinforcing the north proved virtually impossible, with only a handful of aircraft able to run the dangerous gauntlet of crossing Nationalist territory. The only way the Republic could help its northern outpost was by launching an attack in order to draw the Rebels away and buy time for the north to reorganise and refortify. Further, the new People's Army had to go on the offensive; thus far, it had only conducted defences or counter-attacks, never an independent operation of its own. The Republic, which had been expected to collapse months before, sought to prove it had a fighting chance of winning the war, and that it had an army capable of gaining ground, not just defending it. Limited 'pinprick' attacks were launched in Segovia on 31 May, and then at Huesca in Aragon on 12 June, both costing several thousand casualties for very modest gains. These operations highlighted poor communication and coordination in the new army, were launched with too few troops to achieve a meaningful breakthrough, and crucially failed to halt the Nationalist advance on Bilbao. Following these failures, the loss of the Basque Country and the acrimony surrounding the May Days violence, Republican morale was at a low ebb by the early summer. Some sort of success was desperately needed to rouse spirits and prove to Loyalist supporters at home and abroad that ultimate victory in the civil war was possible.

Plans for a major People's Army offensive had been in the works for some time, with Largo Caballero having favoured an attack in Extremadura. This southern agricultural region was weakly held and known to contain many underground Republicans. Further, it would have been difficult for Franco to transfer his forces there from the far north. Rather ambitiously, some also talked of the possibility of splitting the entire Nationalist zone in two, but this would have required a rather unlikely breakthrough of several hundred kilometres. In any case, Rebel communication and supply lines may well have been routed through friendly Portugal had such a feat ever come to pass. However, the Spanish Communist Party and the Russian military advisors preferred an attack in the Madrid sector that would relieve the siege of the capital. The defence of Madrid had been a huge propaganda symbol for the Republic, and around the world the city had been heralded as the 'tomb of fascism'. Its position remained precarious, with Rebel troops still dug in on the outskirts of the capital, at University City and the suburbs of Carabanchel. Nationalist artillery still bombarded the city centre intermittently. Effectively, the former Spanish capital was in a state of siege and there were hopes that an offensive in the vicinity could relieve it. It would also be considerably easier to concentrate the People's Army's best troops and equipment in this battle-scarred sector without arousing too much suspicion, while a significant transfer of forces to the quiet Extremadura front would have been hard to disguise. Rojo defends the choice of an offensive in the vicinity of what he calls 'the heart and brain of Spain' by arguing that only in Madrid could you launch an offensive without weakening the defences of the capital by removing manpower.[7]

The Extremadura plan was shelved for the time being; it had been championed by the now-ousted Prime Minister Largo Caballero, whose military prowess was not held in high regard. Furthermore, the new government of Negrín was keen to distance itself from its lacklustre predecessor and adopting Largo's initiative was not going to help achieve this. On the other hand, the Madrid operation had the support of the PCE, Communist commanders, Soviet advisors and, crucially, Madrid's 'saviour', General José Miaja. Miaja, whose reputation and prestige among the Loyalists made him a formidable figure, flatly refused to surrender troops for the Extremadura operation, although he may well have been motivated more by a desire to retain the best Republican units under his command in the Army of the Centre than any strategic considerations. Colonel Casado in particular is scathing in his memoirs about Miaja's obstinance and Communist interference, for he believed the Madrid operation could not succeed and would result in heavy losses.[8] The battle plan was largely drawn up by Prieto's new chief of the general staff, Colonel Vicente Rojo, the Republic's most able strategist. Brunete, as the battle would come to be known, would be the People's Army's first major offensive of the war, and it was to be the Republic's Somme. In the July of both 1916 and 1937, a new, inexperienced army of citizen soldiers was to launch its first offensive, where its shortcomings were to be exposed.

The offensive was to be carried out by three corps from Miaja's army, in which many of the Republic's most experienced and disciplined formations were concentrated. V Corps was the central element of Rojo's so-called Army of Manoeuvre, a transient body with no single commander, which effectively denoted the units engaged in major offensive operations planned by the general staff. The former militiaman Lieutenant Colonel Juan Modesto commanded V Corps, composed of the 11th, 35th and 46th divisions. The 11th Division, the Listers, contained numerous veterans of the Fifth Regiment, while the 35th Division included the 11th International Brigade. The 46th Division meanwhile had been designated a 'shock division', was commanded by the fearless Valentín González (El Campesino), and had one of the oldest mixed brigades, the 10th. Another divisional commander, Manuel Tagüeña, wrote of his amazement and jealousy at the quality of the equipment dished out to the 46th when compared to the paltry supplies others received.[9]

To their left was XVIII Corps, commanded by Colonel Enrique Jurado, a Loyalist regular officer from the artillery. He had the 10th, 15th and 34th divisions, assembled from west to east. The 10th and 34th were commanded by Enciso and Galán respectively, both junior officers at the war's outbreak, now wielding huge formations. The 15th was an International Division under General 'Gal' (the Hungarian Red Army officer János Gálicz), made up of the 13th International Brigade of Poles and Frenchmen, and the 15th Brigade with one British, two American, as well as Franco-Belge, Balkan and Spanish battalions. The Republican reserve consisted of the 47th Division and the 45th, a new formation under General Kléber (Manfred Stern, commander of the first International units) composed of the 12th Garibaldi International Brigade as well as the newly formed 150th International Brigade of central Europeans.

These two corps, positioned roughly 24 kilometres north-west of Madrid, were tasked with smashing through Nationalist lines and taking a series of

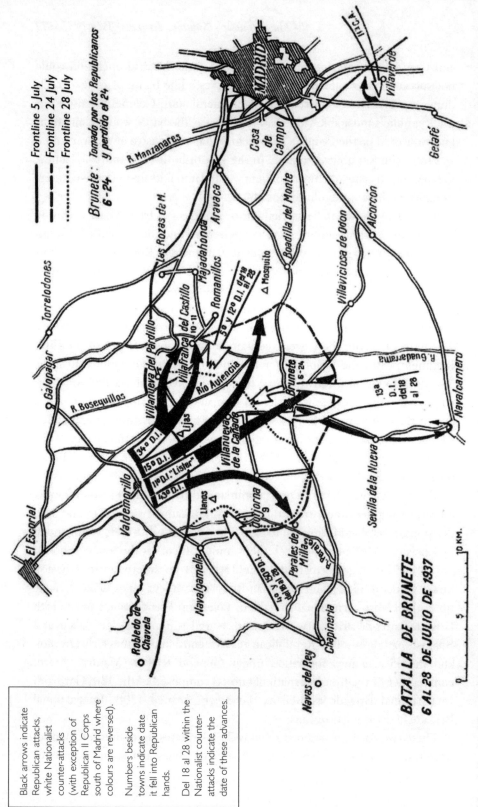

Map 4: Battle of Brunete, showing the advances of Republican divisions (D.I.) and the Nationalist counter-attacks. Note 43 Division on the Republican right is in fact 46th Division.

small towns and villages (one of which was Brunete) on their way to seizing two vital tactical objectives: the Romanillos Heights and the town of Navalcarnero. Navalcarnero was the centre of Rebel logistics on the Madrid front, while the hills west of Romanillos overlooked the roads that supplied Franco's forces besieging the capital. If these objectives could be seized, the position of the Insurgent forces on the outskirts of Madrid would become untenable and they would surely be compelled to withdraw. An additional, supporting attack was to be launched out of the suburb of Carabanchel to the south-east, carried out by II Corps with two divisions, all under professional officers. The aim was to take Villaverde and push on to Alcorcón, a distance of over 12km, before linking up with the main Republican push and therefore completely encircling the Francoists before Madrid. However, the strategic goals of the offensive were wider than simply relieving the capital. It was hoped that Franco would be forced to call a halt to his planned offensive in the north and instead divert forces to deal with this breakthrough. If this could be achieved, then perhaps the battered Northern zone could be bought some breathing space, enough to prepare adequately for the coming Rebel attack on Santander. A significant flaw with the plan was that the only major route with which the offensive was to be supplied and reinforced, and along which the advance was to be centred, was a section of the El Escorial to Madrid road, running Valdemorillo–Villanueva de la Cañada–Brunete. This road was in XVIII Corps' sector, leaving Modesto's V Corps without their own line of communication and reliant on Jurado to clear a path for their own advance to succeed.[10]

The assault force, the largest the Republic had ever concentrated, was crammed into just 10km of frontage, between the villages of Navalagamella in the west and Villanueva del Pardillo in the east. Its exact size is not clear; of an army of roughly 600,000 at this point, estimates range from 50,000 to 85,000 being deployed for the Brunete operation.[11] Given that People's Army divisions rarely, if ever, numbered over 10,000, and the fact that a number of them had two rather than three mixed brigades (and so could have had no more than roughly 6,000 men), a figure towards the lower end of these estimates seems more likely. Additionally, the Republic committed 140 aircraft, although reportedly many of these were not serviceable, having been used constantly for many months without sufficient spare parts.[12] Brunete also marked the apogee of Republican armoured strength; two armoured battalions, one for each corps, would support the main assault, totalling 70 T-26 tanks and 20 armoured cars. Meanwhile, a third battalion with 30 tanks and 10 armoured cars was earmarked for II Corps' enveloping attack south-east of Madrid. A final armoured unit of similar strength was held back in reserve, making a total of 132 tanks available.[13] The picture was less rosy in terms of artillery, with just 130 artillery guns, and not sufficient ammunition for a major offensive.[14] In 1916, the German army had at least 850 pieces of artillery and huge stockpiles of millions of shells, to assist three corps at Verdun, including many heavy howitzers and siege cannons that the Republic simply lacked. The three People's Army corps about to go on to the offensive would be deprived of this vital support.

Despite the fact that an early form of the Brunete plan had been leaked to the Nationalists, Franco's forces were unprepared for an offensive on the central front. Just one rather unremarkable Nationalist division, the 71st, was holding the line where the main attack was to fall, composed of a few Tabors of Regulares (amounting to about 1,000 men) but mostly Falangist troops. However, in the wider Madrid region there was also the newly created 150th Division of recently raised Foreign Legion and Moroccan troops, as well as the 12th Division, a grouping of various units in the sector commanded by Colonel Carlos Asensio, an officer who had distinguished himself in the Army of Africa advances of 1936. The Rebel Army of the Centre was under the command of the aged but experienced General Saliquet, but within a few hours of the offensive starting, Franco had swept him aside and placed the talented Varela in charge of field operations in the sector. This highlights the flexibility of the Nationalist military, for although the dependable Saliquet retained his post, and indeed held it for the war's duration, the Caudillo was free to appoint more dynamic generals to direct his battles on the ground. As has already been described, the bulk of Franco's air power, including most of the Axis squadrons, were based in the north, with only seventeen serviceable Fiat CR.32s operating around Madrid.[15] The one advantage in the Insurgents' favour was that, this being the war's most active theatre thus far, they had a large concentration of artillery, including many of the fine German Pak 36 anti-tank gun. A Soviet report calculated that the Nationalists had 26.6 artillery pieces (of all types) per kilometre of the line, roughly double what the Republicans could muster.[16] The Nationalist lines were thinly held, without adequate manpower or resources for continuous defences or trenches. Instead, the defence of the sector relied on a series of fortified towns, villages and hills, which Republican forces would soon find themselves attempting to storm. Modesto described later how these strongpoints were defended: 'All were organised for circular defence, with trenches and barbed wire, machine-gun nests and positions for anti-tank pieces, defended by forces of one or two battalions, as the case may be.'[17]

The terrain over which the battle was to take place was for the most part wide, arid plains, devoid of cover save a few olive groves. To the east were the commanding Romanillos Heights, the peak of which was a point that became known as Mosquito Ridge. There are several small rivers that criss-cross the area, most notably the Guadarrama and the Aulencia, although the former was to dry up during the battle due to the extreme heat.

Forty-eight hours before the attack was due to begin, Modesto claims he proposed a radical change to the plan at a conference of senior Republican officers. The fiery young V Corps commander suggested that the lead units of both his and Jurado's XVIII Corps should sneak through the gaps in the Rebel lines and position themselves before the main centres of resistance, such as the villages of Quijorna and Villanueva de la Cañada, in order to seize them quickly at dawn. This would clear the way for the bulk of the People's Army's strength to then push on to the more distant objectives. Modesto reports in his memoirs that Jurado rejected this idea, wishing to conduct the offensive in the 'classic manner'.[18] General Miaja vacillated and chose the worst of both worlds: he permitted Modesto to conduct his night advance on V Corps' front, while Jurado was free to opt out. Miaja also dictated that one division from each of the corps was to remain in reserve until he released them, General Walter's 35th and the 10th, representing a third of the total assault force. Even before the troops had gone into action, the plan had begun to come apart.

The battle

On 5 July 1937, Modesto met with his divisional commanders, Líster, Walter and El Campesino, to explain the coming attack. As per Miaja's instructions, V Corps was free to infiltrate the Nationalist lines during the night and this is what the daring Modesto chose to do. By 5.00 am on the 6th, units of the 11th and 46th divisions had sunk between gaps in the Rebel positions and were in place before Brunete and Quijorna respectively. Joaquín Masjuán was a young NCO with the Listers who later wrote the story of his war during the final years of Franco's dictatorship under the pen name Jack Max. He described the initial night advance:

It was ten o'clock on the night of July 5th. We slipped out of [the] thick forest, and crossed the road with weapons at-the-ready, ready for the fight.

Antonio was by my side, with the bulk of the column, which looked like a giant wavy serpent, advancing in absolute silence.

We jumped over a trench, previously occupied by the enemy, whose defenders had been eliminated by an earlier raid, made in silence with bayonets, to clear the way for the bulk of our unit.

The dead were lying on one side of the fortifications, piled up as if they were sacrificed cattle, and I was distressed to see that sorry scene, so frequent in all wars.[19]

The troops of the 11th were able to infiltrate Rebel territory with relative ease, advancing deep behind enemy lines unopposed, as Masjuán found:

Soon we heard the loud roar of the battle that was unfolding in the villages that we had flanked and left behind. We could see in the distance the flames of the explosions of our artillery, and we heard the rattle of machine guns, tanks firing, the crackle of rifles and the sharp bang of hand grenades.

We, on the other hand, advanced with total tranquillity, without tanks, without artillery preparation and without aviation.

We found no resistance anywhere, nor did we detect the enemy. … More than being at war, it seemed that we were taking a collective excursion to a castle where a great feast was waiting for us.[20]

What Masjuán and his comrades could hear was Jurado's 'classic' attack, which began with a half-hour air and artillery bombardment at 5.30 am. Walter Gregory, a British volunteer from Nottingham, who had fought fascist Blackshirts in the streets of his home town, describes the conditions as the Republicans of XVIII Corps marched forward that morning:

The mid-summer heat was almost unbearable and the dust which our boots threw into the air with every stride caught at our throats and produced a raging thirst. Flies swarmed around us in clouds, adding to our misery. … To overcome the problems of thirst we were told to find a small, smooth pebble and suck it. After trying this remedy I quickly abandoned it as it did nothing to quench my desire to drink a bucketful of water, and I seemed to be in constant danger of swallowing the blessed thing.[21]

With clear local superiority in numbers and firepower, and in spite of the overwhelming heat, it was hardly surprising that Galán's 34th Division achieved initial success, breaking through the Rebel lines with ease and streaming into open country. Soon, however, they came up against Villaneuva de la Cañada, a small fortified village defended by a Falangist battalion of the 71st Division with machine guns, two 105mm field guns and two Pak 36 AT guns, one mounted in the church steeple.[22] The T-26 tanks of the armoured battalion assigned to XVIII Corps advanced across the open fields before the village, infantry of the 34th close behind, but they were halted 500m from Villanueva de la Cañada by withering fire. Five attacks were made, all failed, with the German gun in the church tower being credited with twelve tanks destroyed.[23] Gal's 15th Division had been tasked with moving past the village and quickly taking the heights to the south-east, over the river Guadarrama, but were diverted to take Villanueva de la Cañada, with the 15th International Brigade in the vanguard. British Battalion commander Fred Copeman wrote that the fateful order to divert to this strongpoint came from General Miaja himself.[24] The battalions of the 15th Brigade surrounded the village and the British positioned themselves on the road south of Villanueva to prevent any reinforcement or escape. Try as they might, all attempts to advance into 'Canada', as the troops called it, were halted by devastating fire and casualties quickly mounted. The Internationals found themselves with no option but to lie low in the scorching sun and wait for nightfall. Walter Gregory had taken a bullet above the elbow approaching the village and describes the hellish day the Republican forces endured:

> Having fixed the dressing to my arm I crawled forward to rejoin the Battalion which was spread out along a ditch within rifle range of the village. It was the very devil fighting in that heat with no protection from the sun's searing rays. Accurate shooting was impossible because everything was shimmering. The Fascist machine-gunners had no such problem, as all they had to do was to spray bullets around with gay abandon; but rifle-men were shooting at targets which never held still for a second. All day we stayed in that ditch, ducking down low whenever a machine gun swung in our direction and sprayed us with bullets, popping up as soon as it had traversed away and firing back with every weapon at our disposal. It was an awfully long day and as it wore on I found it progressively more difficult to steady my rifle as my arm became increasingly inflexible.[25]

The night drew in without any appreciable progress being made. As darkness fell, a tragic incident occurred on the southbound road, where the British were holding the line:

> It was dusk of the first day when our Battalion had advanced to within about three hundred metres of Villanueva de la Cañada. … Suddenly someone shouted: 'Don't fire; there are children coming from the village.' We looked down the road and saw about twenty-five people, men, women and children. In front was a little girl of about ten years of age. Behind her came an elderly woman, a boy of fourteen or so, a few old men. The remainder were young men. …
>
> Believing them to be refugees, we answered them and called them forward. Some of us were now standing, some walking to meet and welcome them.
>
> Pat Murphy, of Cardiff, was the nearest to them. He approached them, telling them to lay down their arms if they had any. For answer, a revolver blazed. Then the Fascists, who had been driving this group of old men, women and children as cover for them, started throwing hand-grenades in our midst. For a few minutes pandemonium reigned.[26]

A cowardly escape attempt by a group of Nationalists ended in not only their deaths but also a number of civilians whom they had compelled to cover them. Shortly afterwards, the British, Dimitrov, George Washington and Abraham Lincoln battalions of the 15th Brigade moved to storm the doomed village under the cover of darkness. In intense fighting, in which bayonets and hand grenades were the most useful weapons, Villanueva de la Cañada was finally taken, although resistance was not entirely cleared until 7.00 am the following day. Several hundred prisoners were taken as well as a number of heavy weapons. The Republicans had paid a high price for the little village, losing many tanks and international volunteers, not least the popular commander of No. 2 Company, British Battalion, Bill Meredith, as his superior, Fred Copeman, remembered:

> A runner from No. 2 Company reported that Bill Meredith had been killed. I couldn't believe it. I had only spoken to him a moment before. Bill was very sentimental but had a heart of gold. He was a member of the Labour Party, very conscientious, anxious to become a good officer, and even more anxious to make a contribution to the Republic. He had

gone to help a wounded man lying in the road. Bending over in the semi-darkness, he received a bullet in the heart. The lad who reported it was sobbing like a kid. I didn't feel at all nice myself.[27]

Copeman writes that a few minutes later he executed a Nationalist officer brought to him as a prisoner. The first twenty-four hours had not been an overwhelming success for XVIII Corps.

Further west, Modesto's V Corps had achieved mixed results. The biggest coup had been the rapid capture of Brunete, a penetration of some 12km. The crucial town had been taken by Enrique Líster's 100th Brigade, the only unit of his 11th Division not composed of Fifth Regiment veterans. Seizing Brunete by noon on the 6th was a fine achievement for these Andalusian conscripts in their baptism of fire, especially as they had been so far forward, they lacked armour, artillery or air support.[28] Antonio Candela, the illiterate peasant who had joined the Fifth Regiment the previous autumn, described the entry into a war-torn Brunete sometime later:

I saw that one of our tanks had received a direct hit. Apparently it had burst into flames, killing the occupants. It was a horrible sight. The tank was typical of the devastation. Most of the houses nearby had lost their doors and windows and, in some cases, their roofs. There was not even a cat or dog to be seen.

The 11th Division also destroyed a Rebel battalion that was on its way to support Villaneuva de la Cañada. At this point, Líster paused, advancing tentatively 3km south of Brunete but no further. He stretched out his forces, six battalions edging towards Villaviciosa de Odón, where Republican forces advancing from Carabanchel were supposed to meet him, others moving towards Sevilla de la Nueva, on the road to the ultimate objective of Navalcarnero some 14km distant. The conservatism of the supposedly aggressive and fearless Líster has been criticised; the road to Sevilla de la Nueva lay open, save for a few scattered Rebel units. This window of opportunity to redeem the whole offensive was very soon to close. However, the famous major of the militias was reluctant to push on past a series of heights he seized in the aftermath of the capture of Brunete. The reasons for his decision were militarily sound; on his left, the XVIII Corps was yet to appear, still held up at Villanueva de la Cañada, while on the right flank, El Campesino's 46th Division had also not arrived on time. The only road providing communication and supply for the Listers passed through

Villanueva de la Cañada, which remained in enemy hands almost twenty-four hours into the operation. Líster simply did not dare push so far forward alone.[29] To advance without protection on either flank could well have ended in disaster, perhaps the destruction of the 11th, especially given the speed with which Insurgent reinforcements were arriving. Modesto petitioned General Miaja to release his 35th Division and use it to exploit the breakthrough and push on to Villaviciosa de Odón, or even Navalcarnero, which one of Líster's battalions was reportedly in sight of, but the Army of the Centre commander refused, fearing a counter-attack on the western flank.[30] Instead of pushing on, therefore, Joaquín Masjuán and the other troops of the Listers dug in to hold their advanced positions, within sight of the church tower of Sevilla de la Nueva: 'While our other forces were fighting against the enemy in the towns we had left behind and which were surrounded, we frantically built solid fortifications to defend, in case the enemy made a counterattack.'[31]

Why had Líster been left so isolated? Valentín González, the least talented of the famous Communist militia commanders (El Campesino, 'the peasant'), had failed to capture his objective: the village of Quijorna. Like many villages in the sector, Quijorna was well defended with barbed wire and entrenched gun positions, and its defences had been augmented by the arrival the day before of a Tabor of Moroccan troops to bolster the Falange Bandera and regular infantry battalion assigned to defend it. González's men had not reached the village before daybreak, as for instance the Listers had done at Brunete, and therefore the garrison of Quijorna were in their trenches and ready from the early hours of the morning of 6 July as shots began to ring out across the countryside. Instead, as one of the Falangists defending the town, Carmelos Revilla, recounts, from their vantage point in the village's hilltop cemetery, the Rebels could observe practically the entire Republican advance, as if watching a parade.[32] Alert, and able to see the attackers coming, Revilla and his comrades easily repulsed the first attacks on Quijorna, which were not supported with air or artillery preparation: 'Their first attack on the olive grove failed completely; as soon as they came within striking distance, they retreated before the defenders' fire and took advantage of the terrain to conceal themselves.'

The Republican troops sheltered in an anti-tank ditch, which had ironically been dug by the Nationalists in order to protect the village, before coming forward again, using the terrain to get within 300 metres of the Rebel trenches:

Then appeared isolated men, trying to get closer – they were officers and commissars who encouraged their troops to join the assault – but they could not advance far. We were waiting for them, and when they exposed themselves, we fired carefully aimed shots … naturally, they retreated, although not all of them, there were brave men who, standing up to cheer their men on, paid for their courage with their lives.[33]

Further, El Campesino had detached a battalion from his 10th Brigade (that was tasked with capturing the village) in order to take the height of Los Llanos.[34] At 743 metres high and with all-around fortifications, this imposing position some kilometres to the north of Quijorna was garrisoned by the Falangist 5th Centuria of Avila, reinforced by a company of Moorish sharpshooters and an anti-tank gun.[35] The Loyalist attack on the hill began with waves of infantry, according to one Falangist Corporal, there were so many,

> that sometimes the defenders did not know which to aim at. … At midday, the attack was supported by a section of tanks. The anti-tank gun went into action, leaving two of them immobilised while the others retreated in the face of such effective fire, but not before they had directed their fire towards the gun and brought down part of the stone parapet protecting the gun on the head of the gunner.[36]

Both objectives remained in Nationalist hands at the end of the day. The scattered 46th Division was unable to penetrate the Rebel defences, either there or at Quijorna, leaving the attack stalled on its far western flank.

Although the skies were, for the time being, controlled by the Republican air force, a dramatic dogfight developed above Brunete when a small group of Italian Fiat CR.32s engaged Loyalist fighters on bomber escort duty. Captain Degli Incerti scored a kill that day:

> Each one of us chose his quarry and the mêlée began. Our guns splendidly spat out a barrage, and our adversaries replied in kind. It was a matter of life or death. I pounced on a Rata [Rebel nickname for I-16, literally 'rat'] and shot at it. It appeared that I had scored a direct hit. I kept following him until I thought that he was clearly falling away. However, as I broke off my chase he zigzagged, dropped a little further and then climbed. He attempted to turn onto my tail, so I quickly hit him again. He pulled up abruptly after diving down a few hundred feet, so I fired at him once more. It looked to me as if the bullets had found

their mark – the tracers clearly indicated that I was aiming correctly – but the Rata pilot continued to defend himself.

I persevered with my foe, despite now feeling that I was possibly coming under attack. I looked over my shoulder and spotted three enemy aeroplanes, still at a distance, heading in my direction with their guns blazing. Moments later my prey finally fell headlong into a thickly wooded area. Staying with him had made me lose precious height, and as I looked up I could see that the fighting was still continuing above me.

I climbed back up into the battle at full throttle, and saw a 'Red' aeroplane chasing a Fiat. Turning tightly, I managed to get in behind the pursuing fighter. He then tried to disengage, but I made the most of my superior position and fired several long bursts at him. I succeeded in forcing him to take flight. Other enemy survivors duly abandoned the fight, and we reformed on our leader after he waggled his wings. We all landed with visible scars of battle on our aircraft.[37]

In contrast to the weakly held lines around Brunete, the defences in Carabanchel, where the ambitious enveloping hook of the offensive had been launched, were quite formidable. There had been heavy fighting here since the previous autumn and the Nationalists were dug in; their defences consisted of several lines of trenches, two belts of barbed wire, as well as concrete machine-gun nests and artillery observation posts. Four Republican mixed brigades of II Corps, supported by twenty-seven artillery pieces and forty armoured vehicles, were unable to make an impression on these defences, nor hold their first objective of Villaverde. The troops in the vanguard had occupied the trenches in the sector for months and felt exposed advancing in the open. Although they managed to advance to the Toledo road, at dusk the leading units panicked and fled back to their starting positions.[38] Another attempt was launched the next day, but the Rebels were prepared, the element of surprise had been lost and without sufficient artillery support, nothing was achieved.[39] The operation in the south-east was called off after twenty-four hours, meaning there was no hope of linking up with Líster at Villaviciosa de Odón and encircling the Rebel forces in Madrid, and also no diversionary attack to distract Francoist reinforcements.[40]

General Franco had been taken by surprise by the Republican offensive, being given the news as he was getting into his car to be taken to the north.

'They've smashed down the Madrid Front!' he exclaimed; the usually cool, unflappable Generalissimo was, according to one colleague, more upset than at any other moment during the war.[41] Almost immediately, the Brunete offensive achieved its strategic objective, namely drawing the Nationalists away from the Northern zone. Franco ordered two Navarrese brigades as well as the Nazi Condor Legion and Italian Aviazione Legionaria to be transferred immediately from Cantabria to the central front; the Santander operation, which had been scheduled to start in just three days' time, was cancelled. Additionally, the 13th Black Hand Division under General Barrón, in which was concentrated many veteran Army of Africa battalions, was dispatched from south of Navalcarnero. Local reserves, including the largely Moroccan 150th Division, Asensio's 12th, plus the 11th and 108th divisions, were sent to plug the breach in the line. Several of these formations, in particular the 12th, 13th and 150th divisions, were reinforced with extra units on a temporary basis in order to halt the Loyalist advance, for example by mid-July, Colonel Asensio's 12th Division consisted of nineteen battalions, making it roughly equal in strength to the entire Republican XVIII Corps.[42] As has already been mentioned, Franco appointed General Varela as commander of the sector, under the guise of VII Corps, and also set up a temporary HQ for himself at Villa del Prado, from where the Caudillo visited his subordinate every day, keeping a close eye on the battle and infecting his fellow officers with his own supreme confidence and optimism in a final victory.

At 7.00 am on 7 July, the fighter squadrons of the German Condor Legion took off from their bases around Burgos for Ávila and a series of other airfields just a short distance from Brunete. As soon as they landed, their new Messerschmidt Bf 109s were refuelled and took off again to escort bombers headed for the battle zone.[43] The same day, fourteen Italian fighters descended on a group of Republican R-Z light biplane bombers with a fighter escort, downing ten of them.[44] Axis airpower had arrived on the Madrid front. Brunete was to see some of the most epic aerial battles of the entire war, as, for the first time, fast monoplane fighters – namely the German 109 and Russian I-16 – engaged in dogfights. This marked a change in aviation history; dogfights between biplanes took place over relatively small distances, often resembling swarms of insects. The clashes between these new fighters, flying at several hundred kilometres per hour, spread over hundreds of square kilometres of airspace.[45] German pilot Günther Lützow recalled of these trailblazing battles:

It was real war, which we had looked forward to for a long time. We had on average, except for Alarmstarts [scrambles], sortied three times a day. Each sortie lasted about 90 minutes and always went up to an altitude of 6,000–7,000 metres. At that time we flew without oxygen, which after a short while we soon bitterly regretted, as flying high altitude without oxygen makes one extremely tired. We had become somewhat unnerved, for in addition to the purely physical strain of several sorties and Alarmstarts, there was the anxiety about the rare opportunities of being able to achieve confirmed kills.

We constantly had to fight against three- or four-fold enemy superiority. This meant, that one never had the time to 'hang on' to an opponent in the air for a long period of time. One had to see to it that, during the time that our own bombers or reconnaissance aircraft were operating, one kept the enemy at bay and at a distance.[46]

Republican control of the skies had been short-lived, as many of their unfortunate troops were about to find out.

Gal's 15th Division, going practically without sleep after the Villanueva de la Cañada battle, was ordered to march on their original objective, the series of heights several kilometres to the east, dominating the Guadarrama River on one side and the villages of Romanillos and Boadilla on the other. The key objective was the so-called 'Mosquito Ridge', the peak of the heights at 702 metres altitude. These hills would allow the Republicans to observe, and lay artillery fire upon, the Nationalist supply routes into Madrid. Leading the advance was the American George Washington Battalion, for whom the Brunete battle was their first action. Fred Copeman's British Battalion was some way behind them.

I watched them going up the steady slope in front of us. It was easy to pick out their perfect formation. Almost immediately four heavy Caproni bombers [Italian, more likely Savoias] came over, very low down. Our own lads dispersed, and soon seemed a part of the ground itself. There were no faces showing and everyone was as near as possible to the wheat stooks. I looked across at the Washington Battalion, and thought, 'God help them!' The tiny neat arrows almost shouted at us. The earth was shuddering with the vibrations from the engines, and sure enough down came the bombs. I stuck my face into the ground, with one eye squinting up at the small silver dots floating down. Then explosions rent the earth. After that – silence. The bombers departed. We passed on, making our way between huge craters, round the edges of which the bodies of dozens of Americans were still smouldering. They had turned a curious black.[47]

Under aerial bombardment and a scorching sun, and further delayed by a two-hour Rebel artillery barrage, the British and Americans did not reach the base of Mosquito Ridge until the end of the day. By then, the height was occupied by the 8th Bandera of the feared Foreign Legionaries, the lead elements of Asensio's 12th Division deploying on the eastern flank of the Republican advance.[48] Earlier in the day, Loyalist scouts had reported the crest undefended. The exhausted 15th Brigade would have to attempt to storm the hill the next day. Meanwhile, Jurado had activated his reserve division, the 10th, and used it to broaden the front of the attack, pushing south to Villanueva del Pardillo but failing to capture it, while the 34th Division swung east to the castle of Villafranca on the banks of the Aulencia.

In V Corps' sector, the 11th Division of Major Líster, weakened by the need to extend its fronts to cover both flanks, had the displeasure of making contact with the first battalions of the Barrón's Black Hand Division, which occupied a series of elevations south of Brunete known only as 670, 640 and 620. These veteran Regulares were soon engaging the Listers in a series of fierce battles over 7 and 8 July, in which the Nationalists were pushed off one of the hills, 670, but further Republican advance proved impossible.[49] The 35th Division under the Pole General Walter was finally brought into action, but Modesto's original intention of using the 35th to exploit Líster's breakthrough and advance deeper into Nationalist territory could not be realised due to the continued failings of El Campesino. His 46th Division remained tied down at Quijorna and so the 35th was dispatched to the far-right flank of the Republican advance, rather than being committed in the centre. Here, El Campesino's troops finally took the Los Llanos height, taking 100 Moroccans prisoner, according to Modesto.[50] The Falangist Carmelo Revilla disputes this account, claiming that only the dead and those who could not be evacuated were left, the rest of the hill's garrison having destroyed their heavy weapons and slipped away the previous night.[51] Whatever happened, with the strongpoint in Republican hands, 101st Brigade pushed west of Quijorna, the village that still held out against repeated, if unimaginative, attacks from El Campesino's 10th Brigade. Revilla, who was a member of Quijorna's garrison, writes of the repeated frontal infantry attacks they repulsed, which merely served to bleed 46th Division white while achieving little.[52] Walter's 35th Division was deployed beyond the village to secure the western flank of the salient the Republicans had formed, with 11th International Brigade, the famous Thälmanns, in the vanguard. Here, two battalions of the newly arrived 150th Nationalist Division of freshly recruited colonial troops made their first appearance in the battle. They were pushed back by the Thälmann Brigade of German and Austrian anti-Nazis, which advanced to a crossroads 4km south of Quijorna and dug in.[53]

On 8 and 9 July, 15th Division made repeated attempts to dislodge Nationalist forces from the Mosquito Ridge, the height that dominated the whole sector. Having captured some secondary heights to the west, the international volunteers came up against machine-gun, anti-tank and mortar fire that seemed to make further advance impossible. Once out of a protective ravine, and on to the open hillside, the only cover was the long grass. Troops who got pinned down, and indeed the wounded, were stuck where they were until nightfall. Captain Oliver Law, the commander of the Washingtons and the first black American ever to lead whites into combat, fell on Mosquito Ridge, as one of his soldiers remembers:

> We crossed the ravine and as soon as we reached the top of the ridge all hell broke loose, machine guns, shells, everything. After going ahead for about a hundred yards, I hit the ground, breathless. Again, like at La Cañada, I heard the cries for first aid and the moans of the wounded and dying. … Oliver Law got up then. He was about twenty yards ahead of us, standing there yelling and waving his pistol. 'O.K. fellahs, let's go! Let's go! Let's keep it up. We can chase them off that hill. We can take that hill. Come on!' He got hit just about then. That was the last I saw of him. Some of the guys got to him and pulled him off the field, but he died before he could reach hospital.[54]

The Republican attacks were made without artillery, air or armoured support, as Fred Copeman explains:

> Three tanks passed us. I thought, 'At least we've got tank support.' I had spoken too soon. With a chug and a grunt the leading one stopped – it could not make the hill, it was too steep, and an enemy anti-tank battery was covering the approaches. The Rebels seemed to have

got their range quite well and three-pounder shells were exploding dangerously close.[55]

It was impossible to advance in such conditions, and bringing up ammunition, food and water also proved a challenge. The complete absence of artillery support seems criminal for these near-suicidal frontal attacks, but was typical of the People's Army, given their severe deficiencies in this field. The diversion to Villanueva de la Cañada on the first day had proved disastrous, preventing the International Brigaders from taking the hills while they were unoccupied. For four days, the troops were thrown against Mosquito Ridge only to suffer appalling casualties. Having both lost around half their strength, the two American Battalions were merged to form the Lincoln-Washington Battalion. The British Battalion had been reduced to just 150 men and Fred Copeman suffered a nervous breakdown a few days later and was withdrawn.[56] By 11 July, attempts to take the Romanillos Heights had to be abandoned, with both the 13th and 15th International Brigades of Gal's 15th Division exhausted and depleted. Several kilometres further north, a fierce battle for the village of Villafranca del Castillo had tied down the majority of XVIII Corps' forces, and although Republican troops briefly entered the village, they were soon thrown out. Lieutenant Colonel Jurado had taken ill (Modesto claims he was dismissed) and had been replaced with another Loyalist professional officer, Segismundo Casado.[57] Changing commanders mid-battle is always problematic, and now Casado had to help direct an offensive that he had long opposed. Republican President Manuel Azaña wrote in his diary, 'As soon as Colonel Jurado, attacked with angina, left the command, the performance of the eighteenth Corps began to decline,' even though he considered Casado a competent replacement.[58] The near-impossible difficulties of such a situation are described in the colonel's memoirs:

I happened to be in Valencia on the morning after the reported casualty of Colonel Jurado and I received orders to go to Madrid at once, where I should get instructions from the War Minister, Señor Prieto. I arrived in Madrid at nine o'clock at night, wondering why I had been summoned, since at that time I was Inspector General of Cavalry and Director of the General Staff School, and so outside the scope of the action which was proceeding. On my arrival I presented myself to the Minister, and we arranged that on the following morning he should give me my instructions on the mission which I had to fulfil. An hour later the Chief of General Staff [Rojo] ordered me to take charge of the 18th Army Corps.

I told him that I did not know the composition of that Army Corps, its situation, the morale of its troops, or indeed anything about it, and if it had to go into action the following day it would do so without my making previous reconnoitre of the territory. He told me that he understood the difficulties of my task, but that I must go immediately to headquarters where they would give the facts of the situation, which according to him were pretty unfavourable.

At two o'clock in the morning I arrived at what was from that moment to be my Headquarters, and when I asked the Chief of General Staff [*sic*, Chief of Staff, XVIII Corps], Lieutenant-Colonel Ruiz-Fornell, how things were, he told me that two brigades were completely demoralised and a good many troops were simply returning from the Front; that in five days of the offensive our forces were completely spent, for they had had nothing but cold rations and had been mown down by intensive fire from enemy aviation and artillery. The Army Corps which I was to command was composed of four divisions, and I was surprised to hear that I could only count on fourteen pieces of artillery. Three-quarters of our materials had gone to be repaired. In such circumstances I was ordered to continue the offensive. I informed the Command of the uselessness of this, but the order stood.[59]

At the same time, the offensive's reserve was committed in the form of the 45th Division of General Kléber, the Romanian Red Army officer Manfred Stern, who had won a great reputation in command of International units during the defence of Madrid. On 9 July, his 12th Garibaldi Brigade encircled Villanueva del Pardillo from the right bank of the Guadarrama, in support of Enciso's 10th Division, which had been trying to take the village for some time. After intense street fighting, the 10th and the Garibaldis stormed it on the night of 10/11 July, capturing 600 prisoners and two AT guns.[60] At the same time, the new 150th International Brigade of Slavic volunteers, supported by Soviet tanks, pushed up to Cota Mocha, a hill on the north-western edge of the Romanillos Heights.[61] General Kléber himself described the tough task they faced there:

We had to attack the famous Mocha Hill, strongly fortified by the enemy. In front of the hill and the barbed-wire obstacles of the enemy was a deep ravine with steep banks. Our tanks got to the ravine and could not move any farther forward. At that point, the enemy antitank cannon were firing well-aimed shots. My infantry got into the barbed wire of the enemy and could not move any farther forward.[62]

High command ordered a second attack be launched at 11.00 am the following morning (11 July), promising air and artillery support. However, neither materialised and once again, the Republican forces got no further than the enemy wire, suffering heavy causalities, particularly among the officers. Kléber continues his report:

Returning from the field of battle to my command post at 1300 hours, I found out that an order had just been received from the command staff that the attack arranged for 11 o'clock was being postponed because of the flight time of the air force and that it would be repeated at 1900 hours, at a time when the participation of the air force could be ensured.[63]

Kléber rang XVIII Corps commander Colonel Casado, petitioning against this fresh effort, only to be lectured by his superior (and his Soviet advisor) about obeying orders. He was then summoned to see an agitated General Miaja, who again demanded another assault. With the 45th Division having already lost 700 men on the hill, the Romanian protested further, insisting that although he was aware whole units had to be sacrificed sometimes, there were no reserves to exploit any success that might be achieved. No new attack was launched. Kléber's men had injected fresh impetuous into this sector but could push no further, nor take Villafranca del Castillo, held by the 2nd Tabor of Tetuán and the 3rd Bandera of the Foreign Legion, tough colonial troops of Asensio's 12th Division. The words of one eyewitness sum up grimly conditions on the battle's eastern flank: 'The hills of Villanueva del Pardillo and its surroundings resemble immense cemeteries.'[64]

V Corps on the western side of the advance was desperately trying to make up for lost time. On 9 July, Modesto himself had gone down to Quijorna to direct the final assault on the village that El Campesino was supposed to have captured on the first day. Well defended by a Bandera of Falangists, a regular infantry battalion and a Tabor of Moroccans, the 10th Brigade of his 46th Division, had tried and failed repeatedly to breach the Nationalist positions. On observing the defences, Modesto realised how the garrison had stood up to superior firepower for so long:

> Their tactic was simple: when our aviation bombed [the village], they went into the trenches [on the outskirts], and during the artillery preparation they retreated to the town, in improvised caves and shelters, so they could re-occupy the defences before the attackers could reach it [the village].[65]

He therefore came up with a plan to deceive the defenders. At 10.30 am, a brief artillery barrage on the trenches outside Quijorna sent the Rebels running for their bunkers, but almost immediately, precise fire was brought down on their escape routes, throwing the Nationalists into confusion. Six T-26 tanks, with infantry from 10th and 11th brigades close behind, moved in, taking the cemetery and then pushing into the village itself. As Rebel forces retreated out of the northern end of Quijorna, a cavalry squadron was lying in wait to ambush them. It was all over before noon. What had prevented the Republicans from taking this strongpoint sooner had been poor coordination between the various arms, although the job appears to have been made easier by the fact many of the Nationalist defenders had evacuated the village the previous night.[66] After taking Quijorna, the 10th Brigade moved west to a position close to Perales de Milla, between the 11th Thälmann Brigade on their left and the 101st Brigade of 46th Division to the right. On 10 July they held firm against several attacks of up to three battalions' strength by the Nationalist 150th Division, maintaining the western perimeter of the Republican salient. The right flank of the Listers was finally secure, but there was little hope of pushing forward. Moving tentatively south-east towards Villaviciosa de Odón, the 11th Division ran into fierce resistance from the Black Hand Division, with the 1st Bandera of La Legion and the 1st, 5th and 6th Tabors of Melilla fighting to hold the Loyalists at the hills south of Brunete. Despite tenacious resistance from Barrón's colonial troops, the Listers managed to take and hold two heights roughly 3km south of the Brunete–Boadilla road on 9–10 July.[67] Joaquín Masjuán's battalion was deployed on the eastern side of the 11th's frontage, opposite Boadilla, and, after being subjected to a heavy aerial barrage, repulsed an attack by Navarrese troops:

> Through the smoke that rose from the burning undergrowth, we distinguished a battalion of requetés climbing the slope. I started firing the machine gun immediately.

At that moment I became another man, full of fury. The first rows fell dead ...

The hand grenades soon made their appearance, as well as mortar fire and grenade launchers, which threw soldiers into the air.

The attackers, in spite of their courage, were lying on the remains of the barbed wire. Some, wounded, crawled down the hill. I did not shoot at them, they had already done their duty. I still had some remnants of dignity, but some of my colleagues did not think like me: they wanted to make them pay for the death of so many comrades. ...

The whole slope of the mountain was covered with corpses dressed in khaki. Some of the wounded tried to move, but it was useless, and soon they were motionless.[68]

By around the fifth day of the battle, the Nationalists, now with over 150 aircraft, had won control of the skies over Brunete and were carrying out constant air raids on Republican troops. The combination of a smattering of the technologically advanced Messerschmitt Bf 109s and great numbers of the resilient Fiat CR.32 meant that the Rebels had both the quantity *and* the quality to dominate the aerial battlefield. Additionally, however, Rebel air force general Alfredo Kindelán describes how the conservative tactics of the Soviet pilots and their Spanish trainees held back the 'Red' fighters. They tended to only operate in large, rigid formations (whereas the Nationalists patrolled in more flexible, discreet pairs) and would often avoid large confrontations, thereby conceding the skies to their opponents.[69] Without having to worry about the intervention of Russian fighters, Spanish and German-flown Heinkel He 51 fighter-bombers had free reign to strafe and bomb Loyalist positions. Harro Harder, a German pilot, records what happened on one such sortie:

We were greeted by a real display of fireworks. Shells burst beside, above and below us, sometimes almost right in our machines. We went over to a low-level attack and were met by intense 20mm fire from every direction. Everywhere one looked there were He 51s dancing and attacking through the flak. The battle lasted about eight minutes, until we had dropped all our bombs. Although we had almost no ammunition or bombs, we so shook the red infantry that they left their positions and ran in headlong flight.[70]

The experience was even more dangerous for the unlucky Loyalist soldiers on the ground, for whom Nationalist control of the skies presented a serious psychological strain; they were facing an enemy that could strike at any time, while having no way to respond. A member of the Lincoln-Washington Battalion described the experience thus:

> we first heard a low hum. It was low but very strong and it was coming from the Fascist side. It was getting stronger by the second and we knew we were for it. It was a roar that filled the air you were breathing. It was a roar that almost lifted you up, shaking. It was getting stronger and stronger and, Christ, it was coming straight at you ...
>
> I was hugging the earth, pressing into it with my hands, with my feet, with my face, but the roar set the whole ground shaking and the ground was pushing you up, pushing you up higher and higher, shoving you over to them; here he is, don't let 'im get away from you ...
>
> And I felt that I was perched up high and knew that they could spot me from miles. I looked up and there they were, going around and around, the whole sky black with them, manoeuvring into position, crooking their claws to swoop down on you ...
>
> Then they let loose. That awful whistle, scream and rush of the bombs, then the explosion. The whole earth was blasted into pieces. It heaved and rocked and swayed and roared and smoked, and the bombs kept coming down, and everytime [*sic*] you heard that whistle and scream you knew there was a shaft pointing to the small of your back and the bomb would hit you right there and blow you to a million pieces ...
>
> Waiting for that next explosion everything in you would be wound up tighter and tighter till you couldn't stand it any longer and felt like screaming; 'Come on, you bastards, drop it, drop it!'
>
> Then they'd begin bombing again and there you were lying naked. And where was our anti-aircraft, where were our planes, where were our guns to help us, to drive 'em away? They were all killed, the Fascists had everything and we had nothing ...
>
> Then the bombing stopped and they began straffing [*sic*]. Everything was smoke and dirt and dark but you knew the machine guns would see through the dark, and everybody around you was killed, and you were left here alone and the next burst would catch you square across the back and you would be killed, too.[71]

The Republican forces relied for the most part on the road Valdemorillo–Villanueva de la Cañada–Brunete for their rations and supplies to get through and unsurprisingly, the columns of trucks were frequently targeted by Nationalist aircraft. James Yates was an African-American from Mississippi, who worked as a truck driver for the Thälmann Brigade and was forced to take cover multiple times during the battle:

> The following day I was back at the front. I had unloaded food from my truck into the baskets on the backs of the donkeys. Then, all at once, all hell broke out. The poor animals screamed. I looked up and saw wave after wave of bombers and fighters coming through the sky toward us. There were so many of them that they blotted out the sun. Everybody scattered. Once the road was cleared of the donkey carts, I headed toward the scorched field which led to the main road. I spotted a few men scrambling beneath a doorway under a grass mound, jumped out of the truck, and entered behind them.[72]

However, despite the impression given to their ground troops of total Nationalist superiority, the Republican air force maintained enough of a presence throughout the battle, to cause concern to the heavier Axis bombers. By the middle of the month, all but the speedy Savoia 79 were mainly operating at night to avoid the Loyalist Moscas. On 16 July, the Savoias carried out a highly successful raid on the Republican airfield at Alcalá de Henares, which resulted in the death of the base commander.[73] The Duke of Lerma, a Nationalist pilot who was flying bombers at this stage of the war, wrote of the primitive methods used to carry out night raids at this time, which involved lighting a series of large bonfires to mark the flightpath to the target.[74] The Loyalists' response was to set up a Chato night fighter wing, which succeeded in scoring the first two night-time aerial kills in history during the battle.[75]

By 11 July therefore, the Brunete offensive had ground to a halt. In truth, the attacking momentum had been all but lost by the operation's third day, if not earlier, as Francoist reinforcements poured into the sector and multiple units became bogged down in front of hills and villages. However, Miaja had kept throwing Loyalist forces forward, suffering heavy losses for ever-diminishing returns. The hopes of capturing the Romanillos Heights or Navalcarnero, perhaps briefly a possibility on 6/7 July, had disappeared, while II Corps' flanking attack at Villaverde had been beaten back almost immediately. The Rebel forces on the edge of Madrid would be staying put. The extreme heat had also played its part in slowing down the Loyalist advance and exhausting their troops. A Condor Legion pilot describes the conditions typical of the battle:

> At the airfields, an insane heat raged – between 40–45°C in the shade, so that the work of the groundcrews was not exactly easy. The mechanics worked exclusively in their swimming trunks and protected their heads from the scorching heat … with wide-brimmed sombreros. During flight our aircraft just could not be kept cool at all. The coolant was at 120°C and the oil clocked up 110°C.[76]

With the Republicans at a standstill, on 11 and 12 July, Asensio's 12th Division and the 5th Navarrese Brigade (newly arrived from the north) launched a counter along the whole of XVIII Corps' front, supported by sixty artillery pieces and heavy air attacks. The assault was halted, with units of the 15th Division holding the gains they had made in the Romanillos Heights, while 10th and 34th divisions frustrated Rebel attempts to recover Villanueva del Pardillo.[77] A period of bloody stalemate ensued for the next few days, with Republican forces digging in to hold their hard-won gains and limited counter-attacks by the Nationalists. Fred Thomas was a cabinetmaker from London and a communist who had joined the 15th International Brigade's renowned anti-tank battery. In his diary he describes a typical day during the Brunete battle's (relatively) quiet interval:

> The tumult and the shouting dies – for a little while anyway. Both sides are now licking their wounds. The Government has advanced 8 miles, which is a lot of ground, but our sector seems immovable right now, and friend and enemy are digging like mad.
>
> Out of forty at the start we have lost fourteen, which means each gun is being manned by six men.
>
> It's a pity we haven't more aeroplanes. Theirs seem to come over when and where they like. Half a dozen times a day at least we are being bombed.[78]

At the same time, Franco was agonising over his next move. For the Caudillo, there was no question that the ground lost to the Loyalist advance had to be retaken, but at what cost to his northern offensive? And what if the 'reds' were driven back? Should they be pursued all the way to El Escorial, or even Madrid? Colonel Juan Vigón, the Caudillo's chief planner and a strong advocate of the northern strategy, was in a state of hysteria; what would these delays and distractions mean for the postponed attack on Santander? Would Franco abandon the advance in the north altogether? He wrote a series of letters to his friend General Kindelán from 12 to 18 July, expressing his dismay at their superior's decision to fall for the Republic's bait at Brunete, playing into their enemy's hands by switching their attention back to the central front. 'It is crystal clear that in a war of two fronts you must concentrate your materiel in one place,' he wrote, adding, 'It is a torment to see things clearly and not be able to fix them,' being unable to question the Generalissimo's orders.[79] Vigón failed to see the point in a counter-attack now that the lines were secure; wasting reserves in such an offensive would only serve to reduce the Rebels' operational freedom.[80] However, Franco was thinking of the political situation, not just the military one. He wished to deny the Republic a clear victory that could be used by their propaganda outlets in Spain and around the world. The enemy could not be allowed to win the battle; territory lost had to be regained.

By now, General Varela had a force of at least 60,000 men, composed of, from west to east around the Republican salient: the 71st Division, the 150th, 4th Brigade of Navarre, 13th Black Hand Division, 108th Division, Asensio's 12th, 5th Navarrese Brigade and the 11th Division. He also enjoyed an overwhelming superiority in artillery and aircraft, augmented by the transfer of supplies stockpiled for the now-cancelled Santander operation. On the other hand, the Republicans had committed their best troops and resources to the initial assault, and after almost two weeks of battle, the fighting strength of the Loyalist forces was on the wane. The Carlist general now prepared a full-scale counter-offensive, intended to drive the Republic back to its start lines. Varela's attack was launched on 18 July, the first anniversary of the Nationalist uprising in mainland Spain. All units were to go on to the attack, with 71st and 150th divisions pushing Modesto's V Corps from the west, 4th Navarrese Brigade and 13th Division to try to evict Líster from Brunete in the centre and the 11th, 12th, 108th divisions, plus 5th Navarrese Brigade, assaulting XVIII Corps from the east. The ultimate aim was for the flanking attacks to break through and cut off the Republican salient entirely. The calm that Fred Thomas had enjoyed was shattered, as he recorded in his diary:

> The fateful 18th July. One year ago to-day this business started. And as might be expected there is quite a lot of activity this morning. In the

early hours there was a terrific artillery duel. Then came a formidable air-raid of about 30 planes which did their stuff a little too near for comfort. In the middle of all this someone started an attack to our right.[81]

Thomas was wounded in both legs by a Rebel bomb a few days later and would be hospitalised for months. Sixty Nationalist artillery batteries and the entire weight of Axis air power were brought to bear on the exhausted Republicans but they grimly held on. On the other side of the lines, the chief of staff of the Condor Legion, Wolfram Richtofen wrote:

18 July. Attack on red infantry who are much better than expected. Air attacks very good despite strongest red flak as never experienced before. 4 Brigade [4th Navarrese Brigade] gets ahead well. Heavy losses on both sides. 4 Brigade has lost eighteen officers by lunchtime and about 400 men. Art[illery] shot badly. Three waved bombing attack went off well, but it did not help. Right wing did not engage at all as art still not in position. Manaña![82]

So the battle went for the next few days, with Nationalist forces making meagre gains for heavy casualties, despite overwhelming firepower. In scenes reminiscent of the First World War, Brunete developed into a bloody attritional struggle, huge quantities of high explosive and manpower being expended for the gain of a few strategically meaningless kilometres. While fighting desperately to hold their ground, Modesto joked with his divisional commanders that should V Corps indeed be cut off, they would set up their own independent Republic![83] After six days of fighting, the lines were little changed; the 71st Division managed to push El Campesino's 46th back a couple of kilometres eastwards and the 150th had made a salient of about half that depth against General Walter's 35th Division on the south-westernmost tip of the Republican salient. The Listers had held fast south of Brunete itself against Franco's colonial troops, with Joaquín Masjuán taking part in the defence of a hill north of Sevilla de la Nueva:

On 19th July, they obstinately attacked the height of Sevilla de la Nueva, and although their aviation and artillery pounded our positions, thanks to the dense defensive network that we had, they could not break through. We inflicted many more casualties on the enemy, especially the legionaries and the Moors. I baptized this position 'the invincible hill'.[84]

Elements of the Rebel 12th, 13th and 108th divisions had mostly driven the Republicans out of the Romanillos Heights. The 5th Brigade of Navarre, operating on the eastern side of the battlefield, had taken the castle of Villafranca from the Loyalist 34th Division, reaching the Aulencia River on 23 July, and with the support of the Rebel 11th Division advanced a kilometre towards Villanueva del Pardillo, where Kléber's men barred their path.[85] Despite all that had been asked of them in the preceding weeks, and with rapidly diminishing levels of supplies and reserves, Loyalist forces as good as held their ground. Varela's troops were badly mauled, the Navarrese Carlists reportedly suffering 1,000 casualties on the first day alone, but the attack was to continue, the battle turning into the greatest slogging match of the war so far, reminiscent of the great battles of attrition of 1914–18.[86] On 20 July, after exactly two weeks of non-stop fighting, Enrique Líster asked V Corps commander Lieutenant Colonel Modesto if his exhausted troops could be allowed a brief rest from the front lines. Modesto kicked the problem upstairs, directing his Communist comrade to the head of the Army of the Centre, General Miaja. Arriving at the general's headquarters, Líster describes in his memoirs an episode that perhaps should be taken with a pinch of salt: he finds Miaja and Defence Minister Prieto in the canteen drinking champagne. He explains that his 11th Division has suffered 50 per cent casualties and gone weeks without a shower or proper sleep. Prieto, Líster claims, stood up and excused himself: 'Well, as this is a military question, I am going to have a nap.'[87] This laid-back attitude seems rather unlikely given Prieto was a famous pessimist and known for his work ethic. Miaja meanwhile fobs Líster off to Republican Chief of Staff Colonel Vicente Rojo, who requests that the 11th hold on for just two or three more days, a conversation that seems far more believable.[88]

Then, on 24 July, the inevitable happened. Exhausted and depleted by three weeks of continuous combat under a burning sun, the Republican line in the centre gave way. It is important to note that on the right and left flanks, the line held, with gains of at most a kilometre for Nationalist forces. However, the Loyalist centre was about to crumble. The 11th Division had fought harder than perhaps any other Republican unit, having advanced 12km on the battle's first day, pushed further south, albeit with little success against Barrón's Black Hand veterans, and finally over the last few days held off repeated attacks by Carlist and colonial troops despite being well beyond the limits of human endurance. Once again, the Nationalists attacked, concentrating their forces on Brunete with sixty-five artillery batteries and every air crew in the Condor Legion. Modesto claims that units of the fresh Republican 14th Division had been in the process of taking over sections of the line held by the 11th when the attack began, causing further confusion and panic.[89] The famous Listers broke, retreating from their positions south of Brunete and losing the town to the Black Hand before being rallied by the major himself at a cemetery on a hill just to the north that dominates the town.[90] He led a counter that briefly recaptured Brunete but was soon ejected once again. Joaquín Majuán witnessed the rout on what he described as the loudest day of his life:

> Between 9 and 10 o'clock in the morning, our troops began to arrive in clear flight, machine-gunned by the enemy aviation. Our men were in a sorry state; they were dirty, tired, hungry and demoralised. I offered my two canteens of water to the fugitives, who emptied them in a frenzy almost immediately. …
>
> I saw a procession of wounded and dying, many with broken limbs. One of them had his forehead and his eyes blindfolded and exclaimed: 'Don't leave me! Do not leave me!'
>
> An ambulance riddled with bullets hurried past. A young nurse, very pale, had a chest covered in blood.
>
> There were so many wounded, that I put the submachine gun on my shoulder and helped transport the unfortunates. I sweated so much, all my clothes were soaked. This was due to the fact that, in the shade, it was 40 degrees. Exhausted, there came a time when I had no choice but to sit down and rest next to the chapel.[91]

A general collapse took place along the centre of the Republican salient as the Listers withdrew, the line only reforming some kilometres to the rear. In the prevention of a rout, generals Kléber and Walter played a vital role, deploying several battalions of their respective divisions to hold the line. Kléber reported to Moscow on the dramatic events of that day:

> Lister's division wavered. The withdrawal of Lister mushroomed into a general flight of several divisions. Hurriedly gathering three battalions and my squadrons of cavalry, I occupied a line and began to halt those

fleeing from the front. How difficult it was to fight against the mass panic can be seen just from the fact that my cavalry squadrons occupied with restoring order had three men killed and fourteen men wounded in the 'battle' with the panicked floods of armed people fleeing to the rear. …

I sent one battalion into Villanueva de [la] Cañada and dug in on the forward line with another battalion positioned somewhere behind it and, with the remaining forces gathered into a strike force, awaited the enemy. With the actions of my division and Walter's division in the region of Quijorna, the general panic was localised and the forward line was preserved behind us. I can state that we were able to achieve this accomplishment thanks to the fact that I did not carry out the orders of my corps commander [Casado].[92]

Although General Walter later claimed the retreat was largely attributable to 'panic sown by the "fifth column" that the fascists had gotten around our forces', it is clear that cool heads and not a little violence were required to bring the rout under control, with hundreds of deserters reportedly shot.[93]

The British and Franco-Belge Battalions of 15th International Brigade were stationed at the far south-eastern corner of Loyalist lines. While the troops in the centre fell back, orders for the British to withdraw never got through and, alarmingly, they found themselves with their flanks completely exposed and in serious danger of being encircled. In trying to make their way back through enemy territory to Republican positions across the Guadarrama, the British became split into two groups. One of the British parties was led by commissar Wally Tapsell:

No one knows how Hinks [acting British battalion commander] did it, but he got those men out some way or other, and without serious losses. But it was dusk before he and we met, and we had practically given him up for lost. Meanwhile, with Hinks away, we had no machine guns. Our men fought like Trojans, firing their rifles, and using those of the wounded alternately, in order to keep the guns cool.[94]

Tapsell's small troop were separated from Hinks with the battalion's Maxim machine guns for most of that chaotic day. However, on their retreat they picked up various stragglers:

Luck came our way when we found two machine-gunners, one German, the other French. We put one on each flank. At 6pm a Company of Moors tried to cut us off on the right flank. The German gunner mowed them down in heaps. We moved back to another hill. This time the attack was on our left, and the French gunner did his bit. Now we were being heavily pressed all round; the Moors knew our numbers. It was perilous work steering our little band back, trying to ensure maximum cover, stopping every few yards to engage the enemy and keep his fire down. But we made it.[95]

Bill Alexander, an industrial chemist from Hampshire, had been promoted in the field to commissar of the brigade anti-tank battery, which played a key role in the fighting withdrawal. Manhandling the 45mm guns from position to position, he recalls:

When the Nationalists were advancing towards me I was deafened. I was standing there with this gun crew, slightly in front [of the British positions], and saying 'over there, to the left', or 'over there to the right', as we saw a group of men, platoon strength (30 strong), get up and run forward. The gunners were doing an extremely good job: rapidly swivelling and adjusting the sights. With one shell we could actually see bodies flying apart. But we just could not do enough to keep the fascists from breaking through.[96]

At the end of the day, only forty-two men answered the battalion roll call, although many volunteers were by this point in the battle wounded in hospital and would return to the ranks in time.[97] The Franco–Belge 6th February battalion had also ceased to exist as a fighting unit.

Republican Chief of Staff Vicente Rojo's directive for 25 July read, 'It is necessary to convince the forces that it is imperative to resist at all costs … any attempt to retreat will be punished rigorously.'[98] The Loyalists planned to retake Brunete that morning, with Ciprano Mera's 14th Division in position in a series of light woods and olive groves a kilometre north of the town. The counter failed miserably; advancing across open ground, the infantry were cut down by machine-gun and artillery fire. At 2.00 pm, the Nationalist offensive resumed with a huge 100-gun barrage and heavy bombing raids. Líster was finally compelled to withdraw from the hilltop cemetery to the town's north by an all-out assault of Black Hand Regulares and the Republican line was driven north towards Quijorna and Villanueva de la Cañada.[99] Barrón had finally delivered the smouldering ruins of Brunete into Rebel hands. 25 July is the Feast Day of St James, Patron Saint of Spain, and Franco was delighted by his troops' success, linking the Rebel cause to divine providence as he declared: 'The Apostle has granted me victory on his feast day.'[100] Meanwhile, a triumphant Richtofen, whose Condor Legion had played such an important role in the Insurgent counter-attack, wrote in his diary: 'All the red attacks have been rebuffed. … Countless red casualties, which are already decomposing in the heat. Everywhere shot-up red tanks. A great sight! Our Heinkel 51s and Spanish fighters attack north of Brunete.'[101]

That afternoon, another German, Gerda Taro, a Jewish anti-fascist who had worked as a photojournalist for much of the Spanish Civil War, was in the midst of the fighting. Her lover, Robert Capa, who was to go on to become perhaps the most famous war photographer of all time, had warned her against getting too close to the action. However, her dramatic pictures of the Listers taking Brunete justified her fearless approach. Having run out of film, Taro was riding a car full of wounded heading towards the rear when Condor Legion aircraft attacked. The car careered off the road and into a Soviet tank, and the young German was injured fatally.[102] She was the first female war photographer to be killed in the field and she rests in the famous Père Lachaise cemetery in Paris. Overnight, Modesto moved his last reserves, the 32nd Brigade of Walter's 35th Division, into the line, relieving the shattered 14th Division. They held a line just south of the Quijorna–Villanueva del la Cañada road against smaller Rebel attacks throughout 26 July.[103] The retreat was over.

That day, Franco met with Varela, Barrón, Asensio and other Insurgent commanders at Sevilla la Nueva, the town Líster had not dared advance on three weeks before. General Varela was hopeful that he would be allowed to follow up his success at Brunete with a drive on Madrid; the enemy was beaten, their best units shattered, morale broken. Finally, the long-awaited prize of the Spanish capital was within reach. Varela was also keen to justify the huge resources, in terms of both men and materiel, which he had expended to take a small town and a few hills.[104] The Nationalists' most talented commander was to be disappointed. Having pondered over his next move for over a week, the ever-cautious Franco had decided to not to risk another attack on the 'tomb of fascism' but to persist with the northern strategy, telling his audience:

I only have a few weeks in which to carry this out. After that the weather will be our greatest enemy, with fog, rain, and snow. I know we could capture the Escorial, but that would only prolong the fighting in the north indefinitely.[105]

Kindelán and Vigón were delighted, with the former recalling the pleasure with which he received the words when they came out of Franco's lips.[106] The Generalissimo had opted for what would surely be the easier option, winning a quick victory at Santander rather than risk another attritional struggle for Madrid. Additionally, he may have been motivated by a desire not to end the war too quickly, but instead clear each region systematically of 'reds'.[107] On the other hand, if Madrid had fallen shortly after Brunete, then the Northern zone would have likely been irrelevant, and Varela's aide-de-camp was of the opinion that Franco did not wish his subordinate to win too much glory.[108]

The Battle of Brunete was over, with the Republicans retaining a few kilometres of their gains and the villages of Quijorna, Villanueva de la Cañada and Villanueva del Pardillo, for which both sides had fought so hard. The shattered shock troops of the People's Army were withdrawn, but not always to safety. Major George Montague Nathan was the very model of a British officer: tall, slim but muscular with polished boots and never seen without his cane, Nathan had a reputation as an utterly fearless leader, unflinching under fire. He had fought in the First World War and the Anglo-Irish conflict and although of no political party, he was a committed anti-fascist who had risen to become the chief of staff of the 15th International Brigade. On 26 July, while ensuring that food would be ready for the returning troops, Nathan was caught in an air raid. His comrades wrote of him:

> Major Nathan, who throughout the most trying days of the three weeks' fighting had been cool and cheery as if on manoeuvres and who had escaped death by a hairsbreadth a dozen times was wounded by a bomb splinter.[109]

Penny Fyvel, an English nurse serving in the International Brigade medical unit, treated him:

> A casualty was carried into the operating-theatre. A weak voice said, 'Penny, don't you know me?' I had a fearful shock. It was George Nathan.

… He was in great pain. I gave him an injection, put the anaesthetic mask on his face and we began to operate. A piece of shrapnel had pierced the liver, diaphragm and lungs and had lodged in the spine. It was quite hopeless. After the operation we took Nathan upstairs. I stayed with him having given an intramuscular saline infusion and repacked his wounds. Our best officer was dying.[110]

Conclusions

The strategic aim of the Brunete offensive, as conceived by the Republican government and by Chief of Staff Colonel Rojo, had been to delay the Nationalist attack on Santander. Franco's offensive, planned for 9 July, was indeed shelved almost as soon as the battle began, and would ultimately be postponed for five weeks. The hope was that this crucial time bought so dearly by the Army of the Centre would allow the Republic's northern forces to adequately prepare for the coming onslaught. In this sense, and this sense alone, Brunete had been a success for the People's Army. In contrast, it had been a clear tactical defeat; the siege of Madrid had not been raised, nor the Rebel forces on the capital's outskirts encircled. There had been no link-up with the south-eastern push of II Corps, which had proved to be a damp squib. The key objectives of V Corps and XVIII Corps, Navalcarnero and the Romanillos Heights respectively, were never taken, let alone held. A significant portion of the ground gained had been lost, and all at a terrible price. Casualty estimates vary considerably, with figures of 25,000 to 17,000 for the Republicans and 17,000 to 10,000 for the Nationalists.[111] 25,000 Loyalist casualties would have represented close to half the entire assaulting force, and although 50 per cent losses were suffered by some formations right in the thick of the action, such as the Listers, this figure seems far too high for the Republicans as a whole. At the same time, 10,000 seems too low for the Rebels, given the tremendous rates of attrition both sides suffered, especially during the battle's final phase. Hugh Thomas's figures of 20,000 Republican casualties and 17,000 Nationalist seem most reasonable, but there is clearly several thousand leeway for both.

Without doubt this was a tremendous bloodletting for both sides over just a few square kilometres of scorched earth, but it was the People's Army that came off worse. Experienced, disciplined and well-trained formations were hard to come by in the underdeveloped Republican army. The few such divisions that did fit that description, such as the Listers or El Campesino's

46th, had suffered a mauling, and there was not a ready supply of high-quality replacements. Even worse was the situation for the International Brigades. The Internationals had fought well; Walter praised the performance of the 11th, the 12th had taken Villanueva del Pardillo, the 15th Villanueva de la Cañada and Kléber's 150th had shown immense courage. But Brunete had been three weeks of hell: vicious fighting, constant air raids, unbearable heat and never-ending casualties. At the end of the offensive, a Comintern report stated that of a strength of 13,393, the International Brigades had lost 779 killed, 2,329 wounded and 392 disappeared.[112] While Franco's administrators in Spanish Morocco could procure, one way or another, ever more recruits for the Regulares, it was not so easy to replace the Republic's foreign shock troops. The initial glut of volunteers inspired by the Spanish Causa had not been sustained, and as news of the appalling losses suffered by International units filtered home, ever fewer new recruits could be found. Soon, famous units such as the Thälmanns would be just 10 to 15 per cent German, the ranks having to be filled with Spanish troops at a severe cost to cohesion. There were considerable morale and discipline problems in a number of International units following the battle: drunkenness, desertion, requests for leave, complaints about other nationalities. A number of leading figures from the brigades were sent home or left, such as the commander of the Garibaldis or British leader Fred Copeman. The most serious problems occurred in the 13th International Brigade, composed of French and Poles, and, after what amounted to a near mutiny, Republican high command ordered it be dissolved. General Kléber reported what happened next:

> What happened to the 13th Brigade? Colonel Rojo ordered that at the disbanding of the brigade it be cordoned off by carabineros [gendarmes] and that it be disarmed. Comrades Franz Dahlem and Gallo arrived and they began to implement the order on disbanding the brigade. Anyone who felt like it began to pilfer weapons taken from the 13th Brigade – machine guns, antitank cannons, vehicles, medical supplies, and so forth. The carving up of the living corpse took on a disgraceful character.[113]

The 13th Brigade was reconstituted as the Dabrowski Brigade, made up of Central and Eastern Europeans from the units of the original 13th and the now defunct 150th International Brigades. Even more irreplaceable than trained troops were the precious reserves of military hardware that had been committed to the battle. The loss of scores of the fine Russian T-26 would never be made good by the dwindling Soviet supply shipments. Of the 132 tanks committed to the battle (virtually the Republic's entire armoured strength), 21 were destroyed and 26 disabled, a loss rate of over a third.[114] The armour had been spread out rather than committed at any one point, cooperation with the infantry had been poor, and many had fallen prey to Nationalist anti-tank guns and aircraft. In the air, the Republic had also suffered badly. The commonly quoted figure of around 100 Loyalist planes shot down to 23 Nationalist is, in the words of Rebel pilot the Duke of Lerma, 'over-optimistic'.[115] Undoubtedly, however, the Nationalists won control of the skies and inflicted heavy losses on the 'reds' during the battle, with the Condor Legion claiming fifty-nine 'confirmed' kills and twelve 'unconfirmed' while only losing two of their new Messerschmitts.[116] The Republican air force was so weakened by Brunete that it took months for them to recover their strength, especially in terms of fighters. Defence Minister Prieto had met with President Azaña before the operation, telling the Republican head of state that the Army of the Centre's attack represented the best hope of ultimate success, and telling him that it if went wrong, 'There's no choice but to hang on until all this goes down the drain.'[117] The big offensive had failed, and Prieto was thrown into a deep pessimism. The chances of Republican victory in the civil war seemed to have slipped considerably.

Why had the Brunete operation failed? The disaster of II Corps' attack towards Alcorcón left the overall plan in tatters from an early stage. Clearly, not enough resources were committed here to break through the well-entrenched Nationalists at Carabanchel. In overall command, General Miaja's conduct of the whole campaign was lacklustre – reserves were released too slowly, resources were diverted to secondary objectives and divisions were not permitted the rest they so desperately needed, resulting in the final collapse. Negrín described Miaja as 'useless' and 'a joker' during the battle, while Azaña suspected the general was being difficult due to his jealousy of Rojo.[118] Rojo himself blamed the failure on the long delays taking the 'two local problems' of Quijorna and Villanueva de la Pardillo, but points out that had they not been captured, the Francoist counter would have been more successful.[119] The performance of Juardo's XVIII Corps was generally poor, but his replacement with Casado elicited little improvement. El Campesino took far too long to take Quijorna, showing little imagination, and that fact, combined with XVIII Corps' delay at Villanueva de la Cañada, cost Líster his shot at Navalcarnero. Perhaps Modesto should have intervened sooner to get his subordinates moving; it was four days into the battle before he personally oversaw Quijorna's capture, eliciting the support of the 11th International Brigade. General Gal's 15th Division had missed the opportunity to take Mosquito Ridge on the first day while it was undefended, his 13th Brigade ended the battle in a state of mutiny and members of 15th Brigade accused the Hungarian general of incompetence. For these failings, Gal was stripped of his command and returned to Russia. 15th International Brigade was then transferred to General Walter's 35th Division, while the rebuilt 13th Brigade was sent to Kléber's 45th Division in an effort to make the International units more linguistically homogenous. The lack of skilled, trained officers of all ranks resulted in a loss of momentum, confusion, and poor coordination between different units and arms, as illustrated by Kléber's account on the battle for Mocha Hill. President Azaña recorded much the same thing in his diary following conversations with several friends who were loyal professional officers:

> What's wrong is the commanders. The new junior officers do not have enough training or experience to deal with the comfort of the troops, outside of combat. Good battalion leaders are missing. Quite a few larger units have only one staff officer, and as they are generally scarce everywhere, their work is overwhelming. In the larger units, the commanders-in-chief are improvised people, without knowledge: El Campesino, Líster, Modesto, Cipriano Mera … who do good work, but who cannot remedy their incompetence. The only one who knows how to read a map is the one called Modesto. The others, besides not knowing how, believe it unnecessary. Menéndez [a regular lieutenant colonel] has seen how they gave El Campesino a map of the situation, and without looking at it, El Campesino spread it out on the table, face down, to serve as a tablecloth.[120]

This problem was exacerbated by excessively high casualties among the People's Army's lower leaders, the junior officers, commissars and NCOs who led the often suicidal attacks. By way of example, during Brunete, the 15th Brigade lost, killed or wounded from amongst its officers: their commander, Ćopić, chief of staff (Nathan), from the British Battalion, Copeman, his second in command, a company commander (Meredith) and two commissars. The American casualties included Oliver Law, Paul Burns, his adjutant Hans Amlie, and Walter Garland, among others, the anti-tanks lost Captain Malcom Dunbar wounded and his second in command killed, while Commandant Fort of the Franco-Belge was blinded.[121] With such a turnover of lower leaders, who play such an important role in inspiring and motivating the men, it is unsurprising that Republican units lost their impetus and saw a fall in morale. General Walter wrote candidly some months later about the mistakes made during the battle:

> In the Brunete operation we did not show enough tenacity in using the very favourable conditions of the first few days, but then had more than was necessary later on when it was too late. We stubbornly tried to compensate for being caught yawning with local and futile attacks at Villafranca and Mosquite [*sic*] by 18th Corps units that had little fighting value.[122]

The salient point here is that opportunities presented on 6 and 7 July were not seized, while the Nationalists were still reeling from the initial blow. Then, once Rebel reinforcements had stabilised the front, the Republican units had been forced to maintain the offensive, despite the fact they were already worn out and the momentum had been lost. The continued assaults from 9–11 July on various strongpoints, not least Mosquito Ridge, served only to exhaust and deplete the People's Army, meaning it would eventually break in the face of the Nationalist counter. Antony Beevor blames this pointless continuation of the offensive on the Communists' desire for material for their propaganda. However, the ultimate decisions regarding the operation rested with Prieto, Rojo and Miaja, all of whom were not Communists.[123] More likely, General Walter's explanation that the Republican command tried to make up for the early missed opportunities with further repeated attacks was the real cause. This was the Republic's first major offensive operation; mistakes were made, high command overestimated the resilience of their troops and persisted too long with the attack. One only has to think of the BEF's first major offensive, 1916 on the Somme, to see how common these flaws can be with newly built armies. In both cases, the failings of a citizen army were laid bare: inadequate training, a poorly exectued plan and a lack of tactical nous and timing from commanders. Indeed, the stories of waves of infantry hopelessly charging trenches, barbed wire and machine guns is a depressingly familiar one.

Republican propaganda sold Brunete as a strategic triumph and a justification of the new government's 'active war policy', but this was clearly putting a brave face on the realities. The People's Army had never attempted an operation such as this, and ultimately it had failed. While some historians have alluded to an Orwellian 'double-think' consuming the Communists and their Soviet advisors,[124] the Republic hardly stands alone in modern history in turning a defeat into a victory for reasons of morale and political expediency. There was also clearly some reflection in Republican ranks, evidenced not least by Azaña's conversations with officers and ministers that have already been referenced.[125] *The Book of the XV Brigade*, published just a matter of months later by the International Brigade Commissariat, remarked on how the operation revealed 'weaknesses still existing' in coordination between units and arms particularly, while Bill Alexander would later reflect that at Brunete, the Republicans:

> still had insufficient reserves to consolidate and then expand their initial victory. This was still in the early days when many of the Spanish battalions were still badly led and not yet consolidated into a serious army.[126]

Whatever the failings in the People's Army, it is hard to look past the huge superiority in air and artillery power enjoyed by the Nationalists. Despite the high quality of the Rebel infantry that fought at Brunete, without the advantages of close air and artillery support, it seems unlikely that their counter-offensive would have succeeded. The morale of the Republicans was sapped away by the clear evidence of their enemy's superior arsenal, and Insurgent control of the skies made getting food, water and ammunition up to the leading Loyalist units a challenge. Rojo admits the ferocity of Rebel air attacks were something of a revelation at Brunete:

> The performance of the enemy [aviation] was simply overwhelming from the third day: day and night raids were occurring with a frequency and power hitherto unknown. The machine-gunning was almost incessant, forcing our men to stay close to the ground without the possibility of defence or manoeuvring, and at night the harassment actions of our rear guard followed, greatly hindering the services and causing numerous fires.[127]

In contrast to the huge bombardments that accompanied the Nationalist attacks, Republican troops often found themselves charging well-defended positions with little or no support, resulting in murderous losses. The People's Army's paucity of modern artillery and bombers made itself felt at Mosquito Ridge, Mocha Hill and numerous fortified villages, and was paid for in blood. Nevertheless, the Nationalists had fought courageously in attack and defence, and the elite colonial troops had justified their reputations as determined, dependable fighters, even if casualties had been high. In particular, the battle had highlighted the flexibility of the Rebel army, able to react so quickly to the Republican assault and make use of the talents of numerous capable commanders.

For the Nationalists, Brunete was a victory, but not a decisive one. The breach in the line that the Republican offensive had cut was rapidly repaired and the advance halted. Brunete itself and a number of important heights had been recaptured. General Varela had been 'serene' throughout, directing the Nationalist response with composure and cool efficiency, despite the intense pressures of the campaign, which saw several Republican officers crack.[128] However, the Rebel counter-attack had made very limited progress for huge casualties, despite a clear superiority of forces. If Franco had persisted in the Madrid sector then perhaps more substantial gains could have been made. On the other hand, many in the Nationalist command were keen to resume the campaign in the north, and the Generalissimo's very decision to accept the Republican gauntlet at Brunete was controversial, as we have seen. In many ways, the way the battle was conducted was typical of the Caudillo's command style: an emotional aversion to losing ground, a cautious, methodical approach to offensive operations, a reliance on overwhelming superiority in firepower, and always an eye on the political implications. The Spanish military historian Cardona is critical of Franco for calling off Varela's counter, comparing it to his decision in 1936 to take Toledo before Madrid; in both cases, he subordinated the primary objective of the war to a secondary one.[129] However, there were many fine arguments in favour of the northern strategy, and the Nationalist units in the sector were, like their Republican counterparts, depleted and exhausted by the bloody battle. With hindsight, it was probably a mistake for Franco to have called off the Santander operation and diverted so many forces to Bruente; the Republican offensive would likely have run out of steam regardless, stemmed by reserves in the Madrid sector. However, it was important to deny the Republicans any sort of victory that could raise morale and confidence in the Loyalist government, and by crushing the offensive it ensured that the Nationalists would still be perceived as winning the war.

Chapter 5

The Third Siege of Saragossa: Belchite, August–October 1937

Background to the campaign

After the close of the battle around Brunete, Franco once again turned his attentions to the north, eschewing the possibility of further gains in the Madrid sector. The same strategic motives drew the Nationalists to the Republic's beleaguered Northern zone as in the spring; the north was isolated, weakly held, deprived of Soviet arms and even more politically divided than the main rump of Republican Spain. Therefore, on 14 August, the Nationalists' northern offensive resumed.

The attack, led by General Dávila, consisted of the Navarrese Corps (six brigades of fanatical Carlists) and the entire Italian CTV: the motorised Littorio division of Italian army regulars, two semi-motorised divisions of fascist Blackshirt volunteers, and the Black Arrows Brigade of Spanish troops under Italian officers. Once again, the Nationalists enjoyed a huge superiority in artillery, boasting ninety-three batteries to just eighty artillery pieces to service 80,000 Republican troops.[1] Dávila was also supported by the great mass of Italian and German air power present in Spain. In contrast, the air forces available to the Republicans in the north were woefully weak – just four Loyalist fighter squadrons (including only one equipped with the modern I-16 Mosca), totally only forty operational aircraft, faced seven Nationalist squadrons, six Italian CR.32 fighter squadrons and a squadron of the Condor Legion's new Messerschmitt 109s, more than 200 planes. By the time fighting reached Asturias in September, the Nationalists had been reinforced further and benefitted from the firepower of two full squadrons of 109s and two squadrons of the new German Heinkel He 111 bomber. The Republican pilots in the north operated in conditions of extreme disadvantage, flying from rudimentary airfields, sometimes so close to the front that they had to deal with hostile anti-aircraft fire as they took off! With their ranks ever-diminishing and no chance of reinforcement, by the end of the campaign, three or four Moscas were regularly engaging enemy formations of up to seventy aircraft.[2] Control of the skies allowed the Nationalists to interdict any attempt to evacuate the helpless Northern zone, with the Republic's best destroyer and a submarine being sunk by air strikes in the port of Gijón days before it fell, to the fury of Republican Defence Minister Prieto. Woefully outgunned on the ground and in the air, it is little surprise that in the face of this fresh drive on Santander, from the east rather than the south, the Republicans were soon in full retreat. Nevertheless, the fighting was bitter and intense. David Granda was an Asturian Socialist, wounded while fighting with the Republican Army of the North:

> The area in which I fell was a real slaughter-house. The enemy had sustained huge losses too in the same zone around Valduno and Escamplero. Years later, when I returned to Spain, I met some peasants from near Valduno, from Premoño and Ania, who told me that during the war they had stayed behind on their farms when the Nationalists advanced and that they had been forced to go with their ox carts to take out the dead, because there were places in the mountains where a lorry or ambulance couldn't get through. The fighting had been very heavy and the shocktroops were always the Arab regulars from North Africa. When they were mown down they were replaced by another wave. The peasants brought out cartload after cartload, piled high with bodies.[3]

This new crisis in the north necessitated a response from the Republic's government and once again, Colonel Rojo found himself planning a diversionary offensive, which was to be launched just a month after the end of Brunete. The strategic objective was identical to that battle, namely to distract Franco's forces from their northern campaign and buy time for Santander and Asturias. The site of this latest attack was to be Aragon, a region in the north-east of Spain, bordering Catalonia. It would have made little sense to resume offensive operations in the Madrid sector, given that the front was now stabilised and sizeable Nationalist forces remained there.

The Republic chose Aragon for two key reasons. Firstly, it had been, since the war's first few weeks, a quiet sector of the front, where Nationalist forces were weak and thinly spread; across 300km were just three Francoist divisions, the 51st, 52nd and 105th. None of these were remarkable formations and they were concentrated in the towns along the front, with only threadbare positions stretching through the countryside between them. There was little in the way of the Nationalists' feared air power here either, hardly surprising given the fact that none of the war's major battles had yet taken place in this region. An attack would likely achieve a breakthrough and force Franco to commit reserves. High command was keen to 'activate' this front and finally achieve full militarisation there.

The relative calm in Aragon was the result of circumstance. In July 1936, at the outbreak of war, the rightist military uprising in Barcelona had been crushed by the militia of the anarchist CNT-FAI, the most powerful political movement in Catalonia. Once the city was safely in their hands, makeshift columns of workers rushed out of Barcelona to secure the surrounding countryside. The eventual objective of the anarchist militias became Saragossa – the traditional capital of Aragon but also the unofficial capital of the anarchist movement, which had fallen to the Nationalists in the first days of war. Amateurish attempts at recapture by the militia were frustrated by an outnumbered garrison and the front settled down several kilometres east of the city. The mainly anarchist and POUM divisions that held the Aragon front were untouched by the Republic's militarisation process to a greater extent than any other part of the People's Army in the main Republican zone, having only accepted the authority of the War Ministry in the spring of 1937. It was only after the May Days repression that high command took control of the front with the appointment of Loyalist professional Sebastián Pozas as commander of a new Army of the East. Without much in the way of weapons, tanks or air support, indeed without much outside assistance or interference of any kind, the war here was largely run by the anarchist Council of Defence in Barcelona. Communist presence was negligible and so Soviet supplies and advisors were notable by their absence. The anarchists certainly lacked the resources and expertise to engineer a breakthrough; however, contemporary criticisms of the stagnant nature of the war effort in Aragon were not without some merit. After all, as we have seen, the Republic was desperately short of practically every military resource; the government simply could not afford to distribute what little there was to a dormant front where the troops could not be relied upon to obey high command. George Orwell served in a POUM unit on this front during the spring of 1937 and describes well the rather sterile, tedious conditions:

> It was an extraordinary life that we were living – an extraordinary way to be at war, if you could call it war. The whole militia chafed against the inaction and clamoured constantly to know why we were not allowed to attack. But it was perfectly obvious that there would be no battle for

a long while yet, unless the enemy started it. Georges Kopp, on his periodical tours of inspection, was quite frank with us. 'This is not war,' he used to say, 'it is a comic opera with an occasional death.' As a matter of fact the stagnation on the Aragon Front had political causes of which I knew nothing at that time; but the purely military difficulties – quite apart from the lack of reserves of men – were obvious to anybody.

Orwell goes on to explain that the front line consisted of rudimentary trenches dug along hilltops several hundred metres apart, the occasional machine gun sufficing to hold the line. He bemoans the complete lack of artillery among the Republican forces (four trench mortars with fifteen rounds each for the entire sector) and describes how occasionally the Nationalists opposite him would 'bring up a gun or two from Saragossa and fire a very few shells, so few that they never even found the range and the shells plunged harmlessly into the empty ravines.' He neatly summarises the dilemma for these under-resourced units:

> Against machine guns and without artillery there are only three things you can do: dig yourself in at a safe distance … advance across the open and be massacred, or make small-scale night-attacks that will not alter the general situation. Practically the alternatives are stagnation or suicide.[4]

The second reason for choosing Aragon was that by shifting the focus of the Republican military to this region, Negrín and his government could take a big step towards completing their state-building counter-revolutionary project. Catalonia and Aragon were the beating heart of Spain's grassroots revolution and the forces here, as already mentioned, were yet to be properly integrated into the People's Army, even if the anarchist militia columns had formerly been converted into mixed brigades with numerical divisions. As discussed in earlier chapters, this region, and Barcelona in particular, had been the scene of genuine social revolution the previous summer, with workers and unions seizing control of almost every aspect of the economy. The anarchist CNT-FAI militia seized three quarters of Aragon and began evangelising their revolutionary creed, pressuring, cajoling and sometimes forcing local peasantry to collectivise the land. Of a population of less than 500,000 in Republican-held Aragon, by May 1937, 180,000 lived and worked on collective farms.[5] Further, the Republic's urban centres were beginning to suffer acute food shortages, and it was believed that the collectivisation experiment had damaged agricultural production, although the evidence for this is sketchy.[6] Certainly, the 'reforms' carried out on these collectives were some of the most radical in all the civil war, as the secretary of one such Aragonese collective describes:

> We thought that by abolishing money we would cure most ills. From an early age, we had read in anarchist thinkers that money was the root of all evil. But we had no idea of the difficulties it would cause – it turned out to be one of the biggest mistakes. And having different money in each village only added to the muddle ...[7]

The region remained outside the control of central government, run by the anarchist Council of Aragon. For Socialist Prime Minister Juan Negrín, brought to power by factions hoping for a firmer counter-revolutionary line, this was anathema. The Republican state had to control its own territory; it could be the only authority. Dismantling the collectives was a necessary step in achieving the government's goal of breaking the CNT-FAI's regional power. In collaboration with the Communists and high command, his fellow-Socialist, Defence Minister Indalecio Prieto, ordered the dissolution of the Council on 11 August. This truly was a coalition project, uniting the liberal, moderate socialist and communist strands of the Popular Front alliance in a common goal. Communist troops were already in situ, in preparedness to carry out the task, by force if necessary. Major Enrique Líster's elite 11th Division was entrusted with this delicate mission, although historians suspect, acting either on his own initiative, or on Communist Party orders, he overstepped his brief. In the loaded words of La Pasionaria, the famed Communist deputy Dolores Ibárruri, 'Republican order was established.'[8]

Formally, Líster and other communist-led formations of Modesto's V Corps were in Aragon on manoeuvres. Modesto records that his arrival in the region was greeted with thankful women who complained of the looting and mistreatment they had been subjected to before Communist intervention.[9] Líster paints a more honest picture of his infamous exploits in Aragon. In his memoirs, he begins his account of the episode with a denial. How could he have crushed the anarchist revolution, supposedly supported by the great mass of the people, with only 7,000 men? Clearly, there was a degree of smoke and mirrors about responsibility, both at the time, and subsequently, for when Líster arrived and reported to the army commander of the sector,

General Pozas, the general claimed to have no knowledge of Líster's mission. But in a subsequent conversation with Pozas's Soviet advisor, the wily major learnt that his commander was well aware of his special orders. At 11.00 pm on 10 August, Líster received a call from Pozas's headquarters, whereupon the general declared ominously, 'We start tomorrow.' Líster informed his superior that everything was in place and betrayed the brutality of what was to come in his belligerent words, 'If anyone moves, I will crush them.'[10]

On 11 August, the 11th Division, supported by other units, forcibly disbanded the Council of Aragon, arresting perhaps 600 anarchists, some of whom were never released and fell into Nationalist hands still imprisoned. Next, the collectives were dismantled, with machinery, tools and seed redistributed to smallholders. Having just thirteen months previously set out to defend the Republic alongside his fellow villagers with medieval weapons, the teenage Toledo peasant Timoteo Ruiz was now a junior officer in the 11th:

> We were told that the peasantry was hostile to the council and frequently crossed to the enemy lines. When we got there we went round the villages disarming the people. We told them there was a war on, that it was being fought to defend the Republic and ensure the triumph of democracy, and that the peasantry must be respected. What they were doing didn't correspond to the needs of the war. The peasants welcomed us as though we were their liberators, delighted to have their lands, tools and livestock back and to be able to work the land as they wanted.[11]

Certainly, the process was not always as tranquil as Ruiz describes. There was violence (although there is little evidence of any deaths) and unnecessary excesses. One Aragonese foundryman was arrested in his home town by a military patrol, despite being a PCE member. He remembers his captors declaring:

> 'We don't give a damn about anyone or anything here. We're in charge and that's that.' They couldn't have cared less. Líster was proclaimed a liberator by the people. But he overstepped his orders. It required a great deal of care to ensure that in liquidating a bad experiment we didn't go to the other extreme. But that was what happened. We went from an anarchist dictatorship to a communist one.[12]

Another collective member recalled being lined up against a wall one night with other prisoners under car headlights, clearly an attempt to intimidate them with the threat of execution. Anarchist divisions at the front were in uproar, many were keen to defend their revolutionary project with force, but their commanders succeeded in restraining them. The CNT-FAI leadership, emasculated by the events of the May Days, could do little other than petition to avoid executions and launch veiled attacks on 'Russian practices' in the anarchist press. Líster was hauled in front of Prieto, berating him for killing anarchists and informing the major that 'Now they are asking me for your head.'[13] The results are hard to measure. It is unclear whether agricultural production was positively or negatively effected, especially as the harvest was collected before the decree. Republican control was reasserted in the region but collectives were spontaneously re-established over time. The true extent of popular support in Aragon for the Council and the collectives is almost impossible to ascertain, given that the driving force in both their conception and destruction was armed force from outside the region; first the anarchist militias from Barcelona, then the Communist troops of Líster. One outcome that is certain is that it further embittered and alienated the radical elements within the Republican camp and fuelled fear of a communist takeover.

With the rearguard secure, Rojo could focus on putting together his Aragon offensive. The objective was to be Saragossa, the same goal the anarchist militia columns had tried and failed to capture for many months. In fact, although in most accounts of the civil war, the coming battle is described as the Battle of Belchite, the struggle for that town was merely the most intense of a series of attacks designed to capture the much greater prize of the Aragonese capital Saragossa. Twice in the space of a few months, Napoleon's France had besieged Saragossa during the Peninsular War, finally succeeding in storming the city in early 1809. The Spanish defenders then were led by José de Palafox y Melci, a famous general after whom one of the battalions of the Slavic 13th International Brigade was named. One hundred and thirty years later, Saragossa would once again be the objective of a grand military operation, and bitter house-to-house fighting would characterise the struggle. This time, the city itself would, mercifully, be left relatively intact, while the surrounding towns and villages would bear the brunt of the destruction. Capturing Saragossa would be a major propaganda coup for the People's Army; as of yet, the Republic had failed to take any provincial or regional capital from their Nationalist adversary – the war had very much been one-way traffic. Further, Saragossa was the key to the whole Aragon

Front, serving as the centre of the road, rail and communication networks for the region. If it were to be taken from the Rebels, perhaps its fall could provoke a general Nationalist retreat in this sector? Most important of all, Rojo was sure that should the city be taken by the People's Army, Franco would be obliged to call a halt to his drive on Santander and once again shift his focus away from that front, buying a vital respite for the disintegrating Republican Army of the North. It does not appear that any thought had been given to what might happen should the Generalissimo take the bait and launch a full-scale counter-attack, as at Brunete. Likely, Rojo hoped that another battle of attrition would develop and that this time his forces would hold the line, buying their Northern comrades time to recover, resupply and fortify their positions.

To achieve this ambitious goal, Rojo developed a sound plan, arguably superior to the Brunete operation on paper. Saragossa was to be assaulted from three directions simultaneously. First, control of the Aragon front was transferred from anarchist committees to a new Army of the East, under General Pozas. Pozas was a professional army officer in his sixties, a veteran of Morocco and probably only 'geographically loyal'. Like many Loyalist officers, he had fallen into the orbit of the PCE in the war's early months and had previously been an army commander on the central front during the defence of Madrid. Disagreements with Miaja had led to his positing to Aragon. His chief of staff was another veteran of the Moroccan wars and prominent Communist Antonio Cordón, who would later become Under-Secretary for War in Negrn's government. According to Kléber, Cordón was, 'of all the professional officers, perhaps the most valuable for the Communist Party. He knew his business, had authority in the army, and was a sincere communist, putting party above all else.'[14]

These men would have overall direction of the campaign and their forces were split into four 'Battlegroups'.

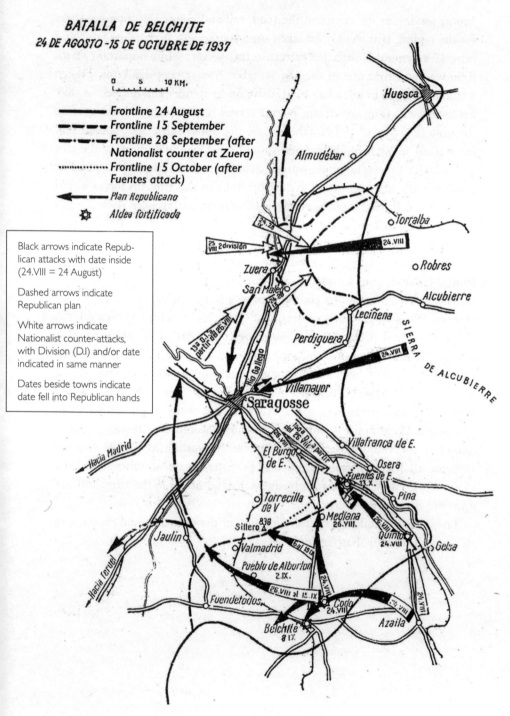

Map 5: Battle of Belchite.

Furthest south, was Battlegroup D under Lieutenant Colonel Juan Modesto, the main body of which was his V Corps from the Manoeuvre Army. This was composed of tried and tested Communist troops: Líster's 11th Division, 46th Division under El Campesino and 35th Division under the Pole General Walter, which contained the largely anglophone 15th International Brigade and the nominally German 11th International Brigade. These units had borne the brunt of the fighting at Brunete and were badly worn out, both in terms of men and equipment. The Listers had been able to quickly receive reinforcements, but the International units were short on replacements and were in most cases at least half-manned by Spaniards. The limited role the 46th Division was to play in the battle suggests it was not back to anything like full strength after the losses of July. The south-western flank of this battlegroup was to be supported by XII Corps of the Catalan 30th Division and anarchist 25th Division. Modesto's task was to push through the towns of Belchite and Quinto, up the road through Fuentes de Ebro and then on to Saragossa from the south-east.

Across the Ebro River was Battlegroup C, a collection of small units including a couple of mixed brigades who merely had to hold the line. Alongside them was Battlegroup B commanded by General Emilio Kléber and consisting of a real hodgepodge of formations. There was his own 45th Division, consisting of the troubled Garibaldi International Brigade (12th) and the 13th International Brigade, which had been dissolved following Brunete and now reconstituted with Slavic volunteers from that formation and from the 150th International Brigade. Kléber had also been awaiting the renowned Dimitrov Battalion of the 15th Internationals to reinforce his new 13th Brigade, but General Walter had declined to hand the outfit over so close to an offensive operation.[15] To support them, he had a battalion of engineers, a small cavalry unit and some anarchists. In terms of heavy equipment, Battlegroup B had only nine aged cannon detached from a local anarchist division, the replacement for the 45th's own artillery units, which were detached by Rojo for reasons unknown (with an unfulfilled promise of their return) after Brunete, according to Kléber's own account. In total, Battlegroup B had 8,400 men with which to drive through a series of fortified hills in the Sierra de Alcubierre to the town of Villamayor and then on to Saragossa itself from the north-east.

Finally, Battlegroup A comprised around 10,000 men, built around the Catalan-communist 27th Division, and would attack towards Zuera before moving on Saragossa from the north. This group enjoyed the support of ten tanks, an additional mixed brigade (127th) and an artillery battery and was commanded by Major Manuel Trueba, a self-educated communist intellectual. The 27th Division had been built out of the Karl Marx communist-socialist militia column and sometimes bore that name, although was also referred to as 'The Witch' after its shock battalion of the same moniker. The two northern drives were, according to Rojo's account, only supposed to draw reserves away from Modesto's main push and to cover the flank of the advance from the north.[16] Hence, Battlegroups A and B combined numbered a little over 18,000, while the forces south of the Ebro (six divisions, fifteen brigades) had a paper strength of 45,000, although given the low unit establishments of the People's Army, possibly it could be as low as 35,000. In total therefore, the assault force numbered somewhere in the region of 55,000, likely smaller than at Brunete and significantly fewer than the common figure of 80,000 given by Thomas, which likely represented the entire strength of Pozas' Army of the East.[17] If two or perhaps all of these assaults were to achieve a breakthrough and quickly take their initial objectives, then the position of Saragossa would very soon become untenable. Should that occur, then Rojo's plan might just come off.

To face this Republican onslaught there were just three Nationalist divisions in the sector, totalling probably 20,000 men to the People's Army's 55,000, a substantially larger Rebel force than held the line at Brunete. As in the previous battle, they were spread thin and composed of undistinguished units under an unfashionable commander; General Miguel Ponte was in charge of a newly formed V Corps based at Saragossa. At his disposal was the 51st Division, strung out north of the city, and the 52nd Division to the east and south. Both had been on this dormant front for some time. Ponte also had three independent mobile brigades, and a handful of outdated Heinkel 51 fighters and He 46 bombers (just fifteen aircraft in total according to Thomas).[18] The recently recruited 105th Division was stationed behind Saragossa in reserve. His men were a mixture of diehard Carlist and Falangist militiamen, integrated into the Nationalist army, and, as with both sides, many rather more reluctant conscripts. It would be a tough test to hold off Pozas's army, supported as it was by 100 tanks and 115 aircraft, many of them the fine Russian I-15 and I-16s.[19]

It was not just the Republicans therefore who had neglected this front to date. There was no organised trench line along the whole length of the front. Instead, as Orwell described, there was a series of strongpoints and machine-gun nests taking advantage of natural features. Aragon has no shortage of hills, valleys and ravines, and without enough manpower to hold the line in the conventional sense it was on these geographical obstacles that the Nationalists were to rely for their defence. Fortresses such as the Purburrel Hill outside Quinto had defences on all sides to account for the lack of a joined-up trench system. Additionally, the towns and villages of the sparse Aragonese countryside served effectively as forts; holding a town allowed you to control the surrounding country and Ponte's men would soon be digging in at Villamayor, Fuentes, Quinto and, most notably, Belchite.

The battle

On the morning 24 August, the three Republican thrusts began, in total, eight separate attacks, as the Army of the East threw themselves at an unprepared enemy. The skies were clear, the temperatures high, the soil arid. There was no preliminary air or artillery bombardment in order to maintain complete surprise, although it seems unlikely the Republic had the resources for a preparatory bombardment on a 100km front. Preparations had not been ideal, with critical shortages of trucks to get the troops into position. General Kléber complained that his Battlegroup B received only half the trucks they had been promised and eighty-four hours late, while Modesto could not begin his attack in full until 10.00 am due to similar problems.[20] Additionally, the drivers were, it turned out, civilians and not suited for work in a combat zone.

The attack of General Kléber's Battlegroup B aimed at reaching the Barcelona–Saragossa highway south of Villamayor, before driving on to the Aragonese capital from the east, but suffered an inauspicious start. Having carried out some rudimentary reconnaissance of the Sierra de Alcubierre, the Romanian commander wished to amend the plan of attack set out by Pozas's headquarters. On his right flank was an exposed, open plain, dominated by Francoist hill forts, complete with concrete fortifications and barbed wire, some kilometres distant. Meanwhile, on the left, the terrain was undulating and covered in thorny undergrowth, not ideal for an advance but not suicidal either. Therefore, Kléber changed the plan, shifting the attack to the left flank and leaving just one battalion to cover the right. However, before the assault was even under way, confusion reigned, clearly frustrating the 'hero of Madrid':

> I went to the headquarters of my brigades to check up on how things were going in preparing for the offensive. To my complete astonishment,

I found Comrade Leonidov [Soviet advisor to General Pozas] in the headquarters of the 12th Brigade, where he was showing the brigade commander Penchienati on the map the advantages of advancing on the right flank, that is, the exact reverse of the decision that had already been made.[21]

Kléber eventually got his way but when the attack began, in Battlegroup B's case during the night of 23/24 August, the 12th International Brigade (the Garibaldis) followed Leonidov's advice and pushed right, while the rest of the attack meandered left. Leading on the left, the Slavic 13th International Brigade drove deep into Nationalist lines, taking positions at bayonet point in the darkness. But by dawn, it became clear that a yawning gap had grown between the two brigades. Penchienati's battalions:

found themselves in the morning to be in a hollow, cut off from all directions. The enemy opened heavy fire on them from the hills, and by the following night both battalions, remaining on the low ground, in a situation where they could neither push forward nor retreat, had sustained losses. At my question about who had given him the right not to carry out my orders, Brigade Commander Penchienati answered that both battalions … had made a wrong turn in the night and that it was an unfortunate accident and not a deliberate act of not carrying out orders.[22]

Alone on the left, and without air, armour or artillery support, the 13th Dabrowski International Brigade was too weak to take the forts, leaving the 45th Division, and thus the battlegroup, stuck. Without artillery, it was near enough impossible to move forward against these fortified positions. Kléber's paltry nine artillery pieces could not assist the Dabrowskis as they spent the entire day desperately trying to help the marooned 12th Brigade with covering fire. Six of the guns broke down in the process, and it became clear that half the shells they had been issued with were either duds or the wrong calibre for their aged cannon.[23]

South of the Ebro, Modesto's Battlegroup D, comprised of the most famous divisions in the People's Army, and enjoying the majority of the offensive's armour and air support, was facing approximately 7,000 men of the Rebel 52nd Division, most of whom were garrisoned in Quinto and Belchite. Jackson gives a figure of 10,000 troops in Modesto's V Corps, but this figure seems rather low given that Líster records his 11th Division alone as being 7,000 strong.[24] One of Líster's brigades, the 100th, was to quickly seize Fuentes de Ebro, on the road to Saragossa, by moving into advantageous positions in the hours of darkness. Meanwhile, General Walter's 35th Division was to secure the 11th's flank by encircling and capturing Quinto. In the vanguard of this attack was the 15th International Brigade under Lieutenant Colonel Ćopić, who tasked his Lincoln-Washington and Dimitrov battalions with seizing the strongly held town, while the British and Spanish 24th battalions remained in reserve. Once the path was clear, Modesto had a motorised column of forty tanks, ten armoured vehicles and the remaining two brigades of the Listers mounted in trucks, which was to race up the road to Saragossa and take it swiftly.[25] The plan was bold and daring, almost reminiscent of German blitzkrieg tactics, but relied on the rapid fall of Fuentes.

The attack began well, as new 15th International Brigade Chief of Staff Major Robert Merriman wrote in his diary: 'At 6 o'clock, barrage started. Tanks followed and our boys with tanks stormed the heights. A more perfect movement I never want to see.'[26] The tall, broad-shouldered Merriman taught economics at Berkeley, although he was from a modest background, the son of a lumberjack. Stoic and always wearing distinctive round spectacles, the American, unlike many International officers, had no party affiliation and was later immortalised as Hemingway's hero Robert Jordan in *For Whom the Bell Tolls*. By noon, Modesto's battlegroup had cleared virtually all enemy resistance between Quinto and Belchite, although both towns remained in Nationalist hands. It was still hoped that Líster might reach Fuentes de Ebro that day. However, things had started to fall apart for the young major at an early juncture. In the small hours of the morning, the 100th Brigade moved up the Ebro valley and took the important hills of Cordero and La Tosqueta, but when they came to attack their main objective, Fuentes itself, the brigade was repulsed. Líster was keen to throw his remaining two brigades, the motorised column, into the attack, but this proved impossible. It was now 7.00 am and the trucks had still not arrived. The 1st and 9th brigades decided to move anyway and set off for Fuentes de Ebro on foot. To Líster's acute frustration, the trucks appeared an hour later, too late to halt 11th Division's advance. Joaquín Masjuán, now a provisional lieutenant, was riding with this motorised column from Azaila:

I ended up riding on the back of the turret of a tank and I started to eat a bread roll. The cavalry accompanied us under a scorching sun and among huge clouds of dust.

The plain we were crossing had a Dantean aspect. In it there were no tracks or practicable roads. On the right I managed to distinguish Quinto and the hermitage of Bonastre.

It was increasingly hot and I ended up drinking the water from the two canteens I was carrying. Although from time to time we would find some pocket of resistance that we eliminated at once, we advanced practically without opposition.[27]

Due to the stuttering nature of the offensive's opening, by 8.00 am General Ponte was clearly already aware of the danger it posed and dispatched reinforcements from his Saragossa mobile reserves to meet the threat posed by Battlegroup D. Despite the ease with which Masjuán and his comrades moved forward, it was not until midday that the rest of the 11th Division reached the 100th Brigade before Fuentes. By then the enemy were well-prepared, the element of surprise had been lost and the town did not fall. Angrily, Líster records in his memoirs that points of resistance should have been ignored and the focus should have been on getting to Saragossa regardless.[28] But given the perilous state of Republican logistics, it seems hard to imagine how Battlegroup D could have got through to the Aragonese capital without using the main roads. Even if Líster had been able to bypass Fuentes de Ebro, how would his crack division have been resupplied? More likely, the headstrong major would have risked an embarrassing encirclement and surely would not have been able to take and hold the city alone. Instead, the 11th had to content itself with repeated failed attacks on Fuentes, which the Nationalists strengthened considerably over the next few days with infantry, artillery and engineers. Líster did detach two battalions that pushed west of Fuentes and captured first Rodén later that day and Mediana on 25 August, as well as blowing up the railway line from Saragossa to Quinto to prevent the Rebels using it to reinforce their garrison at the latter. The Listers had once again advanced further than any other Republican unit, 20 km to Fuentes, and a further 10 km to Mediana. However, they had failed in their primary objective, leaving the whole battlegroup's advance on Saragossa stalled.

The 11th and 15th International Brigades of the Pole General Walter's 35th Division also faced a tougher fight than expected at Quinto. Artillery had been set up on Cordero hill, taken by the Listers earlier, that could bombard the town, but the approaches to Quinto were dominated by the steep, conical Purburrel hill, a fortified height complete with barbed wire, concrete bunkers, machine-gun emplacements and 360° defences. The Dimitrovs and Lincolns had broken through Nationalist lines at 6.30 am in the Azaila area and attacked the hill, without success, before moving round to the town. Under the intense afternoon sun, the Republican air force launched a rare aerial bombardment, and eight tanks were soon brought up to aid the assault. With this support, plus twelve artillery pieces, the most firepower the Americans had ever enjoyed reportedly, the 1st, 2nd and 3rd companies of the Lincoln-Washington battalion attempted to take the town from the plains to Quinto's west.[29] Milton Wolff was a 21-year-old American volunteer from a Jewish family of Eastern European immigrants in New York. Growing up in the Depression, he had become an activist in the Young Communist League and had served at Brunete carrying water for the Brigaders' Maxim machine guns. Now he was commanding an MG section, and advancing across the plain behind the riflemen:

The fascists opened fire with what must have been old artillery pieces, and the shell trajectory was so flat that the shells came whistling by, struck the ground and bounced, and disappeared without exploding. It was like skipping flat rocks over a pond.[30]

Bitter fighting developed in the cemetery on the town's western edge, the work of the Maxims inhibited by Wolff's lack of binoculars. But with the support of the Soviet T-26s, which crushed the Rebel barbed wire, the Americans gained a foothold and forced the Francoist defenders to take refuge in the church. It became the focal point of the defence of the town, the belfry serving as a sniper's vantage point, and withstood repeated artillery bombardments.

Furthest south, the anarchist 25th Division under CNT-FAI militant Major Antonio Ortiz and the Catalan 30th Division were ordered to move on Belchite and the little hilltop village of Codo. Two mixed brigades from each division quickly pushed through the Nationalist lines and by 25 August had completely encircled Belchite, with 117th Brigade of Ortiz's division taking the railway station, bullring and several other buildings on the outskirts of the town. Over the next few days, the Loyalists tightened the noose on the town, capturing the local electricity transformer and water tank, but did not dare assault its impressive defences.

Meanwhile, the Tercio (regiment) of Our Lady of Montserrat, a unit of Carlist Requetès, the red beret-wearing Catholic extremists, held the road from Belchite north towards Mediana. These particular Red Berets were Catholic refugees from revolutionary Catalonia and had more motivation than many to fight for their cause.[31] Their headquarters, as well as 300 Requetès, were based in Codo, atop a commanding hill over 340 metres in altitude, just a short distance north-east of Belchite. Here, the tiny garrison held up two whole Republican brigades, the 116th of 25th Division and 134th from Modesto's battlegroup, for much of the first day. When the village was finally taken, the anarchists and POUMistas of the 25th found graffitied onto walls the slogan 'When you kill a red, you will spend a year less in purgatory'.[32] The Carlists had fought with extreme bravery but paid a heavy price; by 25 August, the Tercio of Our Lady of Montserrat had effectively ceased to exist as a fighting unit. An International Brigader passed through Codo shortly afterwards and described the scene thus:

> Here is the road our Spanish troops came in yesterday. Along the shallow ditch are brown-clad forms. Artillery and shells got them in their last charge. Someone has covered their faces already. We go along, stooping to identify the waxed features. Here the Fascist shells landed. Telephone wires trail to the ground. On the breast of a dead man lies a magpie; the same shell got it on the wires and him on the roadway. Here is another inert figure, a big gash across his chest. Underneath his left arm is tucked a rabbit. How did it get there? Possibly, while they were lying out on the hill beyond, that rabbit had scuttled out from its warren and he clubbed it with a lucky blow. What visions he must have had of the meal he would cook when the town was captured! And this the end of his dreamings.[33]

Searching through the town, the soldier found a composite photo of Franco, Christ and Rebel General Mola, in that order, much to his disgust, before coming to the centre of the village:

> The Shrine of Codo. A commanding knoll, its flat summit encircled by fourteen pillars, with a little chapel in the centre. The chapel overlooked the line of the Republican advance, so the Fascists loopholed and sandbagged it, and built other machine-gun posts beside two of the pillars, just as they also fortify their churches. This is the modern way of fighting for Christianity – turn the churches into fortresses, and then blame the 'Reds' for smashing them up in order to get the garrison

out! There's a cathedral and a few churches over there in Belchite. The Fascists will use them as strongholds too.[34]

The most northerly assault – that of Battlegroup A – had already run into trouble. The Republican achievements in this particular sector were so paltry over the course of the battle that they can be swiftly surmised in a single paragraph. Major Trueba's 10,000-strong force initially enjoyed some success on 24 August, with his 27th Division (referred to variously as either 'Karl Marx' or 'The Witch') of Catalan communists and socialists breaking through Rebel lines after a two-hour battle and pushing towards the village of Zuera on the Gállego River. Meanwhile, the 127th Mixed Brigade, an anarchist unit, covered their northern flank, moving up to the tributary Val de Recordín. Benefiting from substantial (by Republican standards) tank and artillery support, the 27th had taken Zuera by noon. The battle plan dictated that Trueba then move south down the Huesca–Saragossa road but disaster struck. According to Rojo, the unit was drunk with success and failed to regroup for the southern push. Instead, it was taken by surprise by enemy reserves and forced into a disorderly retreat to the other side of the Gállego.[35] Zuera was not retained and by 1 September, with elements of Barrón's 13th Division blocking their path, Battlegroup A had been halted outside the villages of San Mateo and Peñaflor de Gállego, more than 20km from their ultimate objective, Saragossa. Within a few days, all attempts at further advance had been called off, and shortly afterwards, Manuel Trueba was dismissed from his post. On 23 September, the 27th Division, having been transferred further north, was involved in a small-scale action close to the French frontier in a failed attempt to encircle the city of Huesca. However, just a day later, a counter-attack was launched by troops fresh to Aragon: the Black Arrows and Blue Arrows brigades of Mussolini's CTV. These mixed units consisted of Italian army officers and specialists commanding Spanish rank and file and were well equipped with motorised assault battalions and strong artillery support. They quickly pushed Republican forces back from before Zuera and clear of the Huesca–Saragossa highway, ensuring safe communication between these two Nationalist strongholds.[36] The limited achievements of Battlegroup A had been all but undone.

Overall, the first attack had achieved the desired surprise, but did not elicit the desired effect. Franco dispatched reinforcements to the Aragon front, a number of aircraft and two experienced divisions still in the Madrid sector that had played a key role at Brunete. However, he did not call a halt to his Santander operation, nor move key units away from that battle. It was the only time during the war that he permitted his opponents to take territory from him without immediate counter-attack. Listening to the advice of the architect of the northern campaign, Colonel Juan Vigón, Franco agreed that it was wise to concede to the Republicans strategically insignificant ground in Aragon, in order to maintain momentum in the north. In fact, Santander fell on 26 August, with the remnants of the Basque army also surrendering to the Italian CTV. What was left of the Republican Army of the North fled into Asturias. However, the Generalissimo did visit Aragon frequently during the battle and contemplated an offensive to first relieve, later recover, Belchite.[37] In the end, he was persuaded against it in favour of maintaining the effort in Asturias, but the decision clashed with his emotional priorities and henceforth, he blankly refused to accept further loss of ground to the enemy, whatever the cost.[38]

The forces sent to assist General Ponte in his defence of Saragossa were frightening, from a Republican perspective. General Barrón's famed 13th Black Hand Division had been formed out of veteran Army of Africa units and was considered one of the elite formations in the Nationalist army. General Sáenz de Buruaga's 150th Division was composed of more recently recruited Foreign Legionnaires and Moroccan Regulares but had been blooded at Brunete. Barrón deployed north of the Ebro to face Kléber, with some elements of his division being detached to reinforce the Zuera sector. The 150th Division was positioned south of the river to contain Battlegroup D and XII Corps. Just over a month previously, these divisions had been fighting furiously with the finest Republican units on the plains outside Madrid. Now they were in many cases facing the exact same adversaries in Aragon. Rojo's initial plan had relied on the fact that the Saragossa sector was weakly held – within a few days, the arrival of these crack formations, as well as substantial aerial reinforcements, meant that this was no longer that case.

While success on the ground may have been limited, the Republican air force was enjoying some rare victories. As mentioned, they enjoyed a huge superiority in terms of numbers of planes at the outset of the battle, perhaps outnumbering their Nationalist adversaries by more than seven to one. A group of obsolete Heinkel 46 reconnaissance and light bomber aircraft had been deliberately assigned to this quiet sector by Nationalist command to be out of the firing line, highlighting the lack of preparation among the Rebels for a serious battle here. Although the 46s performed with distinction in the skies above Belchite, they suffered many losses, including the squadron leader. Very quickly, however, the Rebels' air arm in Aragon was augmented with around eighty additional aircraft, including forty Fiat CR.32 fighters and twenty Savoia 79 bombers.[39] Command of Nationalist fighter forces on the front was transferred to the Francoists' leading ace pilot, Joaquín García Morato, who would go on to achieve forty confirmed kills during the war. Nevertheless, the Republican air force maintained its presence in the skies above Aragon throughout the battle, competing with the Nationalists in a way that had not been possible at Brunete due to the numerical and technological advantages enjoyed by the Insurgents' air arm. The key reason that these factors did not come into play at Belchite was Franco's decision to leave the Nazi Condor Legion and the bulk of the Italian Aviazione Legionaria on the northern front to continue supporting his operations there. As a result, there were no Messerschmitt 109s at Belchite, and so the Russian-built Chatos and Moscas had more than a sporting chance against Fiat and Heinkel biplane fighters.

Frustrated at the lack of progress on the first day, Battlegroup B's 13th Dabrowski Brigade of the 45th Division devised a plan for a night attack for 24/25 August in the Sierra de Alcubierre. In an audacious strike, the Slavic volunteers broke through and seized the town of Villamayor de Gállago, just 6km north-east of Saragossa. Their commander, General Kléber, clearly proud of the brigade he had rebuilt following its dissolution after Brunete, recounts what happened next:

In Villamayor they captured an enemy headquarters with 150 prisoners of war, mainly officers. Among them were also four Germans with three interpreters. A panic started in Saragossa. The fascists sounded the alarm, and all night long the church bells were ringing. Strong detachments of troops appeared on trucks from Saragossa. The Polish battalions met them in a friendly manner, with machine-gun fire. The battle in Villamayor de Galero [*sic*] continued until 1700 hours, when the enemy, advancing with tanks, forced the Poles from the town. They were already running out of ammunition. At dawn the next day, the Polish battalions, reduced to 60%, began to arrive at our deployment area in groups, carrying with them their wounded and four dozen prisoners. The other captured officers had been shot by them when the prisoners refused to go with them and tried to escape under the cover of night. Separated groups of soldiers made it back through the enemy lines for four or five days more. From Saragossa, the enemy threw three camps [*sic*] of Moroccans at my division, then three battalions of infantry, then five. Rapid-fire batteries and dozens of tanks. Since my groups [*sic*] had gotten closer to Saragossa than the other groups, the enemy considered that the greatest danger to them threatened from that direction, and therefore he threw his reserves specifically at my group.[40]

For a few hours on 25 August, with the capture of Villamayor, the Republican offensive came the closest it would to ultimate success. However, Kléber was powerless to reinforce his brave Dabrowskis in the town, lacking any artillery or armour and with his 12th Garibaldi Brigade still tied down in the open ground before the Sierra de Alcubierre hill forts, he did not have the troops to push through and relieve the Slavs. Had the 12th not mistakenly got themselves pinned down on the first morning of the attack, perhaps the situation could have been saved. Despite the praise he lavishes on his 'Poles', it is clear from Kléber's account that the 13th International Brigade was badly mauled, routed from Villamayor, falling back on Republican lines in disorganised groups. Whether General Ponte in Saragossa had really panicked we do not know, but he acted swiftly and decisively, dispatching elements of his mobile brigades and the 105th Division from his reserves, enough to drive out the isolated Republicans from Villamayor. Over the next few days, Kléber was faced with additional counter-attacks, although he likely exaggerates the scale of such efforts. He did though have to contend with the attentions of Barrón's 13th Division, making any further attempt on Villamayor impossible. Thanks to a combination of blunders, weapon deficiencies and a lack of reserves, the Republic's best shot at Saragossa was lost.

At Quinto, the morning of the 25th began with a Nationalist air attack; the few outdated Heinkel 46 and 51s that were stationed at Saragossa dropped their small payloads on Republican positions, achieving little. At 8.00 am, the battle resumed, with the fighting now taking place in the streets of the town. There was bitter house-to-house fighting, sometimes hand-to-hand. The Dimitrovs, aided by the 3rd company of the Lincolns, seized first the railway station at the town's southern end, and then the well-defended cement factory opposite. The Rebels in the church continued to hold out despite being completely surrounded. A British staff officer, Tom Wintringham, one of the future founders of the Home Guard, was hit by a sniper's bullet while trying to identify a house that could be set alight from which the flames would spread to the church. American volunteer Carl Bradley led a group of ten men attempting to clear out a particularly well-fortified house:

> We went armed with nitro-glycerine bottles and took a position about eight yards from the building. We hid there and waited while the artillery pounded the building to keep the Fascist snipers away from the windows. The artillery accomplished this purpose but couldn't demolish the walls; they were too thick for that.
>
> Two of the men were wounded as we made our way to the building, and three men had to carry them back, which left only five of us to carry on. But five was enough.
>
> Each of us took a bottle of nitro-glycerine, picked out a window and bang! every bottle went home, exploding with tremendous flames inside. … Next we rolled a drum of gasoline inside with a fuse attached to it and waited until it exploded. That finished the job.[41]

However, urban combat like this inevitably meant that civilians found themselves in the line of fire. One group of Brigaders was clearing a street and came across a mother with three small children. As they were being escorted to safety, a burst of machine-gun fire swept the street, wounding one of the Lincolns. Two of the children, 'crazed by terror', ran back to their house and refused to leave:

> Much as we tried, we couldn't induce the children to leave the house. It was necessary to bring the mother back who finally brought them out.
>
> It was horrible to see little children like them going through such terrible agony and there was a big lump in our throat as we watched them being taken back to safety.[42]

Meanwhile, the British Battalion had been called up from reserve and tasked by Brigade Chief of Staff Robert Merriman with taking the intimidating Purburrel Hill.

> There was a little artillery preparation, commensurate with the report that Purburrel was not strongly held. The companies deployed and climbed the slopes of Purburrel.
>
> Then all hell let loose. The Fascist trenches near the summit became one line of continuous crackling machine-gun fire. Not an inch could

we advance in face of such a rain of steel. It was evident that our scouts had been misled. Purburrel Hill was strongly held.

Peter Daly, the gallant Irish soldier who had just been appointed to lead the battalion, was almost the first casualty. He was leading the advance, when he was hit in the stomach by a bullet. Hercules Augherinos, battalion interpreter, gathered a few comrades and brought him back under fire to a dressing-station. Daly lived for several days …

Meanwhile, Paddy O'Daire took over command of the battalion. Realising that it was suicidal to attempt to storm the hill without artillery support, he kept us there, availing of whatever cover there was, until darkness made our withdrawal possible.[43]

Captain O'Daire's cool actions saved many British lives that day, for his orders from Brigade Commander Ćopić were to hold the slopes the battalion were scattered on and from there push on up the hill. Instead, he withdrew his men at the first opportunity and demanded more support. That night, the British captured a Rebel patrol sent out from the hill in a desperate search for water. It transpired that the pipe that supplied the garrison had been cut by the Lincolns and it was only a matter of time before the 500 Nationalists stationed on Purburrel would be compelled to surrender. However, Ćopić's orders were clear; another attack would have to be made the next day. The hill had to fall so that the road to Saragossa could be opened – the British would be climbing the Purburrel again the next day.

All the while, Kléber's battlegroup was fighting hard to hold its positions among the hill forts of the Sierra de Alcubierre, coming under pressure first from General Ponte's reserves then from General Barrón's freshly arrived African troops. Whole battalions of the 45th Division's International Brigades were reduced to company size or smaller, and Kléber notes particularly the exploits of the Đuro Đaković battalion, made up of Bulgarians and Yugoslavs. This Balkan outfit was left with just fifty men (all its officers and commissars became casualties) during a desperate defence of its hill fort against the Black Hand Division, with reportedly the corpses of 800 Moroccans piling up in front of them over several days.[44] On 26 August, the day after his battlegroup's brief stay in Villamayor, Republican Chief of Staff Colonel Vicente Rojo visited Kléber's headquarters:

After my report on the course of the operation, he said, very meaningfully, 'There is still the question of whether your units were actually at Villamayor.' I did not want to answer this question at all. I asked him where the brigade he had promised me in Valencia was and where the three batteries that had been taken away from me where. To this Rojo replied, 'If you take Villamayor, you will get it all.' I rephrased his words, saying, 'If everything had been given me on time, you would be having this conversation with me today in Villamayor de Galero [*sic*], not here.'[45]

Without additional resources, especially artillery, Kléber had no hope of reaching his objective, no matter what the Republican chief of staff might say.

It was not until 4.00 pm on 26 August that the Lincolns flushed the Nationalists out of the church in Quinto. The brave defenders had held it for nearly forty-eight hours, without food or water, but were finally ejected using methods reminiscent of a Medieval siege:

The Dimitrovs who had been cleaning up the streets to the left of the church and the Lincoln-Washingtons who had been doing the same from the right now closed in and partially encircled the church, keeping all openings covered with fire. ... But one side of the church couldn't be covered because it was exposed to fire from strongly-entrenched fascist positions on a neighbouring hill. The church had a door on this side also and many Fascists escaped through it.

While we were giving covering fire the Dimitrovs broke the church door down with a beam. The Fascists immediately opened fire and started throwing hand-grenades at us. We drew to one side to be out of direct fire and then we retaliated in kind.

Next we got bundles of hay, threw them inside the church and pitched grenades on top of them trying to set them aflame. It took a long time before we succeeded.

In the meantime, another group approached the side of the church where there was a small window. A few Fascists were trying to make their get-away through that. But, realising the hopelessness of their situation, they began to surrender and we took 75 prisoners through this small window alone. ...

We kept up our fire and the Fascists, realising that they were completely trapped, all surrendered with the exception of a few officers. Carlists, Phalangists [*sic*], Civil Guards and young conscripts, they were all lined up, many of them badly wounded, many of them terror-stricken.[46]

The same day marked the final assault on Purburrel hill. This time, the British battalion was aided by a handful of tanks, the brigade anti-tank battery, the Spanish battalion of the 15th Brigade and a company of the Lincolns, which attacked the hill from the south, while the British and Spanish advanced from the east. Even with overwhelming firepower, the battle was brutal:

> The battalion was standing to at dawn. Then our artillery opened up. The Anti-tanks did marvellous work. They sent over salvos without a pause, raking the Fascist trenches, searching out the machine-gun nests, and destroying them one by one. Over one hundred shells landed in that kilometre of trenches that encircled the hill. Cheered by the visible damage our guns were doing, we began the advance.[47]

But the Nationalist machine guns kept firing and the British were once again forced to hug the bare earth, desperately seeking any cover they could find. To brigade veterans, it seemed like Mosquito Ridge all over again. With dread, they saw Italian Savoia bombers approaching. However, things took an unexpected turn:

> They believed the town and the hill were ours. They dropped their load, and scored bull's eyes- on the Fascists!
> So, naturally, the Fascists thought they were our planes. Up went the white flag in their trenches. We dashed upwards to take the surrender. The Fascists, realising their error ... hauled down the flag and opened a murderous fire. But we had profited by the incident nevertheless; we had got closer to them, without incurring serious casualties.[48]

According to some accounts, the Nationalist officers actually shot the troops who had raised the white flag, rather than it being a simple mistake. The three-day battle for the hill, and indeed for Quinto, was now reaching its climax:

> Our artillery, especially the anti-tank guns – gave them hell. The little shells went in one continuous scream over our heads and smashed the machine-gun nests. I believe the whole battle lasted five hours. But,

that day, I had no sense of time, and my memory of the sequence of events is faulty.

I remember seeing barbed wire ahead, and the brown earth of parapets. I remember Paddy O'Daire's yell: 'Charge the trench!' As we ran up the last few yards, the trench became alive. A mass of white faces, hands upstretched [*sic*] to the sky, and in cracked voices from parched throats, the cry of *'Agua! Agua!'* And here were these men we had been trying to kill a few minutes before, now drinking out of our water bottles!

Shots rang out further down the trench. It was a group of Fascist officers who had committed suicide. … The trenches stank with the smell of the dead. I came across a Fascist whose head had been completely blown off by a shell. I couldn't find the head.[49]

General Walter declared victory for his 35th Division of Internationals, claiming 350 enemy dead and 1,000 prisoners taken for the loss of only 50 killed and 269 wounded in both the 11th and 15th brigades.[50] However, these figures seem to be a piece of pure propaganda, given the fact that the British Battalion alone had lost 300 men killed, wounded or missing from 400 who had gone into battle. The brigade had fought with courage and skill to clear the town but spirits were low – it had taken too long, cost too many men and the whole offensive had lost momentum. Despite the successes of that day, Republican President Manuel Azaña recorded pessimistically in his diary that he did not think the offensive would achieve anything of note, nor even distract Franco from the north.[51] Perhaps as a result of these frustrations, at least a dozen of the prisoners taken at Quinto were shot out of hand. Several Nationalist officers were executed personally by General Walter as vengeance for the death of his friend, the polish head of 35th Division's medical services, whose body Walter rescued from no man's land.[52] Esdaile quotes a Nationalist prisoner who asserts several hundred were in fact murdered.[53] Merriman was deeply troubled by the indiscipline shown by the Republican troops, which, as well as the killings included taunting of 'brave' prisoners by German volunteers and looting of the town.[54] 44th Division, a unit in reserve, passed through Quinto the following day and amongst its ranks was a Catalan conscript named Lluís Puig. Unlike the Brigaders who had taken the town, Puig's commitment to the Republican cause was near non-existent; he was a former salesman, a staunch Catholic and sympathised with the right. His diary provides an insight into the mindset of so many in the People's Army who were either apolitical or even rightist in their leanings; they simply wanted to survive and the war to be over.[55] Having been recruited earlier in the month, following the advance of V Corps was Puig's first taste of war, and it clearly left a strong impression:

> Quinto! The village where a few hours ago Mass had been celebrated, had just fallen into the hands of the troops in the service of Russia! Quinto! A pleasant and picturesque Aragonese village was now a heap of rubble.
>
> No more than a few dozen houses could still be of any use. All around lay dead bodies, some killed by air raids, others buried under the rubble. We saw horses loose in the middle of the streets. We could hear the pitiful howling of dogs calling their masters. We saw the village without a single inhabitant. …
>
> You cannot imagine how terrible war is until you have seen what I saw with my own eyes.[56]

Battlegroup D of Lieutenant Colonel Juan Modesto had reached a point where further progress on Saragossa seemed impossible. Belchite was still holding out and on 27 August he directed Walter's 35th Division to head for the town after their success at Quinto. Líster had had no luck in taking Fuentes de Ebro; his troops had at one point entered the town but were quickly thrown out. Modesto writes of this frustrating period:

> The attempts of the Republican troops to break the enemy defense at Fuentes de Ebro and to the north of Mediana, during 27th, 28th and 29th of August, were unsuccessful because the enemy had already concentrated enough forces to contain our attacks.[57]

The Nationalist lines had been buttressed by the arrival of Sáenz de Buruaga's African troops and the impetus and momentum of the offensive had drained away. These reinforcements would also push the Listers out of Mediana and although the 11th Division managed to contain the Nationalist counter-attacks for the time being, clearly the Rebels would attempt to relieve Belchite at some point. General Pozas, overall commander of the Republican Army of the East, ordered Modesto to transfer the bulk of his available forces, namely the 35th International Division, to the Mediana sector. They were to attack the following day, 1 September, in the direction of Valmadrid, a village around 10km north of Loyalist-held Puebla de Albortón. Modesto thought this foolish; to undertake the attack, he would have to force-march his men 30km through the night and leave the problematic Belchite unconquered. The young corps commander picked up the phone and requested a day's delay in order to hold a conference with Pozas, his Chief of Staff Antonio Cordón and the main Soviet military advisor in Spain, Gregorovich.[58]

The four men met to discuss the future direction of the offensive. Pozas, a native of Saragossa, was still pushing for further attempts on the Aragonese capital, while Modesto insisted that Belchite had to be the first priority. Although he does not admit it in his account, it appears likely that Modesto had realised that Saragossa could not be taken; the offensive had run out of steam and Nationalist reinforcements were already blocking their path. The 11th Division was facing the Nationalist 150th and 52nd divisions, and the 13th was not far away; it was not a fair fight. Just a month previously at Brunete, the Republicans had kept throwing the troops forward, without any appreciable progress, only serving to exhaust and decimate their own units, leaving them vulnerable to Franco's eventual counter. If Saragossa was not to fall, better to salvage some small success from the operation, namely the capture of Belchite, than let it go the same way. Rather dramatically, Modesto announced that, 'If, despite my proposal, the Army command insisted on its order, I would comply, but I would leave with the 35th Division, taking personal command of it.'[59] Pozas relented, and the order was given to focus on Belchite.

The town was garrisoned by approximately 3,000 Nationalist troops, who had had plenty of time to dig in after being surrounded on 25 August.[60] Antony Beevor claims that there were just a few hundred men in Belchite, which Modesto could rightly have ignored as posing no threat to his rearguard.[61] However, all other accounts of the battle are clear that there were several thousand Insurgent soldiers in the town. This figure would appear far more logical given the ferocity of the struggle that was about to take place, and the fact that various units in the sector, such as the remnants of the Tercio garrisoning Codo, had fallen back on Belchite after the initial Republican assault. In this case, Modesto's reluctance to leave such a large enemy force in his rear is far more understandable, especially as Nationalist efforts to relieve the town could have been complimented by a simultaneous breakout attempt. Had the Rebels been able to rescue the garrison, one way or another, it surely would have represented a huge propaganda coup for Franco and a bitter blow to Republican morale.

Modesto therefore set up a new headquarters on La Tosqueta, a hill 274 metres high that overlooked Belchite but was also just a fifteen-minute walk to Mediana, and had been captured by the Lísters' 100th brigade on the first day of the battle. General Walter's 35th Division of International units had the unenviable mission of capturing Belchite. Meanwhile, the Listers and brigades of the 25th and 30th divisions were to hold a line running south-west from the Ebro, through Fuentes de Ebro, to Mediana and north of Puebla de Albortón. This was not a straightforward task; the main weight of 150th Division, with its feared troops of La Legion and the Regulares, was now deployed in the sector. Already, they had completed their first objective of halting the Republican drive on Saragossa from the south-east. Now they would begin a series of attacks aimed at breaking the Loyalist encirclement of Belchite. Joaquín Masjuán was amongst the Loyalist troops attempting to hold the line:

> On the 27th we retreated 2km from the crossing of the El Burgo de Ebro to Mediana highway, where we had built better fortifications.
>
> The enemy did not take long to appear with numerous troops. They intended to attack us and rescue their 2,500 men surrounded in Belchite, but all their attempts were useless.
>
> Again and again we stopped their attacks. On each occasion they had hundreds of casualties, and although their aviation and artillery bombarded us, they also failed to break us.[62]

Fighting raged from 30 August to 6 September, as strong Nationalist forces, including elements of the three divisions, well supported from the air, pushed hard to rescue their beleaguered comrades.

During the last days of August, fierce fighting had continued in the Sierra de Alcubierre, north of the Ebro. Five fortified hilltops changed hands repeatedly as the under-resourced Battlegroup B of General Kléber struggled in vain to repeat their earlier feat of coming within 6km of Saragossa. The Moroccan Regulares of the Nationalist 13th Division were proving wily opponents, however. Kléber was finally receiving reinforcements, but only in penny packets, and unfortunately for the Romanian, not of the quality of his Slavic International units: 'these were anarchist battalions and battalions of new recruits.'[63] One surprisingly useful outfit that he did acquire was 100 cavalrymen, albeit without their horses, who Kléber claims were mostly former White Russians. Fifth Regiment veteran Antonio Candela encountered some of these men during the Saragossa campaign:

From militia to People's Army – the transformation of Republican forces from the badly organised militia bands of 1936 (**1**) to something approaching a regular army by summer 1937 (**2**).

(3) Troops of the People's Army's 46th Division reviewed by (from left to right) Republican Prime Minister Juan Negrín, President Manuel Azaña, General José Miaja, Major Valentín González (El Campesino), and Major Enrique Líster.

(4) Chief of the General Staff of the People's Army Colonel (later General) Vicente Rojo, visiting the front.

(5) Major Attlee Company, British Battalion. Named after the Labour Party leader, commander Sam Wild is in black crouched by the Maxim machine gun.

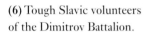

(6) Tough Slavic volunteers of the Dimitrov Battalion.

(7) Men of the Machine Gun Company of the Abraham Lincoln Battalion.

International Brigaders: Fred Copeman (**8, top left**), Royal Navy mutineer and commander of the British Battalion at Brunete; Bill Alexander (**9, top right**), industrial chemist and British Battalion commander at Teruel; Robert Merriman (**10, bottom left**), Economics doctoral student and chief of staff of 15th International Brigade at Belchite; and Milton Wolff (**11, bottom right**), machine-gunner then Lincoln-Washington Battalion commander in 1938.

(12) Ernest Hemingway (centre) conversing with officers of the German-Austrian 11th Thälmann International Brigade.

(13) General José Miaja, 'Saviour of Madrid'.

Nationalist commanders: the Caudillo and Generalíssimo Francisco Franco **(14)** and General José Enrique Varela (seated) with staff **(15)**.

(16 & 17) Propaganda shots of the Nationalist army's advance on Madrid, autumn 1936.

The Rebel elite: General Miguel Cabanellas salutes Moroccan Regulares (18); 'Bridegrooms of Death' Foreign Legionnaires resting at Navalcarnero (19).

The Nazi Condor Legion in Spain: Messerschmitt Bf 109 (**20**), Junkers Ju 87 Stukas (**21**), Heinkel He 111 being armed (**22**), and Flak 36 88mm cannon (**23**).

(24) Major Enrique Líster (centre) with men from his famous 11th Division during the Brunete campaign.

(25 & 26) Lieutenant Colonel Juan Modesto, commander of V Corps, overseeing operations at Brunete.

(27) Major Valentín González, El Campesino, directing Republican troops on horseback during the advance on Quijorna.

The Battle of Brunete: a Soviet-built T-26 passing through Villanueva de la Cañada (28); British machine-gun crews in action (29); the ruins of Villanueva de la Cañada, the church steeple housed an AT gun (30); and Republican transports under bombardment on the road to Brunete (31).

(32) The Belchite siege; the fortified Purburrel Hill outside Quinto.

(33) The old town of Belchite today; the San Martín parish church is visible the background.

(34 & 35) Exterior and interior of the San Agustín, stormed by the Lincolns on 4 September 1937.

(36) Republican troops advance confidently into Teruel, December 1937.

(37) The diversion: Republicans pose with a captured Nationalist placard celebrating the anticipated fall of Madrid to Franco's shelved winter offensive.

(38) People's Army machine-gunner killed in the hills around Teruel.

(39) A T-26 abandoned in the snow.

(40) Republican troops fighting house to house in the city itself.

(41) A Carlist Requeté of the Navarrese Corps in a snowbound Teruel trench, February 1938.

(42) A lone soldier advances on the Teruel bullring.

(43) 'Liberation': Nationalist troops enter the ruined outskirts of Madrid, March 1939, as the populace look on.

One of them was telling me that they were Russians. I was very surprised. I knew that there were Russian technicians teaching Spaniards how to manage complicated armaments and how to fly aircraft, but I did not know that there were Russians in the infantry as well. One of them, seeing that I had been taken aback, hastened to say that they were 'White Russians'. Then I thought, were not the White Russians the Czarist troops who fought against the Bolsheviks? 'So! I take it that you are Fascists?' I said in a very confused voice. … 'But,' he added quickly, 'we are White Russians because we fought against the Bolsheviks. We all want to go back to our country, however, and Stalin has said that if we fight for the Spanish Republic and win this war, we will be able to go back and live there freely.' I was not sure if what I was hearing was true or whether they were pulling my leg, so I asked a Spanish sergeant … 'Of course,' he replied, 'they are White Russians but they are fighting on our side and I can tell you that they are darned good fighters. They are very fine comrades, and we get on very well together.'[64]

According to the account of their commander, Kléber, this unlikely band of exiled horseless cavalrymen acquitted themselves well in the battle, but it was to no avail:

A night assault by these cavalrymen succeeded in pushing the enemy out of the most important fort on Petruso Hill. At night, we began to improve the fortifications at the fort for ourselves. In order to have some reserves free for further action, I pulled the cavalrymen back at night and sent a battalion of anarchists attached to my group into the fort. At dawn the enemy carried out a counteroffensive on the fort with ten tanks. It did not take fifteen minutes before the battalion of anarchists fled from the fort in panic, leaving it to the enemy practically without a fight.[65]

One such Nationalist effort to drive Kléber's men back was launched by the veteran Foreign Legion officer Carlos Iniesta, in temporary command of the 4th Bandera of La Legion. Having dispatched a company and machine-gun section to Zuera to halt Battlegroup A, Iniesta found his unit deployed alongside a Tabor of Moroccan Regulares, whose captain the Legionnaire struck up a friendship with. On 29 August, these two units, supported by five tanks, assaulted a set of Republican-held heights known as Los Galados, close to Perdiguera. Iniesta later wrote:

Hours before starting our attack and knowing the tenacious resistance of the reds in that position, the captain of Regulares told me jokingly: 'Today I think it's going to be a bad day. I think we are going to have a very hard fight, one of these combats in which it would be good to receive a wound, not a serious one, at the beginning, which would be the equivalent of a permit to enjoy some rest.'[66]

Just ten minutes into the Rebel assault, a runner informed Iniesta that the Regulares captain had indeed been wounded and the young Legionnaire found himself in command of both units. As he climbed over the parapet to lead the charge, Iniesta was hit:

I received three bullets: one, in the upper part of my forehead, over my left eye, which, although it was not serious – for it only chipped the bone – it was alarming at first because of the abundant blood that was spurting out. And at the same time the other two bullets caused a bad wound with great tissue destruction and bleeding at a considerable pressure in the right thigh.

One of the two bullets – destroyed because, apparently, it must have hit the stony ground before injuring me – was lodged next to the femur.

The doctor of the Bandera hurried immediately to stop the haemorrhage by placing a firm tourniquet – much more painful, by the way, than the wound – and then I was evacuated on a stretcher to the area protected from fire, from which the ambulances made the transfer to the hospital in Saragossa.[67]

Clearly, although the Republicans could advance no farther, the fight was just as tough and bloody for some of the finest troops in Franco's army.

During the march to Belchite, the British Battalion of the 15th International Brigade was ordered to change direction and march on Mediana. There was a real fear that the Republican forces there would give way in the face of the ongoing Nationalist counter-attacks, after which, the road to Belchite would be clear. The British were naturally unhappy about being divided from their brigade comrades and dispirited by the heavy losses sustained at Quinto, which had included the battalion's commander and commissar. A minor mutiny took place in which a number of soldiers refused to go to Mediana and a party meeting had to be held to agree on the order, almost like the workers' militias of 1936. Eventually, the battalion complied and dug in on broken hills overlooking the village, which the Listers had lost to Rebel forces, almost immediately having to repel an enemy attack. Walter Gregory describes the battalion's experience:

> The fighting at Mediana was short and sharp, and we were able to inflict heavy casualties on the Nationalist troops before they were forced to fall back on Mediana. Now that we knew that the besieged Belchite garrison would remain so for a while, the British Battalion was drawn up in a cordon overlooking Mediana lest another attempt to relieve Belchite be made later.[68]

For the length of the battle for the town, the British and other Republican forces held the line against 'a monotonous succession' of Insurgent attacks and Loyalist counters, their sleep interrupted by two night raids and dramatic thunder storms that illuminated the countryside. When the British were finally relieved after Belchite's fall, the battalion was in 'less than pristine condition'.[69] El Campesino's 46th Division had also joined the fray and penetrated north of Puebla de Albortón to the edge of the village of Jaulín, the closest Battlegroup D got to Saragossa, but was quickly pushed back. Back-and-forth fighting continued inconclusively, with the Nationalists unable to break through to Belchite, nor the Republicans having any real hope of advancing on Saragossa. Antonio Candela vividly described how the hills around Mediana were no less deadly than the streets of Belchite:

> While we were issuing rations to the troops, the enemy artillery started to shell our positions. We threw ourselves to the ground. The soldier lying next to me raised his head, saying, 'Look at that shell flying. Hell, it is going slow.' Then, looking to his right side, he realised in horror that the flying object had not been a shell but his own lieutenant's head. In his terror he went white as a sheet, and I must admit to feeling sick to my stomach. Neither of us could say a word for quite a while; we both lay shaking.[70]

At the same time, Lluís Puig's unit had moved up to relieve some of Líster's tired troops opposite Fuentes. On his way to the front for the first time, Puig had managed to persuade some American volunteers to give him a steel helmet, and the Brigaders had left a decidedly good impression on the committed Catholic.[71] Very soon, he was more than grateful for the gift, as his hilltop observation post came under fire:

> They spotted us from the Nationalist trenches and fired a mortar at us. It fell a few feet away from me and gave me a huge fright. Fortunately, the fact that I was wearing my helmet saved me from the fallout of stones and shrapnel which bounced off it. In order to avoid another one being fired at me, I ran and took refuge behind a rock.[72]

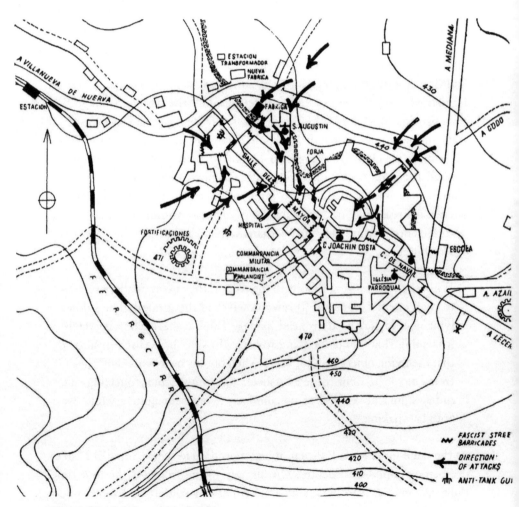

Map 6: The fighting within Belchite.

On 1 September, the same day that Puig was experiencing his first aerial bombardment, Ćopić's 15th International Brigade, minus the British Battalion, began the attack on Belchite. It may only have been a small medieval town of 4,000, but it was a daunting objective to say the least, and brigade Chief of Staff Major Bob Merriman was apprehensive.[73] The garrison was several thousand strong, numerous buildings had been fortified, most notably the churches, machine-gun nests and trenches criss-crossed the town, as did underground tunnels linking the strongpoints, and Nationalist artillery emplacements were dotted around the outskirts and on street corners, firing over open sights. First, the Republican armour was sent into the town, but putting tanks in an urban environment always leaves them vulnerable. Following air and artillery bombardment, the streets were filled with rubble and it soon became clear this would be a job for the infantry of the Dimitrov, Lincoln-Washington and 24th Spanish battalions. Close artillery support was provided by the British-manned brigade anti-tank battery, whose three Soviet 45mm guns fired 2,700 shells on the first two days alone.[74] American volunteer Dave Engels describes his first experience at Belchite, occupying trenches just outside the town:

> These trenches were very shallow, just deep enough to give us cover if we lay down. Once in, we had to lie there all day without food or water. The position was only about sixty yards from the enemy and completely exposed; it was impossible to bring up supplies. The Fascists in the outlying houses raked us with enfilading fire; everybody who as much as sat up in the trench was certain to draw fire instantly.[75]

Milton Wolff's Maxim machine guns were also on the edge of Belchite, trying to suppress one of the Rebel strongpoints. He relates what happened next vividly in his autobiographical novel *Another Hill*, written in the third person with himself as 'Mitch':

> There was a stone retaining wall that held a terrace sloping up to where a church sat, its tower commanding the surrounding terrain … there was a large ragged opening that had been punched in the thick wall by artillery fire. The fascists were in the church, according to Manny. The guns inside had to be silenced for the rifle companies to move into town.[76]

Wolff positioned his three Finnish-American gun crews along a wall to the left of a dirt road, but soon they came under deadly sniper fire:

Before the Finn could fire a burst, there was a sharp snapping sound and the Finn's face disappeared. He fell away from the gun, as though someone had jerked him from behind and sent him sprawling.

Before Mitch could say anything, one of the men pulled the dead man gently aside and himself got behind the gun. The same thing happened to him. A loud snap and he was gone.[77]

An Insurgent sniper in the church was clearly targeting the tiny aiming aperture in the Maxim's gun shield. The third member of the crew took over, with Wolff now watching the shell hole in the church for a muzzle flash. Once again, the sniper scored a direct hit, but this time, the American had seen the flash, deep inside the church:

Holding the image in his mind's eye, he straddled the dead Finn. The gun grips were warm and sweaty. The son-of-a-bitching MG was sighted too low. He unlocked the elevating screw and the traverse clamp and swung the muzzle upward, not bothering to sight in, for he knew that there was no time. A bullet clanged off the shield; moving the gun had saved his ass. He opened fire – a sustained burst and then a short one, and another and another.[78]

The sniper was silenced.

The first couple of days saw intense fighting but little progress and high casualties for both sides, but particularly the exposed Republican attackers. The Lincoln's 2nd Company lost their adjutant and commissar, the 3rd their commander and his adjutant. The 1st Company was pinned down at a series of terraces leading into the town from the Azaila road. Major Merriman demanded that the assault proceed, but the Lincoln-Washington commander Hans Amlie, a Dakotan miner, could not bring himself to ask the men to go forward in the face of withering fire:

the orders kept coming and Captain Amlie kept pocketing the orders. … This one attack, when my platoon leader was killed, twenty-two men started out. None of them made it. Two survived. That was the thing that led to the situation where Hans Amlie would not tell the men to continue the advance.[79]

Very soon, Amlie was a casualty, shot in the head, although not fatally. So too would be Brigade Commissar Steve Nelson, who was sent to reason with the Lincolns' captain:

Amlie's temper was fully as bad as Bob's. 'What the hell is the matter with you guys?' he shouted at me. 'Go forward? How can we go forward? The town's bristling with machine guns. You want to slaughter the whole damn battalion? Where's the artillery?'

'I don't know,' I said, 'but the guys can't stay where they are. And the antitanks can't hang around all day shooting snipers out of the window for us.'[80]

The attack had to go on.

2 September saw a surprise visit to the front; Juan Modesto returned to his hilltop HQ to find Spain's most famous Communist, La Pasionaria, Dolores Ibárruri, awaiting him. The fiery woman's first words to Battlegroup D's commander were, characteristically:

'When are you going to take Belchite?'

'We are on it comrade Dolores.'

'Then I will stay until we get it.'[81]

With some persuasion, she agreed to take Modesto's tent, but was far keener to visit the besieged town:

House by house, street by street, our soldiers were taking the city, demolishing the desperate resistance of the enemy. A flag was placed in every important spot taken in the town by Republican combatants. From Modesto's headquarters situated on the side of a small hill outside the city we could see the flags that marked the progress of the battle.

The seminary at the entrance to the city, converted into a fortress by the Rebels, was destroyed; the Civil Guard barracks were assaulted. Our job was to win every important building where the enemy was holding out. The church and the town hall were the last two points of enemy resistance. When I entered Belchite fighting was still going on.

While crossing a street through a mountain of smouldering ruins, I came face to face with General Walter, who was preparing his men to take the town hall. He instructed me to turn back and stay out of the city until the enemy was completely routed. There were still many snipers hidden among the ruins.

I returned to Modesto's headquarters and in a short while the first prisoners of war began to arrive, soldiers and civilians along with a group of priests dressed in street clothes. All expected to be shot without mercy now they were in the hands of the 'reds'. The stories told about Republican forces by the fascist propaganda would have put to shame the most hair-raising stories about vampires or cannibals.[82]

Rather comically, La Pasionaria conversed with these rural rightists without them recognising her, and they informed her that Dolores Ibárruri was more a beast than a woman, and that she looked like a man. Many other Nationalists were of course still fighting within Belchite, and it was not just the ranks of the People's Army that endured great losses and hardship. One such soldier trapped in the town was Joaquín Moreno, who had volunteered for a Falangist Bandera in Saragossa at the war's outbreak. He later wrote his memoirs, like Milton Wolff, in the third person, with 'Lucas' taking Moreno's place in the story:

> At sunset, Lucas enters a half-demolished house. Looking for water. And when he snoops among the rubble, he seems to hear faint moans. In the shadows he sees a fallen body. From the uniform he notices that he is an enemy and he seems to ask for help. … He offers him a little water from his canteen, which he eagerly drinks. But instantly his head drops and turns white. Lucas' eyes are wet, he leaves the body gently on the ground and rushes outside, where the tragic dance of fratricidal combat continues.

The following day, one of Moreno's comrades is killed in an explosion while manning a mortar:

> A Galician soldier, friend of Lucas, nice and likeable, has been stuck like a puppet to the wall, held by a thick piece of shrapnel from the mortar tube that has pierced his head. Several corpses surround the base of the weapon, among them that of the mayor, Ramón Alfonso Trallero [the Falangist mayor of Belchite participated in the fighting and was killed during the battle]. And Lucas has no tears left to express his pain.[83]

Belchite was not Brunete, and so the air arms of both sides could not dominate the battlefield and terrorise ground units in quite the same way among the hills and valleys of Aragon as the Nationalists had on the wide open plains outside Madrid. As a result, air power did not play the decisive role that it had done in the previous battle. The Duke of Lerma, aristocratic Nationalist pilot, had just been trained to fly fighters and was transferred to Saragossa on 4 September. Flying a Heinkel 51 fighter-bomber, he was:

> kept hard at work strafing the red positions and road transports. The enemy was well supplied with quick-firing 20mm and 40mm A.A. guns, which made things very unpleasant for us as we swept down to ground level. Shells which looked like flaming rockets came swishing up to meet us in great numbers. One could see them coming all the way, which added to our discomfort. We had a rude, unprintable name for these.[84]

He, and the other Nationalist air reinforcements to Aragon, faced a tough aerial battle as well as frequent ground attack sorties to disrupt and harass the enemy, and Lerma describes how on returning from each mission, their fuselages were riddled and splintered. On one such strafing run, the duke spotted a Republican dispatch rider, a tiny black speck leaving a huge cloud of dust down the road:

> I pulled my machine over sharply and pointed her nose in a shallow dive down the road, coming up straight behind the motorcycle. The rider must have realised I was behind him (what a nightmare!) even before I started firing, for he started to zigzag crazily, trying to reach the cover of farm buildings just ahead. I pressed the trigger when I was within 150 metres, and bullets began spitting down the road, throwing up small puffs of dust right up to him. He then made a high somersault straight into a ditch. It looked so comic from the air, but I imagine the poor devil did not think so, if he lived to tell the tale, which I doubt. I hoped he was carrying an important dispatch.[85]

Fighting was still raging further north, where various Republican units were endeavouring to prevent the Nationalists from relieving Belchite. Having only been at the front a couple of days, Lluís Puig's 143rd Brigade of Catalan conscripts got its first taste of battle on 3 September:

> At night, one of our soldiers, a man from Mataró, crossed the lines to the other side. The news had a great effect on the Staff as they thought he would tell those opposite that we were recently called up and that

we were losing our bottle. They were not wrong and not an hour had passed before the enemy started shooting at us fiercely. I was afraid and hid at the bottom of the trench. The bullets whistled and cracked above me, some landing right in the trench. Mortars fell and bombs exploded. Orders were shouted and the soldiers had to take shelter. Next to me I had one who did not stop shouting and swearing. Indeed, more than shouting he was wailing. He was shooting without respite and throwing hand grenades one after another. He realised I was curled up in the hole and called me a chicken because I was not defending myself against the enemy which was approaching. He ordered me to go and get some hand grenades immediately. I brought him a big box so that he would not bother me any more. He was a volunteer from Madrid who had come to reinforce our Battalion. I could hear the Jefe shouting my name and others, but I turned a deaf ear. … It all made such a racket. It seemed as if everything was collapsing around me. The artillery was also in action. The firing lasted about fifteen minutes after which it quietened down until it ended up with isolated gunshots. Then I came out and I reported 'diligently', offering to do whatever was necessary. I was not told off.

It seemed they understood. Quite a few of us had gone missing. Nonetheless they gave me a report to take to one of the companies. There were no casualties but some escaped home.[86]

The problems implicit in using conscription in a civil war were stark, and clearly the motivation and commitment of many soldiers who found themselves in the People's Army did not come close to matching that of the International Brigades and units such as the Listers. Nevertheless, the line held and Belchite remained under siege.

By 4 September, General Walter's men had adopted a more methodical approach to seizing Belchite, with six T-26 tanks, the 45mm guns of the anti-tank battery and the various battalions of the 15th International Brigade working in unison. The outlying buildings had fallen and the fight was very much now in the streets and houses of the town. Key defence points were the churches of San Agustín and San Martín, the town hall and the military command post. The main target that day was the same church before which Milton Wolff had lost his gun crews, the San Agustín. Referred to in some accounts as a cathedral due to its size, it was the main barrier to the advance of the Lincoln–Washington Battalion. The jumping-off point for the attack was a small, one-storey factory just 45 metres from the church, which had been taken by the Dimitrovs the day before. Careful reconnaissance had revealed that the Rebels holding the San Agustín ran out the main doors whenever the church was being bombarded, before quickly running back in when the artillery stopped to man their posts. Two American attacks had failed in this manner, with the Nationalists getting back into the church before the Lincolns could reach it. On the third attempt, the Lincolns creeped as close as they dared while the tanks and AT guns pounded the exterior. Machine guns suppressed the surrounding houses so that the storming parties would not be exposed to Insurgent fire. It was a daring but also well-orchestrated attack. Milton Wolff abandoned his Maxims to join the rush on the church:

> They made their way through a shell hole in the wall, then raced to reach the back entrance, its one door open and held in place by a bent iron hinge. Each man knew it was a matter of life and death to get into the church before the fascists could get back.
>
> The interior of the church surprised Mitch, because there was no smoke or stink of exploded shells. Many holes, big and small, breached the thick walls. …
>
> 'Here they come,' Manny whispered.
>
> Mitch saw them clearly, crowding through the huge wooden doors that now hung lopsidedly inside the front entryway. Some were in uniform, with and without helmets, others in white shirts and blue trousers. …
>
> 'Don't let them back in!' Manny sounded like one of the street kids in Brooklyn. … Mitch and the others rushed forward, shouting *'Viva la Republica! Viva!'* Forgetting to use their weapons, they charged the fascists, who panicked, pushing and shoving in retreat.

Perhaps feeling guilt over compelling his men to push ever forward, Bob Merriman led another of the groups assaulting the San Agustín, and played a key role, as one historian described:

> As he ran forward a grenade exploded nearby, and a few splinters tore into his face and arms. Comrades shouted at him to go back but he refused, and with blood streaming from his wounds he led his troops forward until they swarmed into the cathedral, driving the Rebels out into the plaza and down the open streets where many of them were shot

down and the survivors at last surrendered. Only then did Merriman let himself be led back to the medics to dress his open wounds.[87]

With the church taken in the afternoon, the key to the town's defences was unlocked. The brigade began to move deep into the town from the north and clear it out systematically:

> We were organised into groups to clean up the town street by street, house by house. Each group had grenadiers, riflemen, and men carrying dry twigs and gasoline to set fire to houses where they encountered resistance. When a house was occupied we would put up a red blanket, mattress or bunting in the window to show that the house was ours. Major Merriman and Captain Phil Detro, both good pitchers, could be seen all over the place handgrenading the Fascists.
>
> It was a tough job. The Fascists were resisting fiercely and we were fighting our way from street to street all that night and all next day. We didn't have a minute's rest for two or three days and nights in a row, and we were all groggy with sleep.[88]

At the end of the day, the Republicans held most of Belchite, with Rebels still clinging on to the town hall and the San Martín parish church.

At the same time, Kléber's Battlegroup B had been brought to a standstill in the Sierra de Alcubierre. The Romanian Red Army veteran quite simply lacked the resources to overcome the Nationalist hill forts, reinforced as they were with Barrón's skilful Moroccan troops. After two weeks of chaotic, back-and-forth combat, offensive action was called off and the Republicans switched on to the defensive. In the end, the 45th Division had to satisfy itself with holding two of the five forts, at a cost of 800 casualties for the impressive 13th Dabrowski International Brigade and 250 for the 12th Garibaldis, mostly suffered on the first day when they had mistakenly become pinned down in the open.[89] Villamayor, so tantalisingly close to Saragossa, was a distant memory. General Walter of 35th Division, writing a stern critique of the battle for his superiors in Moscow some months later, bemoaned the futility of Kléber's operation: 'the 45th Division sat around marking time with the half-demoralised and unbattleworthy 12th Garibaldi Brigade and with the 13th Polish [sic] Brigade, which was senselessly, futilely but profusely bleeding.'[90]

Casualties had indeed been high among a clearly talented unit, but all for the paltry return of a few kilometres of insignificant ground and a couple of hilltops.

5 September was to prove the decisive day in Belchite; the parish church of San Martín was captured and the Nationalists were squeezed into a pocket just a few hundred metres across. As the screw was tightened, the garrison made several attempts to break out, all of which failed. With Rebel morale clearly flagging, the newly appointed brigade commissar, 27-year-old Dave Doran from Albany, New York, had a bright idea. Commandeering a propaganda truck with loudspeakers, he wrote a brief speech with the help of a Spanish interpreter and delivered it to the Rebels holed up in the town hall:

> Doran's speech was terrifying in its directness. It stripped the political issues involved to their barest elements until every word became a sledgehammer smashing through sandbags, barbed wire fortifications, battering away on the barricades. It was the heavy artillery of the science of politics … and it laid down a psychological barrage on the most vital centres of resistance.[91]

The commissar refuted the lies about relief that had been broadcast on Nationalist radio, extolled the virtues of the Republic for the common man and ended on a severe threat: 'If you hold out you are doomed. You will all die. There is no escape for you. If you don't come over you will all be killed in the morning.'[92]

One wounded Rebel soldier came over the barricades seeking first aid, but Doran turned him away, demanding he persuade his comrades to surrender first. Half an hour passed with tension mounting before suddenly, the street was filled with 350 Francoist soldiers who gave themselves up in a mass surrender. The writing was on the wall for the shattered remnants of Belchite's brave defenders and a final, desperate breakout attempt was made. On the night of 5/6 September, the 24th Spanish battalion of the 15th International Brigade fought the last action of the siege of Belchite. A group of civilians approached their positions, but when challenged to identify themselves, it transpired that hidden amongst them were Nationalist officers in civilian dress. Lieutenant Hernández y Alcalá recalls:

> The whole affair had taken us by surprise. Then, we had hesitated too much for fear of killing civilians. So the Fascists were able to attack us first. But when it came to a fight at close quarters it was a fight between the Fascist officers and us. Some succeeded in slipping past us, but the

Dimitrov Battalion rounded them up and disposed of them. We also discovered that the Fascist officers had split up into two parties and were trying to break out at two points.

It was terrible fighting for the time it lasted. But every one of the officers met his fate.

One of their commanders was using a dagger as well as a pistol. One of our comrades pluckily wrestled with him and killed him with his own dagger. ...

It was only afterwards when, covered with the blood from our own wounds and those of the enemy, we found out that to us had fallen the task of despatching the last and most tyrannical of the Fascist garrison of Belchite.[93]

As the morning of 6 September dawned, Belchite was in Republican hands. Virtually the entire Nationalist garrison of 3,000 men was either killed or captured, with just a handful escaping in night-time breakout attempts. They had sold their lives dearly and the Loyalists had paid a heavy price to take a town that was now a ruin. Marion Merriman, the wife of the 15th Brigade chief of staff, who performed administrative roles back at base, visited with her husband a short while later:

As we passed a little factory, huge sewer rats scurried into a drain beside the road. They were as large as cats. Even though it was two weeks later, the smell of burned flesh still hung faint and nauseating in the cool dusk. Their forces had far outnumbered ours, but the Fascists had not even attempted to dispose of their dead. They left hundreds of decaying corpses stacked in various buildings.[94]

The scenes that greeted Republican medics when they entered the Rebel hospital in the town were, distressingly, just as bad, with two wounded to a mattress, the floor slimy with blood and vomit and tourniquets turned hard from dried blood.[95] After the war, General Franco decreed that Belchite would not be rebuilt, but instead serve as a monument to the tremendous battle fought there. Its old town still lies in ruins today, much the same as it did after the civil war, a stark reminder of a time when Spain was shattered physically and psychologically.

While troops from both sides had been suffering great hardship in the heat, dust and rubble of Belchite, often short on food and, more importantly, water, Nationalist pilots behind the lines were living the high life. The Duke of Lerma may have been flying dangerous missions by day, but at night, he and his comrades enjoyed themselves without regard for the sufferings of their comrades. 'Saragossa was so gay,' he tells us:

> you would never have thought that the front lines were only a few miles away and that the city was in danger of being captured. The morale of the civilian population was very high. The nightclubs, chiefly the Royal, had a rough time. Whenever a party got wild, which was very often, heads were broken.[96]

Meanwhile, the Republican air force continued to keep the Nationalists busy. They had a found a use for the otherwise obsolete Russian R-5 reconnaissance biplane, namely night raids on Saragossa. The squadron went over one aircraft at a time at twenty-minute intervals for the whole night, dropping their paltry payloads, and keeping both anti-aircraft gunners and the civilian population on edge from dusk until dawn. After their successes, the squadron adopted as their emblem a bat silhouette across a crescent moon.[97]

Officially, Army of the East commander General Pozas had called a halt to proceedings on 15 September, although local Nationalist counter-attacks continued throughout the month. Many of the battered Republican assault units were withdrawn for some much-needed rest and recuperation. In most accounts of the battle, it is seen as to the People's Army's detriment that the capture of Belchite took so long and appeared to drain so much of the offensive's fighting power. Many historians end their story of this campaign with the Republican forces exhausted by the battle for the town and unable to push on further. However, as we have seen, the struggle for Belchite only directly involved the 15th International Brigade, and even then, only three battalions – the Lincoln-Washingtons, the Dimitrovs and the Spanish battalion. While certainly other units will have been on hand, holding the ring around the town, most of Modesto's forces were in fact further north, holding back repeated Nationalist attempts to break through to Belchite's rescue. For the majority of the battle, the majority of Battlegroup D was on the line from Fuentes–Rodén–Mediana–Puebela de Albortón, desperately fighting to prevent General Buruaga and his Army of Africa reinforcements from relieving the town. This is where the attacking power of the Saragossa offensive was drained away, not in the gruelling fight for the streets of

Belchite. Meanwhile, small-scale operations along this line continued throughout September. One such limited offensive was carried out by Lluís Puig's 143rd Brigade on 26 September:

> Thus, at five o'clock [in the morning] on the dot our artillery started to fire at the enemy positions. Several batteries were involved and I had to count the number of shells fired. Tanks were going to help our infantry. Men were very nervous. Almost the whole of the Staff were next to me, watching the attack which in a few minutes' time was going to build up. I had already counted 970 cannon shots; it was morning when they gave the signal to attack. The machine guns began crackling. Our soldiers came out from the trenches and within a few moments, enemy mortars rained down on them. It was impossible to move as the ground was covered with corpses. The Company Commanders ordered a retreat. The tanks fled because they were under constant fire from the Nationalist anti-tank guns and grenades.
>
> The jefes [leaders] were nervous. … They ordered us to come out again and attack but the soldiers refused. … Many had fallen and we had advanced very little. The attack had failed.
>
> The Fascist trenches were animated. We could hear cries of victory. The shouting of *'Franco! Franco! Franco!'* could be heard and the name of Spain repeated many times with deafening *'Vivas!'*
>
> The Nationalist Air Force appeared. Three squadrons of Junkers [Ju 52s] could be seen. Overcome with panic we all took to our shelters, and it was just in time because moments later a series of heavy bombs fell around us. The whole shelter shook and with every bomb that fell our hearts jumped. Our eardrums took a beating as the artefacts exploded. Next to me was a good companion from Mataró, called Coma; he was frail and at every bomb that fell he went into a state of panic and, hardly able to breathe, he would grab me saying: 'Puig, I can't breathe, I need air! I'm dying …!' I would answer: 'Don't be afraid, Coma. Don't you see that I'm alright. If I was worried, then you should be frightened …' But with all sincerity, I was suffering a lot as well, as at every explosion a strong blast of air rushed through the refuge which made me lose my breath and my bearings. What an earthquake!![98]

This botched attack, which enjoyed armour and artillery support, highlights the poor quality of many of the new conscript-heavy formations, and their officers, which made up the majority of the hastily constructed People's Army.

Colonel Segismundo Casado took over command of the sector mid-way through the month, with most units in the sector now reorganised as XXI Corps under his leadership. He and Defence Minister Prieto were keen to attempt another attack on Saragossa. The chief reason was that the Northern zone remained in grave danger – something had to be done to relieve the pressure. A plan was hatched for an attack on Fuentes de Ebro, which, if successful, could clear the road to the Aragonese capital. A brand-new unit was to act as the spearhead, the International Tank Regiment. The regiment was comprised of a small number of Russian crews but mostly Spanish and International Brigader personnel who had just returned from a training course at the Gorky Tank School in the Soviet Union. They were equipped with forty-eight BT-5 fast cruiser tanks, Russian copies of an American design, which had been shipped in that summer. The BT-5 was capable of speeds of 45mph and was equipped with the powerful 45mm gun found on the T-26s in Spain. Soviet advisors were confident that the BT was the best tank the war had yet seen and had high hopes of the International Tank Regiment proving itself a success. A conference was called to discuss the proposals attended by Pozas, Cordón and Modesto, amongst others. Modesto claims he raised objections, which were ignored, and that he initially refused to lead the attack, only to be compelled by Casado.[99]

The list of flaws with the Fuentes operation of 13 October is almost too long to recount and betrays gross incompetence on the part of Republican planners. The International Tank Regiment were brought up 50km the night before the attack (in order to maintain the element of surprise) and thus were not given a chance to survey the ground they would be attacking over, nor train with the infantry they would be working with. The tanks were to go in along a narrow front between the Saragossa road and the Ebro River, where the ground was wet and boggy after heavy rainfall. The town was well-defended, having been under assault on-and-off since 24 August, and high-quality Nationalist units held the line. Finally, the element of surprise that the Republicans had enjoyed at the beginning of the campaign had clearly dissipated now that the sector had been active for close to two months. In his memoir, admittedly with the benefit of hindsight, Líster labels it 'one of the stupidest operations of the whole war'.[100] The 24th Spanish Battalion of 15th International Brigade was to ride the tanks into combat, while the rest of the brigade would attack between Fuentes and the Ebro River. In the intervening period since Belchite, the International Brigades had undergone some reorganisation, the 15th losing the renowned Dimitrov battalion to the 13th Dabrowski Brigade. To replace them, the now entirely anglophone 15th received the new Mackenzie-Papineau Battalion, a nominally Canadian but in fact majority American unit that had trained over the summer under Robert Merriman's tutelage. The brigades of Líster's 11th Division would advance to the west of the town towards Valmadrid. Further smaller-scale pushes would be made north of the Ebro from the ground gained by Battlegroups A and B; Casado was launching almost all his forces into the attack.

Unsurprisingly, things started to unravel quickly. The supposed preliminary barrage amounted to little more than some desultory artillery salvos at around 10.00 am. Eighteen R-5 biplanes dropped their bombs around noon. It was not until 1.30 pm that the BT-5s came roaring into view. The tanks moved so quickly that many of the unfortunate Spanish troops, clinging on for dear life, were thrown off or fell under the treads. One Republican unit had not been warned that the tanks would be passing through their lines and actually fired on the BTs, creating further confusion. Once over the lines, the tanks continued to race forward, well ahead of the supporting infantry attacks, but found themselves stuck – in sugarcane fields, irrigation ditches and before an escarpment of 3–4 metres height. Nationalist artillery and anti-tank guns had easy targets and the tanks became 'tombs for their crews'.[101] One Canadian tanker, William Kardash, later described the disaster, explaining that once his BT reached the Nationalist lines, any infantry still hanging on were shot off. Then, the tank was set alight by a Molotov cocktail and Kardash's crewmates were gunned down as they bailed out. Kardash himself was hit by a grenade but managed to haul himself aboard one of the retreating tanks.[102] As the day wore on, many of the BTs took it upon themselves to limp back to Republican lines, although there was no overall control. The fiasco had cost the International Tank Regiment nineteen of their forty-eight vehicles, with more damaged and a third of the crews killed or wounded.[103] Puig's Brigade was stationed on the flank of the attack and the Catalan conscript witnessed the debacle:

> It was sad but fascinatingly impressive to see dozens of tanks ripping through everything and making straight for the Nationalist positions above Fuentes itself. They destroyed the barbed-wire fences and made their way to positions above the trenches. At that moment Franco's troops came out defending themselves like bulls throwing powerful hand grenades. It was such an unequal battle. Steel monsters fighting against men! However, our infantry failed. The volunteers of the Líster Brigade

did not come out of their trenches and the tanks were left defenceless, and after facing considerable difficulties, they had no alternative other than to retreat. They were forced to leave in the enemy's hands about twenty tanks which were burnt right next to the Nationalist positions. A thick, black smoke signalled the location of the lost tanks.[104]

The Republican infantry either side of Fuentes had also had a tough time. The Canadian Mac-Paps were in action for the first time and went over the top at 1.40 pm, as Milo Makela recounts:

> Joe Dallet, Battalion Commissar, went over with No. 1 Company on the left flank, where the fire was heaviest. He was leading the advance when he fell, mortally wounded. He behaved heroically until the very end, refusing to permit the First Aid men to come over to him in his exposed position.
>
> The advance, which earned the special tribute of Brigade Commander Copic was magnificent and worthy of veterans of many campaigns. Our Battalion advanced between 800 and 900 yards, taking positions and digging in on an important ridge directly facing the enemy strongholds on the outskirts of the town.[105]

Makela was putting a brave face on things; the Mac-Paps suffered more losses than any other unit in the brigade in a real baptism of fire. The Lincoln-Washingtons got as far as the enemy barbed wire, but wisely withdrew when the scale of the disaster became apparent. The British Battalion, just 150 strong at this point, ran into withering fire and lost yet another commander, Harold Fry, as well as their commissar. One Britisher compared the Fuentes tank assault to the Charge of the Light Brigade.[106] Ernest Hemingway asked Milton Wolff about what had happened later:

> 'Fuentes was our big foul-up wasn't it?' said Hemingway. 'Especially with the tanks?'
> 'The tanks? Oh that. I don't know. After all, it was the first time it was tried. Infantrymen riding tanks into the enemy lines. I thought sure as hell they were going to go all the way to Saragossa.'[107]

The operation brought the Republican lines up to the edge of Fuentes de Ebro, perhaps a good jumping-off point for a future assault, as Líster observed, but the attacking potential of the Army of the East had been expended. Prieto, Pozas, Casado, Modesto, Líster – all have been blamed for the disaster. If we accept Modesto's account, responsibility lies with the overall commander, Colonel Casado, for designing the offensive and forcing his subordinates to go along with a bad plan. On the other hand, Modesto may be attempting to shift the blame and perhaps the unforgivable lapses in planning were his own. Petrou cites a Canadian veteran who recalled that the plan was General Walter's imitation of a battle scene from a Soviet propaganda film the Pole had enjoyed.[108] Whatever the truth of the matter, the Fuentes fiasco marked the end of the Republican's attempts to capture Saragossa.

In contrast to failure on the ground, the campaign ended well for the Loyalist air force. On 15 October, the Republicans launched one of their most successful air assaults of the war, against the Sanjurjo-Saragossa air base (rather ironically named after a Nationalist general who had been killed in a flying accident). Sweeping in at dawn, twenty-one I-15 Chatos strafed and bombed the airfield under the cover of forty-three I-16 Moscas, achieving complete surprise. The Nationalist planes were caught on the ground; twelve aircraft were destroyed and sixteen damaged, five of them severely.[109] Amongst the planes destroyed were three German Ju 52 bombers, two He 46s and six of the fine Italian Fiat CR.32 fighters.[110] The Republicans had committed fifty-five modern fighters to the attack, five squadrons worth – quite a gamble considering this represented at least half the total air power they had at the front, and the vast majority of their advanced aircraft. However, the operation was a huge success, catching the Rebels totally unawares and fulfilling that dream of any aerial strategist, eliminating the enemy's aircraft on the ground. Putting twenty-eight aircraft out of action in a single day, even if many could be repaired, was no small feat considering the Nationalists had probably less than 100 planes in the entire sector. The Duke of Lerma was stationed at the base and described it as 'a very nasty jolt', before explaining how his adversaries achieved such a surprise:

The enemy lines were only a few minutes' flight from the airfield. Neither interception nor air-raid warning were possible. During daylight hours we had one or two aircraft constantly on patrol. One of them was just about to take off when the attack began.

Clearly, Republican command had done their homework, calculated that the base would not receive sufficient warning and observed that a dawn raid would miss the patrols. General Alfredo Kindelán, commander of the Nationalist air force, fails to mention the raid in his memoirs …

Conclusions

Rojo's plan had failed on both the tactical and strategic level. In Aragon, Saragossa had not fallen and the Nationalists had not been forced into headlong retreat, merely driven slowly backwards for approximately a week, while taking a heavy toll on their attackers. While no accurate figures seem to exist, both sides evidently suffered thousands of casualties, the Loyalists surely more. Additionally, more of the People's Army's scarce military hardware had been lost irrevocably, not least the new BT-5s. In terms of Republican grand strategy, the failure was even starker. The objective had been to draw Franco away from the beleaguered Northern zone, as had been achieved at Brunete. This time, the Generalissimo had not taken the bait. The offensive had come too late to save Santander, which fell just two days into the Aragon campaign. Barely pausing, and with the battle for Belchite at its height, the Francoist drive into Asturias began on 1 September, showing no regard for the intense fighting further east. Franco had found the resources he needed to reinforce Saragossa from other fronts, rendering the Republican attempts at diversion futile. In a campaign lasting less than two months, the Nationalists crushed the last remnants of the Army of the North in Asturias, capturing the last Loyalist stronghold of Gijón on 21 October. David Granda, an Asturian soldier with the Army of the North, later recalled the tragic chaos at the fall of this final Republican enclave:

> We reached Gijón at nightfall and we began to go round looking for people that we knew, but they had all gone. At the offices of the Socialist newspaper *Avance* we found someone. He said, 'But what the hell are you doing here, get to the port. Everyone has gone from here. Jesus Christ! The fascists are here; they've arrived. You've got to get out!' We went down to the Old Port of Gijón and all hell was let loose. Everyone, men, women, children, soldiers, were in a panic, pushing and fighting their way to the quayside. Some were shouting, 'It's all over, they've freed the prisoners. The fascist prisoners have been released and they are in the street.' The Fifth Column had opened the prison gates. 'The army is here! They are coming! They are coming!' It was pandemonium.
>
> In the port everyone was trying to get onto a little coal ship, a collier. The steamer was keeled over on its side and it turned out that

it had been bombed and was taking in a lot of water. A team of Basque metalworkers was trying to repair the hole in the side by welding on a metal plate. The boat could not get out anyway until the tide came up to float it off. Everyone was trying to get on the ship and a battalion … made a cordon so that women and injured wouldn't be crushed. But what with the general panic and the people screaming that the fascists were coming, things were out of control.[111]

Prieto and Rojo's hope of saving, or at least buying time for, their isolated northern comrades had come to nothing. The defence minister offered his resignation but it was declined by Negrín.

Historians often refer to the Battle of Belchite as effectively another Brunete, and while there are obvious similarities, the differences are stark. In both cases, it is true that the Republican attack achieved surprise and gained ground initially, only to become bogged down within a few days. However, this is the extent of the comparisons. As was discussed in the previous chapter, Brunete was a tactical failure but a strategic success; Franco was forced to halt his offensive in the north, but the ensuing Nationalist counter-attack deprived the Republicans of most of their gains and shattered their forces. On the other hand, Rojo's Saragossa operation had failed on a strategic level; Santander and Asturias had not been saved, nor even bought time. And at a tactical level too, the main objective of the Aragonese capital had never been under real threat. But the Republic did hold on to the majority of its gains – 900km² of fairly insignificant ground – if only because Franco had chosen not to try to take it back. The Generalissimo had conceded a minor tactical defeat in Aragon for a huge victory in the north, probably the best military decision he made in the war and a decision he was not to repeat.

From a Republican perspective, on the first analysis, things may seem bleak, and indeed it is hard to sell Belchite as a success, as Loyalist propaganda at home and abroad was compelled to. 'So many troops to take four or five pueblos does not satisfy the ministry of defence,'[112] ranted a frustrated Prieto to General Pozas. His frustration is understandable; with tens of thousands of troops and most of the Republic's available air and armoured forces at their disposal, the Army of the East had little to show for their efforts. While Rojo admits in his account that the operation was not one for the military textbooks, he does call it a 'concrete triumph and a sacrificial action', referring to the need to launch an offensive so quickly to try to help the north.[113] However, there is evidence that lessons had been learnt from Brunete.

Modesto had the foresight to see that by the end of August, there was no longer any hope of taking Saragossa. Unlike at Brunete, the Republicans did not keep throwing their exhausted troops forward in the vain hope of some last-gasp breakthrough. Instead, Modesto persuaded his comrades that they would be better served by taking Belchite, an achievement that could be billed as a clear success for Republican arms. Many Republican units fought well and gained vital experience. The 15th International Brigade stood out in particular as now being a true shock formation, having been chosen as the tip of the spear at Quinto, Belchite and Fuentes. And, albeit for less tangible results, Kléber's 13th Brigade had battled hard, as had the ever-reliable Listers. The People's Army ended the campaign in far better shape than they had at Brunete; whole brigades did not have to be completely dissolved or reconstituted, there was no breakdown of discipline and there could be pride in a handful of limited achievements.

Nevertheless, the ultimate Republican failure must be accounted for. While many in the febrile political atmosphere of the Republic blamed sabotage, treachery or 'Trotskyist elements', the real reasons are self-evident. Masjuán was probably right when he commented ruefully that had the entire strength of the offensive been concentrated on the initial push south of the Ebro through Fuentes, rather than diluted into three distinct drives, then Saragossa might have fallen quickly.[114] Several historians have rightly pointed to the shortage of quality, experienced junior officers and NCOs in all People's Army units as being a huge hindrance. Without strong company and squad leaders, troops tend to go to ground in the face of machine-gun or artillery fire, and this seems to clearly have been the case at Saragossa. To make matters worse, junior officers and commissars suffered disproportionately high casualties in the battle, as we have seen, with many units losing their commanders. Numerically superior Republican forces were held up time and again by well-sited Insurgent strongpoints and all but the most hardened of the Republic's divisions lacked the lower-level leadership to drive frightened troops forward, to outflank a machine-gun nest or storm a trench. Defence Minister Prieto himself, in a meeting with President Azaña, bemoaned the lack of speed and improvisation and blamed these flaws on the poor quality of the officer corps, also reporting a worrying reluctance to fight among conscripts. Azaña wrote in his diary:

> Prieto believes that the offensive could have given very important results, if everything had worked with the speed and accuracy required

in such cases. It has not been like that. Prieto attributes it to the lack of leaders. As soon as an unforeseen difficulty arises, there is no one who knows how to solve it on the spot.[115]

Clearly, lack of strong communication and intelligence again hindered the Republican offensive efforts. Coordination between different units and arms was poor and between battlegroups seemingly non-existent. The botched advance of General Kléber's Battlegroup B is a perfect case in point; he had absolutely no intelligence on enemy positions, his brigades did not cooperate, and orders were disobeyed, all of which culminated in the failure to seize one of the campaign's biggest opportunities when Villamayor fell. The Fuentes de Ebro tank debacle is another obvious case study in a disastrous intelligence oversight, amongst many other mistakes. Undoubtedly, the Republican commanders also made several tactical blunders. Trueba, the autodidactic commander of Battlegroup A, failed miserably in his task and was sacked shortly afterwards. The Saragossa offensive was by far the biggest test of his military career to date and he failed to make enough headway given the relatively strong force he was assigned. It seems he was out of his depth. The aforementioned Fuentes disaster is also a clear target for criticism and Líster, rather unfairly to say the least, bears the brunt of blame for some historians. The attack was rushed, the tankers had not been allowed to properly prepare and the units they were passing through had not been informed. The relationship between Modesto and Líster, already characterised by jealousy, was irrevocably damaged by mutual recriminations over the acrimonious losses to the International Tank Regiment, suggesting that the latter blamed Modesto for the fiasco. Furthermore, the decision to target Belchite, rather than ignore points of resistance and push on to Saragossa, seems to have angered the temperamental Líster, for confidential Soviet reports refer to the major's 'stubborn unwillingness to carry out the orders of his corps commander … especially in the Saragossa operation'.[116] Kléber's performance was harshly criticised at the time by fellow communists and before long he was relieved of his division and left Spain. Considering the resources he had at his disposal during this battle, this decision seems more than a little harsh, although Rojo criticises the 45th's performance after their brief stay in Villamayor, calling the ensuing battle in the hills east of the village a 'sterile struggle'.[117] This is contradicted by the account we have heard from Legionary Officer Carlos Iniesta, who was seriously wounded in a desperate and futile counter-attack in late August on some of the heights

Battlegroup B had captured. Clearly, the Republicans were hard-pressed to hold what little they had taken and the fighting appears to have been intense. While Kléber was not the military genius that he had been billed by PCE propaganda the previous autumn, he was surely one of the most capable of the Republic's field commanders, dogged, determined and unflappable. He would be missed. Modesto's decisions were perhaps the most significant of the campaign. As we have seen, his influence was decisive in shifting the emphasis of the southernmost attack from Saragossa to capturing Belchite, an ultimately insignificant objective in the grand scheme of the war. A case in his defence has already been made in some detail. In summary, after the energy expended at Quinto, Líster's first failure at Fuentes de Ebro and with Nationalist reinforcements already arriving, was winning a quick victory at Belchite in fact the best option open to Battlegroup D? Antony Beevor is highly critical of the decision, and of Modesto's conduct of the entire campaign,[118] but was the capture of Saragossa even possible by late August? His forces had been fighting hard for a week and were tired and depleted. The Nationalists were already counter-attacking, attempting to relieve Belchite. Better surely to secure the rearguard and free up troops by taking Belchite, before waiting to see if another Nationalist hammer blow would fall, rather than to repeat the mistakes of Brunete. While we cannot know if Battlegroup D had the strength to carry Saragossa, or whether that potential was wasted by focusing on Belchite, it would be wrong to criticise Modesto for not driving mercilessly on, given how recently that approach had come back to bite him.

The extreme heat of the late Aragonese summer doubtless played its part, with water hard to come by, as at Brunete, leading to discipline and drive deteriorating in the attacking troops. Lluís Puig paints a vivid picture of the effect that water shortages had on the men:

> It was very hot. There was no water in the vicinity and we had a raging thirst. The soldiers in the trenches asked for water persistently, but the water did not come. … The water trucks had not been for two days. The soldiers said they were in a desperate situation. They were so thirsty and highly strung that it was rumoured that, if the water did not come, they would defect to the other side. In the afternoon a water truck arrived and the water was distributed to the various positions. Everyone went berserk as if they'd never seen water before.[119]

More than anything else, Republican failure during the battle can be attributed to the dire shortage of artillery and of any real bombing capability.

Milton Wolff's wry observation that their air and artillery support had 'shot their load in the first few days of the Aragon offensive'[120] seems startlingly accurate, and was most likely a result of shortages in ammunition and spares. Time and again, the offensive was delayed by fortified hills or villages, against which the infantry had little firepower. What a battery or two of howitzers could have done for the British Battalion pinned on the side of Purburrel Hill or Kléber's Battlegroup stuck in the Sierra de Alcubierre. With an artillery arm properly befitting an entire army corps, Modesto could have rendered the position of the garrison in Belchite untenable in a matter of hours. For their big raid on Saragossa air base, the Republican air force relied on I-15 fighters, which could carry a few light bombs under the wings. Their SB Katiuskas, the only modern bomber the Republicans possessed, suffered so many losses during the battle that two squadrons had to be dissolved.[121] Almost comically, they resorted to using the R-5 reconnaissance biplane for the strategic bombing of Saragossa. The preparatory bombardment for the Fuentes attack was insufficient to say the least. In the age of the machine gun, infantry alone, no matter how brave, can only take defensive positions at extortionate cost. The Western Front bore this out in 1914–18, so did the Battle of Belchite. Artillery or aerial bombardment were essential in this era to unlocking enemy defences. The People's Army lacked the tools it needed to succeed in this battle, and the primary reason for this was the arms embargo enforced by the British and French.

Credit must be given to the Nationalist defenders for their impressive performance in the face of, at least at first, a vastly superior enemy. The garrisons of Codo, Quinto, Belchite and the sierra hill forts fought with at times incredible tenacity and courage. The long delays in taking these positions drained the momentum out of the Republican assault, cost the Loyalists dear in terms of casualties and bought vital time for reinforcements to arrive and change the complexion of the battle. The 51st and 52nd divisions may have been second-rate outfits, and Ponte an unfashionable general, but their conduct in this campaign cannot be faulted.

In the air, the battle had been more even than at Brunete, but this was naturally because the bulk of Nationalist aviation, including the Condor Legion, had remained on the Northern Front. As we have seen, the Republican air force performed well but Francoist planes were able to harass the Loyalist ground forces with some impunity. No reliable figures for loss of aircraft seem to exist, the Duke of Lerma boasts of thirty red planes being downed in a week over Belchite, while Republican sources claim twenty 'fascist machines' were shot down in the last three days of the offensive.[122]

Both these figures are surely exaggerations, but what is clear is that both sides lost dozens of aircraft over the course of the battle. Ultimately, even though the Republican air force held their own, they could ill afford such losses from their small supply of Russian craft, while the Nationalists could quickly acquire German and Italian replacements.

Overall, Franco could look at the Saragossa campaign with satisfaction. The local units had fought doggedly at Quinto, Belchite, Villamayor and Zuera, taking the wind out of sails of the Republican assault. His decision to only send reinforcements from Madrid, and leave his northern armies largely intact, had paid dividends with the capitulation of Santander and Gijón. Although the failure to relieve Belchite must have come as a frustration, the Nationalists were surely pleased with the position they found themselves in; the northern campaign had been brought to a successful conclusion, they seemed to have absorbed all that the Republic could throw at them and the Generalissimo's advisors now believed the People's Army lacked the strength to launch another major offensive that year. In this, they were wrong.

Chapter 6

Stalingrad in Miniature:
Teruel, December 1937–February 1938

Background to the campaign

The destruction of the Northern zone had given Franco operational freedom, but the Generalissimo was in no hurry, taking his time to consolidate his position and reorganise his forces. The capture of Gijón released 65,000 troops and 100 artillery batteries, meaning the Rebels now had numerical parity with the Republican forces manning the main battlefront, running thousands of kilometres from the Pyrenees to the south coast. Furthermore, the Nationalists 'recycled' more than half of the 100,000 Basque and Republican prisoners of war that were captured in the northern campaign and integrated them into their army. Those who refused found themselves in forced labour camps, working for the Rebel war effort regardless, with some opting to escape imprisonment by volunteering for military service. While the reliability of these troops was naturally low, many were used on quiet fronts or for rearguard, garrison and auxiliary roles, allowing tried and tested units to be concentrated in a new Army of Manoeuvre.[1] The Army of Manoeuvre consisted of five corps in which the vast majority of the Nationalists' best soldiers were concentrated. Franco's most talented commanders were appointed as the heads of these new powerful formations: the Moroccan Coprs under General Yagüe (which included many colonial troops); General Varela had the Corps of Castile; the Galician Corps included the renowned 13th and 150th divisions and was commanded by General Aranda; while the Navarrese Corps contained the best of the Requetés under the Carlist General José Solchaga. Additionally, the Nationalist air force had been reinforced throughout the year with new Axis machines and now numbered over 400 aircraft, with the Spanish contingent receiving an increasing number of modern models handed down by the Germans and Italians. The conquest of the north had brought 1.5 million people under Franco's rule, as well as 36 per cent of Spain's industrial production, and allowed the Nationalist navy to be redeployed to the Mediterranean.[2] Franco had always enjoyed superiority in firepower, logistics and military efficiency, and further boosted by the north's economic resources, it appeared that the Nationalists were ready to deal the decisive blow in the civil war.

The only question was, where should the blow fall? There were a number of options open to the Rebels, now that they felt they held the initiative. Aragon, the scene of the war's most recent great battle, seemed a logical choice, either for a drive into Catalonia aimed at Barcelona or else along the Ebro River to the sea to divide the Republic in two. A number of Insurgent officers preferred this option, including, it appears, General Alfredo Kindelán, who wrote:

> [This operation] is feasible with the following favourable consequences: deprive Catalonia of the aid of the rest of Spain and of a wide area of recruitment, recover thousands of our supporters, occupy an important part of the Mediterranean coast, threaten Valencia, headquarters – for now – of the Red Government, deprive it of irreplaceable aid of Catalan and French industry.[3]

The city of Teruel, the capital of a poor province in southern Aragon, occupied a salient cut deep into Republican lines and could be the jumping-off point for such a drive to the sea. On the other hand, there was Madrid. The Spanish capital still held an emotional grip over the Generalissimo, the failure to take it the previous winter marked the Nationalists' only clear military defeat. While the capture of Madrid would bring tremendous prestige to the Rebel cause and certainly deal a heavy blow to Republican morale, the military benefits of such an operation were not as clear, with Kindelán listing the only obvious advantage being the freeing of a number of divisions tied down on the Madrid front.[4] Initially, Franco began preparations for an offensive in Aragon, but in late November he changed his mind, issuing orders on the 28th to switch to the Madrid plan, the slim chance of winning the war in a single blow proving too alluring.[5] He gathered the largest force the war had yet seen: over 100,000 men with Varela and Yagüe's corps either side of the Italian CTV, plus the Galician and Navarrese (who had seen the heaviest fighting in the north) corps in reserve. In keeping with the flexible nature of the Insurgent army, the composition of each corps could vary from campaign to campaign, and even within each battle, depending on the requirements of the situation. Given the overall strength of 100,000, it is fair to assume each corps consisted of around 20,000 men. This Army of Manoeuvre, under the

Caudillo's command, was deployed along the Guadalajara sector, north-east of Madrid, the same battlefield on which the Italians had failed miserably in March 1937. Was Franco's choice a deliberately petulant attempt to prove Spanish superiority over his Axis allies? His relations with Hitler and, in particular, Mussolini were at a low point that winter. Whatever the motive, the conditions appeared good: with overwhelming force, the Nationalists were to encircle the capital and either compel it to surrender or storm it.[6] The opening of the offensive was set for 19 December. To try to disguise the build-up, the Nationalist air force launched a major raid on the Aragon front on 10 December, involving 190 aircraft and reportedly costing the Republicans twenty-two planes.[7] The fact that the Nationalists were able to conduct such a huge operation as a mere diversion highlights the growing power of their military. It was clear to those in Spain and abroad that Franco was poised to deliver what could be the war's defining moment, and possibly decide the contest; the US media reported that the Generalissimo was 'giving the government five days to surrender before the final triumphal offensive'.[8]

The Republic had other ideas. The Nationalist Guadalajara build-up had been uncovered by anarchist scouts of Cipriano Mera's IV Corps, but while the Loyalists were aware the attack was coming, the question was what to do about it. Defence Minister Prieto had recently promoted Republican Chief of the General Staff Vicente Rojo to the rank of general and his task now was preventing the dreaded Madrid offensive. The government knew that the capital's fall would be a huge blow to Loyalist morale and to the Republic's chances of winning any help from abroad. Communist propaganda had built up the 'tomb of fascism' as a key symbol of the Republican war effort and its loss could prove fatal. Through the autumn, Rojo had been working on a series of initiatives to build on the Brunete and Belchite operations. His most ambitious proposal was devised in October, the so-called 'Plan P', a reboot of Largo Caballero's shelved Extremadura offensive. The operation would involve a massive twenty-five Republican divisions deployed between Peñarroya and Medellín, whose rather unlikely task would be to divide Nationalist Spain in two by penetrating through to the Portuguese frontier.[9] Prieto having rejected this suggestion in the summer did the same again, and therefore Rojo developed two more simple operations, both on the Aragon front, one against Huesca and one aimed at Teruel. The defence minister was rather reluctant to launch another offensive but was overruled by Prime Minister Negrín and the majority of the cabinet who favoured Rojo's 'Strategic Counter-attack Number Two'.[10] With the

Republic already having failed to take Huesca twice, the Teruel operation seemed more appealing, especially given the precarious position the city was in, tucked into Republican lines. Furthermore, in contrast to both Huesca or Extremadura, Teruel was fairly close to both of the Republic's main population and production centres, Barcelona and, in particular, Valencia. On the other hand, the distance to Franco's huge concentration of forces before Madrid was not great either. Teruel was a small, walled city of around 20,000, located in a cold, mountainous corner of Aragon. It is surrounded by a series of imposing heights that were fortified with bunkers and barbed wire and held the key to taking the city. Henry Buckley, *Daily Telegraph* correspondent in Spain for a decade, had visited the city a number of times and described it as:

> a bleak town if ever there was one; it is a sort of Spanish Buxton. It stands on a small hill in a basin surrounded by blunt hills nearly all of which are treeless. In normal times Teruel always scores by having the lowest temperatures of any other important town in the country each winter. … There is a grandeur about this town perched on the top of a low hill, alone in this desolate terrain.[11]

The most notable of the heights was La Muela (the molar) to the south-west, a flat, toothlike hill of 1,520m altitude, which was considered essential to the city's defence. The Puerto Escandón (1,301m) and the Mansueto (1,151m) barred an advance on the city from the south-east and east respectively. Additionally, El Muletón and Santa Barbara (also known as the cemetery hill), both over 1,000m in altitude, dominated the northern and western approaches to the city.[12] The valley of the narrow Alafambra River flows down to Teruel from the north, where it meets with the Guadalaviar and Turia.

The Republican assault, scheduled for 14 December, was to be carried out by the Republican Army of the Levant (bolstered by units from the Army of Manoeuvre) under the command of Colonel Juan Hernández Saravia. Saravia was a retired artillery officer, a close friend and military advisor to the liberal President Manuel Azaña, one of the few Loyalist professional officers who had genuine Republican politics, rather than being 'geographically loyal'.[13] Buckley, who would see much of Saravia during the battle, described him as 'a mild-mannered little man he was always most pleasant to deal with but I never got the impression that he was a very efficient soldier.'[14]

His Army of the Levante was composed of between 80,000 to 100,000 men but only around 40,000 of these would make up the initial Teruel assault force.[15] During the Belchite campaign, Defence Minister Prieto had begun to grate somewhat about Communist domination of the People's Army and as a result the Teruel attack would, at first, see very few of the famous Communist commanders or formations involved. Most importantly, he had allowed the International Brigades a rest, making this an all-Spanish operation. All three corps were commanded by regular officers rather than militia leaders. Colonel Fernández de Heredia's XVIII Corps (34th, 64th and 70th divisions) was to encircle the city from the south, while Colonel Juan Ibarrola, a conservative Basque, would lead XXII Corps (11th and 25th divisions) to do the same from the north. Finally, XX Corps (40th and 68th divisions) under another of Azaña's associates, Colonel Menéndez, would assault Teruel directly from the south-east. Once the pocket was sealed, the 11th and 64th divisions would dig in and await the inevitable Francoist counter-attack, while the remaining divisions from each corps would join the attack on the city from every direction.[16]

The People's Army had developed in size and strength throughout 1937 as the militarisation process reached its climax, but the best units and equipment had been worn out by the brutal battles at Brunete and Belchite, a situation exacerbated by a dearth of Soviet supply shipments from August 1937 to June 1938. It was remarkable that the Republic's tank force was still going, given almost all their T-26s had exceeded their expected mechanical lifespans, but 104 tanks would be available at Teruel from two armoured battalions and the remnants of the International Tank Regiment.[17] As before, they would be split into small groups and deployed with the attacking infantry. This, combined with the unfavourable weather and terrain, meant that the tanks would play a limited role in the battle. The majority of the Republic's dwindling aerial strength (Kindelán puts the total of 'Red' planes in Spain at 320, perhaps a little high[18]), plus thirty-seven artillery batteries, were also committed to the operation.[19] Additionally, cracks were beginning to show under the strain of constant defeat. As has been alluded to, Prieto was increasingly resenting the Communist influence over the war effort, especially as military success had been scant. Further, relations between the famous militia leaders were strained; Modesto and Líster's relationship had deteriorated to such an extent that Líster's 11th Division was removed from Modesto's V Corps. A Soviet report explained:

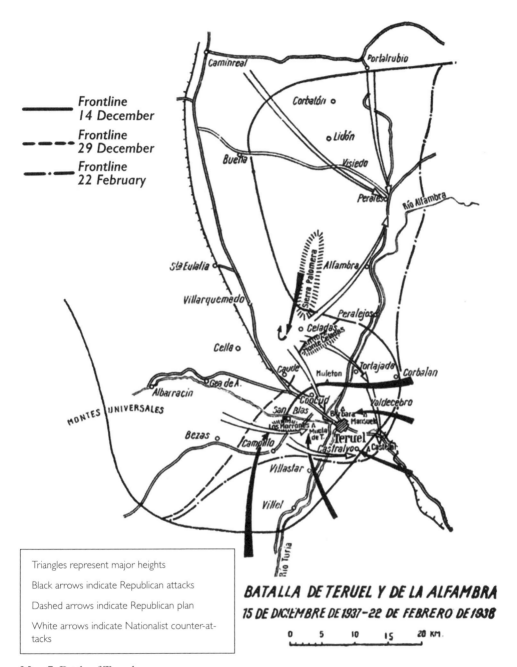

Frontline
14 December

Frontline
29 December

Frontline
22 February

Triangles represent major heights

Black arrows indicate Republican attacks

Dashed arrows indicate Republican plan

White arrows indicate Nationalist counter-attacks

BATALLA DE TERUEL Y DE LA ALFAMBRA

15 DE DICIEMBRE DE 1937-22 DE FEBRERO DE 1938

0   5   10   15   20 KM.

Map 7: Battle of Teruel.

The veiled hostility between Lister and Modesto is widely known in the People's Army. Petty, personal factors – envy and rank – are at the bottom of this. ... Both of them have provided themselves with special people to shadow and collect compromising material on one another. Modesto has used most colourful language about Lister, and the latter has answered Modesto's criticism as a commander with a stubborn unwillingness to carry out the orders of his corps commander, as happened at Brunete and especially in the Saragossa operation.[20]

However, both men would grow to despise their PCE comrade Valentín González, better known as El Campesino. They resented his primitive military methods and wilful ignorance; El Campesino had not shown any progression since being a brave militia battalion leader. It seems unlikely that González would have remained 46th Division commander for so long were it not for his fame and propaganda value. In contrast, Líster enjoyed a positive relationship with his new corps commander, the Basque Ibarrola, of whom he wrote:

Not only did he never hide his deep religious beliefs as a practising Catholic, but he defended them clearly and openly. Because of his simplicity and his cordiality, he quickly conquered all of our hearts. This appreciation was to be increased a couple of weeks later, by observing his courage in the face of the enemy and his companionship and loyalty to his subordinates. Our relations did not last longer than the first phase of the battle of Teruel, but they have left in me one of the best memories of the entire war.[21]

As the ranks of the People's Army had swelled with conscripts and new recruits, it was only natural that the importance of the International Brigades declined, their numbers remaining fairly constant at no more than 15,000 in total. There is also evidence that the International units were in a poor condition after the summer's battles and badly in need of rest. For one, the numbers of Internationals in each brigade had declined considerably due to heavy losses, and most International Brigades were now majority Spanish units, meaning they were not quite such a prestigious elite any more but also creating additional tensions; often Spaniards resented serving under foreign officers and some Brigaders did not have a good relationship with their Spanish comrades.[22] The 11th Thälmann Brigade had a strength going into the battle of 2,899, of whom

22 per cent were Internationals (Germans, Austrians, some Scandinavians) and Soviet reports frequently referred to German 'chauvinism'. Meanwhile, the anglophone 15th Brigade, which had fought well at Belchite, was probably the only International Brigade that still retained much of its original character, with 52 per cent of their 2,463 strength being foreign volunteers.[23] In addition, after the constant hardship that came with repeatedly being used as shock troops, the brigades were in a bad way. They were swept by a typhoid epidemic in October 1937, which 'carried off' more than 1,000.[24] On inspecting the 11th and 15th brigades of his 35th Division before the battle, General Walter was appalled by their combat readiness:

> It is difficult to convey in words the state of [their] weapons and how dirty [they were], especially the rifles. The bores of their barrels were not much different from a seventeenth-century musket barrel found at Belchite. No fewer than 95 percent of the rifles had no bayonet or cleaning rod, all lost since time immemorial. There was only a handful of cleaning rags in the brigade.[25]

It must be added that later in the same report, Walter commented that the two brigades had 'seriously pulled themselves together' in the last few weeks. In December, the morale of the British was boosted by the visit of a delegation from home, which included the Labour Party leader Clement Attlee, with No. 1 Company of the British Battalion being renamed in his honour the 'Major Attlee Company'. The 35th Division was the only International formation earmarked for the Teruel battle, being held in reserve behind the lines, while all the other International units were deployed to quiet sectors, clearly not fit for offensive action.

Facing the People's Army at Teruel was a small, second-rate force of somewhere near 20,000 Nationalist troops, mostly drawn from the 52nd Division and local Falangist units.[26] While few in number, these troops enjoyed strong positions on the fortified heights surrounding the city, complete with linking trench systems, barbed wire and concrete strongpoints. Colonel Rey d'Harcourt, a lifelong soldier, would direct the defence of Teruel, having been given the unenviable posting of military governor of the provincial capital. Overall command rested with General Dávila, who, fresh from his successes in Asturias, remained head of the Francoist Army of the North, now operating on the Aragon front.

Teruel and its surroundings were ultimately of very little strategic value, but this was a key aspect of Rojo's plan. It was far more preferable from a Loyalist point of view for the winter's big battle to be fought here rather than at Madrid, which held such emotional and propaganda value for the Republic. The fall of Madrid might just bring about the end of the war. Rojo's 'Strategic Counter-attack Number Two' sought to choose less significant ground over which to fight Franco's superior army. The question was, would the Generalissimo take the bait?

The battle

The Republic's diversionary offensive was supposed to start on 14 December but was delayed by logistical difficulties exacerbated by the weather. Instead, it started at midnight on the 14/15 December with the most northerly of the assault troops, Líster's 11th Division, crossing the lines in one of their now-trademark night attacks. Líster had gained special permission to carry out this assault from General Rojo and explains why in his memoirs:

> It is not that I had a special preference for that form of combat: it was necessity that imposed it. Night combat was rather like poor man's combat. The enemy fortified himself well, established his fire systems well; during combat ... [their] fighters clung tenaciously to the ground.
>
> To overcome all this, heroism was not enough, resources were needed; powerful artillery fire, aerial bombing – two weapons of which we were very short during the entire war – and therefore, in the absence of them, we had to use forms of surprise to save lives and obtain maximum success.[27]

Moving south, the 9th Brigade of the Listers was led by guides across the Celadas Heights towards San Blas, a village to the west of Teruel where they were due to meet the advance of XVIII Corps to cut the city off. To their right, 100th Brigade was to establish the outer defence perimeter of the encirclement, while 1st Brigade was to take Concud, which would serve as a reserve position. Having been transferred from the 1st to the 9th Mixed Brigade of the Listers, Lieutenant Joaquín Masjuán was part of yet another night-time infiltration:

> We passed through something of an unguarded sector in which there was a small hill. We did it in complete silence, led by four experienced guides from Teruel. My teeth were chattering because of the cold, as there was a chill wind. I could not see where I put my feet. The sparse

vegetation gave the illusion, as it moved in the wind, of hundreds of enemies crawling along the ground. Suddenly, something ran through my feet: it was a frightened dog.

Then I noticed that we were going down a slope. Sometime later we crossed a plain which, due to its length, I reckoned was a valley. To our right we passed the enemy village of Caudé and, to the left, that of Concud.

When the day dawned, we found ourselves crossing this great valley, while we heard the barrage of our artillery.[28]

By 5.00 am, the 9th had advanced 10km to San Blas, but the 1st Brigade had got lost in the night and found themselves in front of, rather than behind, Concud's defences. As Líster writes, 'The surprise had gone to hell and there was no other solution than to take it bare-chested,' and a frontal assault began at 7.30 am, which did not clear the village until the afternoon.[29] Amidst the first Republican troops to enter Concud was Simona Grinchenko, a 19-year-old Russian translator who, despite the orders of her superiors, preferred the front lines to staff postings. Antonio Candela was there too and helped clear out the town and evacuate the civilian population. He relates a startling story of the surrender of the last of Concud's garrison that night, holed up in the church:

A group of Republican soldiers approached the church's huge main door and very cautiously pushed open a small door within the larger one. They tiptoed into the church but it was pitch dark so one bright sergeant had the idea of striking a match and, as it flamed and revealed the surrounding area, they came face to face with a wall of Civil Guards' faces staring at them from just five feet away. The armed Republicans must have given the impression of being jittery, because one of the Civil Guards said hurriedly: 'Don't be alarmed, we surrender!' The personnel inside the church had left all their arms piled up against the church wall.[30]

Starting at 8.30 am, with snow falling steadily, and without air or artillery preparation in order to achieve surprise, the rest of XXII Corps from the north and XVIII Corps from the south crashed through Nationalist lines. Although progress was slower than the Listers, the anarchist 25th Division pushed a kilometre through the fortified positions directly north of Teruel, while the 34th played a similar role to the south. 64th Division managed to link up with

Líster towards the end of the day, having taken Campillo and moved up to the Guadalaviar River.[31] All road and rail communication to Teruel had been cut and XX Corps, along with supporting divisions, had begun the advance on the city itself. Colonel Rey d'Harcourt and his men found themselves in a pocket 1,000km². The Republican plan had gone like clockwork, all at the cost of just 300 casualties.[32] As for Franco's Guadalajara offensive, scheduled for the 19th, it was put on ice for the time being while one of the five Manoeuvre Army Corps, the Galician, was ordered to Teruel, as well as 81st and 84th divisions from Davíla's Army of the North. It would not be until 21 December, with the help of remnants from the 52nd, that the Nationalists would be able to form a continuous line to seal the Republican breach.[33]

On the second day, the snowfall became a blizzard and Nationalist air support was largely grounded, as it would remain for the first week or so of the battle – a huge advantage to the Republic. XX Corps struggled to overcome the strong defences guarding the most direct route into the city, while 6km to the west, 11th and 64th divisions began the unenviable task of digging in and preparing for the Nationalist counter. As Rojo would later explain, Teruel was an 'offensive–defensive' operation, which aimed at compelling the Nationalists to counter-attack rather than completing a deep exploitation into Rebel territory.[34] In terrible conditions of ice, wind and snow, the fighting was bloody. The fortified hills that surrounded the city proved incredibly tough to crack. One of the unique features of the Teruel battle was how close foreign journalists were allowed to get to the action, with the Republic hoping for a major improvement in their international standing should the operation prove a success. Herbert Matthews of the *New York Times* watched the battle from Colonel Hernández Saravia's command post on 18 December:

No worse weather could possibly be imagined for fighting purposes. The effect of it on the writer … is doubtless the same as on the soldiers, although I have only had five hours of it on an exposed mountain-top whereas they have fought through four days and nights of it without relief. It is the cut of the wind that is so distressing.

Nothing is a protection against those icy blasts that come shrieking down from the north, penetrating any amount of clothes. Your eyes fill with constant tears from the sting of it; your fingers swell and become numb and all feeling goes out of your feet except an overwhelming iciness; you gasp for breath and cannot stand in one spot to look through your field glasses for the wind buffets you like a fighter boring in.

That wind has been roaring down at fifty miles an hour throughout these four long days and yesterday and Thursday there was heavy snow, while everything underfoot turned into ice. Through it all the Loyalist soldiers fought steadily forward and most amazing of all Government planes again have taken to the air to bomb and strafe the Rebel positions. Whatever the outcome of this offensive, no one can deny that it has been a triumph of human material and modern aviation under the most trying conditions.[35]

That day, the four Republican divisions attacking Teruel took the cemetery hill and on the 19th, the Puerto Escandón, before assaulting the most of important of all, La Muela, on 20 December. Ernest Hemingway was there too, writing dispatches for the North American Newspaper Association, and described the fighting that day in his typical style:

On Friday, while we watched from a hilltop above the town, crouching against boulders and hardly able to hold fieldglasses in a fifty-mile-an-hour gale which picked up the snow from the hillside and lashed it against our faces, the government troops took the Muela of Teruel, one of the odd thimble-shaped formations like extinct geyser cones which protect the city. Fortified by concrete machine-gun emplacements and surrounded by tank traps made of spikes forged from steel rails, it was considered impregnable, but four companies assaulted it as though they had never had explained to them by military experts what impregnable meant. Its defenders fell back into Teruel and a little later in the afternoon, as we watched another battalion break through the concrete emplacements of the cemetery, the last defenses of Teruel itself were squashed or turned. …

I have been in many dugouts and seen many staffs at work during a battle, but Saturday's was the most cheerful ever seen and as we went below to warm our hands and get the wind out of our eyes, the officers were as jovial as the heat was welcome in the candle-lit underground shelter. For three days they had fought as much against the weather as against the enemy.[36]

Unsurprisingly, Hemingway wanted to get even closer to the action, and on 21 December, as the noose was closed around Teruel, he and a handful of foreign journalists were with the assault troops of XX Corps. His dispatch from that day is probably his most vivid from Spain and is worth quoting at length:

> We lay on top of a ridge with a line of Spanish infantry under heavy machine-gun and rifle fire. It was so heavy that if you had lifted your head out of the gravel you would have dug your chin into one of the little unseen things that made the stream of kissing, whisper sounds that flowed over you after the pop-pop-pop of the machine guns on the next ridge beyond would have lifted the top of your head off. You knew this because you had seen it happen.
>
> On our left, an attack was starting. The men, bent double, their bayonets fixed, were advancing in the awkward first gallop that steadies into the heavy climb of an uphill assault. Two men were hit and left the line. One had the surprised look of a man first wounded who does not realise the thing can do this damage and not hurt. The others knew he had it very bad. All I wanted was a spade to make a little mound to get my head under. But there weren't any spades within crawling distance.
>
> On our right was the great yellow mass of the Mansueto, the natural battleship-shaped fortress that defends Teruel. Behind us the Spanish government artillery were firing, and, after the crack, came the noise like tearing silk and then the sudden spouting black geysers of high explosive shells pounding at the earth-scarred fortifications of Mansueto.
>
> We had come down through the pass on the Sagunto road to within nine kilometres of Teruel and had left our car. Then we walked along the road to kilometre six and there was the front line. We had stayed there a little while, but it was in a hollow and you couldn't see well. We climbed a ridge to see and were machine-gunned. Below us an officer was killed and they brought him back slowly, heavily and laid him grey-faced on a stretcher. When they bring the dead back on stretchers, the attack has not yet started.
>
> The amount of fire we were drawing being incommensurate with the view, we broke for the ridge where the advanced positions of the centre were. In a little while it was not a nice place to be either, although the view was splendid. The soldier I was lying next to was having trouble with his rifle. It jammed after every shot and I showed him how to knock the bolt open with a rock. Then suddenly we heard cheering

run along the line and across the next ridge we could see the Fascists running from their first line.

They ran in the leaping, plunging gait, that is not panic but a retreat, and to cover that retreat their further machine-gun posts slithered our ridge with fire. I wished very strongly for the spade, and then up the ridge we saw government troops advancing steadily. It went on like that all day and by night time we were six kilometres beyond where the first attack had started.

During the day we watched government troops scale the heights of Mansueto. We saw the armoured cars go with troops to attack a fortified farmhouse a hundred yards from us, the cars lying alongside the house and whang, whang, whanging into the windows while the infantry ducked into it with hand grenades. We lay during this in the doubtful lee of a grass-stuffed hummock and the Fascists threw eighty-millimetre trench mortars behind us on the road and in the field, they coming with a sudden whushing drop and cracking burst. One landed in the wave of an attack and one man ran out of the seeming centre of the smoke in a half-circle, first naturally, wildly back, then checked and went forward to catch up with the line. Another lay where the smoke was settling.

No smoke blew that day. After the Arctic cold, the blizzard and the gale that blew for five days, this was Indian summer weather and shell bursts flowered straight up and slowly sank. And all day long the troops attacked, held, attacked again. …

We sat behind trees, comfortable thick trees, and saw twigs clipped from their drooping lower branches. We watched the Fascist planes head for us and hunted shelter in a soil-eroded gulch only to watch them turn and circle to bomb the government lines near Concud. But all day long we moved forward with the steady merciless advance the government troops were making. Up the hillsides, across the railway, capturing the tunnel, all up and over the Mansueto, down the road around the bend from kilometre two and finally up the last slopes to the town, whose seven church steeples and neatly geometrical houses showed sharp against the setting sun.

The late evening sky had been full of government planes, the chasers seeming to turn and dart like swallows, and, while we watched their delicate precision through our glasses, hoping to see an air fight, two trucks came noising up and stopped, dropping their tailboards to discharge a company of kids who acted as though they were going to a football game. It was only when you saw their belts with sixteen bomb pouches and the two sacks each wore that you realised what they were, 'dynamiters'.

The captain said, 'These are very good. You watch when they attack the town.' So, in the short afterglow of the setting sun, with all around the town the flashing of the guns, yellower than trolley sparks but as sudden, we saw these kids deploy a hundred yards from us, and, covered by a curtain of machine-gun and automatic rifle fire, slip quietly up the last slope to the town's edge. They hesitated a moment behind a wall, then came the red and black flash and roar of the bombs, and over the wall and into the town they went.

'How would it be to follow them into the town?' I asked the colonel [likely Hernández Saravia]. 'Excellent,' he said, 'a marvellous project.' We started down the road, but now it was getting dark. Two officers came up, checking on scattered units, and we told them we would stay with them because, in the dark, people might shoot hastily and the countersign had not yet arrived. In the pleasant autumn falling dusk, we walked the road downhill and into Teruel. It was a peaceful-feeling night and all the noises seemed incongruous.

Then in the road was a dead officer who had led a company in the final assault. The company had gone on and this was the phase where the dead did not rate stretchers, so we lifted him, still limp and warm, to the side of the road and left him with his serious waxen face where tanks would not bother him now nor anything else and went on into town.[37]

After close to a week of bloody fighting in the hills and valleys around the city, Republican troops finally entered Teruel late on 21 December, with all the key heights now in Loyalist hands. All the while, the 11th and 64th divisions were holding a line just west of San Blas and Concud against numerous local counter-attacks from the new Nationalist units arriving in the sector. Joaquín Masjuán tells of one such assault in which a middle-aged Requeté died on the barbed wire just metres in front of him. Upon examining his wallet, Masjuán found letters from the soldier's wife and 10-year-old daughter, clearly affecting the young officer, for he wrote, 'I could not get rid of that Requeté from my mind. After 35 years it seems to me that I am still thinking about it.'[38] The struggle was against the cold as well as the enemy however, and Masjuán describes in detail the process of aiding one of his men suffering from frostbite:

On 23rd December, at dawn, I was awakened in the trench by the cries of a soldier complaining about his feet. He was relieved immediately, I took him in the machine-gun nest (I had a lit brazier) and I took off his boots and socks. With cognac from my canteen, I massaged it into both his feet for an hour, until his blood began to circulate normally again. Finally, he bathed them in hot water. ...

I ordered the soldiers to fill their shoes with newspaper and straw from the few mattresses we had, which we emptied completely. I also ordered that fires be lit in all the trenches and that water be heated in all kinds of receptacles, and also that wine and cognac be distributed. The guard shifts were reduced to half an hour.

After a short time, the entire front, on both sides, was full of columns of smoke.[39]

Miguel Hernández was a Communist poet serving in the Listers, who wrote an article entitled 'Firm in Our Posts' describing the actions of the 11th in that first week:

The decisive days we are going through form the anvil where the moral and physical quality of men determined to defeat fascism is put to the test.

In the Sierras de Teruel, where the lowest temperatures in Spain are recorded, the soldiers of the 11th Division have observed and observe an unwavering iron demeanour. ... The snow, the cold, the wind, the enemy, they have bitten with intensity in these days of December and in these crude Sierras, ready to devour the ears, to catch their breath, to take the heat of these soldiers. ...

The soldiers of the 11th Division accept, blithely, the roughest battles with fascism and with the most terrible elements of winter. And they have taken towns from the invaders, Concud, San Blas, and have made possible the siege of Teruel and have repulsed and repel the onslaught of the numerous forces that press to break the siege. ...

The victorious will of these soldiers reached a high point of grandeur on the afternoon of the 19th. Singing the 'Internationale' and shouting 'We are those of Lister!' they checked a column of Legionnaires and Falangists, who attacked protected by heavy artillery fire. The opposing forces had to retreat decimated and beaten by the valour of our soldiers.

If you seek them, you will find them between bullets and explosions; firm in their posts. If you look for them, you will find them in the middle of the snow, attacked by it, melting it with enthusiasm and joy; firm in their posts. If you seek them, you will find them in winter, in the wind, in the cold, lit like bonfires; firm in their posts. If you look for them you will find them conquering fascist towns, snatching arms and land from fascism, saving men, women, children, Spain, from fascism: firm in the positions that the voice of their commander has indicated to them. Firm in their posts.[40]

While clearly a piece of agitprop, the article illustrates the anti-fascist zeal of the 11th Division, explaining in part the impressive combat record of the famous Listers. Antonio Candela, having served under Líster since the days of the Fifth Regiment, later wrote of the struggle to hold the eastern limit of the Republican advance:

We were sent to some hills, a few kilometres to the east [of Concud], to form a new line of defence. As we were approaching the hills we saw a Fascist column coming out of the village called Caude; they entrenched themselves well outside the village on the hills to the east and we also took up positions. A first line was established along the low-lying hills. We stayed there for some fifteen days, and during that time the enemy launched many attacks against our positions. They gained very little ground and we counter-attacked at night, aided by search-lights, which lit up the countryside as if by fierce daylight. With that advantage the enemy could not see us coming and we gained some ground. The news of the 'Reds' advancing by searchlights spread throughout the enemy territory. In early January 1938, there was an aurora borealis in the sky over Seville, and some residents mistook it for the advancing 'Reds'. They began to leave the city to flee for the safety of Portugal.[41]

With the outer defences breached and Republican troops in the city itself, Colonel Rey d'Harcourt, Teruel's military governor, made what Kindelán and others considered a crucial error, pulling his men back from the trenches and fortifications around the outskirts of the city and into a number of well-defended buildings.[42] Roughly 4,000 troops and 2,000 civilian volunteers were holed up in several strongpoints centred on the central Plaza de San Juan: the Bank of Spain, the Civil Governor's Palace, the seminary, and the Convent of Santa Clara. The defenders were further encumbered by thousands of women, children and elderly sheltering with them, who required food and water that was in short supply. On 20 December, with the fall of La Muela, Franco had made the fateful decision to attempt to save Teruel with a counter-offensive. He chose his firefighter, Varela, to go with his Castilian Corps and, alongside Aranda's Galician, break through the Republican lines and relieve the city. Their attack would be supplemented with two Navarrese divisions and the fine Italian artillery group.[43] The aircraft of the Condor Legion and the Aviazione Legionaria, as well as numerous Spanish squadrons, were to be transferred to the Aragon front and the great offensive on Madrid was delayed indefinitely the following day.[44] This move flew in the face of the advice afforded to Franco, both from his own staff and his Axis allies; with the Republicans committed at Teruel (an insignificant objective), surely now was an ideal time to strike at Madrid? Varela, Yagüe, Aranda, the Italians and Germans, all counselled that the Caudillo stick to his guns. And yet it was a decision typical of Franco, in the words of Spanish military historian Gabriel Cardona, 'The Generalissimo did not react as a judicious general but as a bull before a red rag.'[45] Franco simply could not contemplate giving up ground to the enemy without a fight or allowing his adversaries a clear victory. As always, there was perhaps a political element to his decision-making, for he must have realised the propaganda value that a success at Teruel would have for the ailing Republic. On the other hand, all talk of the storming of a provincial capital would surely have been dispelled by the fall of Madrid. Mussolini and his foreign minister, Galeazzo Ciano, were beside themselves, with Ciano ranting in his diary on the 20th about his allies' lack of military vision, and on 23 December he wrote that:

> The Duce is worried about Spain. He doesn't overestimate the red action against Teruel but believes, and rightly so, that it will serve to recharge the morale of the reds. He said that the Spanish, who are the descendants of the Arabs, do not know how to fight a war in its entirety: they lack the essentials and fight individually, as a patrol, or at best a tribe.[46]

The CTV commander General Berti was recalled and discussed the possibility of withdrawing the Italian forces in Spain, railing against the Nationalist command's lack of coordination or haste to bring the war to a conclusion. Ciano commented, 'Franco's star is not as bright as it was some two months ago. … This Spanish affair is long and burdensome.'[47]

Meanwhile, as Mussolini had prophesised, spirits in the Republican camp soared at news of what was in effect the greatest triumph of the People's

Army to date. With the Nationalist garrison confined to just a few buildings, the government declared the fall of Teruel on 23 December. The usually despondent Prieto joked he was now the minister of defence *and* attack, and promoted Hernández Saravia to general.[48] On Christmas Eve, the *Daily Telegraph's* Henry Buckley had supper with the staff officers of a Loyalist mixed brigade in the city, who by all accounts were in high spirits:

> What nice young fellows they were, few of them over thirty; nearly all university students or clerks who had now been trained as officers and were full of enthusiasm. The troops provided a rondalla, or choir of guitar players and singers in the Aragonese fashion, who played and sang magnificently. There was a young Swiss with them. He had been brought up in Spain where his parents had a business, but he had of course no need to do service. He thought it a good idea to strike a blow for Democracy. Despite good wine and singing I was sad, for these boys were so earnest and out beyond the Pyrenees who cared about them?[49]

The excitement in Republican ranks is palpable in Robert Merriman's letter to his wife, who was now back in the United States:

> The fall of Teruel just might mean the completion of our best attack to date, and it was done by Spanish troops and Internationals here held in reserve for the first time. This gives great confidence to the Spanish people. ... Just when the whole world knew the fascists planned an attack we staged a fine one ourselves. Furthermore, it is the first one we have completed just as we planned it. Teruel is our Christmas present to all the anti-fascists in the world.[50]

However, President Azaña refused to be sucked into the euphoria, scrawling pessimistically in his diary:

> They enter Teruel ... Usual haste. Telegrams, addresses, optimism. I abstain: telephone conversations with Saravia. There remain a few redoubts. ... They do not want to give importance to the 'nuclei' that resist. I remember Toledo [where, famously, a Nationalist garrison had held out and been relieved by Franco], for more than one reason.[51]

The reality, of course, as Azaña knew, was that Teruel had not fallen. Fierce street fighting now took place as the Republicans sought to evict Rey d'Harcourt's beleaguered garrison. Nationalist air support was still limited by the weather; on 23 December, the Condor Legion had been transferred to local airfields but a formation of Heinkel He 111s had been scattered by a blizzard, with one force-landing in Republican territory.[52] Even once the Condor Legion and other aerial reinforcements had arrived, it was a struggle to get the planes in the air, as one German pilot remembered:

> None of us had believed it to be possible that in Spain it could become really cold. The scorching heat of the summer had, in fact, helped to give us the notion that we would also experience a warm and pleasant winter. Shockingly, when I made my first reconnaissance flight to the Teruel Front on Christmas Eve, the thermometer showed -18°C. It was especially difficult for our groundcrews at Calamocha. Night after night and hour after hour, a special Kommando [squad] had to rev up the aircraft in order to keep them warm.[53]

The storming of the city was slowed by Prieto's instructions to avoid harming the civilian population by banning the use of heavy artillery, bombing or mines to clear the Rebel strongholds, packed as they were with refugees. This well-intentioned directive was a serious headache for XX Corps commander Colonel Leopoldo Menéndez, as the Rebel-held Seminary and Santa Clara Convent on the town's western edge dominated the Valencia road, effectively meaning all supplies coming to Republican forces in the city had to take an eye-watering 112-kilometre detour![54] Nevertheless, the fighting was bloody and brutal, conditions for soldiers and civilians indescribable. Only tinned food, rock-hard, of course, could make it to the front, while water was frozen solid in the pipes. Furniture was burnt simply to melt the snow for vital water. The position of the Insurgents, trapped in a handful of buildings with thousands of civilians to feed, soon became desperate. Beevor has compared the fighting to that at Stalingrad just a few years later.[55] While Hemingway had departed for home, Herbert Matthews continued to report from the besieged city for the *New York Times*:

> Nowhere in the world will Christmas be so tragic as in this city where two small groups of determined men are selling their lives as dearly as they know how. In the Seminary, not only soldiers and Italian and German officers [*sic*] have taken refuge, but many priests and novices and perhaps even the Archbishop of Teruel.

It is hoped that only soldiers are firing, but many civilians to whom I have spoken in these last few days claim that the novices are armed and have been fighting since the offensive started. The government hopes that they will surrender, in which case they will be treated with due respect, but so long as they remain among these desperate soldiers no choice is seem [*sic*] but to shell and machine-gun the Seminary until its occupants yield.

It appears to be an utterly hopeless struggle. For nine days the city has been cut off; food must be gone, ammunition low and fatigue surely poisoning mind and body. Soon it will be time for the midnight mass and tomorrow will be Christmas. But here in Teruel there will be no peace on earth or good will toward the men who have chosen to die rather than to surrender. ...

In the Civil Guard barracks some 120 men have taken refuge and those remaining are still firing with that deadly marksmanship for which the corps is noted. They are the most hated class in Republican Spain and obviously feel that they can expect no more quarter than they ever gave to the people who are now closing in on them. ...

There is nothing more dangerous in warfare than cleaning up a city, for one is generally dealing with the best-disciplined and most desperate soldiers and they are shooting at close range. The writer on one incursion accompanied a tank which was dragging a six-inch gun to fire at 300-yard range against the Seminary and it was one of the riskiest episodes in my career. Three streets which had to be crossed were dominated by fire, one from only 150 yards. It was a case of sprinting desperately one by one, doubled over to make as small a mark as possible. One man got shot in the stomach and in maintaining liaison two soldiers were killed the same afternoon. But the gun rolled into place and for the last two days we have had the remarkable experience of watching it blast away half of the solid Seminary. It is the first time in this war that such heavy calibered cannon have been used at a range so short that the discharge and shell explosions sound almost simultaneous.

The technique is always the same. Tanks and armored cars manoeuvre, firing, until the snipers and machine-gun nests are silenced; dynamiters make the last charge, while windows are kept under streams of fire to protect their advance; soldiers creep up from every side to dash into the houses.

Almost always they would be received by shouts, and men and women would come out trembling but happy and be evacuated. Sometimes, however, shots would greet the inrushing men and there would be casualties.[56]

Without doubt, the conditions endured by both sides at the battle were the most horrific of the war. Up to half the losses suffered by both sides were on account of the weather, against which troops struggled daily. English writer Laurie Lee served briefly behind the lines with the International Brigades that winter and in his autobiographical novel *A Moment of War* retells the shocking account of a Republican lorry driver:

A van-driver arrived seeking a supply of blankets. It had taken him three days to cover the hundred miles from the front. Here was no hero or victorious eagle but a shivering and ragged man. He told us of pain and snow-blindness, panic and exposure on the road, while his eyes jumped like beans in his head. Oh, yes, we were winning in Teruel. He'd seen the dead stacked like faggots of wood round the walls. Frozen barricades of flesh you could shelter behind, protected from the wind and bullets. He'd seen mules drop dead in the cold, then set stiff and rigid in the road so that they held up the traffic and had to be sawn up in solid blocks and removed. His tales were of a reversal of hell, and he seemed as astonished by them as were his hearers; that he, a Spaniard, had seen such weather in his own country, such acts of slaughter in death's own climate, and the young soldiers, even alive, dressed in sheeted white.[57]

While repeated local counter-attacks against the lines fortified by the 64th Division and the Listers some 6km to Teruel's west had failed to break through, General Varela was preparing for a major operation to relieve the city. He had at his disposal 78,000 men of his own Castilian Corps and Aranda's Galician Corps, including the 13th, 54th, 61st, 62nd, 82nd, 84th, 150th, and the 1st Navarrese divisions, plus an overwhelming concentration of air and artillery firepower – 390 artillery pieces, which included an Italian CTV artillery group and the Condor Legion's deadly flak guns.[58] All he needed now was for the weather to improve. At last, in late December, conditions improved and the Condor Legion was able to get into the air in force for the first time in the battle. At Teruel, these German airmen were to have an even more decisive impact; during their rest period since the end of the northern campaign, the Condor Legion's fighter pilots had been working on new tactics to overcome the Russian I-16 Mosca. At low altitudes, the Soviet fighter was faster and more manoeuvrable, but the Condor Legion's Messerschmitt held a clear advantage over 3,000m. Therefore, the Nazi flyers developed a strategy of sitting at 5,000m, above and behind Loyalist squadrons, which flew in tight formation. The Moscas could not climb to meet their opponents due to their inferiority at higher altitudes, and the Messerschmitts were free to dive down and take out the rookie pilots who would be placed at the rear of Republican formations.[59] This allowed just a handful of 109s to dominate entire squadrons of I-16s and once again demonstrated the tactical, as well as technological, superiority of the Condor Legion over their Russian counterparts. By 28–29 December, the Axis air units were able to begin the process of winning back control of the wintery skies over Teruel. On the ground, however, the offensive, which began on the 29th with an assault by 62nd and 1st Navarrese divisions, did not meet with quite as dramatic a success, at least initially. For two days, they hammered the Republican positions, as the combat reports of the 9th Brigade of Líster's 11th Division attest to:

29th December – Last night, the enemy tried to surprise us with an advance, but was completely repulsed. Today there has been a great deal of aerial and artillery activity, bombarding and shelling our lines intensely. 15 tanks attacked on the right flank of the 100th Brigade. With rifles and machine guns they were twice repulsed. But the tanks attacked again and overran the lines of the 100th Brigade.

30th December – After a huge preparatory bombardment by the enemy aviation and artillery, a furious attack with a great quantity of men and materiel was launched, concentrating mainly in the sector occupied by the 100th Brigade. We have caught the enemy with intense enfilading fire, fending off all their attacks and causing many casualties. This manoeuvre has been done with great speed and audacity.[60]

Joaquín Masjuán was of course fighting with the 9th Brigade at this time and provides a rather more personal account of those hardest of days:

At night, the show was fantastic, as parachute flares were continually being launched over the battlefield, slowly descending, illuminating us as if it were broad daylight, while thousands of tracer bullets passed over the trenches.

On 30th December, when it began to clear, the enemy bombarded our pulverised trenches with artillery fire. Then aviation came to increase the destruction.

When the attackers thought we were finished, we, the survivors, surprised them, because we managed to repulse them three times. Hill 1061 was covered in corpses and wounded. We had not eaten for 20 hours and had almost no sleep.[61]

Major Líster had no reserves left; all his brigades had been committed to hold the line. Despite heroic resistance, on 31 December, Varela got his breakthrough and an advance of 8km was achieved by the Nationalists. Concud and San Blas quickly fell to the Rebel 62nd Division as the Loyalist 64th and 68th divisions crumbled. Next, Navarrese Requetés stormed La Muela, the key fortified height less than 3km south-west of Teruel.[62] The situation seemed lost, and the Republican troops of 40th Division inside Teruel itself, besieging the last few Nationalist strongholds, panicked and swiftly withdrew. The Rebel garrison was alone in the ruined city, but they were unaware that their besiegers had left. 11th Division had been relieved (it is possible Líster took the decision unilaterally)[63] on the night of the 30th, and on the 31st, the Basque XXII Corps commander Ibarrola had arrived at Líster's HQ and requested at least one brigade go back into battle to restore the situation. The young major refused, citing the toll that fifteen days' combat in such cold conditions had taken on his men, not least fifty-eight amputations of frostbitten feet. Perhaps he feared a repeat of the rout at Brunete when the exhausted Listers had lost the town. In his memoirs, Líster claims that on examining his troops, Ibarrola acquiesced to his demand for rest.[64] On the other hand, Republican records show that the Communist's flat-out refusal to carry out orders caused some consternation, and Rojo has received criticism for not taking a firmer line with his famous subordinate.[65] Instead of facing reprimand, the following day Líster was promoted to lieutenant colonel, the first militia leader to reach such a senior rank following the lifting of a bar on promotion for non-military men (Modesto had presumably bypassed this rule having served in the Foreign Legion before the war). Reportedly, many Republican officers were appalled at Líster's insubordination and outraged at his subsequent promotion.[66]

The situation in Teruel was still desperate. Azaña recorded in his diary a bleak picture of the panic:

> First a division [possibly the 11th]. The next day, three divisions did not wait for the fight [the units in the city], and they broke up. Some soldiers arrived in Sarrión [40km away]. Rojo admires the speed. Officers of the headquarters on the Puerto de Escandón, halting the fugitives with pistols. Teruel, abandoned for four hours. A lieutenant of carabineros went to the Rebels, and told what was happening. They did not believe it. That's why all was not lost.[67]

The Army of the Levante, and indeed the Republic, needed a firefighter. Therefore, General Hernández Saravia called Juan Modesto and his V Corps up to the front. V Corps had been weakened substantially, with the Listers obviously detached already, and 46th Division tied down in the Guadalajara sector. It now consisted merely of General Walter's 35th 'International' Division and the 47th Division, commanded by another militia major, Gustavo Durán, who had been Kléber's chief of staff in the defence of Madrid. At this crucial juncture, the weather intervened. On the afternoon of 31 December, with the Republican lines in tatters, Varela just a few kilometres from Teruel, Líster refusing to intervene and the city largely abandoned, the snow began to fall again. It soon became a blizzard. Temperatures plunged to -20°C, the lowest recorded in Spain since the turn of the century, and snowdrifts of over a metre deep deluged the battlefield. Engines froze solid, planes were grounded and the Nationalist troops, who were on the advance rather than in fixed positions, were completely exposed and suffered dreadfully, with scores dying overnight. General Barrón complained that his elite troops of the Black Hand were perishing in large numbers, having 'no protection against the weather' and inadequate winter clothing.[68] The snowstorm lasted for two days and cut off Teruel from outside communication; a traffic jam of 600 lorries blocked the Valencia road, rendering the Republican forces temporarily incommunicado.[69] The weather had bought Modesto the breathing space he needed. At dawn on New Year's Day 1938, the Republican troops belatedly returned to their posts in Teruel, Rey d'Harcourt's garrison none the wiser.[70] Meanwhile, Modesto went about stabilising the situation. He dispatched the 11th and 15th International Brigades of Walter's 35th Division to hold a line west-north-west of Teruel, which included the Santa Barbara and Muletón heights, while Durán's 47th was tasked with retaking the crucial La Muela.

Without it, Teruel simply could not be held. One Republican junior officer later wrote lucidly of the hazardous journey through the blizzard to the front and the subsequent bitter struggle for that queer, molar-shaped hill:

When my unit was sent to the front, the snow had been falling for days. The glassy road winding through the mountains was crowded with trucks inching their way toward Teruel. We forgot the beauty of the place when three of the trucks slipped over the precipices and fell into the ravines below. Then we knew it was bitterly cold, and there was no more dangerous road anywhere on earth. The convoys crawled. There were no guard-rails – only the winding road and the mountains and Teruel a few miles away.

I saw a lot of that road, for I went up and down it on a motorcycle, and I knew the sufferings of the men and felt compassion for them.

Very late in the day I was able to concentrate my unit in a bombed village at the foot of a ravine, but the ravine formed a chimney for the wind, and it was probably colder there than in the mountains. The gutted walls provided no shelter. The men slept by the side of the cliff, huddled together. In this way each man had three or four blankets over him. It was the best way.

Meanwhile I found a small house on the other side of the ravine, and went there to get some sleep. I might have done better in the open. There were sixty men huddled round a fire, and the wind howled through the open roof, and the smoke clogged our eyelids. But we slept a little, and before dawn we were on the march.

Our object was to take La Muela de Teruel, the flat-topped hill on the south bank of the Guadalaviar River, overlooking Teruel. We needed the hill, for it was an excellent observation post and dominated the valley. It was very nearly impregnable, scored with small ravines, and the sides were almost vertical.

We attacked during a blizzard, the temperature below zero. Our men had somehow to climb and grapple their way up the steep slopes of the hill, arm over arm. There was a biting wind and blinding snow, but somehow they succeeded in establishing a foothold, and by mid-day they were occupying half of the hill. It was the better half, looking down on Teruel. It was December 31st, 1937.

The horror was in the cold, the wind, the snow, the absence of footholds. More than half our casualties came from frostbite: many had to have their toes amputated. Still, half the hill was in our possession. I could have pressed my men to take the whole hill 'whatever the sacrifice', and perhaps we might have taken it, but it was impossible to demand any more sacrifices from them. We had to content ourselves with our slice of the hill, with the enemy no more than a few yards away.

It was a strange position up on La Muela, with a wavering serpentine line dividing us from the enemy, our men digging shallow trenches and taking what cover they could.

On one of my inspection tours of the front I found the hill blanketed with fog. I was unable to see more than three or four yards ahead, and often much less. Later the sun burned the fog away, and the whole hill stood out perfectly. I continued my tour of inspection along the erratic forward line, the enemy perhaps three hundred feet away. All this time my orderly was acting in a way beyond my understanding. He kept moving round me. Sometimes he was on my left, sometimes on my right, sometimes behind me or in front of me. I suddenly realised my orderly was trying to protect my life with his own, and I was alarmed. It was strange and wonderful that he should have thought he could protect me on that exposed hill, against bullets which would slice through two men as easily as one. And I marvelled.

Teruel is the coldest town in Spain, but the hill was colder. La Muela was absolutely barren: no trees, no grasses, grew on it. All around Teruel there is this eroded land with deep gulleys, harsh and uninviting. But we clung to our hill. …

One day I accompanied General Hernández Saravia on one of his visits to another sector of the front. We stood on a hill and watched the preparations for the enemy's coming attack. The whole snowy countryside seemed to be boiling under the heavy concentration of fire, from aviation and artillery. Because the ground was covered with ice and the earth was frozen, there was no black smoke in the explosions. All along the front thick white clouds erupted and dissolved and flared up again and melted and reappeared elsewhere, and there was no end to the weight of armour hurling down over the plains of Teruel.

General Saravia was a quiet man. For a while he watched in silence the pounding of our lines, and then he could contain himself no longer. He leaned forward and muttered between his teeth: '*Cobardes! Así se puede ganar la guerra!* Cowards! Is that the way to win a war? Why don't you fight man to man, as we do?'

There was no end to those pure white explosions filled with smoke and ice and expanding gases and the remains of human beings, and no end to the General muttering: '*Cobardes! Que den el pecho, como nosotros!*'[71]

In three days of brutal fighting, with what Modesto labelled 'superhuman' efforts, with tanks and heavy weapons having to be hauled onto the heights, 47th Division managed to push the Nationalists back sufficiently so that Teruel was no longer in immediate danger. Varela's men dug in on the western edge of La Muela. The heroism and bravery of the Nationalists desperately attempting to maintain their foothold was just as impressive, as the operational diary of one Carlist unit stationed on the hills outside Teruel recorded:

> It is worth mentioning the spirit and enthusiasm of the requetés, who, after an artillery preparation and in the hardest moments of the attack, received the enemy with regional chants and cheered by their hand grenades and machine-gun bursts, which decimated the ranks of their adversaries, which left a large number of dead and wounded at the edge of our trenches.[72]

Meanwhile, the Galician Corps had become bogged down in the Celadas Heights further north.[73] As the thermometer had plummeted, the momentum had drained away from the Rebel counter-attack. Modesto's V Corps had, for the time being, snatched some sort of victory from the jaws of disaster.

Despite Franco's failure to relieve the garrison, the siege of the last few Insurgent strongpoints in Teruel dragged on. The Generalissimo telegraphed Colonel Rey d'Harcourt to instruct him to 'trust in Spain as Spain trusts in you', effectively ordering him not to surrender.[74] On 31 December, when Nationalist troops had been so close yet so far, the Rebels had claimed Teruel saved. To try to ascertain the truth of this claim, a carload of foreign journalists working in the Nationalist zone had driven through the blizzard and attempted to enter the city, only to be shelled by Republican artillery. Disregarding the clear dangers of battlefield reporting, Herbert Matthews was back in Teruel by 4 January:

> They [Republican troops] eagerly told us how mines had been exploded in the Civil Governor's building and Santa Clara Convent, where the Rebels were still holding out.

Accompanied by a news photographer, I went quickly to the Governor's building to see for myself. That was the building that one six-inch gun had been punishing from a distance of 300 yards for ten days. What with that and the mine, the whole front facade on the side facing the bridge had collapsed.

On the side I first approached, Loyalists were swarming to attack. My companion and I scrambled up after the soldiers. The building echoed deafeningly with rifle fire, pistol shots and grenade explosions. It needed some cautious manoeuvring to recognize what corner not to go around.

We made our way to the third floor. The Rebels were on the floor below us, firing upward, while the Loyalists shot down or dropped hand grenades.

Shouts of 'Viva Franco' and 'Arriba España' came up clearly, Loyalist militiamen answered with shots and bombs. Once a song floated upward amazingly from that doomed place below. A soldier next to me heard it just as he was about to draw the pin on a grenade.

'They're singing,' he said in a stupefied tone.

The stairway rose a few steps and led into a corridor that swung around to the left. We crept up and around by the wall and peered into room after room, where with slight variations the same scene was being enacted. Men crouched at windows and holes in the floor were firing down or throwing grenades.

The government has really occupied the Governor's building, the seminary and other places, as its communiqués have stated, but underneath these lies a veritable subterranean city. Passages connect the Gobierno, as it is called, with the Hotel Aragon, the Bank of Spain, the seminary, Santa Clara Convent and other places. The importance of what was then happening, however, was that the Loyalists had at last made contact with the Insurgent garrison and driven them underground.

One by one in small groups they are being captured or killed. Three prisoners were taken in the *Gobierno* while we were there. I talked with one of them, a youngster of 19 years, black and grimy, his lips swollen and cracked from lack of water.

He said they had lived on sardines and other canned foods and had plenty of ammunition. Water was rather scarce, although there was enough to prevent desperate thirst. There was no bread.[75]

In the air, the Duke of Lerma, his fighter squadron having been refitted with Fiat CR.32s, had arrived in the sector in late December. Conditions remained difficult for the airmen of both sides, with the Nationalist fighter pilot reporting temperatures of -50°C in the open cockpit of his Fiat biplane. The frozen pilots had to be lifted out of their aircraft by the ground crew, having lost feeling in their limbs. While flying over Teruel, one of the duke's friends was shot down by anti-aircraft fire and in recounting what happened next, Lerma gives an insight into how Spain had been torn in two by the civil war:

He had floated down to the ground and was immediately grabbed by enemy patrol, who marched him off to the nearest command post, where he was led into a dugout. His escort saluted and departed. An officer was sitting at a table, very busily talking over the telephone. Careaga [Lerma's friend] waited in silence, but the fellow paid not the slightest attention to him and carried on with his conversation. He might not have existed as far as the speaker was concerned.

He waited patiently, hoping to get some attention, until eventually he decided to break the ice.

'My name is Careaga,' he said. 'Could I be led to the post commander?' The officer, still on the telephone, suddenly jerked around and in a brusque manner said, 'I am the commander. What the hell do you want?'

They both remained dumbfounded with astonishment and surprise, for recognition was instantaneous. They had been friends in the past in Bilbao, where they both lived. Careaga had been an enthusiastic amateur boxer, and the post commander his instructor.

'I must get you away from here as soon as possible,' he told him, 'before others take a hand in the matter. It is not safe.'

They had been delighted to see each other. It had been so unexpected. Careaga was very relieved to have fallen into the hands of an old friend. Prisoners taken near the front lines usually had a rough time of it. He was taken away under a safe escort to a prison camp in Catalonia, where he remained until the end of the war.[76]

However, it was not all bad for the Rebel pilots. Once again deployed in Aragon, the duke and his fellow airmen could return to some of their old haunts:

Whenever possible we drove a squadron bus into Saragossa in the evenings, over a long and bumpy road. The first thing I usually did was jump into a hot bath at the Grand Hotel. If we were free next day with no flights on the agenda, we were allowed to stay overnight and, naturally, make merry while we could.

The cafés and bars in Saragossa were always very crowded, for they were the general meeting places. You would find a mixed gathering, from plain soldiers and civilians to generals, Requetés from the Navarre brigades, Regulares, Legion, air force, and Falangistmen, in a varied and colorful display of uniforms. Some were fresh from battle, others about to leave, not knowing if they would ever see those bright lights again; many had bandaged heads, arms in slings, or were using sticks and crutches; but all were full of enthusiasm and optimism. One would run into old friends or relations whom one had not seen for months. It was all very gay and exhilarating, and the war would be forgotten for a few hours.[77]

While Lerma was lucky enough to take a bath, drink and make merry, his comrades in Teruel had reached the limits of human endurance. It had become clear that relief was not forthcoming, and with just as many civilians as soldiers under his care, Colonel Rey d'Harcourt was in an invidious position. The Nationalist garrison had now been largely forced underground, holding out in the basements of the city's main public buildings. The final capitulation came on 8 January, and, once again, Herbert Matthews was there:

Today's surrender was partly spontaneous, partly the result of negotiations such as occurred yesterday. Lieut. Col. Rey d'Harcourt, who surrendered yesterday, first offered to go as an emissary to an isolated group of soldiers who had gathered underneath the ruins of the seminary and the Santa Clara Convent, but Indalecio Prieto, Defense Minister, refused to permit this, for fear the Insurgents might try to kill the civil officials and attribute the crime to the republicans 'as being a violation of our promise to respect the lives of prisoners'.

Some Loyalists who went forward this morning to parley were shot at for their pains. Later, contact was made with Colonel Barba, the commander of the Rebel forces [in the Santa Clara], and he proposed that the sick and wounded be evacuated while the others remained.

Señor Prieto again refused and between made his only terms, the unconditional surrender of all. To that Colonel Barba replied that he would consult his fellow-officers.

No reply ever came, but it was not needed, for at various times during the morning Rebels began cautiously to make their way out of the convent with their arms raised. By 2 o'clock 144 had escaped safely.

It must have become obvious to those remaining that resistance was hopeless.[78]

Several thousand Nationalist troops and many more civilians, including the Archbishop of Teruel, handed themselves over on 7–8 January. Rey d'Harcourt was vilified in Francoist Spain as a coward and a traitor, though he and the archbishop would both be shot in the Republic's desperate final days in 1939. Teruel would not be a second Alcázar, there would be no relief, no rescue, no heroes. There was also little joy on the Republican side after the long siege. The Catalan head of propaganda, Jaume Miravitlles, rushed to see Prieto with proposals for a massive campaign to celebrate the victory. However, the eternally pessimistic defence minister poured cold water on the idea, insisting that the city could only be held for three weeks. Miravitlles left the meeting convinced the war was lost.[79] Prieto was clearly aware that much of the Army of the Levante that had been committed to the Teruel fighting was now completely exhausted and depleted. Having fought for three weeks in the worst Spanish winter for a generation, XX Corps and others were due a rest. Many units had lost a third of their strength and half of their armaments.[80] 40th Division, which had borne the brunt of the fighting in the city itself, suffered 25 per cent casualties and was withdrawn.[81] Meanwhile, the anarchist 25th Division had been forced to keep fighting even once the other unit in XXII Corps, the Listers, had been relieved, a decision their commander blamed on Communist favouritism. Clearly in a poor state, the anarchist unit clashed with troops from 40th Division over loot from Teruel and was also taken out of the line.[82]

Meanwhile, the International Brigades of the 35th Division were strung out along the hills and trenches, west of the city, in what their commander, General Walter, called a 'position of honour'. The 11th Brigade had deployed its Thälmann, Edgar André and 12th February Battalions on El Muletón, the height that dominated the northerly approaches to Teruel and the Alfambra valley. The British Battalion of 15th Brigade was deployed on Santa Barbara, with the Canadian Mac-Paps beside them, and the American

Lincoln–Washington Battalion holding positions right on the outskirts of Teruel. Life at Teruel had been fairly uneventful thus far for 35th Division, although the Lincolns' Captain Phil Detro, who had replaced the wounded Hans Amlie at Belchite, was fatally hit by a sniper's bullet on 16 January. The imposing Texan, proud of his Confederate lineage, had neglected to use the communication trenches when inspecting positions on the line and paid the price, later dying when he refused to have his wounded leg amputated.[83] Furthermore, even simply being in the line at Teruel was a trial, as Welsh volunteer medic Alun Williams remembered:

> As far as I was concerned the Battle of Teruel happened at the North Pole. It was a bitter winter. My hands were sticking to metal and frostbite was a major factor. … It was a cruel battle: the cold, the weather, the short days. By this time things were getting short in the war, such as food and clothing. In this battle, I didn't have any shoes, just rope sandals. My feet were killing me and I was wrapping them up in anything I could find.[84]

During this quiet spell on the front, Nationalist Army of the North commander General Fidel Dávila had been preparing another counter-offensive, this time to retake rather than relieve Teruel. Aranda's Galician Corps, with, from north to south, the 13th Black Hand, Sáenz de Buruaga's 150th, the 5th Navarrese Division and 84th Division, would attack through the Celadas Heights, with the latter two divisions targeting the heights of El Mueltón. Meanwhile, units of Yagüe's Moroccan Corps would drive east along the Guadalavier valley to threaten La Muela and Teruel itself from the south-west. In total, twelve divisions and 500 artillery pieces were committed to the attack.[85] The assault began on 17 January with a gigantic air and artillery bombardment. A handful of the soon-to-be-infamous Ju 87 Stuka dive-bombers had arrived in Spain that month, and this battle was almost certainly the scene of their first true combat testing.[86] While the 13th and 150th Nationalist divisions pushed Republican units back several kilometres in the Celadas Heights, the focus of the initial assault fell on El Mueltón, defended by the 11th International Brigade. The American Milton Wolff, now a captain on the 15th Brigade staff, could only watch from a kilometre away as the terrible scene unfolded:

> The fascist planes would come in and circle overhead. One would peel off and dive almost straight down toward the crest of the hill. He could

see the bomb, or sometimes more than one, separate from the fuselage. Then the plane would flatten out and scream upward, bank, and join the circling planes above, one of which would already be on its way down. When the planes had gotten rid of their bombs and the top of the hill was a ball of black smoke, they dived again, one after the other, the rattle of their machine guns clacking through the whine of the wings. …

The cloud of smoke rose to meet the diving planes. They went into it, screaming out as they made their passes. Mitch could see fascist cavalry and foot soldiers forming for the attack, officers moving up and down along the ranks, standard-bearers waving red-and-gold banners to and fro at the foot of the hill. When the planes buzzed off, the artillery began and the formations started up the hill. When they got close to the top, the artillery lifted, the men picked up the pace.

There was a furious rattle of gunfire and the explosion of grenades. The enemy broke ranks and the men fell back in disorder. The planes came in, then the artillery, and then the men, over and over. He had seen all this before. Too many times.

Meanwhile, in the rear, convoys of trucks brought more men and ammo for the artillery that was pounding the hill.

Along with a group of officers from the Brigade, an exasperated Wolff wanted desperately to help his beleaguered comrades, but to no avail.

The Thaelmann Battalion was on that hill. They were Germans, and other central Europeans, all exiles from their own countries. Mitch knew one who had been in the hands of the Gestapo for months, tortured and beaten, but not broken. Now they were in Spain on a hill called El Muletón on the outskirts of Teruel, and they were being pounded by Stuka dive-bombers and German artillery. …

'My God, isn't there anything we can do?' Castle asked. Copic shook his head.

'Dunbar?'

'Nothing. We do not have the means.' His diction was precise, very British. 'All our units are committed.'

'Why don't they take them off the hill? Why are they – '

'They won't come off. They are sworn to hold the hill to the last man.'

'To the last man? That's bullshit.'

'They're Germans.' Dunbar looked like an Egyptian pharaoh, or at least like the photos and drawings Mitch had seen, except he was very white. His face was smooth, no sign of concern wrinkling the surface. Stiff upper lip. 'I suppose they've decided that this is where the battle ends. They've been at it for an awfully long time, you know. One might say since 1930, perhaps before.'[87]

Eventually, after holding out for the best part of two days, the 11th Brigade was compelled to withdraw. Under the most intense of air and artillery bombardments, and constant attack from Carlist and Nationalist infantry, the Thälmanns had fought with dogged determination. However, delaying Dávila's counter-offensive had come at an extortionate cost; while proud of the 'most brilliant' performance of his 11th Brigade, commending the fighting qualities of the new Spanish recruits, General Walter reported that they suffered 1,000 casualties in three days' combat (from a strength of 2,899 before the battle).[88]

19 January was to be the sternest test for the Republicans as the Rebel attack reached its climax. Four hundred Nationalist aircraft were committed that day, flying from dawn until dusk in close support of the Insurgent advance.[89] The Duke of Lerma was in the air for most of that day, in what he described as one of the biggest aerial operations of the war:

> We were briefed that day to escort the Junkers, Savoias, Heinkel 51s, and Romeos; this meant we would be flying in wide circles over the target area, some of us at the same level as our bombers, the rest high above them. An endless relay of light and heavy machines roared in, unloaded, and were out again to leave room for more. The patrols lasted from two to two and a half hours from takeoff to landing; we were over the lines between sixty and ninety minutes. It was a strain on the neck muscles to continually swivel one's head around in all directions, especially above and behind, the two most vulnerable spots, but it was the best way to keep alive. Eyes strained to pick out the slightest movement in the sky. During this period, we were flying two or three patrols daily. General Franco visited the front that day.[90]

Having taken El Muletón, the 5th Navarrese and 84th divisions were free to sweep down the Alfambra valley and outflank the lines held by the Canadian

Mac-Paps. Already on the 18th, some Insurgent units had tried to move down the valley, only to be driven back by the British machine guns. Bob Cooney of Aberdeen remembers what happened next:

> The fascists were bound to attempt to move up the valley again in order to take the Canadians in the rear. In order to prevent this, it was decided the British should occupy the valley. It was an undertaking calculated to make the stoutest of hearts quail, but the British lads went to it with a will.[91]

The British Battalion moved down from their strong position on the Santa Barbara to an exposed line in the valley itself, in order to protect the Canadians' flank. Cooney continues:

> First down was Lieutenant Sam Wild with No. 3 Company. Sam was always at his best in an emergency and, though he probably knew the meaning of fear as well as any other man, he never gave any outward indication of it.
>
> No. 4 Company made the descent next, but were observed and heavily bombarded by the enemy. No. 1 Company brought up the rear and raced down the gully under even heavier fire. Three of the company were killed, but the audacious descent achieved its purpose. The valley was held.[92]

On 19 January, a huge bombardment fell on the British lines, from artillery and aircraft, which lasted several hours, with the Major Attlee Company taking the worst of the enemy fire. Once again, Bob Cooney experienced the drama:

> They fired everything at us. At the height of the bombardment I crouched beside 'Tappy' [Walter Tapsell], the battalion commissar. On top of our position a tank had been abandoned. It drew the fire of the enemy. 'Tappy's' language was lurid as he described in uncomplimentary terms the ancestry of the so-and-so who, with all the battlefield to choose from, had abandoned his tank at that particular spot. We spent an uncomfortable half hour while the fascists tried to blow the tank to pieces. Our trench was destroyed at several points.[93]

Next, when the shelling finally ceased, came the Rebel assault. The battalion's Maxim machine guns had remained on the Santa Barbara hill, ensconced in concrete bunkers that had formed part of the Nationalist defence of Teruel, and were able to fire over the heads of both the British and the Canadians. With the machine-gunners was Bob Clark, a Communist from Liverpool who had just joined the battalion. He later wrote this account of his first combat:

> Suddenly what looked like black ants came crawling up the valley, evidently intent on occupying those forward positions but they had forgotten about us. What a surprise lay in store for them. I for one was almost petrified on looking at hundreds of Fascist troops advancing along the valley, my first view of the enemy. How strange it all seemed. These black objects, could they be men intent on killing me as well as my comrades? It hardly seemed credible. ...
>
> The blowing of whistles which the enemy officers used as a sort of signal, made it all too real. We suddenly sprang to life on the orders of [Sergeant] Cornwallis and in a few seconds had a perfect bead on the advancing enemy. Our heavy gun opened fire and a hail of lead hit the ground a few yards in front of the advancing Fascists, a slight movement of the gun sights and dozens of men collapsed and died. The enemy staggered. At the same time the Canadians on the valley heights opposite opened up with all they had. In a few minutes the valley was completely deserted except for a few score black objects to testify to the enemy's terrible mistake.
>
> We kept on firing for quite a long time. How exhilarating it all was. I felt almost ashamed of myself when I remembered afterwards how full of joy I felt, how exalted, how terrible. How near we all are to animals. The lust to kill is only dormant and is easily aroused. Yet when I thought of what had happened to our lads earlier in the day, I excused myself. This war was like all wars: kill or be killed. Dead silence followed. A few birds flew over the valley but we had no time to waste on birds, more evil kinds might soon return. There was more digging and improving the gun position. We were then eleven feet in depth and had to construct a fire-step to enable ourselves to observe the movements, if any, of the enemy.
>
> As darkness descended we received reports of how gallantly the British infantry had stood up to their ordeal but at a heavy price.[94]

Twenty-one British had been killed but the gallantry of the British and Canadians who had halted the Rebel advance down the Alfambra was praised in Modesto's orders of the day for V Corps. In addition, the commanders of both battalions received promotions.[95] During those days, the situation had been critical and some of the units that had suffered a mauling at Teruel were thrown back into the line. 40th Division, which had done much of the street fighting, was committed at Cemetery Hill on 17 January, covering the British positions. After suffering heavy casualties, on the 20th, one of its battalions refused orders to go up to the line and relieve another. One hundred and six soldiers were disciplined, including forty-six shot for insubordination. The following day, the brigade was pulled out of the line and disbanded.[96] Clearly, many People's Army units were in a bad way. Despite this, the line held, conceding only part of La Muela thanks both to the brave efforts of the Internationals, Modesto's 47th Division and XVIII Corps, which held Yagüe's Moroccan units advancing from the south-west.[97] Nationalist losses had also been heavy, with the 84th Division, which had fought at El Muletón and beyond, suffering 3,500 casualties from 16 to 25 January.[98] By 22 January, Dávila's counter-offensive had petered out, with the Rebels several kilometres closer, but still short of Teruel. It had been hoped that the advance could be continued to the Santa Barbara cemetery, and therefore begin to encircle the city from the north, but in the face of such stiff resistance, and considering the huge losses sustained by the 5th Navarrese Division, the attack was called off.[99]

Throughout January, the Nationalist efforts were supported by the 13th Black Hand Division, which included Commander Carlos Iniesta's 4th Bandera of the Spanish Foreign Legion. They were deployed in the heights north of Teruel around the town of Celadas, tasked with making repeated attempts to push the Republicans back, achieving limited results. Iniesta describes in his memoirs the concrete fortifications and triple lines of barbed wire that made the job of his battalion so difficult, compounded by the difficulty of getting supplies to the front line:

> I remember that period – from January 4th to February 9th – as the hardest, and, undoubtedly, the hardest of the war. The red resistance was so stiff that the Bandera had a large number of casualties. Due to the intense cold … there were also a large number of casualties due to the freezing of extremities. The losses, in total, exceeded 450 in number.
>
> In my modest opinion, the operation – well conceived in the beginning – was badly executed, because … we were forced to carry

out a series of frankly frontal attacks, that could not succeed, in spite of the great heroism that all the legionaries, with their officers at the head, frittered away ... they were stopped by defensive positions and barbed wire hidden by piles of snow, they were swept by machine guns positioned on the flank.

On several occasions we had to remove our dead at night and tied them to ropes with which they had to be dragged to achieve their retrieval, because when standing up we were easily spotted, as our bodies stood out against the ground so white with snow.[100]

For the time being, the Nationalist advance was halted and the International units were withdrawn, and dispatched further north, where they would be making a diversionary attack to try to draw the Rebels away from Teruel. Meanwhile, General Hernández Saravia launched a number of small-scale attacks all along the line from 25 to 27 January to try to improve the Republicans' positions, but with little success against a superior and well-prepared enemy.[101] Higher up, Republican Chief of Staff General Vicente Rojo was worried that Loyalist success could lead to strategic problems. His 'Strategic Counter-attack Number Two' had achieved its aims of distracting Franco from Madrid and capturing Teruel. However, Rojo now feared that with the 'red rag' of a beleaguered garrison now gone, the Generalissimo might return to his Guadalajara plan. The battle in Teruel was over, it appeared; might the Nationalists now launch their own offensive anyway, with the People's Army tied down in Aragon? Clearly, the Republican command took this possibility seriously, for Rojo activated 'Plan P', the much-maligned Extremadura offensive in southern Spain. It was hoped that the Rebels could once again be distracted from Madrid with another diversionary offensive. From mid-January onwards, the slow process of moving vast quantities of troops and equipment to the rural south had begun, with the over-stretched Loyalist logistical system only able to provide 400 trucks and three trains per day for this gargantuan task.[102] But Rojo had jumped the gun. He had misread his adversary, and Republican military intelligence had clearly let him down. Franco was not finished with Teruel.

General Juan Vigón, the Caudillo's chief planner, had put together a more imaginative operation than Varela or Dávila. Vigón transferred the bulk of Nationalist strength well north of the battlefield that the fighting of December and January had criss-crossed. The site for the new offensive was approximately 40km north of the contested city, where Loyalist lines bulged out into the wide open plateau behind the Sierra de Palomera. The Republican defences here were weak, manned by inexperienced conscripts. The Rebels gathered as many as 100,000 men, made up of the Galician, Castilian and Navarrese corps, plus a cavalry division under General Monasterio, and supported, as ever, by Axis air power, tanks, twenty-four batteries of Italian artillery from the CTV, and the formidable flak units of the Condor Legion.[103] Aranda's Corps of Galicia would attack from the south-west, either side of Celadas, towards the Alfambra itself with, from north to south, the 85th, 83rd, 84th and 13th divisions. Yagüe's Moroccan Corps would do the same from the north-west, driving south towards Fuentes Calientes and Perales de Alfambra with 82nd Division, 1st and 4th Navarrese divisions and the 108th in reserve. In the centre, the 1st Cavalry Division under Monasterio and 5th Navarrese Division would push across the plateu behind the Sierra Palomera.[104] The operation was to be a giant pincer that would cut off the Republican bulge and break through to the Alfambra River. Peter Kemp was one of a handful of British volunteers in the Spanish Foreign Legion, and his Bandera was being brought up to take part in the central attack:

> I was standing on a mountainside, about two hundred yards below the crest of a stony ridge connecting two great shoulders of rock that sloped back towards the plain; the whole formed a wide, semi-circular amphitheatre about half-a-mile in circumference. Now its craggy sides were swarming with troops – green-coated legionaries, Requetés in scarlet berets, khaki-clad infantry and gunners. The whole arena teemed with men, horses, mules, guns and equipment. Colonel Sánchez González's 5th Navarre Division, with the 14th and 16th Banderas, was massed below the crest in preparation for a great attack.[105]

As the men moved forward, they noticed an old general on a white horse overseeing the preparations on that bright winter's morning. 'Look, there's Papa Vigón! We'll be all right if he's planned this,' one of the men shouted.[106] It was 5 February and Vigón's masterstroke began with a huge air and artillery bombardment:

> By half past ten the last mist had cleared. We heard a droning in the sky and saw a formation of silver, twin-engined bombers, with an escort of bi-plane fighters, approaching from the west; they flew over us towards

the enemy lines; a minute later we heard the thunder of their bombs. At the same moment our batteries opened fire all round us, from the mountains on either side and from the foothills and the plain behind; the air was alive with the hiss of shells passing overhead. The aircraft returned to circle over us and make a second run; again we heard the roll of bursting bombs.

For two hours the bombardment raged, the guns keeping up an unceasing barrage while waves of aircraft flew over us to unload on the enemy positions. Not a shell came back in reply, nor was there a sign of enemy activity in the air. When the firing began we all made ready to advance, expecting the order at any moment; but as it became clear that the bombardment would be a long one, we gradually relaxed and made ourselves comfortable.[107]

Some of the bombers mistook the assembled Legionnaires for Republican troops and dropped their loads on Kemp's position, causing 500 casualties. Nevertheless, his own Bandera had been lucky, losing just five, and very soon, the offensive was under way:

Half-an-hour after our disastrous bombing the fire of our batteries slackened and we received the order to advance. We climbed slowly to the top of the ridge behind which we had been sheltering all morning, and moved in single file down a narrow, stony track on the further side; the three rifle companies in our van spread out in open order to cross the flat country in front of us. Away on our left the cavalry were racing ahead, widely extended across the plain. We advanced slowly towards a line of low hills. At any moment I expected to hear the patter of bullets falling among us; but the most we encountered were a few 'overs' from far away, and we reached the hills without casualties. The enemy had abandoned their defences under that inferno of bombing and shellfire; after our experience of the morning I could not blame them.[108]

In the face of such overwhelming firepower, the inexperienced Republican troops in the sector, mostly from 42nd Division of XIII Corps, melted away. Monasterio's division achieved one of the last successful cavalry charges in the history of warfare, mercilessly cutting down fleeing infantry as in the great battles of the past.[109] The advance soon became a rout and Kemp never met any enemy resistance, merely abandoned defences and supply depots as the Loyalist forces desperately tried to avoid encirclement. By 7 February, the Nationalists were on the banks of the Alfambra (a 20km advance), having taken a huge swathe of territory (1,300 square kilometres) and captured more than 7,000 prisoners.[110] Many of these came from 42nd Division, which was effectively dissolved and later reconstituted from new mixed brigades. 7 February was also the best day of the battle for the Condor Legion, with the German pilots claiming twelve kills in a single aerial battle, as Gotthardt Handrick explains:

I was underway with two Staffeln providing cover for the bombers, which were scheduled to follow us. I flew with 1. Staffel, and far ahead of us was 2. Staffel. Hardly had we flown over the Front when we caught sight of a large number of aircraft in the east, which were flying exactly opposite to our course. Were these our own bombers which, having performed their task, were already on their way home?

Soon, however, we could make out from their blood-red emblems that these were enemy bombers. They were Martin aircraft, Soviet machines of American design [SB Tupolevs], not dissimilar to our He 111s. 2. Staffel, flying ahead of us, immediately attacked the reds. We also stepped on the gas and took out the aircraft that were there. My heart was beating with joy for up to now we had never seen so many red bombers – there were 22 of them – and we got them under our guns. Not only that, but it appeared as if the bombers were not accompanied by any fighters at all.

When the reds recognised us, they turned away, but it was too late. As they turned our 2. Staffel caught them, and two red machines dived into the depths, leaving enormous trails of smoke behind them. Their crews saved themselves by parachute. The remaining 20 attempted to slip away, but they were already near enough to be held under our fire. In a wink of an eye, eight reds began to burn and crashed like flaming torches. I myself had got to about 150m behind one of the bombers.

I had the aircraft, as large as a barn door, in my sights. I pressed the trigger, but after 14 rounds both weapons jammed – the enemy machine just stayed there. I had to break off from my victim. I could clearly see how its machine-gunner was shooting at me like a savage.

Meanwhile, the enemy fighter cover also showed up on the scene. Three or four squadrons of Ratas [I-16s] suddenly came down on us like a warm rain, and there resulted a wild and lurching twisting and turning dogfight, which ended up with two enemy fighters sharing the same fate as the Martin bombers. For us, it was now high time to protect our own bombers from the fighters. The enemy had, however, obviously lost his appetite. He withdrew in the direction of Valencia and our Kampfgruppe was able to accomplish its task unmolested.[111]

Also, on the 7th, the Rebel 13th Division finally broke through at Celadas and could join the advance, with Carlos Iniesta's men at last breaching the fortifications against which, in the opinion of the Foreign Legion veteran, they had suffered their sternest tests of the war:

> On several occasions, provided with large wire-cutters, we crawled – I include myself in the plural, as I too did it – until reaching the barbed wire of the enemy redoubt and, cutting the wire to the right and left and to the necessary depth, we tied long ropes [to the wire] which we pulled to create gaps, where, the next day, as soon as dawn broke, the assault was attempted. At last, and after multiple battles, the redoubt of Celadas ... was occupied on February 7, 1938.[112]

Even great victories come at a high price in human life, as Priscilla Scott-Ellis was finding out. An English aristocrat, she had defied her parents and gone to Spain to serve as a nurse for the Francoists after the death of a Spanish friend in the conflict. Without any real medical experience other than a first aid course, she found herself in a hospital dealing with the wounded of Vigón's audacious counter:

> This afternoon we had three operations. The first was a red prisoner with a bad head wound, the second was one of the most fascinating things I have ever watched; an operation on an eye. They had to take out some shrapnel and then sew up the actual eyeball. The needles were so small one could scarcely see them. The third was awful. A head wound from shrapnel. It had slit up his cheek and right across the top of his head. When they cut him open there was a hole in his frontal lobe about three inches in diameter; of course when they took out the chips of bone his brains all oozed out to such an extent that one could see right down inside his head to the back of his left eye. One of the nastiest things I have seen yet. The man can't possibly live, which for his benefit under the circumstances is all for the better.[113]

Meanwhile, on the 8th, Peter Kemp's Bandera of crack Legionnaires were tasked with clearing the Sierra Palomera, now cut off from Republican territory:

> All that day we climbed among the ridges of the Sierra Palomera, rounding up the broken remnants of the Republican forces. These were in no state to offer resistance, and only wished to surrender as quickly as possible. They were all Spaniards. In the evening we arrived exhausted at a ruined monastery in the mountains, where we spent the night. … During the whole operation the Bandera had suffered less than half-a-dozen casualties from the enemy; these had been among the rifle companies on the first and third days. But the cold had killed an equal number of us.[114]

It was not until that same day that General Hernández Saravia could put together a force sufficient to stem the tide. Rojo had already dispatched his reserves to Extremadura and there was little chance of getting them back in time, given the perilous condition of the Republic's logistics. A small, unsuccessful counter-attack was organised, but it was clear the situation at the Alfambra was lost. One of the Republican units rushed to the front was the anarchist 25th Division, which had previously been withdrawn following heavy losses. According to the division's commissar, a CNT-FAI activist called Saturino Carod, the division was refused arms by corps staff, who insisted that the commissar accept a Communist Party membership card before the weapons be handed over. Carod refused, and the division was directed to another arms dump, only to find it had been captured by the enemy.[115] Whether the story is true or not, the People's Army was in a bad way and military defeat tended to exacerbate political tensions. On 9 February, Nationalist units pushed across the Alfambra River itself, but by now, despite the dire situation, Republican resistance had stiffened considerably, as the account of another stern test for Commander Carlos Iniesta and his 4th Bandera attests to:

> The enemy, who was in advantageous positions and well-entrenched, opposed our advance with great resilience. …
> Once the red resistance was overcome in the lowest line [Iniesta's men were assaulting a fortified height of over 1,000m altitude], I organised the assault, with the support of a base of fire and a strong barrage from

our 81mm mortars, on the highest position, which was occupied in hand-to-hand combat in the dark around two in the morning.

Once the aforementioned position was occupied, the enemy, with great courage and determination, counter-attacked to recover the lost ground, managing to enter the legionary trenches, which were defended in hand-to-hand combat. ... The confusion was tremendous, because in the darkness the two sides were mixed up.[116]

Due to such dogged resistance, the breach was sealed and the Insurgents held not far from the east banks of the river. When the battle had started, Teruel had occupied a salient within Republican territory. Once again, its position looked incredibly tenuous, but this time it was the Loyalists who were desperate to hold on to the provincial capital and now dangerously close to being encircled. The final word on the Alfambra battle goes to Lieutenant Carmelo Revilla, an experienced campaigner who had been wounded at Brunete and was now an officer with the 1st Navarrese Division:

The result of this operation could not be more encouraging; throughout the Division there had been fewer casualties than in the occupation of any of the heights in the first days of the battle of Teruel; On the contrary, the enemy had suffered significant losses, not only in actual losses due to death, but also deserters and prisoners ... the pocket that was formed in the Sierra Palomera by the joint operation of the three Army Corps [resulted in] about 1,200 killed and more than 6,000 prisoners, in addition to the large area of land conquered and the seizure by the National army of all the ammunition and food found on a quiet front.[117]

In the meantime, Walter's 35th Division of Internationals had been redeployed to a position close to the village of Segura de los Baños, some 80km north of Teruel. Their task was to launch a diversionary attack that would hopefully draw some Nationalist forces away from the main battle further south by capturing Vivel de Río Martín, a road and rail junction that linked the Rebels at Teruel with Saragossa.[118] First, on the night of 16/17 February, the American and Canadian battalions launched an attack on some fortified hills, overseen by Captain Wolff. Delays in reaching their positions meant that the night attack became a dawn raid, which was to have deadly consequences:

The Lincolns took the first hill without a fuss because there were only a handful of men on it. However, the prisoners said there were two companies on the other hill. Conscriptos, peasants and workers like themselves, but the officers – that was another matter. Falangistas.

The battalion headed for the hill in full daylight. A fusillade of rifle and MG fire brought it to a halt. Bill's [Titus] company was chosen to lead the assault on the hill from its side. There would be some artillery, in that a gun or two had been brought up. ...

After awhile the guns opened fire, a few desultory rounds that landed each one far from the one before it, down the slope, up on the crest, and finally over and below the hill. There wasn't anything hitting the gun emplacements or tearing up the barbed wire in front of the trenches.

Titus gathered his section leaders and laid out the plan of attack, which was not much of a plan: first section on the left, second one in the center, and third one on the right, pointing to the slices of the slope each was to use.

'When I give the word, we go up together. Spread out, but keep contact, keep the men firing, fix bayonets, use your grenades to cut the wire, but keep some in reserve for the trenches. I'll take the lead.'

'Don't you think you ought to sit back and see how the sections go up?' Mitch said. Titus's face was chalk white, his lips bloodless, the purple of his irises so deep now as to be almost black. 'If you're going to be up front, I mean, how the hell are you going to control the action?'

'Watch me,' said Titus. He turned away. When the section lead signalled that they were ready, he raised his pistol and fired toward the trenches, then brought it down, his falling arm signalling: Go.

The men came to their feet and began the assault. They reached the wire under the covering fire of the Machine Gun Company. ... Titus was heading for the wire but Mitch hung back to see how it would all go.

The MGs stopped firing and the fascists opened up. They had one machine gun going on the first section's flank and a lot of rifle fire all along the line. The sound of a firefight came from the other side of the hill, where the First Company was attacking. The men who reached the wire first were taking casualties. The slope wasn't very steep, and Mitch had a good view of the strands of wire and trenches below the crest of the hill.

Following the action, Mitch spotted a footpath leading to a gap in the wire, presumably a supply route. He turned to point it out to Bill, but Bill was well on his way to the wire directly ahead.

Mitch started after him and then stopped. He saw that Bill was running right for the wire, but there was no way of going through it except under or over. The way Titus was running and shouting and waving his arms it was clear that he had no intention of doing anything but running right through it.

Grenades exploded all along the strings of barbed wire, rearranging their lines but leaving them largely intact. There was no way to stop Titus. The men nearest him were carried along by his rush, and they too headed for the wire. The section on the left flank stumbled onto the path that Mitch had seen, and they were going up it, getting in each other's way, scrambling and throwing grenades into the trenches whenever they got a clear field. There were a few more shots from the fascists, and then a white flag appeared.

When Mitch got to Titus, he found him hanging on the wire. He knew Titus was dead from the way he hung there. Mitch and some of the men picked him off the wire and laid him on the ground. Mitch looked at him briefly, furious with him for being dead, for being killed the way he'd been killed. He knelt to close the lids over the staring eyes. The irises, seen so close, were no longer violet, but grey and dulling.[119]

The British following up on the American success lacked the strength to punch through to Vivel de Río Martín. Two Banderas (battalions) of La Legion, including Peter Kemp's 14th, were rushed up to Segura de los Baños for a rapid counter-attack. The Rebel assault was hasty and poorly planned, the Legionnaires having to cross over a kilometre of open ground to reach the International Brigade positions along a ridgeline. After the easy advance on the Alfambra, this would be a tougher fight for Franco's elite:

Taking advantage of such cover as the undergrowth afforded, the Bandera advanced down the forward slope against a murderous volume of fire from some hundred heavy and light machine guns. In spite of casualties it crossed the first valley and reached the low ridge of hills about six hundred yards from the enemy. Here de Mora [Kemp's commanding officer] halted and placed his machine guns. When I arrived he was about to continue the attack.

I was put in command of a machine-gun platoon on top of the ridge, on the right flank; two of its four guns had already been destroyed by shell or mortar fire. I hurried off to supervise the distribution of ammunition and arrange for the provision and carriage of fresh supplies during the ensuing engagement; then I prepared to bring my two remaining guns into action, to cover the rifle companies' advance. Across the valley I could make out where the enemy positions were located, well concealed among the pines and dominating our own; my orders were simply to maintain as high and accurate a volume of fire upon them as possible. …

As soon as the rifle companies began to move down through the trees in front, the enemy opened fire all along his line, sweeping the forward slope and the crest of our ridge with a steady rain of bullets, mortar bombs and shells. As I ran from gun to gun, crouching low and taking what cover I could from the formation of the ground, I wondered how anyone could survive in the open against such a devastating weight of fire. I flung myself to the ground beside each gun in turn, straining to mark through my field-glasses the impact of its bursts on the enemy positions, and passing corrections in elevation and direction to the sergeant in command, shouting my orders to make myself heard above the stammer of the gun. I tried to hold the glasses steady, to give my orders without a tremor in my voice and to ignore the vicious spatter of the enemy's bullets.[120]

Waiting for the onrushing Insurgents was Bob Clark, with the Machine Gun Company of the British Battalion of 15th International Brigade:

At about four o'clock the shrill blowing of whistles informed us that the Fascist infantry were attacking. From our position we had a real bird's eye view as we overlooked the valley in front and were nearest the enemy positions. Depressing the sights on our maxim we watched, trembling with excitement, for the first appearance of the enemy. Suddenly, from behind a large number of boulders which were strewn along the valley, the enemy advanced in short rushes. On they came in small formations looking quite determined and almost cocky. They were so close we could distinguish their officers, who curiously to us, were behind their men. This did not mean that they were cowards for we had been informed that the general rule was to urge their men on. …

We in this sector of the line were well below strength and in the event of only a comparatively few casualties would be in a very precarious position. A messenger arrived at this stage with the order to hold the position at all costs and that reinforcements were coming up. The enemy reached only about seven hundred yards away and strangely enough seemed totally unaware of our forward position. In fact they seemed to be advancing diagonally across our line of fire, intent on forcing our centre positions held by the Major Attlee Company. At last we received the order to fire. The effect on the advancing enemy was tremendous. At almost the same moment of our opening fire, someone opened up with a light machine gun and a small mortar. Two of the mortar shells fell very close to the enemy troops.

It was all over in about five minutes; the 'Banderas' hesitated for a moment and then rapidly turned tail leaving a number of killed and wounded on the field.[121]

The 11th Brigade took over the line for 18 February, and Bob Clark comments on the fact that the battered Thälmanns still looked more soldierly and organised than the British.[122] Kemp's Legionnaires were thrown forward again that day, with equally disappointing results, and his superior officer took the decision to defy orders and call off the attack:

A dejected and depleted Bandera dragged itself wearily back to the ridge it had left that same morning. There, after posting guards, we lay down to sleep in the snow, too weary to eat, too sad even to talk of the day's misfortune.

Thanks to de Mora our losses had been remarkably light in the circumstances – four officers and about a hundred men killed or severely wounded; the 16th Bandera had suffered more heavily, losing a large percentage of officers.[123]

Eventually, the corps commander, General Yagüe, arrived, and on inspecting the positions agreed that further offensive action was futile. Nevertheless, the Republican operation fell short of capturing Vivel de Río Martín and ultimately failed to draw significant Rebel forces away from Teruel. The encounter cost the Internationals further losses, including the wounding of the British commander, Bill Alexander, who was replaced by the veteran Sam Wild. A gruff Lancastrian, Wild is generally regarded as the finest leader of the British Battalion and by the war's end would be a decorated major.

Further south, at Teruel itself, the Nationalists launched their final assault on the city on 17 February. Varela's Castilian Corps swept south, attempting to reach the Turia River, and in so doing cut the Sagunto and Valencia highways. Meanwhile, General Aranda's Corps of Galicia assaulted Teruel more directly from the direction of the Santa Barbara. Lieutenant Revilla later wrote that despite the tough fortifications that stood in their path, the Carlist Requetés 'burned with desire' to finally take the positions that had been their objectives two months ago during the first Insurgent counter-attack.[124] Rebel nurse Pip Scott-Ellis was taken to watch the battle unfold from the heights around the beleaguered city:

> When we stopped the car in a dip we could hear the roar of the cannons quite near. So we left the car and climbed up the hill to where lots of German anti-aircraft guns were placed. The Germans were amicable and lent us glasses and explained what was what. The noise was incredible, a continual roar like thunder with intermittent different-toned bangs. The sky was full of aeroplanes shooting up and down the red trenches and the whole landscape all around was covered with pillars of smoke. Bit by bit we wandered from one hill to another amongst all the anti-aircraft and look-out posts until we finally arrived quite close to the action, though out of danger as all the firing was aimed elsewhere. At about 11.30 the bombers began to arrive and came in a continual stream for hour after hour till the red lines were black with the smoke of the bombs. The roar of machines continually coming and going and cannons without cease was deafening. From one hill we could see almost all our batteries firing and the infantry moving up to the front. Occasionally a red shell would wallop down about a hundred metres away aimed at the battery. One could hear it whizz through the air with a high-pitched scream and then crash! and a huge cloud of smoke down below us. We stayed there till 1.30 watching, too enthralled to leave. One could see Teruel about ten kilometres away hidden in a cloud of smoke. … When we left, the air was still full of planes and the roar of cannons as intense as ever, but the red shells were falling nearer so we decided that discretion was the better part of valour and packed off home again to peaceful Cella about six kilometres away.[125]

The following day, the Rebel Castallian Corps took control of all the heights west of Teruel, including Santa Barbara. Republican reserves had been exhausted and the Nationalists were advancing slowly but surely, albeit with heavy losses. Even so, and with the battle reaching its climax, there were still thousands of individual human tragedies being played on both sides of the lines, as Scott-Ellis saw first hand. She found a soldier on a stretcher, fatally wounded in the lungs:

> Consuelo sent for the priest to give him the Last Sacrament and we could do nothing at all, just sat around miserably watching him die. He was unconscious and as pale as a sheet. We looked through his pockets to see if there was any address of his family to write to, but only found one pathetic crumpled letter from his fiancée saying that, after all the difficulties there had been with her family, when he came back from the war they would let them marry and how happy they would be. It was pathetic reading it with him dying at our feet. As there was no address we can't even write to tell her what has happened to him. The worst was that there was a hurry to start operating another, the capitan, who is a brute, got angry and told them to take him away to the mortuary for the dead and the man was still living. Suppose he came to life to find himself just thrown anyhow amongst the dead corpses or buried alive. It must happen to lots of them. I have seen them being taken away to the cemetery just piled anyhow half-naked in a lorry. It is foul and not necessary.[126]

By 20 February, Aranda's forces had entered Teruel and were engaged in fierce fighting with the Republican 46th Division of El Campesino (Valentín González). Both El Campesino's Division and the Listers had been prised out of General Miaja's hands in the wake of the crisis on the Alfambra. The obstinate commander of the Army of the Centre had initially refused to surrender these elite formations from his sector, but the rapidly deteriorating situation at Teruel necessitated their release. They had been transferred to Modesto's V Corps (which was missing the Internationals of the 35th Division engaged at Segura de los Baños) and the Lieutenant Colonel had once again taken over the last-gasp defence of the city on 19 February.[127]

What happened next remains a matter of historical controversy and was certainly not fully understood by Republican high command at the time. The position of the maverick Major González was precarious – Teruel was cut off by Varela's Corps and as good as surrounded on all sides, just as the Nationalist garrison had been two months before. Both Modesto and Líster write in their memoirs that their forces were holding a position just south-east of Teruel, around the Puerto Escandón, maintaining some sort of contact with El Campesino. In the early hours of 22 February, they were about to launch a counter-attack to relieve the city when news came through that El Campesino had abandoned his post and the 46th had fled Teruel (Modesto writes that this took place the following night but he is undoubtedly mistaken; Pip Scott-Ellis was in Teruel by the 22nd).[128] On the other hand, the illiterate González supposedly wrote his own version of the disaster in the early fifties:

> I was left with my men to defend a forlorn hope to the last. If we all were killed, if I was killed, the Communists would be able to blame Prieto for the loss of Teruel – and for the loss of El Campesino. Modesto and Gregorovich [chief Soviet advisor in Spain] had decided that I should render this final service to the Party. The only thing was, they failed to inform me of it. …
>
> The advanced positions were lost, and I quickly found my force of 16,000 men surrounded [this figure seems too large]. Outside the town, Lister and Modesto commanded six brigades and two battalions. They could have helped me. They did nothing of the kind. Even worse: when Captain Valdepeñas wanted to come to my rescue, they prevented him from doing so.
>
> But I have little taste for martyrdom. I fought back. Shut up in Teruel, besieged and encircled by the Fascists, my men fought on splendidly. Of the nine hundred men of my 101st Brigade, who bore the brunt of the attack, only eighty-two survived. I decorated all of them when the battle was over. …
>
> There was no hope of holding Teruel any longer. Now the task was to try to save my men and as much as possible of our equipment. We fought our way out, through the encircling forces, at a cost of a thousand men.[129]

González goes on to claim, quite ridiculously, that the loss of Teruel was deliberately orchestrated by the Communists in order to discredit the Socialist Defence Minister Prieto. Anthony Beevor repeats El Campesino's version of events, Alpert tentatively supports it, while Hugh Thomas and Esdaile sit on the fence somewhat. However, Preston and Southworth come to quite a different conclusion.[130] In particular, Herbert Rutledge Southworth had carried out a methodical demolition of González's story in his article 'The Grand Camouflage'. In the 1980s, one Julián Gorkin admitted to an historian that he had written El Campesino's account after spending time with him following the latter's escape from the Soviet Union.[131] Gorkin had been the co-leader of the anti-Stalinist POUM, which had been brutally supressed by the Communists after the Barcelona May Days. By the late 1940s, Gorkin was working for the CIA through their front organisation, the Congress for Cultural Freedom, which sought to discredit communism by publicising the works of left-wing dissidents. In this context, we can only see El Campesino's account as a piece of Cold War propaganda designed to smear the Soviet role in the Spanish Civil War.[132] In the immediate aftermath of the withdrawal, Prieto wrote to General Rojo, calling El Campesino a liar and saying he had never had to fight his way out, while Rojo himself reported large numbers of troops fleeing the battle without weapons on 22 February.[133] In González's defence, Alpert cites the fact that just a few months later, 'presumably after an exhaustive investigation', El Campesino received the Medal of Valour.[134] However, Alpert presumes that the medal was awarded for González's actions at Teruel, rather than, for instance, his defence of Lérida in March–April 1938 and provides no evidence for this supposed enquiry. What we can say is that the 46th Division fought hard and suffered heavy casualties, as Rebel reports from the time indicate, and that over 1,000 of González's troops were left in Teruel when it finally fell.[135] Another Nationalist combat report stated: 'The enemy, broken and shattered, surrendered in large groups, others managed to flee by the river-bed during the night.'[136] Was this González and a portion of his men slipping away? Lieutenant Carmelo Revilla wrote that his Navarrese unit 'observed at midnight symptoms of general retreat' and the next day took 2,000 prisoners, among whom were a divisional commissar, brigade commander and chief of staff, all of which points to a rather disorderly and incomplete withdrawal.[137]

On the balance of evidence, the most likely scenario seems to be that late on 21 February, El Campesino and men from his division fled Teruel in a fairly chaotic manner, without informing his superiors. In their escape, it appears that elements of the 46th had to fight their way out (Revilla mentions some neighbouring units engaging the fleeing Republicans that night),[138] but we only have El Campesino's word that he directed these breakout efforts. By González's own admission, Modesto and Líster were poised with enough troops to save him, verifying the latter two's claims, and rather undermining his decision to evacuate the city. Five months later, El Campesino would be sacked for cowardice at the Battle of the Ebro and never held a combat command again.

Whatever transpired the previous night, on the morning of 22 February, the battle was over. Teruel was in Francoist hands. Modesto managed to form a defensive line several kilometres east of the city, preventing a further rout. That day, Rojo wrote to his defence minister of the young V Corps commander, praising:

> the skill which he has shown in handling his units, since the collapse which we have seen here has been has been completely halted in his sector. Since he has taken over command, total order has been restored within the difficulties inherent in the tactical situation which he had to resolve.[139]

Hardly the sort of report one would expect if Modesto had indeed deliberately lost the city, as El Campesino claimed. Nationalist nurse Pip Scott-Ellis arrived in the ruins of Teruel on the afternoon of the 22nd, and recorded in her diary her impressions of the city that had been so bitterly contested for more than three months:

> The town is utterly destroyed. I didn't see a single whole house, they are all covered in bullet holes and shot to bits by cannons with great gaping holes from air bombardments. The filth was incredible, dust everywhere. The streets littered with paper and rubbish and sandbag barricades in all the side streets and squares. The shops were just a shambles and the soldiers were busy looting all they could, which was very little. We wandered in and out of all the shops and collected a bracelet and some much-needed field-glasses. In one bar in the middle of a complete shambles was an untouched grand piano which I played tunes on for fun. Everyone was crazy with joy and all the soldiers were dancing about in the streets with queer straw hats on which they had looted.[140]

The Italians were keen to unleash their motorised CTV and pursue the battered Republicans down the Valencia road. Franco refused, insisting on a delay to rest and reorganise his troops before offensive action be resumed. The frozen hills of Teruel were finally his.

Conclusions

The months-long struggle over the same few kilometres of ground with vast bombardments, the like of which had not been seen before in Spain, was in many ways reminiscent of the worst battles of the First World War, as was the intense suffering endured by the troops. As has been mentioned, comparisons have also been drawn to Stalingrad, another winter bloodbath where the besiegers would eventually become the besieged. The People's Army had been totally shattered by the battle for Teruel. Once again, multiple divisions were decimated, both experienced and green formations, along with huge quantities of equipment wasted. Twenty-four priceless tanks were lost, supply dumps were abandoned in the routs of February and so many I-16 Moscas had been shot down that two squadrons had to be disbanded.[141] Total casualties for the Republicans were, historians agree, certainly higher than those of the Insurgents (Thomas says up to 50 per cent higher) but the best estimate seems to be 60,000, including thousands of soldiers taken prisoner in the Alfambra retreat.[142] This is a staggering figure considering only 40,000 were deployed for the initial assault; however, as we have seen, more and more divisions were thrown into the 'cauldron' of Teruel, as Franco called it. The Nationalist forces, dispatched to relieve Teruel, lost in the battles of late December, January and February, 14,000 dead, 16,000 wounded and 17,000 sick (almost all due to the extreme cold). On top of this must be added the Rebel forces caught within the initial Teruel pocket, which numbered close to 10,000 and were practically all either killed or captured.[143] This gives us total Francoists losses of approximately 57,000. Perhaps a third of the huge force that the Generalissimo committed to save a wholly unimportant objective ended up becoming casualties. Given that Teruel saw the highest casualty figures for both sides in any single battle of the war, it would be fair to call it the greatest battle of attrition of the conflict, if not its most important battle. It was, in Preston's opinion, 'the military turning point of the Civil War'.[144]

And it had been a decisive victory for General Franco, regardless of his appalling losses and meagre territorial gains. With military success and a conciliatory letter, the Caudillo won back his incensed Italian allies, so frustrated by the cancelation of the Guadalajara rerun.[145] The outcome of the battle had also restored total confidence in the Generalissimo following the doubts that had surfaced. With his enemy exhausted, the initiative was back with Franco; he could now pick and choose when and where to fight the war's next battle. Losses had been high, but they could be replaced, not least thanks to the continued flow of munitions from the Axis powers. The services of the Italian CTV had not even been required and they were fresh and ready to serve as the spearhead for Franco's next offensive, with Mussolini having been talked out of withdrawal. Once again, the Nationalist forces had performed well; the garrison of Teruel had fought doggedly (despite Rey d'Harcourt's vilification) and the dramatic Alfambra operation had demonstrated tactical nous and fine planning on the part of Vigón. Varela's first counter-attack would almost certainly have relieved Teruel earlier were it not for the timely arrival of both a snowstorm and Juan Modesto. The counter-offensive of 17–22 January had on the other hand achieved relatively little and the entire campaign had been highly expensive in terms of manpower. From many of the first-hand accounts, it appears that the Rebel army was just as reliant on the bloody infantry charge as the Republicans, albeit compensated for by overwhelming air and artillery support that time and again rendered Loyalist positions untenable. The importance of the Condor Legion had reached its zenith, with the German Messerschmitts clearing the skies and Stuka dive-bombers seeing their first deadly action. The Italians too had contributed handsomely, with the Fiat fighters performing solidly as always and the bomber squadrons distinguishing themselves in particular.[146] The People's Army's early success had worried Franco, who commissioned General Kindelán to write a report on their enemy's performance during January 1938. However, the air force commander concluded that in fact the Republican forces had not improved, rather that they had won only a temporary advantage at Teruel and that 'the cold was to blame for everything'.[147]

Why had the Republic been defeated once again? The battle had started so well, with Rojo's plan coming to fruition in the first few days. Furthermore, the strategic objective, namely distracting Franco from his Madrid offensive, had been achieved within a week, although ironically the Republican high command were clearly not aware of how committed their opposite number was to recovering Teruel. Líster's insightful critique of the battle draws out the main Republican flaw:

> What happened was that the Central Staff spent the whole battle obsessed by the fear that the enemy would suspend their attacks against Teruel and unleash their offensive on Madrid or another front. The proof … is that, twice, the Central Staff terminated the battle of Teruel by removing forces and material from the front and sending them to other fronts, then having to move them back to Teruel hastily.[148]

The irony was that the Teruel offensive worked better than the Loyalists had dared hope. Once the garrison surrendered, they presumed that Franco would revert to his Guadalajara operation. The decision of General Rojo to activate 'Plan P' and transfer a great quantity of men and materiel from the Manoeuvre Army to Extremadura was a fatal error, which directly led to the catastrophe on the Alfambra in February and the subsequent loss of Teruel itself. Rojo's own account of the battle omits any mention of this mistake and the general felt it necessary to give just a single, dismissive sentence to the successful Nationalist counter, attributing Rebel success to nothing more than superior numbers. Instead, for Rojo, Teruel marks the moment the People's Army came to maturity and carried out its first successful offensive operation, his meticulous planning finally bearing fruit in what he labels as 'a lesson in the art of war'.[149] Writing soon after the war, it appears the former Chief of the General Staff was more interested in aggrandising his own military triumphs than providing a thoughtful analysis of the battle.

On the other hand, and far more realistically, both Modesto and Lister are highly critical of the Republican high command at Teruel.[150] As well as Rojo's 'Plan P' blunder, General Hernádez Saravia wasted his precious reserves on a series of pointless local attacks just days before the Rebels swept to the Alfambra. Additionally, diverting the Internationals to Segura de los Baños was a fruitless venture and deprived Teruel of fine troops. Otherwise, the Army of the Levante commander seems to have performed reasonably well, and his decisions to twice commit Modesto's V Corps at critical moments were certainly justified. Modesto and his men deserve huge credit for saving Teruel at the turn of the year, when all seemed lost, although the weather also played a huge part. That the city could not be held in February was, perhaps, down to El Campesino's controversial retreat, or perhaps was inevitable after the Alfambra disaster. Despite his subsequent promotion, Líster's refusal to send his division back into battle on 31 December, while driven by well-intentioned concern for his men, was very nearly a catastrophic mistake. A worrying trend of stubborn insubordination tarnishes the career of the famous Communist. Unlike at Brunete and Belchite, there is little cause to criticise the junior leadership of the People's Army, save perhaps the unnecessary abandoning of Teruel on that same 31 December, which was ultimately without consequence. The first phase of the offensive went like clockwork and in defence, many Republican units held their ground with extreme courage. The Republicans should probably have pitched their initial defences of the Teruel pocket farther west to give more breathing space, and

Líster is almost certainly right to point out that too many divisions were committed to the fight for the city itself and the hills around it, rather than to the defensive perimeter that Varela was soon to penetrate.[151] The whole operation has been criticised by Beevor as a futile sacrifice of troops fighting for an insignificant city.[152] However, this critique misses the point of Rojo's 'Strategic Counter-attack Number Two'. The whole purpose had not been to take Teruel, an incidental objective, but to choose strategically unimportant ground over which to fight a battle and force Franco to expend his resources there rather than risk losing Madrid and potentially the war that winter. That the Republic came off worse was the inevitable result of Nationalist military superiority. Unfortunately, however, starved of victories for close to a year, Loyalist propaganda had leapt on the early successes of the operation and it appears the capture of the city had created genuine optimism in Republican ranks. Laurie Lee writes of people talking of 'tides turning, and paths to victory reopening at last'.[153] This made final defeat even harder to bear and left the People's Army morale in dire straits, as Lee, admittedly with the benefit of hindsight, wrote: 'The gift of Teruel at Christmas had become for the Republicans no more than a poisoned toy. It was meant to be the victory that would change the war; it was indeed the seal of defeat.'[154]

The Battle of Teruel left General Franco in a supremely strong position, in spite of his heavy casualties. The enemy had suffered worse, suffering to a far greater extent than at Brunete or Belchite, and it was impossible to replace much of what they had lost, both in terms of men and equipment. The struggle for the city had been considerably longer than expected, with a prolonged intensity not seen thus far in the civil war, and thus also more draining than those earlier battles. Moreover, Republican morale was devastated by such a substantial defeat, especially after so much had been made out of Teruel's capture. Prieto's pessimism reached new heights and before long he would be forced from the cabinet for what amounted to defeatism. The great irony was that of all their offensives, this had in many ways been the People's Army's most successful. It had been too successful, however, drawn too much of Franco's superior army to the sector and finally ended in decisive defeat. Had the Republic more time, lessons could have been learnt; there were signs of progress in the performance of their young military. The Republic did not have the luxury of time, and before it could catch its breath, the Generalissimo would deliver the fatal blow.

Chapter 7

A Slow Agony: the Defeat of the Republic, March 1938–April 1939

On 7 March 1938, Franco launched his Aragon offensive. More than 160,000 men and the biggest concentration of tanks, planes and guns the war had yet seen were deployed along a 160-kilometre front, stretching almost from Saragossa to Teruel. The line was mainly held by inexperienced People's Army divisions, with the veteran troops resting in the rear after the winter's long campaign. The results were catastrophic for the Republicans. Within a few days, the front in Aragon had completely collapsed. The ruins of Belchite were stoutly defended by the Americans who had fought so hard to take it, but by 10 March it was in Nationalist hands. Rojo, who had been caught completely off guard, tried to organise a defence around the town of Caspe. On 16 March it was encircled by Varela's Castilian Corps and the following day the troops defending it surrendered.[1] The Loyalists were in full retreat for over a month; every unit that made a stand soon found its flanks collapsing and had to withdraw in fear of being surrounded. British volunteer Walter Gregory referred to the news of being surrounded as a 'regular occurrence' during this chaotic time.[2] Republican soldiers were frustrated at not being able to stand and fight, but there was no choice other than to retreat, day after day, or else face inevitable capture. Robert Merriman wrote to his wife back home in the US a letter describing the retreats on 28 March 1938:

> The loss of some of the territory was not important, however it makes one feel badly to see the civilian population fleeing before the battle. They take small bundles and leave the rest of their belongings in their life-long homes. The peasants work the land until the last hoping to be able to retain and then at the last minute they have to leave.
>
> It is a sad sight to see some of the villages now. Destroyed by planes which bomb them every day. If you thought Belchite was wrecked when you were there, you should see some of these towns now …

I think of you always – love you more and more and hope that we are together again soon. Love and then some. Bob.[3]

Merriman was killed five days later in a desperate night-time breakout attempt, the Lincolns having been surrounded once again. El Campesino's 46th Division fought doggedly to hold the Rebels at Lérida for a week as March became April, but the advance went on. On 15 April, Carlist troops reached the Mediterranean at Viñaroz, cutting Catalonia off from the rest of the Republic, which was now divided in two. By the end of the month, Franco held an 80-kilometre strip of coastline running south from the mouth of the Ebro.[4]

Map 8: Territorial division of Spain by summer 1938, after Teruel and the Nationalist drive to the sea. Republican-held territory is dark, Nationalist light. Note the impossibility of the Republican position even before the Ebro battle.

The heart had been ripped out of the People's Army. Irreplaceable men and equipment were lost; the 15th Brigade lost their famous Soviet AT guns, never to be replaced, Robert Merriman, as we have seen, and British Commissar Wally Tapsell, who ran into an Italian tank column and was machine-gunned, amongst many others. After the Aragon retreats, the International Brigades became, in effect, Spanish conscript units with a core of foreign officers and NCOs. Almost every Republican formation in Aragon was devastated, often broken up and disorganised in the rout. Many deserted, surrendered or simply fled, some for the frontier, others for home, assuming the war was over, including both the volunteer Antonio Candela and the conscript Lluís Puig. Candela was on leave in Madrid after the Teruel fighting when the Nationalist hammer blow was struck, and eventually came to the conclusion that all was lost:

> No matter what we did our efforts would be wasted. That is what was in my mind as was the case with others, although not many people talked a lot about it at the time. ... By this time I began to see that we could not possibly win the war, although there was always an element of hope on my part. ...
>
> With these thoughts in my mind, I decided, when my leave ended, to remain in Madrid and there I stayed until about the end of April. Then I began to go from place to place, eating and sleeping in temporary army barracks. ... I felt totally lost, and in the end decided to go back to Extremadura [Candela's native region].[5]

A Soviet report from August 1938 is even more damning of the state of the People's Army during those fateful spring months:

> The most unbelievable and disturbing rumours about our supposed hopeless situation and the treachery of the commanders got out of hand among the soldiers and command staff; they carried out almost open agitation for surrendering and going over to the enemy and forcibly taking their officers and commissars with them; the soldiers were persuaded to throw away their weapons because, they said, every armed [man] caught by the fascists would defintiely be shot.[6]

Why had the Republicans crumbled so dramatically? Part of the explanation lies in the overwhelming superiority in firepower that Franco's forces had been able to achieve by early 1938, exemplified at Teruel. While Axis aid to the Nationalists had been stepped up through 1937, Soviet support to the Republic was on the wane, in part due to Italian piracy, but also as Stalin increasingly realised the civil war would bring Russia no closer to France and Britain. In fact, between August 1937 and June 1938, Soviet shipments were so meagre that just twenty-five tanks and thirty-one fighter aircraft reached the Republican zone.[7] While suffering from ever-worsening supply shortages, undoubtedly the People's Army, and in particular its shock units, had been badly worn down by the successive battles of Brunete, Belchite and Teruel. In contrast, Franco had been able to make good his losses in these battles thanks to the destruction of the Northern zone, which had freed up 65,000 troops, with tens of thousands of Republican and Basque prisoners being integrated into the Nationalist army (the recycling process discussed previously). Therefore, by early 1938, the People's Army was tired, demoralised after repeated failure and short on both quality manpower and materiel. The opposite was true of the Francoists, who were coming off the back of considerable triumphs in the north and at Teruel, and had more troops and equipment than ever before. What is remarkable is that the Republic was not totally defeated at this stage, but in fact resisted for almost another year.

Many in the Republic considered the war now lost; how could the divided and broken Loyalists resist the unstoppable Nationalist army? Defence Minister Prieto and President Azaña both advocated suing for peace. However, Franco would accept nothing less than unconditional surrender. Prime Minister Negrín and the Communists were determined to fight on, their new slogan being 'To resist is to win', but Negrín was humiliated and undermined when the French ambassador asked him whether he shared his defence minister's opinion that the war was over.[8] Unable to tolerate a defeatist in the War Ministry, and with mounting Communist agitation calling for his head, the prime minister forced his friend and mentor Indalecio Prieto to resign, the most high-profile victim of the Aragon retreats.[9] The unified counter-revolutionary coalition of moderate Republicans, Socialists and the PCE that had come to power in May 1937 and overseen the 'active war policy' was now shattered. For the remainder of the war, the direction of the Republican government effort fell into the hands of Negrín (with a narrow base within the Socialist Party) and the Communists.

With the situation so desperate, how was it that the Republic clung on? In the midst of the crisis, Negrín had flown to Paris and persuaded the

Blum administration to temporarily open the border, allowing a final glut of arms to arrive in Catalonia. However, the stay of execution was in no small part down to General Franco. After the success of his Aragon offensive, the Generalissimo was in an exceptionally strong position, to the extent that preparations for the end of the war were under way.[10] However, Franco then made another decision that would cost his side dearly. Rather than push on into Catalonia – which practically stood open for him – he decided to drive south towards Valencia, through difficult, mountainous terrain. The Republicans had prepared a series of trench lines, well-sited in the sierra, with barbed wire, concrete machine-gun nests and overlapping fields of fire, typical perhaps of First World War defensive positions. The XYZ Line, as it was known, was to prove too great an obstacle even for the supremely powerful Nationalist forces. Despite repeated offensives, Insurgent progress towards Valencia was painfully slow. The Rebels suffered 20,000 casualties to 5,000 Loyalist losses.[11] Payne defends Franco's decision to advance on Valencia by claiming that the Generalissimo was bowing to German pressure not to attack Catalonia (the Germans at this stage secretly wanted to prolong the war to distract from their own expansionism).[12] However, this argument does not stand up given Franco's refusal to heed military or diplomatic advice, from both his Axis allies and from his own staff, on so many previous occasions.

The decision not to crush Catalonia led directly to the Republic's Ebro offensive of 25 July 1938. The drive on Valencia afforded some breathing space to the remnants of the People's Army stranded in Catalonia, which included the famous Communist formations and the International Brigades, driven back after the spring retreats. The units were reformed, reorganised, reinforced with a fresh class of conscripts and rearmed with the last of the Soviet supplies that made it across the French frontier. Modesto was given command of the new Army of the Ebro, with Líster in command of V Corps. General Rojo planned yet another diversionary offensive, aimed at distracting Franco from his current Valencia push, which appeared to be finally bearing fruit, and proving to the world that the Republic was not dead in the water. The Ebro is often held up as the greatest battle of the civil war, somehow the peak of the conflict's military history, and often receives more detailed coverage than the battles primarily discussed in this book (it is for instance the only civil war battle to be covered by Osprey's famous Campaign series). However, it was in reality little more than a desperate last gamble, by an army that was already beaten. While the strength of the Army of the Ebro is often listed as high as 80,000, in Esdaile's words 'the greatest [array] in the history of the Republican war effort',[13] there is substantial evidence that by now, the People's Army was far weaker than it had been at Brunete, Belchite and Teruel. For one, reportedly only a handful of tanks supported the offensive, and according to Henry's figures, only 129 artillery pieces were available to the two corps carrying out the main attack.[14] The Republican air force would also find itself totally overwhelmed in the battle, with Bf 109s now present in such large numbers that they were being handed to Spanish pilots as well as German. Nationalist aircraft would be bombing and strafing the Republic's river crossings from the battle's first afternoon, severely restricting the reinforcements and supplies that made it to the assault troops. Not only did the People's Army lack the firepower it had enjoyed in previous offensives, it was also short on quality, experienced manpower at the Ebro battle. The famous formations, such as the 11th, 35th and 46th divisions, which led the way once again, had been ripped to shreds just months previously during the Great Retreats through Aragon. Their ranks were swiftly filled with Catalan conscripts; the draft was widened to include all from 16-year-olds to the middle-aged, and Barcelona's industry sifted ruthlessly for able-bodied men.[15] The International Brigades participating in the attack were now overwhelming Spanish units, commanded by Spaniards, the Red Army officers such as Walter and Kléber having been withdrawn by an increasingly uninterested Stalin. The main thrust of the attack was carried out by just six divisions in two corps: XV Corps under Tagüeña and the famous V Corps. Given that People's Army divisions numbered less than 10,000 on the whole, this assault force could not have numbered many more than 60,000. Simply put, rather than representing the Republican military's zenith, the Army of the Ebro was, even by the low standards of the People's Army, a badly under-resourced and inexperienced force.

Nevertheless, the operation started well, with Republican forces carrying out an audacious night-time river crossing on 24/25 July, surprising the three Rebel divisions (the 13th, 50th and 105th, which amounted to around 40,000 men) holding the Ebro line and achieving an impressive advance. By 26 July, Modesto's troops had seized a pocket of 800km². Yet once again, the extreme summer heat took its toll on the attackers, and after an initial breakthrough, the offensive stalled. The advance was held up at the town of Gandesa and the fortified heights around it, reinforced swiftly by Modesto's old adversaries, Barrón's Black Hand 13th Division, who had undertaken an impressive forced march to ensure the town was adequately defended on the battle's second day. Here, repeated assaults by 35th Division failed to capture the town, supported as they were by what little armour and artillery the Republicans could get across the Ebro. The river swelled dangerously after the Nationalists opened the dams upstream, and anti-air defences were wholly inadequate against the might of the Condor Legion, which targeted the river crossings.[16] 15th International Brigade was tasked with securing Hill 481 overlooking Gandesa and paid a heavy price. Bob Cooney recalled the hell the British Battalion endured assaulting yet another fortified height:

We attacked the 'Pimple' for six successive days. The battle reached its climax on 31st July, when we came within an ace of capturing the hill. Again and again our marvellous fellows charged and got near enough to lob their grenades at the enemy, but weight of numbers in men and guns plus steel and concrete barriers told against us.

The story of No. 2 Company gives some idea of what our lads endured that day. When the company made its first assault, Lieutenant John Angus was in command. He fell seriously wounded in the chest. His successor, Lieutenant Walter Gregory, got a bullet in the neck. Sergeant Bill Harrington took over, till he too was seriously wounded and Corporal Joe Harkins – my companion in escape at Calaceite – assumed command. Joe Harkins fell, mortally wounded, just before Lieutenant Lewis Clive, the original company commander, returned from hospital. Clive was killed on the following day.[17]

It was an unenviable task for the battalion's commissars and commanders to motivate the troops to assault the same position the next day, but once again the British advanced:

Some of them fell as they cheered in their first leap from the trench. Their comrades carried on. Up the hill, back again, up to within twenty metres from the top, only to be driven back again by a fury of hand-grenades and machine-gun fire.

For twelve hours the bloody struggle raged; from climax to greater climax. In every critical situation the sangfroid of Sam Wild, greatest of all battalion commanders, inspired the men to pull out yet another bit extra. Seven times that bank holiday the battalion went over the top, each time with a brave British cheer. Not one man thought of letting up. We were there to take that Pimple. Up the ravine till the concentrated fire of the enemy made further progress impossible. 'Lie flat, wriggle over behind that stone. Wait for the fire to slacken. Now! On again, a hundred metres to go – fifty – thirty, twenty. Get down!' …

The battle went on with increasing fury. To add to our difficulties the battery which had been given the job of softening up the enemy fortifications made a mess of its calculations and shelled us. It was heart-breaking, but our lads never gave up.[18]

Flanking efforts by XII Corps further north and several mixed brigades, including the 14th International Brigade, downstream failed to achieve much other than to temporarily distract local Nationalist forces. Across the front, by the end of July, the Rebels had stabilised the line and halted the Loyalist advance.

Through August, the Nationalists gathered a force not only superior to the Republicans in sheer numbers, but amply supported with the sort of firepower the Republic could never compete with: 300 artillery guns, 500 planes and for once, a Nationalist advantage in armour, with 100 tanks.[19] A slow, grinding, bite-and-hold counter-offensive began, with Franco using his huge material superiority to slowly push back the People's Army, which was well dug in, the pocket they occupied being dominated by a series of limestone sierras that proved formidable obstacles for the Rebels. Joaquín Masjuán was, as ever, in the thick of the fighting, defending against one of the many Nationalist counters:

The artillery bombardment having come to an end, the … enemy infantry began to advance. As they did however, we saw the majority of them go down. A few of them tried to take shelter in the indulations of the terrain, but our artillery soon drove them out into the open, where our automatic weapons did the rest. In all, they launched three consecutive attacks, and all three failed with heavy losses … we destroyed three enemy tanks, each reduced to a smoking heap of scrap metal.[20]

Despite enjoying huge materiel superiority, Franco's Ebro counter would drag on for three months of grinding attrition. This was the point when dissatisfaction with the General's leadership reached its height, particularly among senior Nationalist officers. Even apologists for the Caudillo present the Ebro campaign as his darkest hour; Crozier describes an incident in which a frustrated Franco laments his staff: 'They don't understand me! I have the best of the Red Army locked up in an area 35 kilometres long, and they don't understand me!'[21] Franco's press and propaganda officer Luis Bolín defended the slowness of the Ebro campaign (it took three months to retake the ground lost in a week) as 'the reds had dug themselves into the Sierras de Pandols and de Caballs, and before they could be dislodged and forced across the river both ranges had to be carried. Our opponents fought well, at times outstandingly well.'[22] The same source also tells of the Nationalist leader regularly breaking down upon reading the day's casualty reports. This begs the question, why did Franco choose to fight there at all? He was correct in surmising that he had the best of the People's Army holed up in a small pocket with their backs to a river. Why then did he opt to attack them head-on? With the Loyalists in such a perilous position, he could have launched an attack in northern Catalonia against a practically undefended Barcelona, potentially ending the war in the summer of 1938.[23] He could quite easily have encircled Modesto's beleaguered forces by crossing the Ebro himself, up and downstream of the Republican salient. Both options would have brought a far swifter, more decisive and less bloody conclusion to the Ebro battle. Yet Franco lacked the vision to carry out such operations. The stalemate produced hysterical reactions in Rome, where Mussolini declared Nationalist defeat inevitable: 'The reds are fighters, Franco is not,' he moaned, adding his own critique of the Generalissimo's plodding approach: 'Calm optimists get run over by a tram.'[24] It was not until mid-November that the Republicans were finally driven back across the river to their start lines. By now, thousands on both sides had been killed. Some historians list the Ebro as the war's bloodiest battle, and it certainly did see murderous attritional fighting over a prolonged period. Esdaile quotes casualty figures of 70,000 for the Republic and 60,000 for Franco's forces. On the other hand, most historians pitch the final figures substantially lower; Thomas estimates Republican dead at 10,000 to15,000, Jackson at 10,000 to 12,000, and Preston gives figures of 7,150 killed. Their estimates for Nationalists killed range from 5,000 to 10,000. Henry estimates total casualties of all kinds at around 40,000 on both sides.[25] Whichever of these figures we plump for, we still find ourselves well short of the casualty count for Teruel, which, if only due to the extreme cold and the many lives it claimed, ranks in the opinion of the author as a bloodier battle. Whatever the exact figures, the slaughter at Teruel took place within a substantially shorter window, almost exactly two months, compared to the long, drawn-out struggle on the Ebro, making Teruel a significantly more intense battle. Furthermore, Teruel ranks as a far more important one because, as we have seen, by the time of the Ebro offensive, the war was already lost, the People's Army already as good as beaten. It was an attack launched in desperation, to try to forestall imminent Republican defeat. In this aim, it succeeded to some extent, once again distracting Franco and drawing him into a prolonged battle away from his primary objective of Valencia.

The Ebro campaign may not have been a showcase of expansive generalship but it was the last throw of the dice for the Republic. They had committed the last of their reserves and modern hardware, and ultimately achieved little. The shattered Army of the Ebro was driven back to its start lines by mid-November, four months after they had crossed the great river with such optimism. Furthermore, during the battle, Negrín's hopes that the western democracies would stand up to European fascism, and then perhaps come to the Republic's aid, were dashed by Chamberlain's capitulation at Munich, appeasement's high-water mark. In December, Franco launched an offensive into Catalonia and soon had the broken Republicans on the run. By now, the People's Army no longer had enough rifles to arm its brigades while the Rebels had never been stronger, fresh German weaponry arriving with the signing of a new mineral deal. Henry Buckley was one of a handful of foreign journalists still taking an active interest in the now-decided conflict and visited a desperate Líster as he tried in vain to hold back the Insurgent tide:

> Out at Castelldans I and Herbert Matthews and Willie Forrest found Lister with his Army Corps headquarters in a cave about a mile from the front line holding on grimly while the Italian troops in front battered furiously against his positions. The air was full of Nationalist planes. The Franco guns thundered mightily and were only faintly answered by the few Republican guns. Lister, usually polite and communicative, swept by black and grim as the craggy hillside where he had been holding out for eight days, with a dry *'Buenos dias!'* His chubby-faced Political Commissioner, Santiago Alvarez, was more communicative. We did not need telling that things were bad. Shells were dropping all around. The second-line troops were huddled against a ditch only a quarter of a mile from headquarters. The Italians had been held by a tremendous effort but now there was a tremendous push down towards the southern flank. …

The officers who knew us spoke freely enough. Up in the mountains defending the approach of Valls and Tarragona young Tagueña over lunch told us: 'We have an average of one or two machine guns for each battalion. We have twenty-eight guns for the whole Army Corps. At one time two were functioning only. The men work miracles. The fitters repair the guns in their positions. But they are falling to pieces. Yesterday a tank was set on fire by an incendiary shell. It was towed back by another tank. The charred remains of the crew were taken out, it was disinfected, repaired and to-day it is in action again.' It was the same tale everywhere. Nothing like enough machine guns, scarcely a single anti-tank gun, the artillery few in number of pieces and all worn out from the tremendous usage they had received on the Ebro.

It was a situation nobody could do much about.[26]

On 26 January 1939, Nationalist forces entered an abandoned Barcelona. The capital of the Spanish revolution fell without a fight; few wished to die for a lost cause. Half a million Republican refugees crossed the Pyrenees to France, a mixture of soldiers and civilians terrified of Francoist reprisals. Fearing this influx of potentially dangerous radicals, the French herded the majority into makeshift internment camps, some completely exposed to the elements. Many Republicans were still being held by the time of the fall of France in 1940 and would end up in Nazi concentration camps, the most famous example being former Prime Minister Largo Caballero. Several hundred Spanish Republican veterans volunteered for the French Foreign Legion and would find themselves part of Leclerc's famous 2nd Armoured Division fighting with the Free French during the Second World War. These Spaniards were part of an advance force that entered Paris on 24 August 1944, the first Allied troops to do so, riding halftracks named 'Brunete', 'Santander', 'Guadalajara' and other Republican monikers. After much hard fighting, they would end the war at Hitler's mountain retreat at Berchtesgaden.[27] Many other Republican exiles would fight in the French Resistance. Returning to the narrative, in February 1939, both President Azaña and General Rojo, having escaped to France, refused to return to what was left of the Republic, knowing the war was over. Yet the rump of Republican Spain, which still consisted of 30 per cent of the country, including Madrid, Valencia and a significant portion of the south, had many hundreds of thousands of men under arms. Prime Minister Juan Negrín insisted the struggle continue, knowing the war was lost but desperately hanging on to his last card in negotiations with both Franco and the outside world; the threat of continued resistance.

However, there was little appetite for fighting on in the starving and war-weary Republic. Ironically, the civil war, which had begun with a military coup, ended in the same fashion in March 1939. Colonel Segismundo Casado, with a ragtag group of professional officers, anarchists, Fifth Columnists and dissident Socialists, launched an anti-communist coup aimed at ousting Negrín and the PCE. General Miaja was won over by the cabal with the promise of serving as head of state and he ordered the arrest of all Communists in Madrid. Casado and the plotters naively hoped that once the Communists were gone, Franco would be willing to come to a fair peace deal with the Republic. Negrín had already tried and failed to secure peace, both through international mediation and secret approaches to the Caudillo. His policy of fighting until the end was his last resort, designed to buy time for as many Republicans as possible to escape. Instead, the Republic descended into chaos as pro-Casado forces clashed with units loyal to the government. Realising the situation was finally lost, the prime minister and what was left of his administration fled the country on 6 March. There was no organised evacuation for the majority of Republicans and now the Nationalists could advance unopposed.[28] On 1 April 1939, Francisco Franco officially declared the end of the Spanish Civil War. A terrible fate awaited those Loyalists, including the thousands of veterans of the People's Army who had failed to get away: imprisonment, labour camps, blacklisting, poverty and the execution of thousands for the ironic charge of 'military rebellion'.

Chapter 8

To Resist is to Win: The Performance of the People's Army

The Republican People's Army will not go down in the annals of history as one of the world's great fighting forces. The problems it endured will be by now familiar to the reader; it was under-armed, lacking in quality firearms and artillery, ammunition and bomber aircraft. Uniforms were often irregular and equipment was scarce, steel helmets by no means ubiquitous. Discipline and motivation in many units was low, while leadership was generally of a poor quality from squad level upwards. The organisational system of the mixed brigade was wasteful and bureaucratic, while logistics were often found wanting and training was rarely sufficient. Political rivalries and intrigue racked the Republican military throughout its existence. Cooperation between various nationalities in the International Brigades, between Russian advisors and their Spanish advisees and between jealous and suspicious commanders, often left much to be desired. Yet, this unlikely people's army, born out of civil war and riddled with fatal flaws, was able to just about hold its own in combat and somehow managed to retain the initiative on Spain's main battlefront for the majority of 1937 thanks to three audacious surprise offensives. When assessing the combat performance of the People's Army, all its flaws and the constraints under which it operated must be taken into consideration. When one lists the problems and challenges the army faced, it is remarkable that the Republican forces managed to achieve anything at all.

The Communist policy in the Spanish Civil War has been much criticised from right and left in the subsequent decades. However, as Esdaile has pointed out, the only thing that prevented a swift Rebel victory in the conflict was the formation of the People's Army.[1] While it was not capable of winning the war, this force could at least put up a real fight, launch serious offensive operations and hold their ground at times. This was substantially more than the revolutionary militias had been capable of and ensured that the Republic would survive from its existential crisis of 1936 up until the spring of 1939. This is the greatest and perhaps sole achievement of the Republican People's

Army. 'To Resist is to Win' was Negrín's famous slogan as the war continued to go from bad to worse, and the hard fight the Republican army put up for two and a half years from its inception to its final collapse is the only thing that stood in the way of Franco's seizure of power. The revolutionary approach advocated by the anarchists and POUM, which still finds sympathy with modern authors such as Beevor, offered nothing militarily and could only have ended in the rapid defeat of the Republic.

While we cannot compare directly to the First World War for reasons that should now be obvious, it is worth noting some difficulties shared between the People's Army and fighting forces of the First World War. Whereas most European nations had a history of conscription and therefore a huge pool of reservists upon which to call up at the outbreak of war, this was not the case for the United States. America had to build a citizens' army from the ground up, like the Spanish Republic in 1936–37, albeit with more time, space and money. The difficulties encountered by the Americans in attempting to build their AEF (American Expeditionary Force) during wartime exemplify how the People's Army's struggles were not unique to the Spanish Republic, nor neceisarrily the fault of its leaders. The Americans of 1917–18 enjoyed a number of huge advantages over their Spanish Republican counterparts. For one, the United States was an economic powerhouse, with a sizeable domestic arms industrial base, with little threat, other than the sinking of Atlantic shipping, to her own production. Spain, on the other hand, had been economically backward by European standards before the war, and possessed only a meagre armaments industry. During the war, the Republic faced four huge economic barriers: 1) the constant loss of territory, manpower, resources and industry to Nationalist conquest, most notably the Northern zone; 2) the struggle to contain and reverse the social revolution of 1936, and the economic dislocation it had precipitated (the flight of foreign capital, even the abolition of currency in some localities); 3) the conversion of Barcelona, Spain's foremost industrial centre, from predominantly textile and chemical production to that of war materials; 4) the physical destruction and interdiction of the war economy by Nationalist bombing and blockade. These barriers necessitated the Republic's (and indeed the Nationalists') reliance on imported munitions and supplies, with all the problematic implications that came with.

Despite all of this, the Republic built and mobilised divisions quicker than the USA in the First World War, even with all advantages that America possessed. Admittedly, the USA faced no immediate threat and therefore was not under pressure to mobilise straight away. However, despite the benefit of time, all the equipment and expertise they could ask for from their allies and huge economic strength (all advantages that the Republic lacked), not only was America slower to mobilise, but it could be argued that it did so less effectively. The first American attack of the war was conducted on 28 May 1918, by a single regiment on the Somme. It had taken over a year since the American entry into the war to mount any kind of independent offensive operation – and this from a nation that had mobilised 200,000 men in 1916 for a short war with Mexico. The Republic built their army in a far shorter time period and without an existing military to expand, nor the advice and support of allies who had been at war for years. Only nine months after its conception, the People's Army launched an ambitious combined arms assault at Brunete with tens of thousands of troops in three corps, supported by tanks and aircraft. The AEF's operations in 1918 show how difficult it is for a new army to achieve success quickly. During its relatively brief participation on the Western Front, the AEF suffered from severe logistical difficulties, a lack of adequate planning and high casualties due to the inexperience and poor training of the troops. Their commander, General Pershing, was under-qualified for the sizeable task of leading an entire army; he saw his role as merely 'driving them [his subordinates] on, while monitoring the command performance of his generals to ensure that they demonstrated sufficient vigour. Of sophisticated tactics he knew little.'[2] The Americans' only major offensive of the war was the Meuse-Argonne of September-October 1918, which some historians contend is the bloodiest battle in US history. The AEF suffered 122,000 casualties, fighting a German army whose morale was collapsing and that was in full retreat on other parts of the Western Front. This figure represents a tenth of the 1.2 million American personal in France, a startlingly high casualty rate, even by First World War standards. Close to half the German losses during the campaign were prisoners taken by the Allies, highlighting the poor condition that the kaiser's armies were in by this time and their willingness to surrender. Against a broken enemy, America's new army suffered appalling casualties. Not only that, but the Allies enjoyed total material superiority by this time, with control of the skies, hundreds of tanks and a domination in artillery. While the Republicans never faced the kind of fortifications that the Americans encountered in the Argonne, it is clear that many of the deficiencies of their army, such as poor command and inadequate training, are common issues with hastily built fighting forces, and even nations as great as the USA can be susceptible to such shortcomings. In this light, the efforts of the new People's Army against Franco's army, confident, better trained and far better equipped than them, seem rather more impressive.

Open warfare, as occurred during the great Republican advances, is extremally challenging and requires great skill from junior officers and NCOs to be conducted effectively. We have already seen how the deficiencies in this area within Loyalist ranks led to offensives breaking down. In October–November 1918, when the British had broken the German lines and a war of movement returned to the Western Front, the BEF found itself with fresh problems. For one, its infrastructure and logistics began to break down under the strain of constant advance, and certainly we can see that the People's Army's logistics often left much to be desired also. However, perhaps more importantly, the British were psychologically and tactically dislocated by open, mobile warfare. As John Terraine writes, 'Great responsibilities now devolved on junior officers, most of them mere boys with very little training (many battalion commanders at this stage were only in their twenties).'[3] This profile of a young, inexperienced officer corps, inadequately trained for mobile, offensive operations, could equally be applied to the junior officers, and to some extent field commanders (such as Líster and Modesto) of the People's Army. While the certainties of defensive battles, trench warfare and meticulous planning from professional senior officers could mask these inadequacies at times, in the dynamic, ever-moving, ever-changing scenarios that attacking troops find themselves in, the junior officer is the lynchpin of any army. A shortage of experienced junior officers (and NCOs to assist them) severely hampered the Republican forces and took the impetus out of their offensives once the initial breakthrough, planned by Rojo and his staff, had been achieved. Open warfare, was, as Haig had labelled it in 1918, 'a platoon commanders' war' and the Republic did not have enough platoon commanders. As we have seen from the accounts in this story, the men who ended up as lower leaders, such as Milton Wolff or Joaquín Masjuán, had no qualification other than a track record of bravery in combat, and Wolff admits candidly in the latter stages of his novel, when he found himself in command of the Lincoln-Washington Battalion, that he was disorientated and unprepared to lead a large body of men.

Nevertheless, the People's Army's commanders of all ranks also suffered far more handicaps than American or British leaders. Firstly, the Republic simply did not have the men, *materiale* or money that world powers had at their disposal and neither had they the luxury of time to learn from their mistakes. On the Western Front, it took the Allies four bloody years and millions of casualties to learn the art of trench warfare, and crucially, how to break it. The People's Army never had that opportunity. Secondly, the personnel of the People's Army at all ranks, and most significantly in command, had little to no military experience. The militia leaders such as Líster and Modesto simply had to learn on the job how to lead a corps or division. The minority of Spain's professional officers who did remain loyal often found themselves catapulted into lofty commands, such as Rojo, who went from a major in June 1936 to the chief of staff of the People's Army and the Republic's strategic planner less than a year later, or Miaja, who had never handled more than a regiment in combat before the civil war, in which he commanded armies and army groups. While they and others did the best they could in the circumstances, perhaps they were not ready for the gravity of the task they faced. Not only that, but Spain had not fought in the First World War, and many of the Loyalist officers were of the Peninsula Army and had not even fought in the Rif. Therefore, many regular officers in the People's Army had no more combat experience than the militia officers, and had rarely been on manoeuvres thanks to the poverty of the pre-war army, so could bring little more expertise than that learnt from a textbook. The People's Army simply did not have the time or the resources to develop the tactical doctrines and techniques needed to mount successful offensives in modern war, never mind have the chance to carry out these attacks in the face of a superior foe with better quality equipment. Without time, resources, any meaningful military tradition or relevant experience, it is remarkable that the People's Army managed to carry out an offensive at all.

That being said, there was a clear difference in fighting quality between formations in the People's Army. Throughout the conflict, the standard line divisions and brigades, composed largely of conscripts, performed poorly in battle, conceding ground on the defence and struggling to make headway in the attack. It appears that perhaps the majority of Republican divisions could do little more than hold the line, and indeed many were rarely asked to do more. This was disappointing and frustrating for figures such as Rojo and Prieto, but understandable considering People's Army formations were by and large composed of green conscripts, militia and inexperienced officers, and lacking in weapons and equipment. Furthermore, almost all units lacked a combat tradition and cadre of veterans, both of which would be key to the integration of new recruits in most militaries. Just a few People's Army formations stand out as exceptions to that rule, most notably the divisions that served in Modesto's V Corps. The Listers of 11th Division achieved the greatest advance in all three Republican offensives described in this book, and did so quicker than all other units engaged in the attacks. They mastered the art of the infiltration night attack and fought tenaciously in defence time and again. The 11th clearly possessed that combat tradition and core of dependables that meant that despite repeatedly suffering heavy casualties, the division's combat performance remained strong. While the Listers did break on 24 July 1937 to lose Brunete, and were irresponsibly withdrawn from the front at Teruel as Varela's counter was in full swing, in both cases the division had been in constant combat for weeks, in conditions of extreme heat and cold respectively. It certainly cannot be denied that Lister's famed 11th was the finest Spanish unit in the People's Army.

Also in V Corps throughout 1937 was General Walter's 35th 'International' Division. The International Brigades in particular have been the victims of extremes in the historiography; either they are a heroic elite or incompetent and over-hyped. To quote Charles Esdaile's recent military history of the war, 'It is difficult to escape the feeling that militarily, the International Brigades contributed very little – whether at Madrid, the Jarama, Brunete, Belchite, Teruel, the Ebro, they performed no better than the Spanish units around them.'[4]

What Esdaile and others miss is the nuance of the combat performance of the Internationals. The International Brigades are almost universally in the history of the war referred to as one monolithic organisation. Judgements passed on the brigades are passed on the organisation as a whole. In fact, clear distinctions can be drawn between the different brigades and battalions, and similarly there are differences over time. For instance, the 14th International Brigade of largely French volunteers never covered itself in glory, from its first disastrous action in late 1936 at Lopera, to the abortive Segovia offensive of May 1937. It played no part in the subsequent great Republican operations of Brunete, Belchite and Teruel as a result of its poor performance. Additionally, while the 12th Garibaldi Brigade unquestionably fought well at Guadalajara in March 1937, after repeated bloodletting and devastating losses at Huesca and Brunete, we have seen its subsequently lacklustre showing at Belchite under General Kléber. The brigade was a spent force and like the 14th was no longer a go-to formation, not being deployed for offensive operations again for almost a year. The 13th Brigade effectively mutinied after Brunete and was dissolved, but after being reconstituted with reliable Slavic battalions, including the Dimitrovs, the 13th Dabrowski Brigade became a battle-hardened unit, as we saw at Belchite, with Milton Wolff refering to them as 'the Poles, Hungarians and Palestinian Jews, European hard-fighting IB'ers'.[5] The records of the 11th and 15th International brigades stand out. The Austrian and German anti-fascists of the Thälmanns fought with incredible bravery, albeit at huge cost, in the battles for Madrid from November 1936 to March 1937. In spite of these casualties, the 11th Brigade still put in respectable showings at Brunete and Belchite, and as we have seen, fought extremely hard at Teruel. It is difficult to imagine many units in the People's Army replicating the Thälmanns' three-day stand on El Muletón. Esdaile's analysis seems especially inaccurate when one looks at the 15th International Brigade, which has occupied a central role in this book's story. Once again, there are nuances; the 15th's first combats at Jarama saw great bravery but also tragic levels of incompetence and inexperience. However, at Brunete, the 15th took Villaneuva de la Cañada, succeeding where Spanish troops had failed, and was left stranded holding the line during the rout of 24 July as many Republican units, including the Listers, melted away. At Belchite, the 15th Brigade was repeatedly selected by Modesto as the tip of the spear, storming Quinto, Purburrel Hill and Belchite itself. Few other units in the People's Army would have succeeded in taking first Quinto, then Belchite itself in the space of a few days against such determined opposition. At Teruel also, the Brigade fought well to hold a Nationalist counter in mid-January. As we have seen in the case of the 14th, it was simply not the case that Loyalist commanders always threw International Brigades into the toughest fights; rather, the 15th was a tried and tested unit that was clearly considered reliable and capable. Furthermore, the battalions of the International Brigades were repeatedly worn down to double figures and yet the fighting calibre of the 11th and 15th remained high despite an ever-increasing number of rookie replacements from Spain and abroad filling the ranks. Most Republican units that suffered such heavy losses ended up being disbanded, hence the stories of whole mixed brigades written off after Bruente and even during the Teruel struggle. The 11th and 15th brigades, as well as the Slavic units across numerous brigades but later concentrated into the 13th, stand out as examples of reliable, motivated formations that, thanks to a core of veterans and something approaching a combat tradition, managed to maintain a level of performance above that of most Republican troops, in spite of repeated maulings. Thus, Esdaile's comment that they performed no better than Spanish units is somewhat wide of the mark;

throughout this text we have seen the unreliability of many conscript-based units, in both attack and defence, for instance Puig's 44th Division at Belchite or the untested troops who faced Vigón's Alfambra counter. Other modern scholars have asserted, without evidence, that the Internationals' status as an elite was merely a product of propaganda, with one even going so far as to imply this made the volunteers virtual victims: 'they were forced to act as storm troops in the bloodiest battles, for the simple reason of exploiting their propaganda value.'⁶ Yes, the international volunteers were poorly equipped and trained, and, at times, poorly led. But so was virtually every formation in the People's Army. The most ludicrous element of this assertion is that the men who led the People's Army would willingly subordinate the prospects of Republican victory to the propaganda needs of the Comintern. Would Negrín, Prieto or, most importantly, Rojo, have been prepared to assign low quality troops to tough objectives, simply to make Moscow happy? Were the communist commanders such as Modesto and Líster so brainwashed as to prioritise the prestige of their international movement over military necessity and the very fate of their country? To take the Saragossa operation as an example, would Prieto have been so enraged by its failing if it had been a mere propaganda stunt? Would it have so poisoned the relationship between Modesto and Líster if all that was at stake was a few headlines in party newspapers around the globe? The men who commanded the People's Army, it should go without saying, cared deeply about Spain and the outcome of the conflict. This was their country; they were fighting a bitter civil war against a murderous enemy. The stakes could not have been higher; therefore to suggest that Republican leaders used the International Brigades as shock troops simply for column inches is an unsubstantiated, nigh on offensive, assertion. They wanted to win the war, so they gave the toughest assignments in their most ambitious operations to troops who were reliable – who were committed and hard fighting in defence and attack. In the context of the People's Army as a whole, which was not an efficient or especially effective fighting machine, some of the International units really did stand out as veteran troops who, unlike many of the Republic's reluctant warriors, could be depended upon to stand and fight (and indeed die), no matter the situation. While not an elite in the sense that military historians might be used to (they had no special training or equipment), certain International units were clearly superior to the average line division in the People's Army and this must surely have been the overwhelming reason they were used as shock units.

Modesto's (and later Líster's) V Corps therefore stands out markedly. The 11th Division was a first-rate formation, who cannot be blamed for the unpredictability of their commander. The 11th and 15th International brigades of General Walter's 35th Division were high-quality units within the context of the army they were part of. In both cases, high motivation, a nascent combat tradition and an increasingly experienced set of officers and squad leaders helped maintain their elite status as battle-hardened divisions. While it cannot be argued that either the 11th or 35th would compare favourably to the elites of other twentieth-century militaries, in the context of the improvised, poorly led and under-equipped People's Army, these troops certainly stood out. Most pertinently, they proved in combat on many occasions to be the equal of the finest troops in the Nationalist army, such as the 13th Black Hand Division or the Navarrese formations.

What of the Republican commanders? The 'geographically loyal' generals such as Miaja and Pozas were lacklustre and passive on the whole and lacked the combat experience, energy and commitment to succeed. Many militia brigade and divisional commanders were also totally out of their depth; the examples of El Campesino and Manuel Trueba spring readily to mind. The notable exception, Enrique Líster, clearly possessed the gift of leadership but showed himself to be dangerously unreliable at crucial moments. Modesto and Rojo are the two most obviously talented amongst the Republic's senior officers. We have already assessed in some detail their successes and failings. Esdaile highlights the flexibility that Rojo showed in abandoning the traditional preliminary barrage, knowing his forces lacked the firepower to carry out massive bombardments, drawing particular attention to the People's Army's infiltration tactics.[7] Modesto, the 30-year-old lieutenant colonel from the militias, undoubtedly benefitted from his experience in Morocco with the Foreign Legion and his Moscow training. His forthright and uncompromising attitude perhaps speaks of his Africanista background, showing some similarities to the brutal personas of Nationalist leaders such as Yagüe. He was certainly unique among the militia officers in that he possessed both the courage *and* the skills required to lead, but lacked the bravado and popularity of Líster or El Campesino. While it appears he was not the easiest commander to work under, Modesto consistently got better results than his professional regular officer counterparts, and Rojo, always disdaining of the Spanish officer corps' ignorance, seems to have preferred working with the young Andalusian. This may simply be because much of the best troops and equipment were concentrated in his hands, as a trusted, Moscow-trained Communist. While such an approach was frustrating for non-communist personnel, it was not without logic or merit. The Republic, as we know, was almost always desperately short of arms and equipment. In these circumstances, it would have made little sense to distribute the highest quality material evenly throughout the army. Parts of the People's Army, especially the divisions holding the quiet sectors, such as Aragon (up to August 1937) or Extremadura, often lacked any real combat experience and bore worrying resemblances to the militias long after militarisation had supposedly taken effect. The CNT-FAI and POUM militias in Aragon had only accepted the military authority of the central government as late as March 1937. To have sent the invaluable Soviet aid to these formations would, frankly, have been a waste.

On the issue of Republican leadership and strategy, Antony Beevor has written that 'Franco did not so much win the war: the Republican commanders, with the odds already stacked heavily against them, squandered the courage and sacrifice of their troops and lost it.'[8]

He argues that not only were the Brunete, Belchite, Teruel and Ebro offensives ill-conceived and futile operations, but also that they were 'launched for propaganda considerations', i.e. simply to justify exaggerated Communist propaganda claims.[9] Instead, he suggests an alternative approach:

> a far more effective conduct of the war would have been to combine a strong defensive strategy with short, sharp probing attacks at different points to confuse the Nationalists. The People's Army's tank forces should have been held back in an armoured reserve ready to counter-attack any Nationalist breakthrough.[10]

Let us deal with these points in turn. First, the assertion that the Republic's big offensives lacked military purpose and merely served as promotional material for PCE and Comintern propaganda, achieving nothing other than to wear out their own army and ultimately hand Franco victory. This is quite a ridiculous argument; for one, these offensives were ordered by Defence Minister Indelacio Prieto, a social democrat who fiercely resisted Communist domination of the Republic and its army. Further, the operations themselves were devised and planned by General Vicente Rojo, a Catholic conservative professional officer. The battles of Brunete, Belchite and Teruel, far from being prestige operations, had clear strategic and tactical goals, as has been discussed at some length in this book, and to a greater or lesser extent, the strategic aims of the operations were achieved.

Secondly, the supposed alternative of fighting a defensive war with occasional raids and a large reserve to meet Nationalist attacks. The war's main front was thousands of kilometres long, larger than the First World War's Western Front, stretching from the Pyrenees to Spain's south coast in a winding scythe. Given that Spain's infrastructure at this time left a lot to be desired, the idea that the Republic's armoured forces could flit from sector to sector wherever trouble arose is quite fanciful. There were no panzer divisions or mechanised infantry in the Republican military that could move so rapidly. However, what of Beevor's wider point that a defensive approach would have better suited the People's Army? For one, it was impossible for the Republic merely to adopt the defensive in 1937. Franco was preoccupied with the conquest of the north and so did not launch an offensive of his own on the main battlefront from March 1937 to the same month the following year. For the People's Army to have simply sat static during this period would have been intolerable for several reasons. It would have meant the undignified abandoning of the Northern zone, which almost certainly would have collapsed significantly faster, thus speeding up Franco's overall victory. However, even more important, it would have been an unacceptable situation to the army rank and file and to the civilian population. For, to adopt a defensive posture while the enemy is otherwise preoccupied would have been nothing short of an admission of the Nationalist's superiority and therefore the hopeless position of the Republic. How could there be any hope of winning the civil war if the Republic was incapable of attacking? Popular support for the war would have dried up and morale collapsed. A combatant who knows victory is out of reach quickly folds, as shown by the Germans (both at the front and at home) from the summer of 1918. Indeed, when in the winter of 1938–39 it became clear to all that the Republic's hopes of victory had disappeared, the Republican will to resist evaporated. Despite the fact that the Republic still held 30 per cent of Spain and had thousands of men under arms, once it had become clear to the civilian population and elements within the army that victory was beyond their grasp, further resistance was deemed pointless. Those who advocated it, namely Prime Minister Juan Negrín and the PCE, were the targets of the military coup in March 1939 that effectively brought the war to an end. Therefore, it is unthinkable for the Republic to have effectively admitted the impossbility of their situation so openly in mid-1937, and to have done so by switching over to the defensive while the enemy was occupied elsewhere, crushing their allies to the north, could have been fatal to the Republican war effort.

The second reason why this argument is so deeply flawed is that it is a fallacy to believe that the defensive is less costly than the offensive. The idea that the Republic could have preserved its strength by simply sitting on the defensive is not one based in reality.[11] Fighting a defensive battle can be just as costly in terms of men and material as launching an attack, as shown by German casualties during five months on the Somme or at Passchendaele, French losses at Verdun, or those of the Russians at Stalingrad. General Ludendorff wrote of Passchendaele (a pointless bloodbath of an offensive in the British psyche) that it was 'the greatest martyrdom of the German army', which had torn its heart out and reduced it to a mere 'militia'.[12] In modern war, holding ground can be extremely costly, especially when the enemy has superior firepower, and it is certainly no live-saver. Given the huge superiority of the Nationalists in terms of shells and aircraft, the losses that could have been inflicted on the People's Army in defence would have been immense. While Beevor might point to the XYZ line as his case in point, in the context of the civil war it looks rather more like the exception that proves the rule. One simply has to look at the desperate attempts to hold on at Brunete and Teruel, or even more pertinently the battles around Madrid and at Jarama in the winter of 1936–37, to see that the Republic suffered just as many, if not more, casualties than the Nationalists when they were on the defensive. Losses would surely have been heightened by the fact that much of the People's Army lacked the resources and technical expertise to build high quality fortifications or defence-in-depth systems. In this situation, with the Republic sitting back, Franco would have been able to choose the battlefield, a luxury he was denied in 1937, and target the most vulnerable Republican sectors. Here, in flimsy defences, the weaker elements of the army would have been sitting ducks for the Nationalists' superior air and artillery firepower.

For these reasons, the Republic had no other option but to attack in 1937 and to do otherwise could well have spelled disaster and brought a swifter end to the conflict. It is therefore nonsense to argue that there was some 'better way' for the Republic to fight, that somehow it would have paid off to preserve their inferior forces and simply wait for Franco to launch an offensive at his leisure. On the contrary, the damage to army and civilian morale that such an admission of weakness would have engendered, and the inevitable heavy losses of men, material and territory that would have ensued, could well have brought about the Republic's defeat far sooner. Unfortunately, there was no alternative but to go on the offensive, to try to aid the north, to deny Franco the initiative and, quite simply, to give any chance of victory in the civil war. Can we hold it against the Republic's commanders that their operations were not overly successful, nor tactically innovative, given the parlous state of the army they led? Surely, it would be far more surprising to see radical tactical and operational innovation from the People's Army than the inverse. The Republicans were more than capable of creating breaches in the Rebel lines, but once a breakthrough had been achieved, no other tactic existed at that time than to commit men and material to try to exploit it. This is precisely what First World War and indeed many Second World War commanders used time and again. The Republic simply did not have the resources with which to exploit a breakthrough once it was obtained. To demonstrate this point, we need only look at the famous Battle of Amiens in August 1918, a battle still renowned for its tactical innovation. Here, three British and Commonwealth army corps were supported by 552 tanks in achieving a stunning 12.5-kilometre breakthrough, arguably the first major mechanised, combined-arms offensive in military history.[13] The figure of 552 tanks is substantially more than the Republic received for the entire duration of the Spanish Civil War (385 according to Esdaile's figures, which includes 64 useless FT-17s).[14] At its height, the People's Army's tank force numbered around 130 machines, which were concentrated to support the three corps participating in the Brunete operation. The Republicans simply never had enough tanks, regardless of the superiority of their T-26s over the Rebels' Panzer Is and Italian tankettes. Although historians are right to point out that the Republic's use of tanks was poor and unimaginative (one has to think only of Fuentes de Ebro here), there was never any possibility that the People's Army could have launched a mechanised assault of the kind seen in the latter stages of the First World War, never mind mimicked the blitzkrieg of the Second. It would therefore be fair to say that while the Republic's offensives were well concieved and adequately planned for the most part, the People's Army was not strong or experienced enough to execute them. The Republicans could achieve advances when Franco was distracted with other theatres, but were not capable of breaking through or holding ground against the main body of the Nationalist army. While progress was almost certainly made, as evidenced by the relative success of the Teruel operation in comparison to prior offensives, the Republic was only able to achieve phyrric victories.

To conclude, while the Republican People's Army was not a great fighting force, it can be argued that the Loyalists did close to the best they could with what they had. Organisation, logistics, training and leadership were poor, and probably the Republic was guilty of not making the best of the scant military resources they acquired. However, Spain was fighting a civil war; troops were needed at the front immediately and there was no time for specialist training, tactical innovation or a thorough theoretical assessment of the military situation. That the Nationalists were able to manage their resources better and make the best of their own, less substantial deficiencies is patently obvious by the final outcome of the conflict. But the People's Army did give them an extremely tough fight, and in the end, that was the greatest achievement of this unique, improvised army.

Firearms of the Spanish Civil War
by Freddy Clifford

I: RIFLES

The repeating rifle was the standard infantry armament of the late nineteenth to early twentieth century, and it usually came in the form of bolt-action designs. Spain's rifle of choice was a specially commissioned 7x57mm version of the famous Mauser rifle, renowned for its excellent accuracy and smooth action. This rifle – commonly known as simply the 'Spanish Mauser' – was adopted by the Spanish army in 1893 and was still in service by 1936. It was the most numerous rifle of the Spanish Civil War.

The Republican government entered the war short on rifles, and thus encountered difficulty in arming its own soldiers. This forced them to turn to foreign aid, primarily from international arms dealers and the politically sympathetic Soviet Union. The providers of this aid saw the war primarily as an opportunity to offload old and obsolete rifles at exorbitant prices. On the other hand, the Nationalist rebellion had a plentiful supply of Spanish military rifles, and also had the backing of Nazi Germany and fascist Italy, who were able to provide thousands of their own rifles to Franco's army.

Republican rifles

About 500,000 Mauser rifles were in Spanish service by 1936, but much of the country's arms and ammunition were taken up by the Nationalists when the war broke out. The government was left with about 200,000 Mausers, and only a fraction of these were actually useable, as many of the bolts were missing – they had been removed and kept in separate storage, allegedly as a security measure against military malpractice. Ironically, this did nothing to prevent the July coup attempt and the general uprising that followed, and only served to upset the government's own efforts to arm volunteers in Madrid, who received only around 7,000 fully-functioning Mauser rifles. Subsequent losses of military arsenals to the Nationalists ensured that the

Republic's supply of rifles quickly dwindled, and foreign aid was therefore required with great urgency. The government set up an arms purchasing commission to aid these efforts.

Most of the Republic's foreign imports came from Poland, the USSR, and private contractors. Poland's anti-communist government publicly supported the Spanish Nationalist movement, but under the table it sold large quantities of armaments to the Republic. The motive for this was purely to turn an easy profit, as Poland had no desire to see the Republic victorious – as such, their arms deals were practically fraudulent, charging obscene amounts of money for what were predominantly German and Austrian leftovers from the First World War that Poland had acquired in the post-war period but no longer required. This included the Imperial German Mauser, known as the Gewehr 98, and the Austrian Mannlicher rifle. The Gewehr 98 was a chambered in the standard German cartridge, 7.92x57mm, but otherwise it would have been instantly familiar to anyone who had trained with the Spanish Mauser. The Mannlicher gun was a little different in that it utilised a straight-pull bolt mechanism, which was faster to operate than a conventional bolt but not as safe or reliable. It also had a unique feature in that the loaded clip would eject from the bottom of the internal magazine once it was expended. Poland sent about 27,000 Mannlichers and another 10,000 French-made Lebel rifles to Spain, but a good portion of these shipments were intercepted by Franco's forces and pressed into service with the Nationalists.

The Soviets supported the Republic on ideological grounds, hoping to stifle the strong anti-communist influence of Hitler, Mussolini and Franco. Initially Russian support was strong. Russia had a huge arsenal of surplus weapons that it had acquired during the First World War and Russian Civil War, largely supplied by the Allies. A large portion of these were subsequently given to the Spanish Republic. Among the Soviet donations were 20,000 Enfield P17 rifles in .303 British, 9,000 lever-action Winchester 1895s, and about 5,000 Arisaka rifles in the 6.5mm. The Enfields were British designed and American produced, and were sent to the White Russians by the US during the Russian Civil War. Upon their arrival in Spain, they were rather suitably issued to British and American volunteers. The Winchesters were also American designed, but produced in Russia under licence and chambered in the Russian 7.62x52mm cartridge. The Arisakas were particularly well travelled. They were Japanese in origin, but had been sold to the British during the First World War as auxiliary rifles for the Royal Navy. Later,

Britain sold them to the White Russians, and then they were captured by the Soviets, who sold them to Spain. This constant changing of hands tells us much about the contemporary opinion of the rifle – it never stayed in service with any one country, other than Japan, for very long. This can be attributed to the underpowered cartridge that it fired.

As the war progressed, Soviet support fizzled out when it became obvious to Stalin that the Republican cause was a lost one. The Republic was receiving ever fewer imports from Russia by 1938, compared to the consistently strong support the Nationalists received on behalf of Germany and Italy. Later support did come from Czechoslovakia, who sent about 50,000 Vz.24s, their own version of the Mauser rifle. These were used extensively at the Ebro and were very efficient guns. Franco's forces were sufficiently impressed by the quality of these Czech rifles upon capture and confiscation from the Republicans, and used them for themselves where they could.

In early 1937, the Republic received a large shipment of Russian Mosin-Nagant rifles, which they allocated to the International Brigades. These rifles became known by British and American volunteers as 'Mexicanskis'. There are several theories as to why this nickname came about, but it is generally thought that it is because the rifles were supplied by the Mexican government, who had received them from Russia at an earlier date. The manufacturers of these rifles varied, as during the First World War Russia had not only produced them domestically at Tula Arsenal, but also contracted the American firms of Remington and Westinghouse to produce additional models. Either way, Russian or American made, the rifles did not impress the Brigaders, as they were said to have arrived in bad condition and lacked reliability. The International Brigades were more receptive to Canadian-made Ross rifles that they acquired in the low hundreds. The Ross was, like the Mannlicher, straight-pull, and was deemed defective by British authorities during the First World War due to its poor reliability in harsh conditions, but nevertheless, it was popular with sharpshooters and boasted exceptional accuracy at long range.

The USSR also used the Spanish war as a proving ground for new and experimental weapons. The Republicans were supplied with small quantities of Simonov self-loading rifles that were newly developed in 1936. These guns were actually selective-fire and could fire in fully-automatic, like a precursor to the modern assault rifle. Less than 100,000 were made and of these, probably only a few hundred – if even that – were shipped to Spain. Experimental semi-automatic Tokarev rifles were also tried out, and the feedback from

Spain was likely evaluated by the Russians in developing improvements for both guns. Another self-loader, the Mondragon, appeared in Spain during the civil war and it seems the Republic received small numbers of these guns at some point between 1936 and 1938. The Mondragon was a revolutionary Mexican-designed rifle that was produced by a Swiss company, SIG, from 1908, and supplied in rather meagre quantities to pre-revolutionary Mexico and Imperial Germany. Only about 4,000 were made in total, and SIG failed to sell them all. Given that SIG sold KE7 light machine guns to the Republic, it is possible that they also tried to offload some unsold Mondragons. Alternatively, the supplier could have been Mexico.

The poorest guns to grace the Republic's ranks came in the form of nineteenth-century single-shot rifles, including thousands of old Vetterli and Gras rifles from Poland. Additionally, some obsolescent weapons that remained in Spanish arsenals were pressed into emergency service with the People's Army, including single-shot Remington Rolling Block rifles from the 1860s. In a twentieth-century war, these guns were not much use and it is doubtful they were received with any enthusiasm.

The Civil Guard

The Guarda Civil, Spain's paramilitary police force, was divided by the civil war, with its ranks split relatively evenly between pledging their allegiance to the government and the Francoists. Their job was predominantly to enforce order within populated cities and towns, which became especially crucial in quashing the mob violence that marked this politically turbulent period. Officers of the Civil Guard were mainly equipped with what was known as 'El Tigre'. This rifle was actually just a Spanish-made copy of the lever-action Winchester 1892, produced in Eibar from around 1915. The Tigre rifle was very popular, perhaps more due to its connotations with the American West rather than its combat efficiency, and it was made in large volumes. By the time of the civil war, many thousands were in circulation. They were chambered for the flat-nosed .44-40 Winchester cartridge, which was basically antiquated by the 1930s but was in ready supply in Spain.

Another indigenously produced rifle of note was the Destroyer Carbine, a short, compact rifle chambered for 9mm pistol rounds. It was also produced in Eibar and was intended for the Civil Guard, but production came along slowly and by the time of the civil war it had failed to replace the Tigre. The quality of the rifle was excellent but, being a pistol calibre, it was not much good for anything other than law enforcement purposes.

Nationalist rifles

The Nationalist forces, controlling most of the pre-war Spanish army, had the largest portion of Spanish Mauser rifles at their disposal when the war began: about 300,000. This was already far more than the Republic, so from the start the Nationalists were at a distinct advantage in equipping their troops. It was this rifle that would serve as the primary weapon of all Nationalist troops throughout the war, and its use in the conflict only reinforced its already positive reputation. In addition to the standard Mauser rifle, the Army of Africa also had in their arsenal some 5,000 Mauser 1891 carbines bought from Germany. These were chambered in 7.65mm rather than the 7x57mm Spanish cartridge, and consequently were not interchangeable with the Spanish Mauser.

Compared to the desperately under-equipped Republican forces, the Nationalists did not rely as heavily on imported arms, but nevertheless as Franco's cause attracted recruits in the thousands, donations from Germany and Italy were accepted. Both countries sent large shipments of their standard service rifles; from Germany it was the Mauser, and from Italy it was the Carcano rifle. The Mauser was without a doubt the better gun, and was supplied in both its older First World War Gewehr 98 model and the newer carbine version, known as the Karabiner 98k – the Wehrmacht's rifle of choice. The Carcano, while very accurate, was of average reliability and was chambered for the underpowered 6.5mm Italian cartridge. The numbers in which both the German and Italian rifles were supplied totals at about 200,000 each.

It also possible, though hard to ascertain, that the Nationalists may have fielded small numbers of the self-loading RSC rifle. These rifles were made in France from 1917, and during the 1920s, they were sold to Spanish elements in Morocco as part of France's aid to Spain in the Rif War. Therefore, it is entirely possible that the Army of Africa could have had these rifles in limited service when the civil war began.

II: SUBMACHINE GUNS

The submachine gun (SMG) was still a new concept in 1936, having been developed during the latter stages of the First World War. Often considered to be the first effective submachine gun was a German design by Hugo Schmeisser – the MP18. Produced by the Suhl factory of Theodore Bergmann, the MP18 was used only in the last months of the war. Its impact, however, was felt during the interwar period, when it spawned countless derivative designs from around the world, seeing use in conflicts in China, South America, and, of course, Spain.

The Spanish Civil War was, in fact, one of the first conflicts to see submachine guns used on a large scale, and it was their use here that sold the German army on the weapon, realising that the SMG was an incredibly effective tool for close-range urban combat. France and Britain did not heed the same lessons from Spain and entered the Second World War without ready supplies of SMGs, and ultimately suffered for it.

Republican submachine guns

When the war began, the Basque firm Star, primarily a manufacturer of inexpensive pistols, had just developed Spain's first indigenous submachine gun, the Si35. This gun, chambered in the Spanish 9mm Largo cartridge, was built to a good standard but was very expensive and needlessly complex. It puzzlingly featured two fire selector levers on the left side of the receiver, one to activate or deactivate the safety and the other to switch between single shots or full auto. Why the designers felt it necessary to separate these functions between two levers is a mystery only they could have answered.

Star seems to have intended to supply these guns not only to the Spanish army but also for international export sale, but the civil war interrupted these plans. Initially, the Star factory was loyal to the Republican government and supplied them with a quantity of Si35s, although given the high production costs and manufacturing time, numbers were likely very low. Star was quickly captured by the Nationalists in 1937 and from then on was required to produce guns for Franco. The Nationalists do not seem to have made any significant orders for Si35 submachine guns and thus the gun disappeared after the war.

When the Star factory fell, the Republic's Comissió d'Indústries de Guerra (War Industries Commission) commissioned a heavily simplified version of the Si35 to be produced at factories in Barcelona and Olot. This gun became known as the Labora and was a rare wartime design. It was intended to be a cost-efficient submachine gun that could be produced and issued in large volumes, but the project did not realise its full potential. The manufacturers still insisted on using high-quality materials and expensive machining processes, which dragged down the production significantly. It only proved to be a strain on already dwindling resources and by the end of the war, nowhere near enough had been produced. The exact number is contested, but it is generally agreed to have been around 2,000–3,000.

The fate of the Labora guns is a mystery, as very few have survived today. Republican remnants in 1939 were determined not to let their weapons fall into the hands of Franco's forces, and thus many were taken to France to be confiscated by the authorities there. The Laboras do not seem to have been among these guns, however, and it has been speculated that rather than handing them over to the French, the Republicans instead buried them somewhere around the border.

Beyond the Si35 and Labora, the Republic relied heavily on foreign imports. Estonia supplied a few hundred MP18 copies produced by Tallinn Arsenal, although these were chambered in 9x20mm Browning, a cartridge not readily available in Spain, and were therefore useless. The USSR saw the war as an opportunity to put their own submachine gun, the PPD, to the test; these guns fed from high-capacity drum magazines fired at around 1,000 rounds per minute, consequently earning the nickname 'La Regadera' ('shower') from Republican troops. Poland provided some old German MP18 submachine guns and about 3,000 EMP-35 submachine guns (see Nationalist submachine guns below). But the main submachine gun fielded by the Republic during the war was the MP28, an improved version of the MP18 developed by Schmeisser. Restrictions on Germany's arms industry after the First World War initially prevented Schmeisser from producing and exporting his gun in Germany, but by 1928, he and the firm Haenel that he was working for had decided that the Versailles treaty no longer applied to them and began mass-producing the MP28 for international sales, including to the Spanish Nationalists.

The Republic did not get their MP28s from Germany, but rather reverse-engineered examples captured from the Nationalists. Republican MP28s were produced in various factories and workshops in the Levante region, and these guns were christened the 'Naranjero' after the orange trees that grew around the Republic's wartime capital city, Valencia. This colloquial term remains a common Spanish nickname for submachine guns of any type. The so-called Naranjero gun was mechanically identical to the original German MP28 that it was copied from, but was often built with a large, cylindrical cocking handle that was unique to the Spanish version. Since the production of the Spanish MP28 was an unofficial undertaking, no data exists pertaining to the numbers made, although thousands of examples circulated around the world after the war.

Nationalist submachine guns

The Nationalists' supply of submachine guns came entirely from Germany, on whom they heavily depended. As previously mentioned, the MP28, produced by Haenel, was supplied to the Nationalists as part of Germany's aid. The MP28 was the archetypal submachine gun, operating on a basic blowback mechanism and offering rapid fire at 500–600 rounds per minute in a compact and lightweight package, chambered for the ubiquitous 9x19mm Parabellum cartridge that was used by all subsequent German submachine guns.

The most numerous submachine gun that was supplied to Franco's Rebels was the EMP, produced by the Erfurt-based firm Erma. Although basically a derivation of the MP28 design, the EMP was easily identifiable by its distinctive wooden foregrip and utilised a bolt delay device that kept the fire rate at a controlled 550 rounds per minute. It was a popular pre-Second World War submachine gun, with sales to Poland, Yugoslavia, Bolivia, and Mexico, among others.

During the mid-1930s, the EMP was offered in two forms: the EMP-34 and EMP-35, although there was little difference between the two variants other than an improved safety latch on the latter. The EMP-34 seems to have been the version supplied to the Nationalists, built with a tangent rear sight, and it proved to be a popular weapon with the troops; so much so, in fact, that after the war ended, the new Francoist government set up licensed domestic production of the gun at Coruña Arsenal. Hence, the gun would earn the nickname '*La Coruña*'. The Republicans also had large quantities of the EMP-35. After the war, these guns were taken by the fleeing Republicans to France, where they were confiscated by the French authorities and, ironically, ended up back in fascist hands when the Germans invaded in 1940.

The Germans also sent some Bergmann MP34/I submachine guns. This SMG, designed by the son of Theodore Bergmann, was the primary competitor to the Erma gun and was ultimately the less successful of the two. Not only was it expensive to produce, but it also exhibited a design eccentricity in which the magazine fed from the right side of the receiver. This did not prove to be a popular feature and made it rather awkward to reload the gun. It also featured a two–stage trigger mechanism in which half-pulling the trigger would give single shots and pressing it down fully would give automatic fire. The performance of the Erma and Bergmann guns in Spain were evaluated carefully by the Germans and led directly to their development of the MP38 and later MP40, the now-famous submachine guns fielded in great numbers by the Wehrmacht during Second World War.

The Italian troops supporting the Nationalist Rebels were equipped with small numbers of the Revelli submachine gun or 'OVP', a 1921 design that was based on a First World War gun. It fed magazines from the top and was chambered in the underpowered 9mm Glisenti round. Although made to a good standard, it was not as effective as Germany's offerings and saw very little use. The Italians also fielded some First World War-era Beretta Mod.1918 submachine guns; this was actually the very first true SMG to see any form of military service, predating the Bergmann MP18, and was largely constructed from components of other guns, including the Carcano and Vetterli rifles. It is not known that the Italians spared any SMGs for their Francoist allies.

III: MACHINE GUNS

The machine gun emerged in the latter part of the nineteenth century, with the British-American inventor Hiram Maxim being generally credited with its invention. The Maxim gun would make its bloody mark on history during the First World War, when it proved to be an indispensable infantry weapon for both sides, accounting for a large portion of the excessive casualties of the conflict. The deadly effectiveness of the machine gun would result in a permanent change in infantry tactics and the early twentieth century saw a worldwide rush to produce and stock up on machine guns in large numbers.

Before the civil war, the Spanish army equipped itself with the French Hotchkiss machine gun. Most of these were allocated to the Army of Africa, who would, under Franco's leadership, initiate the rebellion against the Republican government. The Loyalists retained only about a quarter of the pre-war machine guns in Spanish service. Thus, when the war began, the Republic was desperately short of machine guns, and relied heavily on foreign imports. These came in various different calibers, which caused endless ordnance issues for the Republicans.

Republican machine guns

The aforementioned Hotchkiss was initially the primary machine gun of both the Republican and Nationalist war efforts. This was a gas-operated design, originally developed in France in 1897, and was produced under licence in Spain at Oviedo Arsenal from 1903. Production before the war totalled at about 2,000 units. It was chambered in the Spanish rifle cartridge, 7x57mm Mauser, and fed not from a belt or magazine, but from horizontal-loading strips of thirty rounds. The fire rate was slow at about 400 rounds per minute. Although it was reliable enough, the Hotchkiss was outdated and was incapable of producing the volumes of fire exhibited by the Maxim gun, and by the 1930s there were much better machine guns available. The Republican government actually acknowledged this in 1933 and ordered the development of a replacement weapon, designed by an artillery officer named Andres Trapote. By the time the civil war broke out, however, only 400 Trapote guns had been made, and the project was terminated in 1936.

The Soviets, as part of their support for the Republic, decided to offload many of their old and obsolete machine guns. These included Colt M1895s and Maxim 1910s, both in the standard Russian rifle cartridge, 7.62x54mmR. The Colt gun was a nineteenth-century relic popularly known as the 'Potato Digger' due to its distinctive swinging lever action that operated the mechanism. It was not popular with the troops due to its poor reliability; this was probably not helped by the fact that the Republic already had a limited quantity of these guns in service *before* the war, which were chambered for the 7x57mm Spanish Mauser cartridge, which inevitably will have caused some confusion. Over 1,000 Russian models were sent to Spain and were generally relegated to second-line troops and foreign volunteers.

The Maxim gun, on the other hand, was warmly received. As a tried and tested design that had dominated the battlefields of the First World War, it could hardly fail. The Russian version, produced by Tula Arsenal from 1910, was mounted on a wheeled 'Sokolov' carriage. It was heavy and cumbersome, and designed to be operated by a crew of at least three. But it was chambered for a powerful cartridge and, as a belt-fed weapon, provided a distinct firepower advantage over the strip-fed Hotchkiss. The only major flaw was that after prolonged use, breakages of the firing pin were reported, but this was not a hugely common occurrence and did little to hamper the positive reputation of the weapon. The Republic received 3,221 Maxims from Russia and put them to effective use.

Poland also sent some Maxims in the form of the German-made MG08 and the Polish 1910/28 model. Both were chambered in 7.92x57mm Mauser. The 1910/28 models started life as Russian 1910s that the Poles had acquired after 1918 and converted into the 7.92mm cartridge for their own use in 1928. This meant that their outward appearance was basically identical to the Russian 7.62mm model but they would not fire the Russian cartridge – another ordnance nightmare for Republican troops.

It is also known that the Republic acquired small quantities of .303-caliber Vickers guns, the British-made version of the Maxim. The Vickers was smaller and lighter than the German and Russian models and was of superior quality, but the .303 round was not abundant in Spain so any Vickers guns that were available probably did not see very much use. It is likely that these guns were allocated to International Brigades; probably the British and American volunteers.

Besides Maxims, there was a wide range of other machine guns acquired by the Republic during the war, which were generally considered second-rate in comparison. The French St Étienne M1907 machine gun in 8mm Lebel was initially one of the main machine guns in Republican service, but because of its slow fire rate and notorious unreliability, it was quickly phased out of use by the Maxim. The Poles sent some Italian 6.5mm FIAT machine guns that were not particularly popular in Italy during the First World War and were especially unpopular in Spain during the civil war. Along with these, there were some Austrian Schwarzlose 1912 MGs that were heavier and less reliable than the Maxim, and basically offered no advantage over it. The Polish version of the Browning M1917 machine gun was also received in 1937, known as the Wz.30. Over 1,000 models were sent to Spain and, being based on a good design, there could hardly have been any complaints.

Republican light machine guns
The civil war also saw the wide use of light machine guns, a concept pioneered by the Danish Madsen gun in the late nineteenth century and further expanded upon by the French with the Chauchat during the First World War. In fact, both of these weapons would see use in Spain during this period, along with a variety of other international designs. Light machine guns, while rarely offering the same degree of firepower and accuracy as a medium machine gun, were smaller and lighter than a Maxim and could be operated by a single man with relative ease.

Before the civil war, Spain had a relatively small number of light machine guns in service, most of which were Hotchkiss guns produced at the Oviedo Arsenal. These included the M1909 'machine rifle' and M1922 model. Combined, there were probably about 1,000 in Spanish service in 1936, the large majority of which were acquired by the Nationalists. These guns were, like the larger M1897 model, fed from thirty-round strips and had a slow fire rate. During the war, the Republic acquired quantities of the M1926 model from foreign imports, which was merely a detail improvement of the M1922. The Republic also had small amounts of pre-war Astra machine guns, a gun that had been pegged to replace the Hotchkiss in 1927 but had failed to do so. So few were produced that wartime service would have been incredibly limited.

The Soviets sent some old Madsen machine guns in 7.62mm, which were originally used during the First World War but had since been taken out of Russian service. The Madsen was a mechanically complex and very heavy LMG, and was showing its age by the 1930s. It was fed from a top-loading thirty-round magazine. Estonian Madsens were also sold to the Republic, which had been converted into the British .303 caliber by Tallinn Arsenal, and as such were probably not much use to the People's Army. Russia also sent some MG08/15s that they had captured from Germany during the First World War, although these guns were very heavy and cumbersome.

Among the better machine guns fielded by the Republicans were the Polish Wz.28 and the Russian DP-28. The former was a licensed copy of the M1918 Browning Automatic Rifle (BAR), the American machine gun that earned a famous reputation during the world wars. Like the original model it was based on, the Polish version was a highly reliable and accurate assault weapon. It was chambered in the plentiful 7.92mm Mauser cartridge and was a popular weapon, although with less than a thousand being imported from Poland, there were never enough of them.

The DP-28 was the then-new Russian light machine gun that had been adopted by the Red Army in 1928. In accordance with the USSR's support of the Republic, they sent about 5,000 DP-28s. It was chambered in the 7.62x54mm rimmed cartridge, shared by the Mosin-Nagant, and fed from a top-mounted, circular pan magazine. Despite its unconventional appearance, it was a good light support weapon, but did not quite provide the level of reliability offered by the Wz.28. The USSR also provided 2,000 belt-fed Maxim-Tokarev light machine guns; as the name suggests, these were derived from the Maxim gun, with modifications made by the Russians to decrease the weight and size. It omitted the water-cooling barrel jacket present on the Maxim 1910 and added a conventional shoulder stock in place of the spade grips. These proved to be very effective guns and were popular with both the Republican troops they were intended for, and the Nationalists who pressed captured examples into their own service.

Also sent from Poland were several thousand French-made Chauchat machine guns in 8mm. Originally conceived as a lightweight machine gun for trench assaults during the First World War, the Chauchat earned a reputation as one of the poorest-made and least reliable machine guns to see widespread military service. It did not do well in rough conditions and at least part of its low standard of quality can be chalked up to the fact that it was hurriedly mass-produced by a bicycle manufacturer in 1915. The distinctive semi-circular magazine was also known to be of poor quality. Even if the gun had been expertly made, it still had issues inherent in the design: the magazine held only twenty rounds, and the fire rate was very slow at 250 rounds per minute. For these reasons, it was not a popular weapon with any of its users. Despite placing an order for over 5,000 Chauchats, the Republic only received 400 – most of the shipments were captured by Franco's forces.

Towards the end of the war, the Republic managed to acquire a few thousand Czech Zb.26 light machine guns. The Zb.26 was an excellent design of the utmost quality, and was the basis for the famous Bren gun used by the British in the Second World War. It was chambered for 7.92mm Mauser and fed from top-loading magazines. It saw use during the Battle of the Ebro and the skirmishes that followed, but ultimately came too late to make an appreciable impact. Unsubstantial quantities of the KE7 light machine gun, produced by the private Swiss firm of SIG in the 1920s and 1930s, also reached Republican ranks and while these guns were also high standard, there is no data on their use during the civil war.

Nationalist machine guns

Like the Republican government, Franco's Rebels started the war with the 1897 Hotchkiss machine gun. Since most of these guns were fielded during the Rif War, they were in the inventory of the Francoist Army of Africa when the civil war broke out. While the Nationalists had the advantage of having acquired most of Spain's pre-war arsenal, they were soon faced with Republicans armed with foreign-supplied Maxim guns, which were far superior to the Hotchkiss. Thus, Franco's army was more than happy to receive about 5,000 German machine guns as part of the Nazi aid to the Nationalist war effort.

The German version of the Maxim gun, the MG08, was supplied in large quantities and was equivalent in performance to the Russian 7.62mm model that the Republicans were using. The only difference was the calibre, as the MG08 was in 7.92mm Mauser. It was a well-made and highly effective machine gun, certainly more so than Italy's offerings, which were not as welcomed. These were largely comprised of First World War leftovers, including about 500 of the rather defective St Étienne M1907 (also used by the Republicans) and about another 500 Schwarzlose 1912 machine guns, which, as previously described, offered no advantage over the Maxim. Both were in their respective countries rifle cartridges, 8mm Lebel (France) and 8x50mm Mannlicher (Austria).

Italy provided some of their own domestically designed machine guns, produced by FIAT, although these were not much better. The M1914 machine gun was an unusual design fed from a 'cage' consisting of ten five-round clips stacked on top of one another, which would be fed into the receiver one after the other. It was far less practical than a simple belt feed or magazine and was prone to stoppages and jams. With a slow fire rate and firing the underpowered 6.5mm Carcano cartridge, the M1914 was already unpopular with Italian troops, so it was not particularly appreciated by the Spanish Nationalists.

The M1935, which was merely an improved M1914, was also used. This was a lightened model that replaced the poorly functioning feed system of the M1914 with a more reliable belt feed. It was chambered for the more powerful 8x59mm Breda cartridge and was a marked improvement over its predecessor, but was still subject to complaints about its reliability. Combined, about 2,500 M1914 and M1935s were supplied by Italy to Franco's troops.

In the later stages of the civil war, Italy sent about 2,500 Breda 37 machine guns, which were derived from the Breda 30 LMG detailed later in this chapter. As a brand new design from 1937, this gun was supposed to represent the cutting edge in Italian military armaments, but in actuality it was a very outdated design, firing from small twenty-round strips and firing at only 400 rounds per minute. Unlike the Hotchkiss, the spent strips had to be manually removed before loading a fresh one. For a modern gun, it was too heavy, too antiquated, and ultimately too unreliable.

Nationalist light machine guns

Before the civil war, Spain's light machine gun arsenal consisted only of about 1,000 Hotchkiss LMGs, both M1909 and M1922 models. These were built under licence at the Oviedo Arsenal in Asturias. When the war broke out, the military garrison at Oviedo pledged their support for Franco, and despite repeated Republican efforts to regain control of the arsenal, the

Nationalists repelled them. Therefore, the majority of the existing Spanish LMGs were taken into Nationalist service, and continued production of the Spanish Hotchkiss provided Franco's army with a steady supply of light machine guns.

The Hotchkiss M1910 was a rather compact, lightweight machine gun that was marketed as a 'machine rifle'. It had seen extensive use by the Allied forces during the First World War and was not well liked by American troops due to its apparent tendency to break. In addition, it was perceived as being difficult to operate at night, hence earning it a derogatory nickname of the 'Daylight Gun'. Like most Hotchkiss designs, it was fed from a thirty-round strip. The M1922 was an improved post-war model that was offered with either a strip feed or a top-loading box magazine; the Spanish government sensibly chose to produce the magazine model. Both guns were produced in the Spanish rifle cartridge, 7x57mm Mauser, and had fire rates of around 400–450 rounds per minute, thus could not produce particularly large volumes of fire.

Like the Republic, the Nationalists also received many LMGs through foreign supplies, again from Germany and Italy. Germany gave some of their tried-and-tested wartime guns, all in 7.92mm, such as their lightened version of the Maxim known as the MG08/15 – although it was still very large and heavy, and could not practically be fired from anything but a prone position. This was, in part, down to the fact that it made use of a large water cooler around the barrel, whereas most light machine guns were air-cooled. There was in fact an air-cooled model of the 08/15 that was supplied to the Nationalists during the war, known as the lMG 08/18, although it was still much larger than other designs.

The Dreyse MG13 was another German-supplied gun, which began life as a First World War water-cooled machine gun but was converted in the early 1930s into a light air-cooled gun as part of the rearmament program for the German army. However, in 1936, the Wehrmacht upgraded to the more modern MG34, and thus had no need for the MG13, offloading a large quantity to Spain. It could feed from twenty-five-round box magazines or seventy-five-round drums, and had a better fire rate than the Hotchkiss guns at 600 rounds per minute. The MG13 must have been well thought of, as it remained in Spanish service after the civil war ended.

Through good fortune, the Nationalists managed to intercept a shipment of about 1,500 Bergmann MG15 light machine guns from Poland that were intended for the Republicans. This was a German attempt to produce a belt-fed light machine gun during the First World War, which was largely eclipsed in wartime service by the more cumbersome MG08/15. The MG15 used a 'bullpup' layout in which the trigger was forward of the belt feed and the firing mechanism was located in the stock. Thus, it had a compact overall length while retaining good accuracy.

Italy, rather mercifully, only supplied the Nationalists with one of their latest offerings, the Breda 30. This gun, chambered in the weak 6.5mm Carcano cartridge, was fed from small twenty-round stripper clips that were fed into an opening fixed magazine on the right side of the receiver. This was a very poorly designed machine gun that was prone to jamming, largely down to the awkward feeding system. In order to facilitate the feeding of the bullets into the chamber, the magazine included an inbuilt lubricator that oiled the cartridges; what the designers evidently did not anticipate was that in certain conditions, the lubrication would cause sand and dirt to stick to the cartridges and cause feeding issues. Over 2,000 Breda 30s were supplied by Italy and were probably the worst machine guns available to the Nationalists during the war.

IV: PISTOLS

Self-loading pistols emerged at the turn of the century, with the first successful example being the German-made Mauser C96, which saw wide use around the world by military officers, police forces, and criminal gangs. Preceding the self-loading pistol was the revolver, the popularity of which was never fully diminished by the advent of automatics, and was still preferred by many officers on account of its reliability.

Although not weapons of much tactical importance, being traditionally issued only to officers, tankers and pilots, Spain was one of the world's largest producers, if not the largest producer, of pistols in the early twentieth century. The vast majority of these Spanish-made guns were inexpensive pocket pistols in small calibers, such as the popular 7.65mm Mauser and the Spanish 9mm Largo cartridge. The First World War saw a huge expansion of Spanish pistol production due to a rather farcical state of affairs that emerged in 1914; the French army, woefully under-equipped like almost every country in Europe at the start of the war, sent out an open-ended contract to the Guernica-based firm Gabilondo, requesting 10,000 of their 'Ruby' brand self-loading pistols per month. In keeping with the increasing pressures of the war, the request was soon raised to

30,000 per month. Gabilondo was a young and relatively small company that lacked the manufacturing capacity to meet these demands, so they sub-contracted several other Spanish firms to assist with the production. These firms, in turn, sub-contracted other firms and soon enough almost every gunsmith in Spain was producing Ruby-type pistols to sell to the French, who were hardly picky about the source of the weapons. The most prominent place of production for Spanish pistols was the Basque city of Eibar.

By 1918, many thousands of Ruby and Ruby-like pistols had been produced by various Spanish firms, and with the French no longer taking them, they instead flooded the civilian market under various marketing names. Without a doubt, Rubys would have been the most common type of pistol used during the Spanish Civil War, as they were in endless supply. The Ruby would have been carried by Nationalists and Republicans alike, although they were not in formal issue and would have been privately purchased or obtained. It was a popular gun due to its simplicity, and the quality of any given example depended entirely on the manufacturer, although generally most examples were serviceable, as it was not a particularly difficult gun to produce.

There was also an unusual Spanish pocket pistol in circulation during the interwar period known as the Jo-Lo-Ar. The name was derived from the designer's initials, Jose Lopez de Arnaiz. Originally intended as a self-protection gun for civilian use, the Jo-Lo-Ar was cocked by way of a large lever protruding from the side of the gun, located in front of the guardless trigger. This made it very easy to operate with one hand. The Republicans joked that the pistol was designed for José Millán-Astray, the one-armed Francoist army officer.

The Mauser C96 was produced in Spain by the firm of Astra Unceta, based in Guernica. This company was founded in 1908 by Pedro Unceta and was predominantly a manufacturer of pistols, although it had been known to branch out into other arms, including a failed attempt to introduce a new machine gun into Spanish service in 1927. Their pre-civil war output largely consisted of Ruby clones under various marketing names and Mauser copies. Astra also took on a design from the Count of Campo-Giro, Colonel Venancio López de Ceballos y Aguirre. His pistol, which became known simply as the Campo-Giro, was in official Spanish service for a short-lived period from 1912 to the early 1920s. It was not considered particularly reliable and was difficult to repair. Nonetheless, thousands were produced and were not uncommon in 1936.

The Astra-made Mauser, known as the Astra 900, was introduced in the 1920s as an attempt to capitalise on the post-war fame of the C96 pistol. Astra's version was externally identical to the German model but internally cut some corners for the sake of ease of production. 34,325 Astra 900s were produced from 1928–37, and were primarily in service with the Civil Guard. Some models were in 7.63mm Mauser but most were in 9mm Largo.

Astra also introduced a fully-automatic modification for the Mauser pistol, which they produced in various iterations as the Astra models 901, 902, 903, and 903E. The 901 model was simply an Astra 900 with the selective fire switch that allowed it to fire rapidly at 850 rounds per minute, but with such a small magazine of only ten rounds, this feature was practically useless. Beginning with the 902 model, Astra introduced an extended twenty-round magazine that allowed the gun to fire for twice as long, which – with such a blistering fire rate – was all of about two seconds. This was probably one of the first 'machine pistols' ever developed, and while impractical, it earned some recognition as a poor man's submachine gun, ideal as a backup weapon for vehicle crews. It was such an intriguing concept at the time that in 1932, the Mauser firm copied their own imitators by producing their own rapid-fire model, known as the Schnellfeuer. About 2,000 selective-fire Astra pistols were in service with the Civil Guard by 1936. Rapid-fire Mausers with finned barrels were also produced by the firms of Zulaica y Cia and Eulogio Arostegui of Eibar, known as the 'Royal' and 'MM-31' models respectively. These firms seem to have disappeared during the Civil War and their output was limited.

The final Astra pistol of note was their Model 400, a 9mm Largo pistol derived partially from the earlier Campo-Giro, but of much better quality. It was adopted by the Spanish army in 1921 and over 100,000 were produced before production ended in the early 1940s. This was the primary service pistol of both the Republican and Nationalist factions during the war, and had such a good reputation that during the Second World War, the Germans – an ally of Francoist Spain – ordered 10,000 models for their own troops. During the conflict, Astra was in a precarious position. Being based in Guernica, the factory narrowly avoided complete destruction during the bombing of the city by the Luftwaffe in 1937. While its owner, Pedro Unceta, was a Nationalist, his employees largely held Republican sympathies and many of them fled to Barcelona to work at the government factories there. The Nationalists seized control of the factory after the bombing of

Guernica and appropriated its machinery to produce arms for themselves, thus depriving the Republic of another valuable source of arms.

There were so many more Spanish-made pistols that would have seen wide circulation during the civil war that it is not possible to list them all here, but other popular examples included the Echeverria Star M1919 (popular with CNT militias), the Star M1920 (a Colt M1911 copy), and the various models of Ruby pocket revolvers in .38 calibre that were formerly used by the Spanish army before war. All of these guns no doubt saw much carry, if little actual combat use, during the conflict.

Foreign-imported pistols included 1,200 Russian-supplied Tokarev automatics and Nagant revolvers for the Republicans, as well as a few hundred Browning automatics and Lebel revolvers from Poland. The Nationalists were equipped with a few thousand 9mm Bergmann 1903 pistols that were in service with the Army of Africa during the Rif War, as well as some German-supplied Mausers and Lugers. Italy probably donated some old First World War pistols too, likely Glisentis (which were poor) and Berettas (which were excellent). Realistically, though, pistols were considered low priority by both sides and neither made any significantly large orders for foreign-supplied pistols.

For more on firearms history and unusual guns, visit the Firearms Curiosa at http://firearms.96.LT/Homepage.html.

Sources

Cadiou, Yves & Richard, Alphonse, *Modern Firearms*, Routledge & Kegan Paul, 1977.

Cormack, A.J.R., *Small Arms Profile #15: Astra Automatic Pistols*, Profile Publications, 1972.

Esdaile, Charles J., *The Spanish Civil War, A Military History*, Routledge, 2018.

Hobart, Frank, *Pictorial History of the Machine Gun*, Ian Allan Ltd, 1971.

Hogg, Ian & Weeks, John, *Pistols of the World*, Arms and Armour Press, 1978.

Howson, Gerald, *Arms for Spain: The Untold Story of the Spanish Civil War*, John Murray, 1998.

Nelson, Thomas & Musgrave, Daniel, *The World's Machine Pistols and Submachine Guns, Vol I & II*, TBN, 1962, Chesa, 1980.

Quesada, Alejandro de, *The Spanish Civil War 1936–39 (1), Nationalist Forces*, Osprey, 2014.

Quesada, Alejandro de, *The Spanish Civil War 1936–39 (2), Republican Forces*, Osprey, 2015.

Swenson, G., *Pictorial History of the Rifle*, Ian Allan Ltd, 1971.

Walter, John, *Allied Small Arms of World War I*, Crowood Press, 2000.

Appendix II

Glossary of Organisations and Parties

Organisations and Parties that supported the Republic (Loyalists, reds)

CNT-FAI: Spain's large and radically revolutionary anarcho-syndicalist/anarchist movement.

PCE: the Spanish Communist Party, grew rapidly in size and prominence during the war.

Popular Front: An electoral alliance of the Republican parties, Socialists, PCE and POUM, amongst others, that won the February 1936 elections.

POUM: a small anti-Stalinist Marxist party, created by an associate of Trotsky, Andrés Nin.

PSOE: the Spanish Socialist Party, the biggest party of the Left, although it was divided between moderates, led by Indalecio Prieto, and a radical wing under Largo Caballero.

Republican Parties: term denotes the various liberal parties of the centre/centre-left, such as Manuel Azaña's Izquierda Republicana.

Note: The Republic was also supported by various Basque and Catalan Nationalists.

Organisations and parties that supported the Nationalists (fascists, Insurgents, Rebels)

Carlists: an ultra-conservative Catholic monarchist party, powerful in the rural north.

CEDA: Spain's pre-eminent rightist party before the war, led by José María Gil-Robles.

Condor Legion: an elite unit of German air and ground personnel sent by Hitler to fight for the Nationalists and test new weaponry.

CTV: Corpo Truppe Volontarie, the Italian corps of army regulars and fascist Blackshirt volunteers who fought for Franco.

Falange: Spain's fascist party, translates as 'Phalanx', founded by José Antonio Primo de Rivera and split between radicals and traditionalists.

FET y de las JONS: the single party that Franco created by merging all political forces in Nationalist Spain in 1937, often known simply as the Falange or the Movimiento.

Note: The Radical Party was a key element of the pre-war right but had all but disappeared by 1936. Various monarchist factions also made up the Nationalist coalition.

Appendix III

Republican Orders of Battle

Bold indicates commanders drawn from the militias, rather than professional officers, and have their party affiliation indicated. Note also that Kléber, Walter and Gal were Red Army officers.

Battle of Brunete

Under overall command of Army of the Centre (Miaja)

V Corps (**Modesto – PCE**)
11th Division (**Líster – PCE**), 1st, 9th, 100th brigades
35th Division (Walter), 11th International Brigade, 32nd, 108th brigades
46th Division (**El Campesino – PCE**), 10th, 101st brigades

XVIII Corps (Jurado, later Casado)
10th Division (Enciso), 2nd, 3rd brigades
15th Division (Gal), 13th, 15th International brigades
34th Division (Galán), 3rd, 16th, 68th brigades

II Corps (Romero)
4th Division (Bueno), 19th, 41st brigades
24th Division (Gallo), 6th, 7th, 21st brigades

Reserve
45th Division (Kléber), 12th, 150th International brigades
47th Division (**Durán – PCE**), 69th, 94th brigades

From Late July
14th Division (**Cipriano Mera – CNT**), 65th, 70th, 72nd brigades

Battle of Belchite

Under overall command of Army of the East (Pozas)

Battlegroup A
27th Division (**Trueba – PCE**), 122nd, 123rd, 124th brigades
127th Brigade

Battlegroup B
45th Division (Kléber), 12th, 13th International brigades

Battlegroup D
V Corps (**Modesto – PCE**)
11th Division (**Líster – PCE**), 1st, 9th, 100th brigades
35th Division (Walter), 11th, 15th International brigades, 32nd Brigade
46th Division (**El Campesino – PCE**), 10th, 101st brigades
102nd, 120th, 134th brigades

XII Corps (Sánchez Plaza)
25th Division (**Ortiz – CNT**), 116th, 117th, 118th brigades
30th Division (Pérez Salas), 131st, 132nd brigades

Reserve
24th Division (Gallo), 6th, 21st, 134th brigades
44th Division (Peire), 143rd, 144th, 145th brigades

Battle of Teruel

Under overall command of Army of Levante (Herández Saravia)

XVIII Corps (Heredia)
34th Division (**Vega – PCE**), 68th, 94th, 224th brigades
64th Division (**Martínez – PCE**), 16th, 81st, 83rd brigades
70th Division (**Toral – PCE**), 32nd, 92nd, 95th brigades

XX Corps (Menéndez)
40th Division (**Nieto – PSOE**), Paramilitary Police Unit
68th Division (Trigueros), 218th, 219th, 220th brigades

XXII Corps (Ibarrola)
11th Division (**Líster – PCE**), 1st, 9th, 100th brigades
25th Division (**Vivancos – CNT**), 116th, 117th, 118th brigades

Reserve
39th Division (Alba Rebullido), 22nd, 64th, 96th brigades
41st Division (Eixea), 57th, 58th, 97th brigades

From Late December
V Corps (**Modesto – PCE**)
35th Division (Walter), 11th, 15th International brigades, 32nd Brigade
46th Division (**El Campesino – PCE**), 10th, 101st brigades
47th Division (**Durán – PCE**), 49th, 69th brigades

Foreign Arms Supplied to the Nationalists and Republicans

	Republican	Nationalist
Military Aircraft	854	1,544
Tanks and armoured vehicles	535	284
Field and Heavy artillery	1,180	992
Anti-tank, Anti-air and other support artillery	1,240	999
Artillery shells	>4 million	8.8 million
Machine Guns	30,000	29,000
Rifles	628,000	447,000
Small arms cartridges	862 million	577 million

Note: While on the surface, it appears the two sides enjoyed relative parity in foreign supplies, it will have become clear through the text and especially Appendix I that qualitatively, the Nationalists were at a significant advantage. Russia and Poland took the civil war as an opportunity to offload much unwanted old equipment, often in poor condition and originating from a huge range of countries, while Italy and Germany, on the whole, only provided domestically produced weapons. To give just one example, the British rifles and machine guns that found their way into Republican hands were not especially useful due to the scarcity of the .303 cartridge. Further, the types of all arms supplied to the Republic were much more varied, a logistical nightmare – compare fourteen models of field and heavy artillery sent to the Rebels to forty supplied to the Loyalists. The shortage of shells on the Republican side has also already been commented upon. Additionally, we should note that the Nationalists seized control of the majority of Spain's pre-war arsenal at the outbreak of war.

Sources

Alpert, Michael, *The Republican Army in the Spanish Civil War, 1936–1939*, Cambridge University Press, 2018.

Esdaile, Charles J., *The Spanish Civil War, A Military History*, Routledge, 2018.

Howson, Gerald, *Arms for Spain, The Untold Story of the Spanish Civil War*, John Murray, 1998.

Notes

Introduction

1. Buckley, *The Life and Death of the Spanish Republic, A Witness to the Spanish Civil War*, I.B. Tauris, 2014, p.261.
2. Beevor (2007) gives a total of 200,000 murdered by the Nationalists and 38,000 killed in the Republican 'Red Terror' (pp.94, 81), while Preston (2012) puts Nationalist killings at 130,199 confirmed, with the total figure being something over 150,000 (p.xviii) and victims of the Republic at a shade under 50,000 (p.xvi).
3. Payne, *The Spanish Civil War, the Soviet Union and Communism*, Yale University Press, 2004, pp.310–11.
4. Ibid, p.310.
5. Esdaile, *The Spanish Civil War, A Military History*, Routledge, 2018, pp.312–13.

Chapter 1

1. Quoted in Fraser, *Blood of Spain: The Experience of Civil War, 1936–1939*, Penguin, 1981, p.256.
2. Howson, *Arms for Spain, The Untold Story of the Spanish Civil War*, John Murray, 1998, p.84.
3. See Alpert's *The Republican Army* for a detailed breakdown of the split of the Spanish army in 1936.
4. Esdaile, pp.37–42.
5. Quoted in Preston, 'Italy and Spain in Civil War and World War, 1936–1943', in Balfour & Preston (eds.), *Spain and the Great Powers in the Twentieth Century*, Routledge, 1999, p.163.
6. Quoted in Balfour, *Deadly Embrace: Morocco and the Road to the Spanish Civil War*, Oxford University Press, 2002, p.297.
7. Alpert, *The Republican Army in the Spanish Civil War, 1936–1939*, Cambridge University Press, 2018, p.27.
8. Fusi, *Franco, A Biography*, Unwin Hyman, 1987, p.30.
9. Hugh Thomas, *The Spanish Civil War, Fourth Edition*, Penguin, 2012, pp.438, 492. For an in-depth analysis of these early battles, see Esdaile.
10. Esdaile, pp.174–6.

Chapter 2

1. Quoted in Hugh Thomas, pp.237–8.
2. For the most comprehensive study of violence and atrocities on both sides, see Preston, *The Spanish Holocaust, Inquisition and Extermination in Twentieth-Century Spain*, Harper Press, 2012.
3. Quoted in Smyth, "We are with you': Solidarity and Self-interest in Soviet Policy towards Republican Spain, 1936–1939' in Preston & Mackenzie (eds.), *The Republic Besieged: Civil War in Spain 1936–1939*, Edinburgh University Press, 1996, p.98.
4. See Government chapter of Buchanan, *Britain and the Spanish Civil War*, Cambridge University Press, 1997.
5. Radosh et al, *Spain Betrayed, The Soviet Union in the Spanish Civil War*, Yale University Press, 2001.
6. See works of Helen Graham, most notably,*The Spanish Republic at War, 1936–1939*, Cambridge University Press, 2002, 'War, Modernity and Reform: The Premiership of Juan Negrín 1937–1939', in Preston & Mackenzie (eds.), *The Republic Besieged: Civil War in Spain 1936–1939*, Edinburgh University Press, 1996, *Socialism and War, The Spanish Socialist Party in power and crisis, 1936–1939*, Cambridge University Press, 1991.
7. See Payne's argument in *The Spanish Civil War*, Cambridge University Press, 2012.
8. Quoted in Fraser, pp.256–7.
9. Martin Blásquez, *I Helped to Build an Army, Civil War Memoirs of a Spanish Staff Officer*, Secker and Warburg, 1939, p.185 & pp.124–5.
10. Graham, *The Spanish Republic at War*, pp.149–50.
11. Max, *Memorias de un Revolucionario*, Plaza & Janes, 1975, pp.48–51.
12. Candela, *The Adventures of an Innocent in the Spanish Civil War*, United Writers Publications, 1989, pp.43–4.
13. Esdaile, pp.100–101.
14. Casado, *The Last Days of Madrid*, Peter Davies, 1939, pp.59–60.
15. Graham, *The Spanish Republic at War*, p.146.
16. Esdaile, p.101.
17. Casado, p.58.
18. See James Matthews's study of conscription on both sides of the civil war, *Reluctant Warriors, Republican Popular Army and Nationalist Army Conscripts in the Spanish Civil War, 1936–1939*, Oxford University Press, 2012.
19. Howson, *Arms for Spain*, p.248.
20. Ibid, p.277.
21. Ibid, p.110.
22. Ibid, pp.302–303.
23. Horne, *The Price of Glory, Verdun 1916*, Penguin, 1993, p.43
24. Terraine, *To Win a War, 1918: The Year of Victory*, Cassell, 2000, p.187.

25. Howson, *Arms for Spain*, pp.250–1.
26. Fischer, *Men and Politics: An Autobiography*, Duell, Sloan & Pearce, 1941, p.593.
27. Hemingway, *For Whom the Bell Tolls*, Arrow, 2004, p.241.
28. Azaña, *Obras Completas, Volumen VI, Julio 1936/Agosto 1940*, Taurus/CEPC, 2008, p.389.
29. Martin Blásquez, pp.282–3.
30. Alpert, pp.93–5.
31. Fischer, p.543.
32. Tagüeña, *Testimonio de dos guerras*, Planeta, 1978, p.128, Azaña, p.421.
33. Alpert, p.132.
34. Tagüeña, p.128
35. Hemingway, *For Whom the Bell Tolls*, pp.238–9.
36. Howson, *Arms for Spain*, p.28.
37. Alpert, p.150.
38. Darman, *Heroic Voices of the Spanish Civil War, Memories from the International Brigades*, New Holland, 2009, p.12.
39. See Richardson, *Comintern Army: The International Brigades and the Spanish Civil War*, University Press of Kentucky, 1982.
40. See Baxell, *Unlikely Warriors, The British in the Spanish Civil War and the Struggle Against Fascism*, Aurum Press, 2014 and *British Volunteers in the Spanish Civil War, The British Battalion in the International Brigades, 1936–1939*, Warren & Pell, 2007.
41. Quoted in Darmen, p.23.
42. Baxell, *British Volunteers*, pp.28–9.
43. For extensive criticism of the Brigades' methods see Richardson.
44. Baxell, *British Volunteers*, p.139.
45. Darman, p.14, Baxell, *British Volunteers*, pp.139–40.
46. Richardson, p.168.
47. Michael Petrou, *Renegades: Canadians in the Spanish Civil War*, Warren & Pell, 2008, pp.113–14.
48. Baxell, *British Volunteers*, pp.144–6.
49. Petrou, pp.136–7.
50. See Beevor, *The Battle for Spain, The Spanish Civil War 1936–1939*, Phoenix, 2007 for a generally hostile account.
51. Baxell, *Unlikely Warriors*, p.159.
52. Beevor, p.216.
53. Sid Hamm's diary is included in the publication of the memoirs of Franco volunteer Frank Thomas, *Brother against Brother: Experiences of a British Volunteer in the Spanish Civil War*, Sutton, 1998.
54. Richardson, p.178.
55. Beevor, p.219.
56. Hemingway, *For Whom the Bell Tolls*, pp.241–2.

57. Modesto, *Soy del Quinto Regimiento (Notas de la Guerra española)*, Colección Ebro, 1974, p.133.
58. Gregory, *The Shallow Grave, A Memoir of the Spanish Civil War*, Gollancz, 1986, p.58.
59. Merriman, Lerude, *American Commander in Spain, Robert Hale Merriman and the Abraham Lincoln Brigade*, University of Nevada Press, 1986.
60. Howson, *Aircraft of the Spanish Civil War*, Putnam, 1990, p.20.
61. Howson, *Arms for Spain*, pp.302–303. The figure of 1,000 aircraft supplied by the Soviets to the Republic is often quoted, based on Hugh Thomas's classic 1961 work. Howson's exhaustive investigation into the Republic's struggle for arms gives the much more likely figure of 623.
62. Howson, *Aircraft*, p. 198.
63. Alpert, p.225.
64. Radosh et al, pp.488–91.
65. Esdaile, p.208.

Chapter 3

1. Balfour, *Deadly Embrace*, pp.211–12.
2. Jensen, *Irrational Triumph: Cultural Despair, Military Nationalism, and the Ideological Origins of Franco's Spain*, University of Nevada Press, 2002, p.146.
3. Paul Preston, 'The Theorists of Extermination: The Origins of Violence in the Spanish Civil War' in Carlos Jerez-Farrán and Samuel Amago (eds.), *Unearthing Franco's Legacy: Mass Graves and the Recovery of Historical Memory in Spain*, University of Notre Dame Press, 2010, p.52.
4. Preston, 'Theorists of Extermination', p.48.
5. Jensen, p.153.
6. Paul Preston, 'The Answer lies in the Sewers: Captain Aguilera and the Mentality of the Spanish Officer Corps', *Science & Society*, 68, 3, 2004, 277–312, p.286.
7. Ibid, p.289.
8. Quoted in Cardozo, *The March of a Nation, My Year of Spain's Civil War*, Right Book Club, 1937, pp.151–2.
9. Balfour and Laporte, 'Spanish Military Cultures and the Moroccan Wars, 1909–1936', *European History Quarterly*, 30, 3, 2000, pp.307–32, p.318.
10. Lowe, *Catholicism, War and the Foundation of Francoism: The Juventud de Acción Popular in Spain 1931–1939*, Sussex Academic Press, 2010, p.169.
11. Blinkhorn, *Carlism and Crisis in Spain, 1931–1939*, Cambridge University Press, 1975, p.261.
12. Preston, *Franco, A Biography*, Fontana, 1995, p.13.
13. Quoted in Balfour and La Porte, p.315.
14. Sánchez, *Franco: The Biography of the Myth*, Routledge, 2014, pp.65–7.
15. *Documents on German Foreign Policy, 1918–1945, Series D Volume III, Germany and the Spanish Civil War, 1936–39*, HMSO, 1951, p.7.

16. Ibid, p.40.
17. Leitz, 'Nazi Germany's Intervention in the Spanish Civil War and the Foundation of HISMA/ROWAK' in Preston & Mackenzie (eds.), *The Republic Besieged: Civil War in Spain 1936–1939*, Edinburgh University Press, 1996, pp.53–6.
18. Payne, *Franco and Hitler: Spain, Germany and World War II*, Yale University Press, 2008, p.27.
19. Ibid, pp.80–1.
20. Preston, 'Mussolini's Spanish Adventure: From Limited Risk to War', in Preston & Mackenzie (eds.), *The Republic Besieged: Civil War in Spain 1936–1939*, Edinburgh University Press, 1996, p.25.
21. Ibid, p.45.
22. Ibid, p.49.
23. Payne, *The Franco Regime, 1936–1975*, Phoenix, 2000, pp.113–14.
24. Hodges, *Franco, A Concise Biography*, Weidenfeld & Nicolson, 2000, p.106.
25. Crozier, *Franco, A Biographical History*, Eyre & Spottiswoode, 1967, p.214.
26. Ibid, p.179.
27. *Documents on German Foreign Policy*, p.87.
28. Preston, *Franco*, p.195.
29. Preston, *Franco*, p.255, Hodges, p.127.
30. Preston, *Franco*, p.258.
31. Ibid, p.266.
32. Ibid, pp.268–9.
33. Payne, *Franco and Hitler*, p.14.
34. Sánchez, p.76.
35. Hodges, p.135.
36. Payne, *Franco and Hitler*, p.15.
37. *Documents on German Foreign Policy*, p.712.
38. Balfour, *Deadly Embrace*, p.292.
39. Preston, *The Spanish Holocaust*, p.179.
40. Ibid, p.292.
41. Koestler, "Dialogue with Death', in Valentine Cunningham (ed.), *Spanish Front: Writers on the Civil War*, Oxford University Press, 1986, p.141.
42. Collier, *Socialists of Rural Andalusia: Unacknowledged Revolutionaries of the Second Republic*, Stanford University Press, 1987, pp.162–3.
43. Balfour, *Deadly Embrace*, p.306.
44. Preston, *Spanish Holocaust*, pp.182–3, 186, 194.
45. Gibson, *The Assassination of Frederico García Lorca*, Penguin, 1983, p.97.
46. A.R. Vilaplana, *Burgos Justice, A Year's Experience of Nationalist Spain*, Constable, 1938. Whitaker, John, *We Cannot Escape History*, Macmillan, 1943, pp.28–31.
47. Richard Barker, *Skeletons in the Closet, Skeletons in the Ground: Repression, Victimization and Humiliation in a small Andalusian Town: The Human Consequences of the Spanish Civil War*, Sussex Academic Press, 2012, p.61.

48. Ibid, p.76.
49. Collier, p.146.
50. Blinkhorn, pp.261–2.
51. Preston, *Spanish Holocaust*, p.183.
52. Ibid, p.194.
53. Vilaplana, p.29.
54. Lowe, pp.33–4.
55. Anderson, *The Francoist Military Trials: Terror and Complicity, 1939–1945*, Routledge, 2010, pp.42–3.
56. Quesada, *The Spanish Civil War 1936–39 (1), Nationalist Forces*, Osprey, 2014, pp.8–9.
57. Cardozo, p.57.
58. Quoted in Balfour, *Deadly Embrace*, p.291.
59. Kemp, *Mine were of Trouble*, Cassell, 1957, p.116.
60. Quesada, *Nationalist Forces*, pp.22–3.
61. Balfour, *Deadly Embrace*, p.313.
62. Ibid, pp.290–1.
63. Ibid.
64. Ibid, pp.278–9.
65. Ibid, p.312.
66. Ibid, pp.307–308.
67. Quesada, *Nationalist Forces*, pp.12–13, see also Matthews, who estimates only 100,000 Nationalist volunteers, with perhaps a million men conscripted.
68. Quoted in Cardozo, p.312.
69. Kemp, p.23.
70. Blinkhorn, p.256, Quesada, *Nationalist Forces*, p.14.
71. Coverdale, *Italian Intervention in the Spanish Civil War*, Princeton University Press, 1975, p.181.
72. Ibid, p.393.
73. Lerma, *Combat Over Spain: Memoirs of a Nationalist Fighter Pilot, 1936–1939*, Neville Spearman, 1966, p.149.
74. Coverdale, pp.393–4.
75. Ibid, p.396.
76. Payne, *Franco and Hitler*, p.32, Whealey, *Hitler and Spain: The Nazi Role in the Spanish Civil War, 1936–1939*, University of Kentucky Press, 2005, p.102.
77. Caballero, *The Condor Legion, German Troops in the Spanish Civil War*, Osprey, 2006, p.32.
78. Ibid, p.22.
79. Ibid, p.41.
80. Ibid, p.24.
81. Payne, *Franco and Hitler*, p.33, Caballero, p.30.

82. Caballero, pp.44–5, Zaloga, *Spanish Civil War Tanks, The Proving Ground for Blitzkrieg*, Osprey, 2010, pp.31–2.

83. Whealey, p.136.

84. Whealey, p.136, Caballero, p.32, Alpert, p.245, Coverdale, p.393.

85. Quesada, *Nationalist Forces*, p.19.

86. Coverdale, pp.311–12.

87. Ciano, *Diary 1937–1943, The Complete unabridged Diaries of Count Galeazzo Ciano, Italian Minister for Foreign Affairs, 1936–1943*, Phoenix, 2002, p.37.

88. Hodges, p.138.

89. Balfour, *Deadly Embrace*, pp.308–309.

90. Quoted in S. Payne, *Spanish Civil War*, p.197.

91. Coverdale, p.395.

92. Caballero, pp.46–7.

93. H. Matthews, *The Yoke and the Arrows, A Report on Spain*, George Braziller, 1957, p.94.

94. Payne, *Franco and Hitler*, pp.13.

95. Ibid, pp.13–14.

Chapter 4

1. Quoted in Preston, *The Spanish Civil War, Reaction, Revolution and Revenge*, Harper Perennial, 2006, p.266.

2. Cardozo, p.277.

3. Beevor, p.262, Permuy, *Air War over Spain, Aviators, Aircraft and Air Units of the Nationalist and Republican Air Forces, 1936–1939*, Ian Allen, 2009, p.57.

4. Beevor, p.263.

5. Kindelán, *Mis cuadernos de guerra*, Planeta, 1982, p.127.

6. Quoted in Preston, *The Spanish Civil War*, p.272.

7. Rojo, *España Heroica, Diez bocetos de la Guerra española*, Ariel, 1975, pp.88–9.

8. Casado, pp.70–3.

9. Tagüeña, pp.108–109.

10. Modesto, p.104.

11. Beevor, p.311, H. Thomas, p.689, Jackson, *The Spanish Republic and the Civil War, 1931–1939*, Princeton University Press, 1967, p.394.

12. Beevor, p.311.

13. Zaloga, p.27.

14. Beevor, p.311.

15. Logoluso, *Fiat CR.32 Aces of the Spanish Civil War*, Osprey, 2010, p.45.

16. Zaloga, p.29.

17. Modesto, p.103.

18. Modesto, p.105.

19. Max, p.85.
20. Ibid, p.86.
21. Gregory, p.67.
22. Modesto, p.110.
23. Zaloga, p.28.
24. Copeman, *Reason in Revolt*, Blandford Press, 1948, p.125.
25. Gregory, p.70.
26. Ryan, Frank (ed.), *The Book of the XV Brigade, Records of British, American, Canadian and Irish volunteers in Spain 1936–1938*, Warren & Pell, 2003, p.141.
27. Copeman, p.131.
28. Líster, *Nuestra Guerra aportaciones para una historia de la Guerra nacional revolucionaria del pueblo español 1936–1939*, Editions de la librairie du Globe, 1966, pp.135–6, Modesto, p.108.
29. Cardona, *Historia military de una Guerra civil: estrategias y tácticas de la Guerra de España*, Flor del Viento Ediciones, 2006, p.177.
30. Modesto, p.109.
31. Max, p.88.
32. Revilla, *De esos tenemos tantos como el que más*, G. Del Toro, 1976, pp.158–9.
33. Ibid, pp.161–2.
34. Modesto, p.108.
35. Revilla, *De esos tenemos*, pp.91–3.
36. Ibid, p.95.
37. Quoted in Logoluso, pp.45–6.
38. Rojo, p.96.
39. Cardona, p.177, Rojo, p.96.
40. Modesto, pp.101, 104.
41. Preston, *Franco*, p.281.
42. Modesto, p.116, Lerma, p.121.
43. Forsyth, *Aces of the Legion Condor*, Osprey, 2011, p.62.
44. Logoluso, p.46.
45. Howson, *Aircraft*, p. 233.
46. Quoted in Forsyth, p.65.
47. Copeman, p.133.
48. Landis, *Death in the Olive Groves, American Volunteers in the Spanish Civil War, 1936–1939*, Paragon House, 1989, p.44.
49. Modesto, p.111.
50. Modesto, p.111.
51. Revilla, *De esos tenemos*, pp.108–10.
52. Ibid, p.162.
53. Modesto, p.111.
54. Quoted in Landis, p.45.
55. Copeman, pp.133–4.

56. Baxell, *Unlikely Warriors*, p.233.
57. Modesto, p.112.
58. Azaña, p.417.
59. Casado, pp.74–5.
60. Ibid, p.114.
61. Cardona, p.179, Hurtado, *Las Brigadas Internacionales*, Dau, 2013, p.45.
62. Stern, Document 60 in Radosh et al, p.339.
63. Ibid.
64. Quoted in Hurtado, p.45.
65. Modesto, p.113.
66. Ibid, Revilla, *De esos tenemos*, p.258.
67. Ibid, p.114.
68. Max, pp.95–6.
69. Kindelán, pp.201–202.
70. Quoted in Forsyth, p.70.
71. *Book of the XV Brigade*, p.146.
72. Yates, *Mississippi to Madrid: Memoir of a Black American in the Abraham Lincoln Brigade*, Open Hand Publishing, 1989, pp.137–8.
73. Howson, *Aircraft*, p.272.
74. Lerma, p.120.
75. Permuy, *Air War*, p.62.
76. Quoted in Forsyth, pp.63–4.
77. Modesto, p.114–15.
78. Fred Thomas, *To Tilt at Windmills: A Memoir of the Spanish Civil War*, Michigan State University Press, 1996, p.38.
79. Kindelán, pp.132–4.
80. Ibid, p.135.
81. Fred Thomas, p.40.
82. Quoted in Beevor, p.315.
83. Modesto, p.117.
84. Max, p.105.
85. Hurtado, p.46.
86. Lerma, p.122.
87. Líster, p.137.
88. Ibid.
89. Modesto, pp.117–18.
90. Cardona, p.180.
91. Max, p.108.
92. Stern, Document 60 in Radosh et al, p.341.
93. Walter, Document 76 in Radosh et al, p.481, Beevor, p.316, Cardona, p.180.
94. *Book of the XV Brigade*, p.165.
95. Ibid.
96. Quoted in Darman, p.123.

97. Baxell, *Unlikely Warriors*, p.233.
98. Quoted in Hurtado, p.45.
99. Cardona, p.180, Modesto, p.118–19, Lerma, p.122.
100. Quoted in Hodges, p.133.
101. Quoted in Beevor, p.316.
102. Rogoyska, *Gerda Taro, Inventing Robert Capa*, Jonathan Cape, 2013, p.216.
103. Modesto, p.119.
104. Kindelán, p.131, Cardona, p.180.
105. Quoted in Lerma, p.123.
106. Kindelán, p.137.
107. Preston, *Franco*, p.283.
108. Ibid.
109. *Book of the XV Brigade*, p.136.
110. Fyvel, *English Penny*, Arthur H. Stockwell Ltd, 1992, p.29.
111. Cardona, p.180, Beevor, p.318, Jackson, p.396, H. Thomas, p.694.
112. Longo, Document 47 in Radosh et al, p.238.
113. Stern, Document 60 in Radosh et al, p.348.
114. Zaloga, p.29.
115. See H. Thomas, p.694, Lerma, p.123.
116. Forsyth, pp.71–2.
117. Quoted in Preston, *Comrades! Portraits from the Spanish Civil War*, HarperCollins, 1999, p.267.
118. Azaña, p.389.
119. Rojo, p.97.
120. Azaña, p.420.
121. *Book of the XV Brigade*, pp.132–5.
122. Świerczewski, Document 77 in Radosh et al, p.489.
123. Beevor, p.319.
124. See Beevor, pp.319–20.
125. Azaña, pp.389, 416–17, 420.
126. *Book of XV Brigade*, p.130, Alexander quoted in Darman, p.124.
127. Rojo, p.100.
128. Kindelán, p.131.
129. Cardona, p.180.

Chapter 5
1. Modesto, pp.121–2.
2. Howson, *Aircraft*, p.200.
3. Quoted in MacMaster (ed.), *Spanish Fighters, An Oral History of Civil War and Exile*, Macmillan, 1990, p.75.
4. Orwell, *Orwell in Spain*, Penguin, 2001, pp.54–5.
5. Fraser, p.348.
6. Graham, *Republic at War*, pp.314–15.

7. Fraser, p.354.
8. Ibárruri, *They Shall Not Pass: The Autobiography of La Pasionaria*, Lawrence & Wishart, 1966, p.297.
9. Modesto, p.124.
10. Líster, p.154.
11. Quoted in Fraser, p.391.
12. Ibid.
13. Líster, p.155.
14. Stern, Document 60 in Radosh et al, p.354.
15. Ibid.
16. Rojo, p.107.
17. H. Thomas, p.704.
18. Ibid, p.705.
19. Ibid, p.704, Beevor, pp.332–3. Thomas gives a rather high figure of 200 Republican aircraft, more than what they had at Brunete, which seems unlikely given the planes lost in that battle.
20. Stern, Document 60 in Radosh et al, p.354–5, Modesto, p.128.
21. Stern, Document 60 in Radosh et al, p.355.
22. Ibid, p.356.
23. Ibid, Jackson, pp.397–8.
24. Jackson, p.397, Líster, p.151.
25. Modesto, p.127.
26. Merriman, Lerude, p.163.
27. Max, pp.118–19.
28. Líster, pp.163–4.
29. Landis, p.70.
30. Wolff, *Another Hill*, University of Illinois Press, 2001, pp.69–70. Copyright 1994, by the Board of Trustees of the University of Illinois. Used with permission of the Illinois Press.
31. Blinkhorn, p.256.
32. H. Thomas, p.704.
33. *Book of the XV Brigade*, p.258.
34. Ibid, pp.258–60.
35. Rojo, p.112.
36. Cardona, p.193.
37. Preston, *Franco*, p.288.
38. Hodges, pp.134–5.
39. H. Thomas, p.705.
40. Stern, Document 60 in Radosh et al, p.356.
41. *Book of the XV Brigade*, p.249.
42. Ibid, pp.248–9.
43. *Book of the XV Brigade*, p.254.
44. Stern, Document 60 in Radosh et al, p.357.

45. Ibid, p.358.
46. *Book of the XV Brigade*, p.250.
47. Ibid, p.255.
48. Ibid.
49. Ibid, pp.255–6.
50. Landis, pp.76–7.
51. Azaña, p.458.
52. Baxell, *Unlikely Warriors*, p.268, Palfreeman, *Salud! British Volunteers in the Republican Medical Service during the Spanish Civil War, 1936–1939*, Sussex Academic Press, 2012, pp.135–6.
53. Esdaile, p.236.
54. Merriman, Lerude, p.165, Carroll, *The Odyssey of the Abraham Lincoln Brigade, Americans in the Spanish Civil War*, Stanford University Press, 1994, p.155.
55. Puig, *Personal Memories of the Days of the Spanish Civil War, in Catalan and English*, Edwin Mellen Press, 1999, pp.3–4.
56. Ibid, pp.73–5.
57. Modesto, p.131.
58. Ibid, p.132.
59. Ibid.
60. Hurtado, p.50.
61. Beevor, p.334.
62. Max, p.120.
63. Stern, Document 60 in Radosh et al, p.357.
64. Candela, p.66.
65. Stern, Document 60 in Radosh et al, p.357.
66. Iniesta, *Memorias y Recuerdos, Los años que he vivido en el proceso historic de España*, Planeta, 1984, p.117.
67. Ibid.
68. Gregory, p.81.
69. Ibid, *Book of the XV Brigade*, p.274.
70. Candela, p.103.
71. Puig, p.77.
72. Ibid, p.83.
73. Carroll, p.157.
74. Alexander, *British Volunteers for Liberty: Spain 1936–1939*, Lawrence & Wishart, 1982, p.151.
75. *Book of the XV Brigade*, p.261.
76. Wolff, p.76.
77. Ibid, p.77.
78. Ibid.
79. Quoted in Landis, p.79.
80. Quoted in Landis, p.79.

81. Modesto, p.134.
82. Ibárruri, pp.297–8.
83. Quoted in *El Mundo*, http://www.elmundo.es/cronica/2014/03/30/5336b1beca47418d308b456d.html accessed 14/10/18.
84. Lerma, p.144.
85. Ibid, p.145.
86. Puig, pp.83–5.
87. Rosenstone, *Crusade of the Left, The Lincoln Battalion in the Spanish Civil War*, Pegasus, 1969, p.209.
88. *Book of the XV Brigade*, p.269.
89. Stern, Document 60 in Radosh et al, pp.357–9.
90. Świerczewski, Document 70 in Radosh et al, p.437.
91. *Book of the XV Brigade*, pp.277–8.
92. Ibid, p.278.
93. *Book of the XV Brigade*, pp.284–6.
94. Merriman, Lerude, p.169.
95. Palfreeman, pp.132–4.
96. Lerma, p.145.
97. Howson, *Aircraft*, p.264.
98. Puig, p.99.
99. Modesto, pp.135–6.
100. Líster, p.168.
101. Tagüeña, p.113.
102. Petrou, p.76.
103. Zaloga, p.35.
104. Puig, p.109.
105. *Book of the XV Brigade*, p.292.
106. Baxell, *Unlikely Warriors*, pp.271–2.
107. Wolff, p.117.
108. Petrou, pp.74–5.
109. Permuy, *Air War*, p.63.
110. Howson, *Aircraft*, p.209.
111. Quoted in MacMaster, pp.91–2.
112. Quoted in H. Thomas, p.705.
113. Rojo, p.115.
114. Max, p.120.
115. Azaña, p.465.
116. Document 76 in Radosh, p.484.
117. Rojo, p.112.
118. Beevor, pp.3334.
119. Puig, p.85.
120. Wolff, p.82.
121. Howson, *Aircraft*, p.278.
122. Lerma, p.144, *Book of the XV Brigade*, p.244.

Chapter 6

1. Alpert, p.158, Beevor, p.338.
2. H. Thomas, p.712.
3. Kindelán, p.141.
4. Ibid, p.140.
5. Preston, *Franco*, p.292, Kindelán, p.141.
6. Cardona, p.215.
7. Kindelán, p.141.
8. Hemingway, *By-Line: Selected articles and dispatches of four decades*, Arrow, 2013, p.288.
9. Cardona, p.216.
10. Ibid.
11. Buckley, p.340.
12. Cardona, p.217, Modesto, p.139.
13. Alpert, pp.94–5.
14. Buckley, p.342.
15. Rojo, p.122, Cardona, p.217, Beevor, p.352, Jackson, p.398, H. Thomas, p.768.
16. Líster, p.172, Thomas, p.768, Modesto, p.138.
17. Zaloga, pp.38–9.
18. Kindelán, p.148.
19. Modesto, p.139.
20. Document 76, Radosh et al, pp.483–4.
21. Líster, p.173.
22. Document 70, Radosh et al, pp.452–3, 459.
23. Ibid, pp.450–1.
24. Document 76, Radosh et al, p.482.
25. Document 70, Radosh et al, p.444.
26. Cardona, p.217.
27. Líster, p.173.
28. Max, p.128.
29. Líster, pp.174–5.
30. Candela, pp.107–108.
31. Cardona, p.218, Modesto, p.140.
32. Rojo, p.123.
33. Revilla, *Tercio de Lácar*, G. Del Toro, 1975, p.126.
34. Beevor, p.352.
35. H. Matthews, *New York Times* Article, 20 December 1937.
36. Quoted in Merriman, Lerude, pp.19–4.
37. Hemingway, *By-Line*, pp.285–8. Reprinted with the permission of Scribner, a division of Simon & Schuster, Inc. All rights reserved.
38. Max, pp.139–40.
39. Ibid, p.138.
40. Quoted in Líster, pp.176–7.
41. Candela, pp.109–10.

42. Kindelán, p.151, Cardona, p.218.
43. Beevor, p.354.
44. Preston, *Franco*, p.293.
45. Cardona, p.219.
46. Ciano, pp.38–9.
47. Ibid, p.40.
48. Beevor, p.356.
49. Buckley, p.347.
50. Merriman, Lerude, p.192.
51. Azaña, p.573.
52. Howson, *Aircraft*, pp.182–3.
53. Quoted in Forsyth, p.88.
54. Buckley, p.351.
55. Beevor, p.355.
56. H. Matthews, *New York Times* article, 26 December 1937.
57. Lee, *A Moment of War*, Penguin, 1992, p.121.
58. Cardona, p.220, Revilla, *Tercio*, p.127, Hooton, p.162.
59. Howson, *Aircraft*, p.233.
60. Quoted in Líster, p.178.
61. Max, p.141.
62. Cardona, p.221.
63. Azaña, p.576.
64. Líster, p.179.
65. Alpert, p.97, pp.129–30.
66. Azaña, p.576.
67. Ibid, pp.574–5.
68. Bolín, *Spain: The Vital Years*, Cassell, 1967, p.300.
69. Buckley, pp.348–9.
70. Cardona, p.221.
71. Quoted in R Payne (ed.), *The Civil War in Spain: 1936–1939*, Secker & Warburg, 1963, pp.289–92.
72. Quoted in Revilla, *Tercio*, p.132.
73. Kindelán, p.154.
74. Thomas, p.770.
75. Matthews, *New York Times* article, 5 January 1938.
76. Lerma, p.152.
77. Ibid, p.160.
78. Matthews, *New York Times* article, 9 January 1938.
79. Fraser, p.440.
80. Cardona, p.223.
81. Quesada, *The Spanish Civil War 1936–39 (2), Republican Forces*, Osprey, 2015, p.22.
82. Alpert, p.144.

83. Landis, p.108, Wolff, p.172.
84. Quoted in Darman, p.128.
85. Cardona, p.223, Hurtado, p.55.
86. Howson, *Aircraft*, p.212.
87. Wolff, pp.173–4.
88. Świerczewski, Document 70, Radosh et al, p.459.
89. Forsyth, p.88.
90. Lerma, pp.160–1.
91. Cooney, *Proud Journey, a Spanish Civil War memoir*, Marx Memorial Library/Manifesto Press, 2015, pp.47–8.
92. Ibid.
93. Ibid.
94. Clark, *No Boots to my Feet, Experiences of a Britisher in Spain, 1937–38*, Student Bookshops Ltd, 1984, pp.51–2.
95. Baxell, *Unlikely Warriors*, p.283, Landis, p.114.
96. Quesada, *Republican Forces*, p.22, Alpert, p.169.
97. Modesto, p.143.
98. Lerma, p.155.
99. Revilla, *Tercio*, p.133.
100. Iniesta, p.119.
101. H. Thomas, p.772.
102. Cardona, p.224.
103. Beevor, p.358, Modesto, p.147, Cardona, p.224.
104. Revilla, *Tercio*, pp.96–7.
105. Kemp, p.135.
106. Ibid, p.136.
107. Ibid, pp.136–7.
108. Ibid, p.140.
109. Cardona, p.225.
110. H. Thomas, p.772.
111. Quoted in Forsyth, pp.89–90.
112. Iniesta, pp.119–20.
113. Scott-Ellis, *The Chances of Death: a Diary of the Spanish Civil War*, Michael Russell, 1995, p.36.
114. Kemp, p.143.
115. Fraser, pp.440–1.
116. Iniesta, p.120.
117. Revilla, Tercio, p.141.
118. Baxell, *Unlikely Warriors*, p.284.
119. Wolff, pp.197–8.
120. Kemp, p.147.
121. Clark, pp.54–5.
122. Ibid, p.57.

123. Kemp, p.150.
124. Revilla, Tercio, p.145.
125. Scott-Ellis, p.40.
126. Ibid, pp.41–2.
127. Modesto, p.149.
128. Modesto, p.150–1, Líster, p.182, Scott-Ellis, pp.43–4.
129. González, *Listen Comrades, Life and Death in the Soviet Union*, Heinemann, 1952, pp.25–6.
130. Beevor, pp.258–9, Alpert, pp.135–6, H. Thomas, p.773, Esdaile, p.261, Preston, *Spanish Civil War*, pp.280–1, Southworth, "The Grand Camouflage': Julián Gorkin, Burnett Bolloten and the Spanish Civil War' in Preston & Mackenzie (eds.), *The Republic Besieged: Civil War in Spain 1936–1939*, Edinburgh University Press, 1996, pp.277–81.
131. Southworth, pp.262–7.
132. Ibid, Preston, *The Spanish Civil War*, p.281.
133. Alpert, p.136, Southworth, p.279.
134. Alpert, p.135.
135. Alpert, pp.135–6, Southworth, p.279.
136. Quoted in Southworth, p.280.
137. Revilla, *Tercio*, p.149.
138. Ibid.
139. Quoted in Alpert, p.132.
140. Scott-Ellis, pp.43–4.
141. Zaloga, p.39, Permuy, *Air War*, p.64.
142. Beevor, p.359, H. Thomas, p.773, Jackson, p.400.
143. H. Thomas, p.773.
144. Preston, *The Spanish Civil War*, p.281.
145. Ciano, pp.65–6.
146. Howson, *Aircraft*, p.275.
147. Kindelán, p.152–6.
148. Líster, p.187.
149. Rojo, pp.127–31.
150. Modesto, pp.151–3, Líster, p.184–6.
151. Líster, p.184–186.
152. Beevor, p.359.
153. Lee, p.120.
154. Ibid, p.158.

Chapter 7
1. H. Thomas, p.778.
2. Gregory, p.105.
3. Merriman, Lerude, pp.207–208.
4. Jackson, p.409.

5. Candela, pp.112–13.
6. Document 76 in Radosh, p.485.
7. Howson, *Arms for Spain*, pp.298–300.
8. Jackson, pp.409–10.
9. Preston, *Comrades*, pp.270–2.
10. Payne, *Franco Regime*, p.149.
11. Beevor, pp.386–7.
12. Payne, *Hitler and Franco*, p.27.
13. Esdaile, p.284.
14. Henry, *The Ebro 1938, Death Knell of the Republic*, Osprey, 1999, p.22, Beevor, p.393.
15. Beevor, p.389.
16. Henry, pp.37, 40.
17. Cooney, p.96.
18. Ibid, pp.97–8.
19. Beevor, p.398.
20. Max, p.270.
21. Crozier, p.279.
22. Bolín, p.314.
23. Preston, *Franco*, pp.311, 315.
24. Ciano, p.119.
25. Esdaile, p.291, Jackson, p.527, Preston, *Spanish Civil* War, p.291, Henry, p.84.
26. Buckley, pp.406–407.
27. See Robinson, Seignon, *Division Leclerc*, Osprey, 2018, for more.
28. For the best account of the Casado coup and the end of the war, see Preston, *The Last Days of the Spanish Republic,* William Collins, 2017. For Casado's self-defence, see *The Last Days of Madrid*.

Chapter 8
1. Esdaile, pp.312–13.
2. Hart, *The Last Battle, Endgame on the Western Front, 1918*, Profile Books, 2018, pp.56–8.
3. Terraine, *To Win a War*, pp.202–203.
4. Esdaile, p.293.
5. Wolff, p.371.
6. Daniel Pastor García & Antonio R. Celada, 'The Victors Write History, the Vanquished Literature: Myth, Distortion and Truth in the XV Brigade', *Bulletin of Spanish Studies*, 89:7–8, 2012, pp.307–21.
7. Esdaile, p.305.
8. Beevor, p.476.
9. Ibid, pp.674–6.
10. Ibid, p.675.

11. See Terraine, *The Smoke and the Fire, Myths and Anti-Myths of War, 1861–1945*, Pen & Sword, 1992 for a comprehensive argument on this point.
12. Terraine, *To Win a War*, p.160, also see Terraine's *The Smoke and the Fire*.
13. Sheffield, *Forgotten Victory, The First World War: Myths and Realities*, Review, 2002, p.240.
14. Esdaile, p.344.

Bibliography

Primary sources

Azaña, Manuel, *Obras Completas, Volumen VI, Julio 1936 / Agosto 1940*, Taurus / CEPC, 2008.

Blásquez, José Martin, *I Helped to Build an Army, Civil War Memoirs of a Spanish Staff Officer*, Secker & Warburg, 1939.

Bolín, Luis, *Spain: The Vital Years*, Cassell, 1967.

Buckley, Henry, *The Life and Death of the Spanish Republic, A Witness to the Spanish Civil War*, I.B. Tauris, 2014.

Candela, Antonio, *The Adventures of an Innocent in the Spanish Civil War*, United Writers Publications, 1989.

Cardozo, Harold G., *The March of a Nation, My Year of Spain's Civil War*, Right Book Club, 1937.

Casado, Segismundo, *The Last Days of Madrid*, Peter Davies, 1939.

Ciano, Conte Galeazzo, *Diary 1937–1943, The Complete unabridged Diaries of Count Galeazzo Ciano, Italian Minister for Foreign Affairs, 1936–1943*, Phoenix, 2002.

Clark, Bob, *No Boots to my Feet, Experiences of a Britisher in Spain, 1937–38*, Student Bookshops Ltd, 1984.

Cooney, Bob, *Proud Journey, a Spanish Civil War memoir*, Marx Memorial Library / Manifesto Press, 2015.

Copeman, Fred, *Reason in Revolt*, Blandford Press, 1948.

Darman, Peter (ed.), *Heroic Voices of the Spanish Civil War, Memories from the International Brigades*, New Holland, 2009.

Del Vayo, Alvarez, *Freedom's Battle*, Heinemann, 1940.

Fischer, Louis, *Men and Politics: An Autobiography*, Duell, Sloan & Pearce, 1941.

Fraser, Ronald, *Blood of Spain: The Experience of Civil War, 1936–1939*, Penguin, 1981.

Fyvel, Penelope, *English Penny*, Arthur H. Stockwell Ltd, 1992.

González, Valentín (El Campesino), *Listen Comrades, Life and Death in the Soviet Union*, Heinemann, 1952.

Gregory, Walter, *The Shallow Grave, A Memoir of the Spanish Civil War*, Gollancz, 1986.

Hemingway, Ernest, *By-Line: Selected articles and dispatches of four decades*, Arrow, 2013.

Hemingway, Ernest, *For Whom the Bell Tolls*, Arrow, 2004.

Ibárruri, Dolores, *They Shall Not Pass: The Autobiography of La Pasionaria*, Lawrence & Wishart, 1966.

Iniesta Cano, Carlos, *Memorias y Recuerdos, Los años que he vivido en el proceso histórico de España*, Planeta, 1984.

Kemp, Peter, *Mine were of Trouble*, Cassell, 1957.

Kindelán, Alfredo, *Mis cuadernos de guerra*, Planeta, 1982.

Koestler, Arthur, 'Dialogue with Death', in Valentine Cunningham (ed.), *Spanish Front: Writers on the Civil War*, Oxford University Press, 1986.

Larios, José (Duke of Lerma), *Combat Over Spain: Memoirs of a Nationalist Fighter Pilot, 1936–1939*, Neville Spearman, 1966.

Lee, Laurie, *A Moment of War*, Penguin, 1992.

Líster, Enrique, *Nuestra guerra: aportaciones para una historia de la guerra nacional revolucionaria del pueblo español 1936–1939*, Editions de la librairie du Globe, 1966.

MacMaster, Neil (ed.), *Spanish Fighters, An Oral History of Civil War and Exile*, Macmillan, 1990.

Marshall-Cornwall, James, et al (eds.), *Documents on German Foreign Policy, 1918–1945, Series D Volume III, Germany and the Spanish Civil War, 1936–39*, HMSO, 1951.

Matthews, Herbert, *The Yoke and the Arrows, A Report on Spain*, George Braziller, 1957.

Matthews, Herbert, Selected Stories in *The New York Times*, 1937, 1938.

Max, Jack, *Memorias de un Revolucionario*, Plaza & Janes, 1975.

Merriman, Marion & Lerude, Warren, *American Commander in Spain, Robert Hale Merriman and the Abraham Lincoln Brigade*, University of Nevada Press, 1986.

Modesto, Juan, *Soy del Quinto Regimiento (Notas de la guerra española)*, Colección Ebro, 1974.

Moreno Miranda, Joaquín, extracts from memoirs cited in *El Mundo*, http://www.elmundo.es/cronica/2014/03/30/5336b1beca47418d308b456d.html accessed 14/10/18.

Orwell, George, *Orwell in Spain*, Penguin, 2001.

Payne, Robert (ed.), *The Civil War in Spain: 1936–1939*, Secker & Warburg, 1963.

Puig Casas, Lluís, *Personal Memories of the Days of the Spanish Civil War, in Catalan and English*, Edwin Mellen Press, 1999.

Radosh, Ronald et al (eds.), *Spain Betrayed, The Soviet Union in the Spanish Civil War*, Yale University Press, 2001.

Revilla Cebrecos, Carmelo, *De esos tenemos tantos como el que más*, G. Del Toro, 1976.

Revilla Cebrecos, Carmelo, *Tercio de Lácar*, G. Del Toro, 1975.

Rojo, Vicente, *España Heroica, Diez bocetos de la guerra española*, Ariel, 1975.

Ryan, Frank (ed.), *The Book of the XV Brigade, Records of British, American, Canadian and Irish volunteers in Spain 1936–1938*, Warren & Pell, 2003.

Scott-Ellis, Priscilla, *The Chances of Death: a Diary of the Spanish Civil War*, Michael Russell, 1995.

Tagüeña Lacorte, Manuel, *Testimonio de dos guerras*, Planeta, 1978.

Thomas, Frank, *Brother against Brother: Experiences of a British Volunteer in the Spanish Civil War*, Sutton, 1998.

Thomas, Fred, *To Tilt at Windmills: A Memoir of the Spanish Civil War*, Michigan State University Press, 1996.

Vidal, César, *Recuerdo 1936: una historia oral de la guerra civil Española*, Planeta, 2008.

Vilaplana, A.R., *Burgos Justice, A Year's Experience of Nationalist Spain*, Constable, 1938.

Whitaker, John, *We Cannot Escape History*, Macmillan, 1943.

Wolff, Milton, *Another Hill*, University of Illinois Press, 2001.

Yates, James, *Mississippi to Madrid: Memoir of a Black American in the Abraham Lincoln Brigade*, Open Hand Publishing, 1989.

Scholarship and secondary material

Alexander, Bill, *British Volunteers for Liberty: Spain 1936–1939*, Lawrence & Wishart, 1982.

Alpert, Michael *The Republican Army in the Spanish Civil War, 1936–1939*, Cambridge University Press, 2018.

Anderson, Peter, *The Francoist Military Trials: Terror and Complicity, 1939–1945*, Routledge, 2010.

Balfour, Sebastian, *Deadly Embrace: Morocco and the Road to the Spanish Civil War*, Oxford University Press, 2002.

Balfour, Sebastian & La Porte, Pablo, 'Spanish Military Cultures and the Moroccan Wars, 1909–1936', *European History Quarterly*, 30, 3, 2000, pp.307–32.

Barker, Richard, *Skeletons in the Closet, Skeletons in the Ground: Repression, Victimization and Humiliation in a small Andalusian Town: The Human Consequences of the Spanish Civil War*, Sussex Academic Press, 2012.

Baxell, Richard, *British Volunteers in the Spanish Civil War, The British Battalion in the International Brigades, 1936–1939*, Warren & Pell, 2007.

Baxell, Richard, *Unlikely Warriors, The British in the Spanish Civil War and the Struggle Against Fascism*, Aurum Press, 2014.

Beevor, Antony, *The Battle for Spain, The Spanish Civil War 1936–1939*, Phoenix, 2007.

Blinkhorn, Martin, *Carlism and Crisis in Spain, 1931–1939*, Cambridge University Press, 1975.

Bradley, Ken, *International Brigades in Spain, 1936–39*, Osprey, 1994.

Buchanan, Tom, *Britain and the Spanish Civil War*, Cambridge University Press, 1997.

Caballero Jurado, Carlos, *The Condor Legion, German Troops in the Spanish Civil War*, Osprey, 2006.

Cardona, Gabriel, *Historia militar de una guerra civil: estrategias y tácticas de la guerra de España*, Flor del Viento Ediciones, 2006.

Carroll, Peter, *The Odyssey of the Abraham Lincoln Brigade, Americans in the Spanish Civil War*, Stanford University Press, 1994.

Casanova, Julián, *The Spanish Republic and Civil War*, Cambridge University Press, 2010.

Collier, George, *Socialists of Rural Andalusia: Unacknowledged Revolutionaries of the Second Republic*, Stanford University Press, 1987.

Coverdale, John F., *Italian Intervention in the Spanish Civil War*, Princeton University Press, 1975.

Crozier, Brian *Franco, A Biographical History*, Eyre & Spottiswoode, 1967.

Esdaile, Charles J., *The Spanish Civil War, A Military History*, Routledge, 2018.

Forsyth, Robert, *Aces of the Legion Condor*, Osprey, 2011.

Fusi Aizpurúa, Juan Pablo, *Franco, A Biography*, Unwin Hyman, 1987.

Garcia, Daniel Pastor & Celada, Antonio R., 'The Victors Write History, the Vanquished Literature: Myth, Distortion and Truth in the XV Brigade', *Bulletin of Spanish Studies*, 89:7–8, 2012.

Gibson, Ian, *The Assassination of Frederico García Lorca*, Penguin, 1983.

Graham, Helen, *The Spanish Republic at War, 1936–1939*, Cambridge University Press, 2002.

Graham, Helen, *The Spanish Civil War, A Very Short Introduction*, Oxford University Press, 2005.

Graham, Helen, 'War, Modernity and Reform: The Premiership of Juan Negrín 1937–1939', in Preston & Mackenzie (eds.), *The Republic Besieged: Civil War in Spain 1936–1939*, Edinburgh University Press, 1996.

Graham, Helen, *Socialism and War, The Spanish Socialist Party in power and crisis, 1936–1939*, Cambridge University Press, 1991.

Hart, Peter, *The Last Battle, Endgame on the Western Front, 1918*, Profile Books, 2018.

Henry, Chris, *The Ebro 1938, Death Knell of the Republic*, Osprey, 1999.

Hodges, Gabrielle Ashford, *Franco, A Concise Biography*, Weidenfeld & Nicolson, 2000.

Horne, Alistair, *The Price of Glory, Verdun 1916*, Penguin, 1993.

Howson, Gerald, *Aircraft of the Spanish Civil War*, Putnam, 1990.

Howson, Gerald, *Arms for Spain, The Untold Story of the Spanish Civil War*, John Murray, 1998.

Hurtado, Víctor, *Las Brigadas Internacionales*, Dau, 2013.

Jackson, Gabriel, *The Spanish Republic and the Civil War, 1931–1939*, Princeton University Press, 1967.

Jensen, Geoffrey, *Irrational Triumph: Cultural Despair, Military Nationalism, and the Ideological Origins of Franco's Spain*, University of Nevada Press, 2002.

Keene, Judith, *Fighting for Franco: International Volunteers in Nationalist Spain during the Spanish Civil War, 1936–1939*, Leicester University Press, 2001.

Landis, Arthur H., *Death in the Olive Groves, American Volunteers in the Spanish Civil War, 1936–1939*, Paragon House, 1989.

Leitz, Christian, 'Nazi Germany's Intervention in the Spanish Civil War and the Foundation of HISMA/ROWAK' in Preston & Mackenzie (eds.), *The Republic Besieged: Civil War in Spain 1936–1939*, Edinburgh University Press, 1996.

Logoluso, Alfredo, *Fiat CR.32 Aces of the Spanish Civil War*, Osprey, 2010.

Lowe, Sid, *Catholicism, War and the Foundation of Francoism: The Juventud de Acción Popular in Spain 1931–1939*, Sussex Academic Press, 2010.

Matthews, James, *Reluctant Warriors, Republican Popular Army and Nationalist Army Conscripts in the Spanish Civil War, 1936–1939*, Oxford University Press, 2012.

Petrou, Michael, *Renegades: Canadians in the Spanish Civil War*, Warren & Pell, 2008.

Palfreeman, Linda, *Salud! British Volunteers in the Republican Medical Service during the Spanish Civil War, 1936–1939*, Sussex Academic Press, 2012.

Payne, Stanley G., *Franco and Hitler: Spain, Germany and World War II*, Yale University Press, 2008.

Payne, Stanley G., *The Franco Regime, 1936–1975*, Phoenix, 2000.

Payne, Stanley G., *The Spanish Civil War*, Cambridge University Press, 2012.

Payne, Stanley G., *The Spanish Civil War, the Soviet Union and Communism*, Yale University Press, 2004.

Permuy López, Rafael A., *Spanish Republican Aces*, Osprey, 2012.

Permuy López, Rafael A., *Air War over Spain, Aviators, Aircraft and Air Units of the Nationalist and Republican Air Forces, 1936–1939*, Ian Allen, 2009.

Preston, Paul, *Comrades! Portraits from the Spanish Civil War*, HarperCollins, 1999.

Preston, Paul, *Franco, A Biography*, Fontana, 1995.

Preston, Paul, 'Italy and Spain in Civil War and World War, 1936–1943', in Balfour & Preston (eds.), *Spain and the Great Powers in the Twentieth Century*, Routledge, 1999.

Preston, Paul, 'Mussolini's Spanish Adventure: From Limited Risk to War', in Preston & Mackenzie (eds.), *The Republic Besieged: Civil War in Spain 1936– 1939*, Edinburgh University Press, 1996.

Preston, Paul, 'The Answer lies in the Sewers: Captain Aguilera and the Mentality of the Spanish Officer Corps', *Science & Society*, 68, 3, 2004, pp.277–312.

Preston, Paul, *The Last Days of the Spanish Republic*, William Collins, 2017.

Preston, Paul, *The Spanish Civil War, Reaction, Revolution and Revenge*, Harper Perennial, 2006.

Preston, Paul, *The Spanish Holocaust, Inquisition and Extermination in Twentieth-Century Spain*, Harper Press, 2012.

Preston, Paul, 'The Theorists of Extermination: The Origins of Violence in the Spanish Civil War' in Carlos Jerez-Farrán & Samuel Amago (Eds.), *Unearthing Franco's Legacy: Mass Graves and the Recovery of Historical Memory in Spain*, University of Notre Dame Press, 2010.

Quesada, Alejandro de, *The Spanish Civil War 1936–39 (1), Nationalist Forces*, Osprey, 2014.

Quesada, Alejandro de, *The Spanish Civil War 1936–39 (2), Republican Forces*, Osprey, 2015.

Richardson, Dan R., *Comintern Army: The International Brigades and the Spanish Civil War*, University Press of Kentucky, 1982.

Rogoyska, Jane, *Gerda Taro, Inventing Robert Capa*, Jonathan Cape, 2013.

Rosenstone, Robert A., *Crusade of the Left, The Lincoln Battalion in the Spanish Civil War*, Pegasus, 1969.

Sánchez, Antonio Carzorla, *Franco: The Biography of the Myth*, Routledge, 2014.

Sheffield, Gary, *Forgotten Victory, The First World War: Myths and Realities*, Review, 2002.

Smyth, Denis, "We are with you': Solidarity and Self-interest in Soviet Policy towards Republican Spain, 1936–1939' in Preston & Mackenzie (eds.), *The Republic Besieged: Civil War in Spain 1936–1939*, Edinburgh University Press, 1996.

Southworth, Herbert Rutledge, "The Grand Camouflage': Julián Gorkin, Burnett Bolloten and the Spanish Civil War' in Preston & Mackenzie (eds.), *The Republic Besieged: Civil War in Spain 1936–1939*, Edinburgh University Press, 1996.

Stradling, Robert, *The Irish and the Spanish Civil War, 1936–39*, Mandolin, 1999.

Terraine, John, *The Smoke and the Fire, Myths and Anti-Myths of War, 1861–1945*, Pen & Sword, 1992.

Terraine, John, *To Win a War, 1918: The Year of Victory*, Cassell, 2000.

Thomas, Hugh, *The Spanish Civil War, Fourth Edition*, Penguin, 2012.

Whealey, Robert H., *Hitler and Spain: The Nazi Role in the Spanish Civil War, 1936–1939*, University of Kentucky Press, 2005.

Wyden, Peter, *The Passionate War, The Narrative History of the Spanish Civil War, 1936–1939*, Simon & Schuster, 1983.

Zaloga, Steven J., *Spanish Civil War Tanks, The Proving Ground for Blitzkrieg*, Osprey, 2010.

Illustration Sources
Photographs

1. Imperial War Museum © IWM.
2. © Gerda Taro/International Center of Photography/Magnum.
3. Public Domain, sourced from Wikimedia Commons.

4. Imperial War Museum © IWM.
5. Imperial War Museum © IWM.
6. Reproduced from *The Book of the XV Brigade*.
7. Public Domain, sourced from Wikimedia Commons.
8. Reproduced from *The Book of the XV Brigade*.
9. Reproduced from *The Book of the XV Brigade*.
10. Reproduced from *The Book of the XV Brigade*.
11. Reproduced from *The Book of the XV Brigade*.
12. German Federal Archive, reproduced under Creative Commons Sharealike 3.0 Germany (CC BY-SA 3.0 DE), full licence below.
13. Public Domain, sourced from Wikimedia Commons.
14. Public Domain, Biblioteca Virtual de Defensa, Creative Commons CC0 1.0, sourced from Wikimedia Commons.
15. Reproduced from *The March of a Nation*.
16. Reproduced from *The March of a Nation*.
17. Reproduced from *The March of a Nation*.
18. Public Domain, Biblioteca Virtual de Defensa, Creative Commons CC0 1.0, sourced from Wikimedia Commons.
19. Reproduced from *The March of a Nation*.
20. Public Domain, Biblioteca Virtual de Defensa, Creative Commons CC0 1.0, sourced from Wikimedia Commons.
21. Public Domain, Biblioteca Virtual de Defensa, Creative Commons CC0 1.0, sourced from Wikimedia Commons.
22. German Federal Archive, reproduced under Creative Commons Sharealike 3.0 Germany (CC BY-SA 3.0 DE), full licence below.
23. Public Domain, Biblioteca Virtual de Defensa, Creative Commons CC0 1.0, sourced from Wikimedia Commons.
24. © Agencia EFE/La Fototeca.
25. Reproduced from *Soy del Quinto Regimiento*.
26. Reproduced from *Soy del Quinto Regimiento*.
27. Reproduced from *The Book of the XV Brigade*.
28. Reproduced from *The Book of the XV Brigade*.
29. Reproduced from *The Book of the XV Brigade*.
30. Reproduced from *The Book of the XV Brigade*.
31. Reproduced from *The Book of the XV Brigade*.
32. Reproduced from *The Book of the XV Brigade*.
33. Shutterstock.com/Pedrosala – 40324780.
34. Ecelan, sourced from Wikimedia Commons, reproduced under Creative Commons Attribution 2.5 Generic (CC BY 2.5), full licence below.
35. Ecelan, sourced from Wikimedia Commons, reproduced under Creative Commons Attribution 2.5 Generic (CC BY 2.5), full licence below.
36. Imperial War Museum © IWM.
37. Imperial War Museum © IWM.

38. © Agencia EFE/La Fototeca.
39. Public Domain, sourced from Wikimedia Commons.
40. Public Domain, sourced from Wikimedia Commons.
41. © Agencia EFE/La Fototeca.
42. Shutterstock.com/Everett Historical – 238328791.
43. Shutterstock.com/Everett Historical – 251930548.

Maps
1. Spain with administrative divisions, Shutterstock.com/Peter Hermes Furian – 720418006.
2. Map of Spanish Civil War in July 1936, Wikimedia User Nordnordwest, modified by Sting, Grandiose, sourced from Wikimedia Commons, reproduced under Creative Commons Attribution-ShareAlike 3.0 Unported (CC BY-SA 3.0), full licence below.
3. Map of Spanish Civil War in March 1937, Wikimedia User Nordnordwest, modified by Sting, Grandiose, sourced from Wikimedia Commons, reproduced under Creative Commons Attribution-ShareAlike 3.0 Unported (CC BY-SA 3.0), full licence below.
4. Map of Battle of Brunete, reproduced from *Soy del Quinto Regimiento*.
5. Map of Battle of Belchite, reproduced from *Soy del Quinto Regimiento*.
6. Map of Belchite siege, reproduced from *The Book of the XV Brigade*.
7. Map of Battle of Teruel, reproduced from *Soy del Quinto Regimiento*.
8. Map of Spanish Civil War in July 1938, Wikimedia User Nordnordwest, modified by Sting, Grandiose, sourced from Wikimedia Commons, reproduced under Creative Commons Attribution-ShareAlike 3.0 Unported (CC BY-SA 3.0), full licence below.

Creative Commons licences can be viewed in full at the following addresses:
CC BY-SA 3.0 DE – https://creativecommons.org/licenses/by-sa/3.0/de/legalcode
CC BY-SA 3.0 – https://creativecommons.org/licenses/by-sa/3.0/legalcode
CC BY 2.5 – https://creativecommons.org/licenses/by/2.5/legalcode

Disclaimer
While every effort has been made to trace copyright holders, if any have inadvertently been overlooked, please contact the publishers, who will be pleased to acknowledge them in any future editions of the work.

Index